Imagery and the Threaten[

Imagery is important in cognitive therapy because images often trigger strong emotions, and imagery techniques such as imaginal reliving and imaginal rescripting are increasingly used in therapeutic treatments. *Imagery and the Threatened Self* considers the role that images of the self play in a number of common mental health problems and how these images can be used to help people to recover.

Stopa and her contributors focus specifically on images of the self which are often negative and distorted and can contribute to both the cause and the progression of clinical disorders. The book includes chapters on current theories of the self and on imagery techniques used in therapy, alongside chapters that examine the role of self-images and how images can be used in the treatment of disorders including:

- social phobia
- posttraumatic stress disorder
- eating disorders
- depression
- bipolar disorder.

Imagery and the Threatened Self is an original and innovative book that will appeal to both clinicians and students who are studying and practising cognitive therapy.

Lusia Stopa is a Senior Lecturer in Clinical Psychology and Director of the Cognitive Therapy Programme at the University of Southampton, and an Honorary Consultant Clinical Psychologist for the Hampshire Partnership Trust.

Imagery and the Threatened Self

Perspectives on mental imagery and the self in cognitive therapy

Edited by Lusia Stopa

Routledge
Taylor & Francis Group

LONDON AND NEW YORK

First published 2009
by Routledge
27 Church Road, Hove, East Sussex BN3 2FA

Simultaneously published in the USA and Canada
by Routledge
270 Madison Avenue, New York, NY 10016

*Routledge is an imprint of the Taylor & Francis Group,
an Informa business*

© 2009 selection and editorial matter, Lusia Stopa;
individual chapters, the contributors

Typeset in Times by
RefineCatch Limited, Bungay, Suffolk
Printed and bound in Great Britain by
TJ International Ltd, Padstow, Cornwall
Paperback cover design by Sandra Heath

British Library Cataloguing in Publication Data
A catalogue record for this book is available from the British Library

Library of Congress Cataloging-in-Publication Data
Imagery and the threatened self : perspectives on mental imagery
and the self in cognitive therapy / edited by Lusia Stopa. – 1st ed.
    p. cm.
  Includes bibliographical references and index.
  1. Imagery (Psychology)   2. Cognitive therapy.   I. Stopa, Lusia
Aldona, 1954–
BF367.I458 2009
153.3′2–dc22

                                      2008046078

ISBN: 978–0–415–40759–5 (hbk)
ISBN: 978–0–415–49430–4 (pbk)

For my mother, Jo Stopa (1917–2005)

Contents

Contributors

Gillian Butler is an Associate, Oxford Cognitive Therapy Centre, Warneford Hospital, Headington, Oxford, UK.

Myra J. Cooper is a Senior Research Tutor, Oxford Doctoral Course in Clinical Psychology, University of Oxford, UK.

Samantha Day is at the Sub-department of Clinical Health Psychology, University College, London, and Solihull Child Psychology Department, Birmingham, UK.

Paul Gilbert is Professor, Mental Health Research Unit, Kingsway Hospital, Derby, UK.

Nick Grey is at the Centre for Anxiety Disorders and Trauma, South London and Maudsley NHS Foundation Trust, and Institute of Psychiatry, London, UK.

Ann Hackmann is at the Department of Psychiatry, University of Oxford, and Oxford Cognitive Therapy Centre, Warneford Hospital, Headington, Oxford, UK.

Sarah Hodson is at the School of Psychological Sciences, University of Manchester, UK.

Emily A. Holmes is Royal Society Dorothy Hodgkin Research Fellow, Department of Psychiatry, University of Oxford, UK.

Michelle Luke is a Research Fellow, School of Psychology, University of Southampton, UK.

Warren Mansell is a Senior Lecturer in Psychology, School of Psychological Sciences, University of Manchester, UK.

Lusia Stopa is Director, PgDip in Cognitive Therapy, School of Psychology, University of Southampton, UK.

Jennifer Wild is at the Department of Psychology, Institute of Psychiatry at King's College, London, UK.

Acknowledgements

I would like to thank my family for their love, support and patience while I was writing and editing this book.

Chapter 1

Imagery and the threatened self

An introduction

Lusia Stopa

> For what other dungeon is so dark as one's own heart! What jailer so
> inexorable as one's self!
>
> (Nathaniel Hawthorne, *The House of the Seven Gables*)

The self can be a prison from which to view the world and for many people
suffering from psychological disorders the building blocks of this prison
are the distorted and dysfunctional images that they have of themselves,
which are often based on past memories. The principal aims of this book
are to explore the ways in which images of the self can contribute to the
cause and maintenance of psychological disorders and to examine how
imagery can be used in treatment to help people overcome their psychological
difficulties. Imagery is one of the 'hot topics in modern cognitive behaviour
therapy' (Holmes, Arntz, & Smucker, 2007, p. 298) and the publication of
two journal special issues over the past five years attests to the theoretical
importance of imagery as well as to its clinical relevance (see *Memory*,
July 2004, vol. 12, no. 4 and *Journal of Behaviour Therapy and Experimental
Psychiatry*, December 2007, vol. 38, no. 4). This introductory chapter
describes the rationale for looking specifically at images of the self and
provides the reader with a map of what the book covers. The chapter starts by
defining imagery and considering why it is important in cognitive therapy,
and goes on to look at the links between imagery and self-representation that
form the core of the book. The final part of the introduction provides a brief
summary of the content of the subsequent chapters.

What is a mental image? An image is a mental representation that occurs
without the need for external sensory input. An image may represent the
memory of an object, a place or an event; so, for example, I may see a bright
red apple in a bowl before I leave for work and then have an image of
the apple later in the morning when I start feeling hungry. We can create
images of simple objects such as shapes (imagine a square) or use images
to remember more complex autobiographical events (e.g. my first day at
school). Images can be a direct reflection of reality; for example, it is possible

to imagine a horse, or a particular experience such as rowing a boat, or sitting by the fireside. However, we can also create images of fantastical objects or of events that did not occur. Images occur in every sensory modality, so it is possible to have auditory, olfactory and tactile images as well as visual images. In posttraumatic stress disorder, re-experiencing can involve any or all of the sensory modalities; for example, an individual could re-experience a smell that was a characteristic of the trauma, such as burning rubber in a car accident or the smell of blood if the trauma involved injury. A great strength of imagery is its plasticity: people can imagine different outcomes, face their fears, rehearse behavioural sequences, transform old and painful memories, and create images that represent desired and feared parts of their selves.

In the field of psychology in general, the study of imagery has had a fairly chequered history, moving from being a central feature of enquiry in the early part of the twentieth century to being almost completely banished when behaviourism was at its peak (Baddeley & Andrade, 2000). The resurrection of imagery as a legitimate form of enquiry was largely due to Paivio's (1965, 1969, 1971) application of experimental techniques to the study of imagery, which divorced it from earlier introspective approaches in which the phenomenonal features of imagery were examined through self-observation and self-report. Paivio (e.g. 1969) used a paired associates task, in which participants read pairs of words and then had to remember the second word when presented with the first, in order to examine the role of imagery in learning. Concrete words, which are more imageable, were easier to remember than abstract words, and Paivio formulated the dual coding hypothesis to explain this effect. According to the dual coding hypothesis, there are two independent but interacting systems – a verbally-based system and an image-based system – and concrete words are easier to remember because they can draw on information from both systems, whereas abstract words only have access to information encoded in the verbal system.

Paivio's work provided the impetus for the systematic experimental investigation of imagery, which has taken place over the past 30 to 40 years in the field of cognition and in the field of learning and memory (see Baddeley, 1997, or Parkin, 2000, for an overview). One principal controversy concerns the best way to understand and conceptualise the underlying nature of the imagery system and whether imagery should be seen as the product of an analogue or a propositional system. Proponents of the analogue argument base their case on a substantial body of evidence that demonstrates similarities between scanning visual images and visual perception (e.g. Kosslyn, 1980; Shepard & Metzler, 1971). According to the analogue view, images can be seen essentially as mental percepts that can undergo transformations. The contrasting propositional view, advocated in its most extreme form by Pylyshyn (e.g. 1981), is that images are an epiphenomenon of a propositional system of representation in which knowledge is represented as a collection of propositions that are unrelated to any specific sensory modality. Kosslyn's computational model of imagery (e.g. 1980), while being firmly positioned within the analogue camp, demonstrates how propositional knowledge can be integrated with analogue representations. He argues that there are two different types of information that are stored about objects: one is in the form of an image file that stores basic information about features of the image such as shape, and the other is a propositional file that contains information about the properties of an object.

There are a number of interesting implications from this brief review of some of the key points and controversies that have arisen in the study of imagery. First, in psychology generally, most studies of imagery have concentrated on visual images and have looked primarily at single images or at images of objects such as shapes. While discrete images can play a role in psychological problems (e.g. the image of a specific phobic stimulus such as a snake or spider), imagery is commonly much more complex and frequently represents events and/or people. Importantly in the clinical field, images often represent the self in relation to events and/or in relation to other people. This area of imagery has been almost completely ignored, other than in the clinical field. Second, although there has been no explicit examination in cognitive therapy of whether the system underlying imagery is essentially analogue or propositional, there is a clear implicit assumption in the field that images are analogue representations, and importantly that it is both possible and beneficial to manipulate these representations through techniques such as imagery rescripting. Indeed, the assumptions behind imagery rescripting seem to be entirely consistent with Kosslyn's (1980) proposal that images contain both representational and propositional codes, but it includes the assumption that changing representational codes can influence propositional codes. Finally, the current focus on imagery in cognitive therapy seeks to combine a cognitive science approach through experimental assessment of the features and impact of images (e.g. Holmes *et al.*, 2007) with a phenomenological approach that asks patients to describe their images and then uses this information to intervene (e.g. Hackmann, Clark, & McManus, 2000).

Historically, imagery has been used as a therapeutic technique in a number of schools of psychotherapy. In his book *Imagery in Psychotherapy*, Jerome Singer (2006) presents a useful typology in which he divides therapies into two broad categories: therapies that have a 'narrative, experiential, imagery emphasis' and therapies that emphasise 'rational thought and cognitive approaches' (p. 69). The former, which includes Freudian and Jungian therapies, is heavily dependent on imagery, often realised in the form of fantasy images and dreams. Until recently, the latter, which includes behavioural and cognitive therapies, has apparently relied less on imagery; but, as Singer points out, behavioural methods such as systematic desensitisation have always relied on imagery when they employed techniques such as imaginal exposure. Lang's work (e.g. 1977, 1978, 1994; Lang, Levin, Miller, & Kozak, 1983) on the role of imagery in the development and maintenance of fears was particularly influential in legitimising both the study and the therapeutic use of imagery, and more cognitively based therapies are increasingly using imagery as part of a repertoire of therapeutic techniques.

Lang's bio-informational theory of emotion (Lang, 1977; Lang, Cuthbert, & Bradley, 1998) proposes that emotional episodes are coded in memory as a series of interlinked units that form an emotion network. When one unit is activated, this activation can spread to adjacent units, and if enough units are activated or if the strength of the overall activation is exceeded, then the whole emotion episode is triggered. The activation of a network through any route (e.g. verbal, visual, somatic) is important because it triggers emotions, which Lang conceptualises as action dispositions, i.e. preparatory states such as flight or fight that are designed to help the organism to survive in response to actual or perceived threat. A fundamental premise of this theory in all its variants is that emotion networks are dependent on language and that they can be activated by any matching input, e.g. an external stimulus, an internal image, a symbolic representation, a feeling state.

Imagery is particularly important in this theory because 'images of *action and emotion* prompt activation in the appropriate efferent system' (Lang *et al.*, 1998, p. 659, emphasis added). In other words, an image creates the same outputs in the response systems as does the actual experience itself. Lang's work on the role of images in emotion and on the effects of systematic desensitisation follows directly from this assertion and paved the way for the development of imagery-based treatments. However, despite the influence of Lang's work on using imagery in treatments such as systematic desensitisa-tion, it is only relatively recently that imagery-based interventions such as imagery rescripting have become mainstream methods within cognitive therapy. Imagery rescripting, which is discussed in more detail in Chapter 3, is a method of restructuring meaning that was originally developed for the treatment of sexual abuse and trauma (Smucker & Dancu, 1999) and for personality disorders (Arntz & Weertman, 1999). Despite the recent developments in its use in cognitive therapy, imagery rescripting is not an entirely new technique and has its roots in Janet's work on hypnosis at the beginning of the twentieth century (see Edwards, 2007, for a more detailed discussion).

Why are images important? To begin with, images are often associated with high levels of affect in therapy. The assumption that imagery has a particularly strong association with emotion had not been systematically investigated until recently, when Holmes, Mathews, Mackintosh, and Dalgleish (2008) demonstrated that participants had stronger emotional responses to images of word–picture combinations than to sentences. Their study directly compared imagery with verbal processing and showed not only that imagery produces stronger emotional responses than verbally presented material, but also that imagery appears to have a causal effect on emotion and on evaluative learning. The images used in this study were based on pictures of people in different situations (e.g. a skier at the edge of a slope, a person riding a bicycle) and of objects and places (e.g. a knife, a cliff edge, a flight of stairs). These images do not necessarily have personal meaning and resonance for the participants, but the increased emotional responses that they provoked compared to their verbal counterparts raises a question over the potential impact of images that are personally meaningful, and in particular of images that represent the self.

Our ability to create images of the self is the central theme of this book. Self-representations that take the form of images are likely to have direct and important emotional consequences because perception of self is fundamental to the individual's mood, functioning, and psychological well-being (see Chapter 2). There is some preliminary evidence to support this idea. Positive images of the self in social anxiety reduce anxiety in social situations, improve self and observer ratings of performance, and increase the accessibility of positive memories (Stopa & Jenkins, 2007). Conversely, negative images of the self increase anxiety and impair performance in confident speakers, block benign inferences, and increase accessibility of negative memories (Hirsch, Meynen, & Clark, 2004; Hirsch, Mathews, Clark, Williams, & Morrison, 2006; Hirsch, Clark, & Mathews, 2006; Stopa & Jenkins, 2007). Imagery rescripting usually involves manipulating the self in the image in some way, either by bringing in a different self (e.g. bringing the adult self into a memory of the child self) or bringing another person in to rescue or comfort the self in the distressing memory. Recently, imagery rescripting has been used successfully to treat distressing memories in social phobia (Wild, Hackmann, & Clark, 2007, and see Chapter 4) and in depression (Wheatley et al., 2007).

In order to understand how and why images of the self can play a pivotal role in the development and maintenance of psychological difficulties, we need to consider the triadic relationship between imagery, autobiographical memory and the self. There are well-acknowledged links between the self and autobiographical memory (see Conway & Pleydell-Pearce, 2000, for a review). The autobiographical memory store contains different types of information that Conway and Pleydell-Pearce categorise as knowledge about life time periods (e.g. when I was at school/university), memory about general events (e.g. travelling to work, learning to drive), and event-specific memories (e.g. my wedding day, falling off the climbing frame and breaking my leg). This store of memories provides the knowledge base from which individuals construct representations of self. Memories that are critical in shaping our sense of who we are have been called 'self-defining memories' (Singer & Salovey, 1993) and are discussed in more detail below. The autobiographical memory base is the bedrock of the individual's identity and provides a sense of stability and continuity.

Self-defining memories are those memories that seem to encapsulate the individual's life-story (Beike, Kleinknecht, & Wirth-Beaumont, 2004). They are usually associated with high levels of emotion and are critical to an individual's sense of well-being and to his or her goals (Singer & Blagov, 2004). Self-defining memories can, of course, be either positive or negative, but in clinical practice we are much more likely to encounter and have to deal with negative self-defining memories. This particular type of memory often seems to confirm or define how an individual sees himself or herself. A child who has been bullied, for example, may remember one particular incident that confirmed that he or she was different and would never fit in. Traumatic memories may represent a special kind of self-defining memory for some people. An individual who saw himself or herself as strong and competent prior to the trauma, and then experienced intense feelings of helplessness while witnessing other people being harmed, might conclude that the pre-trauma self was false and that the real self was one in which he or she was weak and selfish. Recurring images of the trauma would serve to confirm the truth of the 'new' self and reinforce the negative self-beliefs.

Images frequently accompany or represent autobiographical memories of all kinds. In many disorders, the individual's self-images that occur as part of these memories are highly distorted and represent the actualisation of his or her worst fears. So for example, a person with body dysmorphic disorder who believes that he has an enormous and disfigured nose might see a mental image of himself that represents this distortion when in reality his nose is of an unremarkable size. This mental image could have a significant role in maintaining the disorder because the individual sees it in his mind's eye and believes that this is a realistic representation and that it is what others see when they look at him. This constructed image of his appearance might also act as a filter through which he perceives actual images of himself such as mirror views. Furthermore, the distorted self-image may carry a number of meanings about the self such as 'I'm weird' or 'I'm unlovable', which have a major impact on both affect (feeling despondent, for example) and behaviour (e.g. avoiding other people because of expectations of rejection).

Images, according to Conway, Meares, and Standart (2004), are the language of goals. They argue that goals are processes that cannot be represented directly and therefore these goals are consciously expressed or represented by images. These goals are closely aligned to Conway and Pleydell-Pearces's concept of the 'working self', which they see as analogous to working memory that was discussed earlier in the chapter (Baddeley, 1993). The working self is the set of self-schemas that is active at a given time and in a given context. Self-images may be a shorthand representation of the current working self that integrates conceptual and event-specific knowledge about the self and guides actions and goals as a result. If this is the case, then dysfunctional, distorted, or negative images of self are likely to influence the goals that an individual is trying to achieve. So, for example, a socially phobic individual, who has an image of herself as red and sweating profusely while having a conversation with another person, may be motivated to avoid interacting with others so as to escape from the perceived humiliation that is implicit in the image.

Over the past 20 years or so, the development of disorder-specific models, particularly in the field of the anxiety disorders, has alerted us to the fact that disorders are the end result of a number of interacting processes. Some of these processes are common to a number of disorders, i.e. transdiagnostic (Harvey, Watkins, Mansell, & Shafran, 2004), whereas others are specific to a particular disorder. Rumination, for example, occurs not only in depression but also in a number of anxiety disorders (Watkins, 2008). However, flashbacks to the self performing or failing to perform a particular action during a traumatic event are likely to be specific to posttraumatic stress disorder. Imagery and the processes that interact to create the experience of self could represent both transdiagnostic and disorder-specific processes. The growing evidence base on imagery suggests that it occurs in all disorders, as the chapters of this book will illustrate. However, the content of images and the ways in which they represent the self may be more specific; for example, in social phobia distorted images of self are more likely to represent a self that is socially inept and visibly anxious (see Chapter 4), whereas in the eating disorders the critical images may be those that focus on body weight and shape and link the attainment of a 'perfect body' to high self-esteem (see Chapter 8).

Imagery has a powerful impact on emotion, but it is also a powerful tool in alleviating emotional distress (Holmes *et al.*, 2007). We know for example that images of feared stimuli or events can arouse high levels of anxiety and that imaginal exposure or rehearsal can reduce this anxiety and help an individual to cope better with the feared situation. What happens when these images are images of the self? The basic premise of this book is that self-imagery provides a potent form of self-representation and that in many disorders these self-images are significantly distorted and, as a result, they act as maintaining factors in a number of psychological problems. The self has played an important part in cognitive accounts of disorders from the inception of cognitive therapy. A core constituent of Beck's cognitive triad of depression (Beck, Rush, Shaw, & Emery, 1979) is the notion of the self as worthless, and Beck and colleagues have stressed the role of dysfunctional self-schemas in the maintenance of depression and anxiety, and even more critically in the personality disorders (Beck, Freeman, Davis, & Associates, 2004).

The self is a complex and puzzling entity, particularly when we consider the fact that all individuals potentially have multiple self-representations and yet manage to retain a core sense of who they are. One argument proposed by Luke and Stopa in Chapter 2 of this book is that cognitive therapy has relied too heavily on the concept of self-schemas to describe self-representations in clinical disorders. The self that is experienced by an individual is the end result of multiple processes, some of which are accessible through conscious reflection and others which are unconscious and automatic and yet still shape how we feel about ourselves. A good example of this is self-esteem, which is known to be a problem for individuals across many disorders (see Fennell, 1999).

Self-esteem describes an attitude towards, or an evaluation of, the self. This self-evaluation process is generally thought of as a conscious deliberative process that occurs through introspection and is often conducted by asking oneself questions such as 'how do I feel about myself, or, am I as confident as I would like to be?'. However, information about the self and attitudes towards the self are represented at both a conscious level and an automatic or intuitive level (Greenwald & Farnham, 2000). Accordingly, we can identify two components of self-esteem: an explicit component that refers to conscious and accessible thoughts about our worth and value; and an implicit component that refers to unconscious, automatic attitudes that we hold about ourselves.

Explicit and implicit self-esteem both contribute to our overall attitude towards ourselves and can influence thoughts, feelings, and behaviour (Spalding & Hardin, 1999). However, they are only weakly correlated (Bosson, Swann, & Pennebaker, 2000), which suggests that they are two distinct processes, although the precise relationship between them is still a subject for debate (Gebauer, Riketta, Broemer, & Maio, 2008). Historically, research into self-esteem in clinical disorders has focused almost exclusively on explicit self-esteem, and it is only very recently that researchers have started to look at implicit self-esteem. Implicit self-esteem is generally positive in healthy individuals and is probably an automatic process that helps to maintain an overall positive sense of self. In contrast to explicit self-esteem, implicit self-esteem remains positive in individuals suffering from depression (e.g. De Raedt, Schacht, Franck, & De Houwer, 2006), although it is less positive in high compared to low socially anxious individuals (Tanner, Stopa, & De Houwer, 2006) and more positive in depressed individuals with suicidal ideation (Franck, De Raedt, Dereu, & Van den Abbeele, 2007) and eating disorders (Cockerham, Stopa, Bell, & Gregg, in press).

The chapters that follow present our ideas about why images of the self are important and how they contribute to a variety of different disorders. In order to do this, the reader needs to be familiar with the various ways that self has been described and conceptualised, and the range of processes, beyond schemas, that have been used to explain how the self is formed and maintained. This is the function of the next chapter, which draws on the rich literature on the self in social psychology and asks how the various theories of self developed over the past few decades can help us to understand clinical disorders. One aim of Chapter 2 is to stimulate research into self-processing and another is to provide clinicians with some conceptual tools for thinking about the self beyond the schema concept. This is quite difficult to achieve because the research agenda requires a level of detail that might at times obscure the more general clinical points. We have dealt with this problem by dividing the chapter into six parts and providing a brief introduction and summary to each part. These introductions and summaries are intended to give an overview of the key points and to link the theories of self described in the section to specific clinical problems in order to illustrate how these theories may inform our understanding. Consistent with the general theme of the book, we have highlighted the different ways in which images can represent the self.

Chapter 3 focuses specifically on imagery and how it has been used therapeutically in cognitive-behavioural therapy. The chapter starts by looking at how imagery can be used in assessment and goes on to examine imagery techniques that can be used as an intervention either to complement more traditional cognitive-behavioural therapy (CBT) techniques or in their own right. As well as describing the various techniques, the chapter includes case vignettes to illustrate how the techniques are used. The intention is to provide the reader who wishes to use imagery as part of his or her practice with a practical resource.

The remaining chapters each focus on a specific disorder. In Chapter 4, Wild examines the role of negative self-images in social phobia. She looks at the content of socially phobic individuals' negative self-images and asks where these images come from and why they persist, as well as discussing a number of CBT techniques aimed at modifying negative self-images, which is a key focus of current cognitive treatments of social phobia (Clark *et al.*, 2003). Wild discusses her own recent work on imagery rescripting, which offers a promising approach to updating the early memories on which many of the negative images that socially phobic patients report seem to be based. She also asks an interesting question about the role of positive self-images in social phobia and points to the wealth of evidence for the beneficial effects of positive imagery in sports psychology as well as the more limited experimental evidence that constructing and holding positive self-images can reduce anxiety and improve perceptions of performance in socially anxious individuals, at least in the short term.

Hackmann, Day, and Holmes study the role of distressing images and early memories in agoraphobia in Chapter 5. They address the puzzling question of why some individuals with panic disorder go on to develop agoraphobia whereas others do not. Their qualitative approach to the study of images in agoraphobia reveals not only fears of impending catastrophe represented by the images, but also beliefs about inability to cope and themes of self-blame and unlovability. Current images were closely linked to childhood memories, which were often traumatic or memories of abuse. Hackmann, Day, and Holmes suggest that early experiences, particularly self-defining moments, may provide one of the pathways to agoraphobic avoidance in later life and stress that assessment and treatment of agoraphobia should include attention to spontaneous imagery and views of the self.

Chapters 6 and 7 both focus on the effects of trauma. In Chapter 6, Grey examines intrusive posttraumatic images and focuses predominantly on adult onset trauma following a single traumatic event or a limited number of traumatic events, whereas in Chapter 7, Butler and Holmes concentrate on the impact of prolonged trauma during childhood. In his chapter, Grey looks in particular at the way in which many intrusive posttrauma images represent a psychological threat to the self. Some posttrauma images are veridical and represent an actual moment or sequence of events during the trauma, whereas others are non-veridical and represent things such as a 'worst case scenario'. Grey makes an important distinction between images that arise directly from the trauma itself and images that are associated with later appraisals, which are often associated with emotions such as fear and guilt. He presents a series of examples to illustrate how different types of meaning can be associated with intrusive images in trauma and to describe ways of working therapeutically with these images. In one case, Grey describes the use of drawings in conjunction with imagery work, a theme that is elaborated on in the following chapter.

In Chapter 7, Butler and Holmes focus on people who have suffered emotional, physical, or sexual abuse in childhood and who feel that they 'do not exist' and that they have no real self. Butler and Holmes argue that this lack of a clearly defined sense of self is often associated with difficulties in cognitive therapy because people are not able to access thoughts and feelings, or to identify specific and discrete experiences on which the clinician can focus therapeutically. According to Butler and Holmes, one answer to the challenges posed by this set of clients is for cognitive therapists to extend and develop the range of ways in which they understand and work with 'meanings'. Butler and Holmes stress the potential benefits of working with imagery to explore meanings, but point to the need to externalise images in the form of drawings, sketches, or other concrete media as a way of capturing meanings about the self. They discuss how cognitive therapists can approach this externalisation of images in therapy to explore meanings and to facilitate change.

Chapter 8 moves away from the anxiety disorders, to tackle the role of imagery in eating disorders. Cooper points out that although imagery has been relatively neglected in cognitive approaches to eating disorders, the self has recently become an important focus and features in a number of recent models. Cooper points to the importance of images of self in a number of personal accounts that have been written and she presents emerging work on imagery in the eating disorders and discusses how this imagery can link with the self. As with other disorders, imagery in eating disorders is linked to autobiographical memories. However, Cooper discusses the fascinating possibility that imagery may not be limited to our traditional conceptions of what constitutes a mental image but may include pre-verbal, pre-conceptual body images that incorporate some of the ways that infants learn about the world through movement, proprioception and sensory experiences. These 'image schemas' or 'embodiments' may provide the foundations of the self.

Cooper concludes with a discussion of novel treatments for eating disorders that incorporate imagery work.

In Chapter 9, Gilbert links the use of compassionate imagery to evolutionary development and contrasts the ability of mental imagery to stimulate and arouse on one hand, and to reduce fear and to soothe and calm on the other. Gilbert proposes that compassionate imagery activates neurophysiological systems that are linked to the evolutionary pathways to affiliative and attachment behaviours. This is particularly important for clients who have high levels of shame and self-criticism and who often fail to benefit from traditional cognitive therapy. He points out that compassionate imagery has been part of various religious systems, perhaps most notably of Buddhism, for thousands of years, and he speculates over whether it is more effective to help patients generate idiosyncratic compassionate images than to draw on pre-existing images in order to promote self-soothing. Gilbert also stresses the importance of creating an image that is in some way sentient; it does not have to be a *person* but he reports that the image does seem to be more effective if it has the qualities of a person (e.g. a mind and an ability to understand other minds and to comprehend distress) rather than being some sort of nebulous healing entity or energy. Gilbert provides instruction and examples of how to work with compassionate images in the chapter. He also alerts therapists to the fact that some clients become distressed when trying to create compassionate images, and suggests ways to work with this distress.

In the final chapter, Mansell and Hodson concentrate on imagery and the self in bipolar disorder. They acknowledge that the study of imagery in bipolar disorder has lagged behind the anxiety disorders, but note that there has been increasing interest in recent years in the self and self-concept in bipolar disorder. Negative self-concepts have been identified at all stages of the bipolar cycle, but surprisingly there is little or no evidence of an increased positive self-concept even during hypomanic and manic states. Mansell and Hodson argue that imagery may be a particularly important way of representing self-concept because of the extreme fluctuations in mood state experienced by individuals with bipolar disorder. They link these images with early memories and report a new analysis of an earlier study (Mansell & Lam, 2004) of autobiographical memory, which provides evidence of an extreme and pervasive self-concept that was often linked to the experience of depression itself. Mansell and Hodson consider a number of theoretical accounts of memory and representation and highlight the tension between theoretically rich accounts of the mechanisms that link images, self, memories, and emotion, and the need for simpler models that can provide the basis for individualised formulations in CBT. In the final part of the chapter, Mansell and Hodson present case examples and discuss working with imagery and the self in bipolar disorder patients.

The chapters on the different disorders in the book are a testament to the novel and innovative work that is currently being done on imagery and show

how, in many cases, the images that patients spontaneously experience and that often cause high levels of distress are frequently linked in some way to the self. Research into the self in clinical psychology is lagging behind the research being conducted on imagery, and I hope that this book will stimulate readers to rethink how we approach the self in cognitive models of disorders and stimulate research into this fascinating area. Clinical treatments are always developing and, although imagery has a long-established history in various therapeutic schools, it has only recently become a core technique in cognitive treatments. Each of the authors in this book has discussed some of the ways in which imagery is currently being used, and Chapter 3 in particular provides the practising clinician with a description of some of the most common imagery interventions. Imagery can be used to tackle a number of different problems, but in this book we have focused on how imagery can be used in CBT to help people to develop more functional and healthy views of self. This research is in its infancy, and we can hope for and expect significant developments over the next few years.

References

Arntz, A., & Weertman, A. (1999). Treatment of childhood memories: Theory and practice. *Behaviour Research and Therapy*, *37*, 715–740.

Baddeley, A.D. (1993). Memory – verbal and visual subsystems of working-memory. *Current Biology*, *3*, 563–565.

Baddeley, A.D. (1997). *Human memory: Theory and practice*. Hove, UK: Psychology Press.

Baddeley, A.D. (2002). *Your memory: A user's guide*. London: Prion Books.

Baddeley, A.D., & Andrade, J. (2000). Working memory and the vividness of imagery. *Journal of Experimental Psychology: General*, *129*, 126–145.

Baddeley, A.D., & Hitch, G. (1974). Working memory. In G.A. Bower (Ed.), *Recent advances in learning and motivation, Vol. 8* (pp. 47–89). New York: Academic Press.

Beck, A.T., Freeman, A., Davis, D.D., & Associates (2004). *Cognitive therapy of personality disorders*. New York: Guilford Press.

Beck, A.T., Rush, J.T., Shaw, B.F., & Emery, G. (1979). *Cognitive therapy of depression*. New York: Guilford Press.

Beike, D.R., Kleinknecht, E., & Wirth-Beaumont, E.T. (2004). How emotional and nonemotional memories define the self. In D.R. Beike, J.M. Lampinen, & D.A. Behrend (Eds.), *The self and memory* (pp. 141–159). Hove, UK: Psychology Press.

Bosson, J.K., Swann, W.B., & Pennebaker, J.W. (2000). Stalking the perfect measure of self-esteem: The blind men and the elephant revisited. *Journal of Personality and Social Psychology*, *79*, 631–634.

Clark, D.M., Ehlers, A., McManus, F., Hackmann, A., Fennell, M.J.V., Campbell, H., et al. (2003). Cognitive therapy vs fluoxetine in generalized social phobia: A randomized controlled trial. *Journal of Consulting and Clinical Psychology*, *71*, 1058–1067.

Cockerham, E., Stopa, L., Bell, L., & Gregg, A. (in press). Implicit self-esteem in bulimia nervosa. *Journal of Behavior Therapy and Experimental Psychiatry*.

Conway, M., Meares, K., & Standart, S. (2004). Images and goals. *Memory*, *12*, 525–531.

Conway, M.A., & Pleydell-Pearce, C.W. (2000). The construction of autobiographical memories in the self-memory system. *Psychological Review*, *107*, 261–288.

De Raedt, R., Schacht, R., Franck, E., & De Houwer, J. (2006). Self-esteem and depression revisited: Implicit positive self-esteem in depressed patients? *Behaviour Research and Therapy*, *44*, 1017–1028.

Edwards, D. (2007). Restructuring implicational meaning through memory-based imagery: Some historical notes. *Journal of Behavior Therapy and Experimental Psychiatry*, *38*, 306–316.

Fennell, M. (1999). *Overcoming low self-esteem: A self-help guide to using cognitive-behavioural techniques*. London: Robinson Publishing.

Franck, E., De Raedt, R., Dereu, M., & Van den Abbeele, D. (2007). Implicit and explicit self-esteem in currently depressed individuals with and without suicidal ideation. *Journal of Behavior Therapy and Experimental Psychiatry*, *38*, 75–85.

Gebauer, J.E., Riketta, M., Broemer, P., & Maio, G.R. (2008). 'How much do you like your name?' An implicit measure of global self-esteem. *Journal of Experimental and Social Psychology*, *44*, 1346–1354.

Greenwald, A.G., & Farnham, S.D. (2000). Using the implicit association test to measure self-esteem and self-concept. *Journal of Personality and Social Psychology*, *79*, 1022–1038.

Hackmann, A., Clark, D.M., & McManus, F. (2000). Recurrent images and early memories in social phobia. *Behaviour Research and Therapy*, *38*, 601–610.

Harvey, A., Watkins, E., Mansell, R., & Shafran, R. (2004). *Cognitive behavioural processes across psychological disorders: A transdiagnostic approach*. Oxford, UK: Oxford University Press.

Hirsch, C.R., Clark, D.M., & Mathews, A. (2006). Imagery and interpretations in social phobia: Support for the combined cognitive biases hypothesis. *Behavior Therapy*, *37*, 223–236.

Hirsch, C.R., Mathews, A., Clark, D.M., Williams, R., & Morrison, J.A. (2006). The causal role of negative imagery in social anxiety: A test in confident public speakers. *Journal of Behavior Therapy and Experimental Psychiatry*, *37*, 159–170.

Hirsch, C., Meynen, T., & Clark, D. (2004). Negative self-imagery in social anxiety contaminates social interactions. *Memory*, *12*, 496–506.

Holmes, E.A., Arntz, A., & Smucker, M.R. (2007). Imagery rescripting in cognitive behaviour therapy: Images, treatment techniques and outcomes. *Journal of Behavior Therapy and Experimental Psychiatry*, *38*, 297–305.

Holmes, E.A., Mathews, A., Mackintosh, B., & Dalgleish, T. (2008). The effect of mental imagery on emotion assessed using picture-word cues. *Emotion*, *8*, 395–409.

Kosslyn, S.M. (1980). *Image and mind*. Cambridge, MA: Harvard University Press.

Lang, P.J. (1977). Imagery in therapy: An information processing analysis of fear. *Behavior Therapy*, *8*, 862–886.

Lang, P.J. (1978). Language, imagery, and emotion. In P. Pliner, K.R. Blankstein, & I.M. Spigel (Eds.), *Advances in study of emotion and affect, Vol. 5: Perceptions of emotion in self and others* (pp. 107–117). New York and London: Plenum.

Lang, P.J. (1994). The varieties of emotional experience: A meditation on James-Lange theory. *Psychological Review*, *101*, 211–221.

Lang, P.J., Cuthbert, B.N., & Bradley, M.M. (1998). Measuring emotion in therapy: Imagery, activation, and feeling. *Behavior Therapy, 29*, 655–674.

Lang, P.J., Levin, D.N., Miller, G.A., & Kozak, M.J. (1983). Fear behavior, fear imagery, and the psychophysiology of emotion: The problem of affective response integration. *Journal of Abnormal Psychology, 92*, 276–306.

Mansell, W., & Lam, D. (2004). A preliminary study of autobiographical memory in remitted bipolar and unipolar depression and the role of imagery in the specificity of memory. *Memory, 12*, 437–446.

Paivio, A. (1965). Abstractness, imagery, and meaningfulness in paired-associate learning. *Journal of Verbal Learning and Verbal Behaviour, 4*, 32–38.

Paivio, A. (1969). Mental imagery in associative learning and memory. *Psychological Review, 76*, 241–263.

Paivio, A. (1971). *Imagery and verbal processes*. New York: Holt, Rinehart & Winston.

Parkin, A.J. (2000). *Essential cognitive psychology*. Hove, UK: Psychology Press.

Pylyshyn, Z.W. (1981). The imagery debate: Analogue media versus tacit knowledge. *Psychological Review, 86*, 16–45.

Shepard, R.N., & Metzler, J. (1971). Mental rotation of three-dimensional objects. *Science, 171*, 701–703.

Singer, J.A. (2006). *Imagery in psychotherapy*. Washington, DC: American Psychological Association.

Singer, J.A., & Blagov, P. (2004). The integrative function of narrative processing: Autobiographical memory, self-defining memories, and the life story of identity. In D.L. Beike, J.M. Lampinen, & D.A. Behrend (Eds.), *The self and memory* (pp. 117–138). Hove, UK: Psychology Press.

Singer, J.A., & Salovey, P. (1993). *The remembered self: Emotion and memory in personality*. New York: Free Press.

Smucker, M.R., & Dancu, C.V. (1999). *Cognitive-behavioral treatment for adult survivors of childhood trauma: Imagery rescripting and reprocessing. New directions in cognitive-behavior therapy.* Northvale, NJ: Jason Aronson.

Spalding, L.R., & Hardin, C.D. (1999). Unconscious unease and self-handicapping: Behavioral consequences of individual differences in implicit and explicit self-esteem. *Psychological Science, 10*, 535–539.

Stopa, L., & Jenkins, A. (2007). Images of the self in social anxiety: Effects on the retrieval of autobiographical memories. *Journal of Behavior Therapy and Experimental Psychiatry, 38*, 459–473.

Tanner, R.J., Stopa, L., & De Houwer, J. (2006). Implicit views of the self in social anxiety. *Behaviour Research and Therapy, 44*, 1397–1409.

Watkins, E.R. (2008). Constructive and unconstructive repetitive thought. *Psychological Bulletin, 134*, 163–206.

Wheatley, J., Brewin, C.R., Patel, T., Hackmann, A., Wells, A., Fisher, P., *et al.* (2007). 'I'll believe it when I can see it': Imagery rescripting of intrusive sensory memories in depression. *Journal of Behavior Therapy and Experimental Psychiatry, 38*, 371–385.

Wild, J., Hackmann, A., & Clark, D.M. (2007). When the present visits the past: Updating traumatic memories in social phobia. *Journal of Behavior Therapy and Experimental Psychiatry, 38*, 386–401.

Chapter 2

Psychological theories of the self and their application to clinical disorders

Michelle Luke and Lusia Stopa

The experience of self is fundamental to who we are. In many clinical disorders there are disruptions to the individual's sense of self. On one hand, the self may be experienced as mad, bad, dangerous, or disgusting. On the other hand, disruptions may involve the continuity of selfhood (at their most extreme in dissociative disorders) or the person may fail to develop a sense of self and may experience the feelings of emptiness and numbness that are characteristic of many personality disorders (see Chapter 7 for further discussion).

In psychiatry, interest in the self has traditionally focused on schizophrenia, where patients may feel disconnected from their bodies, cut-off from everyday reality, and experience symptoms of delusions and hallucinations that profoundly affect their sense of who they are (Kircher & David, 2003). However, disturbances in a person's sense of self, or in the relationship between different parts of the self, are also common in anxiety disorders, depression, eating disorders, and dissociative disorders. Until recently, with the exception of eating disorders (see Chapter 8), the role of the self in anxiety disorders and depression had not been a primary focus of research despite the clinical importance of self-perceptions of worthlessness in depression and vulnerability in anxiety. Research that has looked at the self has concentrated on the negative content of self-beliefs and will be reviewed later in the chapter. Less attention has been given to the processes that contribute to a sense of self. In general, people are motivated to maintain and enhance a positive self-view (Sedikides & Gregg, 2003, 2008). However, in clinical disorders this process is disturbed, or even reversed in cases where patients appear to seek out evidence that confirms their view of the self as defective and flawed. For some patients, particularly those with a history of childhood trauma and/or abuse, negative views of self are intractable and persistent. These cases present a significant therapeutic challenge, because the individual finds it hard even to conceive that there may be another way of perceiving and relating to the self. The debate in the field of personality disorders over whether therapeutic effort is best spent challenging negative beliefs about the self or developing new, more functional beliefs is important here, but this debate needs to be informed by a better conceptualisation of how the self is formed, developed, and maintained.

Changes in the content of a person's self-view are common in depression and in many types of anxiety disorders. In other disorders, the disturbance may constitute a sense of loss or absence of self. In posttraumatic stress disorder (PTSD), for example, patients frequently describe the experience of having lost the 'self' that they were before the trauma, or, more graphically, claim that their old self has 'died'. The core of depersonalisation disorder is that people feel detached or disconnected from their selves, and they often describe this by saying 'I feel as if I don't exist'. The self is usually experienced as a broadly unitary entity even though people experience changes across time and across different situations. However, in dissociative identity disorder, the experience of selfhood is radically altered and individuals may have two or more 'distinct identities or personality states' (American Psychiatric Association, 2000, p. 484).

How do people create and maintain this complex construction that provides the most essential definition of who they are and how they experience the world and their relationships with other people? The self is unique in that it is both subject and object; in other words, the self can be simultaneously experienced and observed. William James (1890) described this phenomenon succinctly in his description of the self as knower and the self as known. This duality of self allows us to think and to talk about ourselves as both 'I' and 'me', and as a result, it is possible for these two aspects of self to 'talk' to each other or to have a dialogue. So, you may hear someone say 'I gave myself a good talking to' or 'I told myself not to be stupid'. This ability both to reflect on and to experience the self is a key reason why the self has a role in the development and maintenance of disorders, but also why self-processes can be utilised in therapy. The aim of this chapter is to review some key theories of self that seek to explain how people construct and maintain self-definitions and to suggest how these processes may contribute to clinical disorders.

The majority of the theories that we will discuss are drawn from social psychology, because it is in the field of social rather than clinical psychology that most advances have been made in understanding how the self is constructed and regulated. We have chosen the theories that we think are currently the most important and influential. It is disappointing that, with a few notable exceptions (e.g. Kowalski & Leary, 2004), there has been relatively limited cross-fertilisation between social and clinical psychology in the field of the self. Understanding how self and identity are constructed and maintained in healthy individuals provides us with conceptual and analytical tools for examining how the self changes and why distorted negative self-views persist in clinical disorders or how a person can report an experience of loss of self. At the same time, clinical disorders provide a fertile and challenging testing ground for the robustness of these self-processing theories.

The experience of a continuous and coherent self is the outcome of successful interactions between knowledge, memory, experience, and various self-regulatory processes. In order to help the reader to make sense of the theories that follow, we have divided the chapter into six parts that are represented in Figure 2.1. As shown in Figure 2.1, four parts of the chapter appear in the 'self' box to indicate that theories discussed under these headings reflect personal and internal processes. Part 1 concentrates on self-definition and self-representation, and looks at theories that describe the self-concept directly. Part 2 discusses how the self is experienced through time, and focuses particularly on memory. Memory is important because some theorists argue that the experience of self is critically dependent on autobiographical memory. Part 3 looks at how people maintain self-representations, and Part 4 examines the self as agent. The other two parts of the chapter describe theories that provide an interface between the self and other people on one hand, and between the outside world or external processes on the other hand. Part 5 looks at theories of self-awareness and self-consciousness, and Part 6 looks at how the self develops and changes within particular sets of social interactions. The principal focus of this book is on images of the self in clinical disorders, and therefore we will provide clinical examples where possible and also point out where images of self might be relevant to the various theories that we are presenting. However, because this chapter concentrates on reviewing current theories of self, there will inevitably be less discussion of imagery here than in the following chapters.

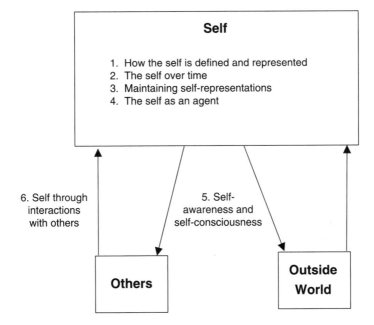

Figure 2.1 Diagrammatic representation of the chapter structure.

Part 1: How the self is defined and represented

One of the principal ways in which the self is represented in cognitive models of both Axis I and Axis II disorders is through the concept of self-schemas, which can be defined as templates that represent connected beliefs about the self. In some early work, Beck, Rush, Shaw, and Emery (1979) argued that schemas are a fundamental way of organising information about the world, including information about the self. Beck *et al.* claimed that, in depression, an individual's idiosyncratic schemas are activated and this schema activation drives the faulty information processing that is characteristic of the disorder. Later work has built on these foundations, and Young's (1999) schema-focused therapy gives primacy to the need to work directly on dysfunctional schemas about the self and others. Wells (1997) describes the current family of anxiety disorder models as schema theories, because they share the idea that danger schemas drive information processing and influence both the content of thinking (e.g. negative automatic thoughts) and the related processes (e.g. attention and memory).

Despite the fact that Beck and later theorists have recognised that schematic beliefs about the self have an important role in the maintenance of anxiety and depression, clinical research on the self specifically has lagged behind research into other aspects of disordered information processing, such as attention, interpretation bias, and memory. In order to redress this gap, we will concentrate on theories about self-concept in this section. We will start by looking at the relationship between self-schemas and self-concept and will then introduce the idea of the working self-concept, which provides an explanation for how individuals construct moment-to-moment self-representations from a vast array of information about the self. Once we acknowledge that the self-system is fluid and dynamic, then we have to account for discrepancies between different parts of the system or, as we will refer to it here, discrepancies between different selves. This creates a challenge for the individual who has to integrate different actual and hypothetical views of self. The degree to which an individual succeeds in this task and has a clear, well-defined, and continuous sense of self is defined as self-concept clarity and this will be discussed next. In the last section of this part of the chapter, we move away from theories that describe the contents of self-representation to theories about how the self is organised.

Self-schemas and their relationship to self-concept

The self-concept comprises the particular schemas that people have about themselves. Markus (1977) first introduced the concept of self-schemas, which are cognitive structures that help to organise, summarise, and explain behaviours in a particular domain. Self-schemas aid in the processing of information about the self, contain behavioural evidence, allow for the prediction of a specific behaviour in a particular domain, and help individuals to resist information that is counter-schematic. Indeed, people who hold a particular self-schema are quicker to indicate that a trait associated with the schema is self-descriptive than people who do not hold that self-schema (Markus, 1977; Sedikides, 1995). Important to the clinical domain is the fact that depressed individuals are quicker to indicate that a negative trait is more self-descriptive than non-depressed individuals (Bargh & Tota, 1988). As such, Markus's earlier concept of self-schemas is consistent with Beck's formulation of schemas and provides support for Young's conceptualisation of early mal-adaptive schemas as 'stable and enduring themes' (Young, 1999, p. 9) that incorporate both cognitive and affective content.

The self-concept is often seen as a global view (set of cognitions) about one's attributes, and a substantial body of research confirms that people with depression have more negative self-concepts than people without depression (see Markus & Wurf, 1987, for a review). Nevertheless, it is misleading to think of the self-concept as a single unitary entity, because one is likely to have several views of the self, and the current self-view is often referred to as the *working self-concept* (Markus & Nurius, 1986). The self-concept is dynamic in the sense that it is the collection of self-representations that are active at any one time (i.e. working self-concept) that regulates both interpersonal and intrapersonal behaviour. In Beck and Young's terms, the working self-concept could be seen as the activation of a particular set of schemas, or in Young's more recent work, the activation of a mode (Young, Klosko, & Weishaar, 2003). The notion of the working self-concept was elaborated in later work by Conway and Pleydell-Pearce (2000), who stressed the fundamental link between autobiographical memory and the self. In some disorders, the current working self-concept can be represented through self-images. For example, a socially phobic individual who has an image of himself/herself shaking, sweating and trembling while giving a presenta-tion at work has constructed a visual representation of the current work-ing self-concept that might incorporate memories of previous presentations as well as encapsulate the beliefs that he or she is incompetent and a failure.

Possible selves

The fact that the self-concept is dynamic means that it can take on the form of 'possible' selves. This idea was introduced by Markus and Nurius (1986, 1987), who argued that possible selves are cognitive structures that represent ideas about what a person may become, including what he/she would like to become and what he/she is afraid of becoming. Furthermore, possible selves act as incentives for future behaviour and give rise to evaluative and inter-pretative information about one's working self-concept. Crucially, people with positive possible selves persist longer on tasks and are more likely to endorse a successful possible self than those with negative possible selves (Fleury, Sedikides, & Donovan, 2002; Ruvolo & Markus, 1992). Furthermore, if an individual experiences positive (negative) affect when a particular possible self is activated, he/she will experience enhanced (impaired) performance on a task relevant to meeting a specific goal (Markus & Ruvolo, 1989).

The role of negative or positive possible selves in clinical disorders and in their treatment has not been extensively studied. There is some work on discrepancies between ideal and actual selves, and this is discussed in more detail below. However, the potential role of possible selves in maintaining disorders is intriguing, as evidenced by the following example of a belief that is often reported by individuals with panic disorder or posttraumatic stress disorder. A common fear in both disorders is 'I'm going mad', and the intensity and perceived uncontrollability of symptoms, such as perceptual disturbances and thoughts racing out of control or intense and disturbing intrusive images, appear to provide corroborating evidence for this belief. In some cases, patients have images of themselves being taken away to a lunatic asylum or they will see an idiosyncratic image of themselves that represents 'madness'. In these cases, the feared 'possible' self is represented by an image and provides a powerful incentive that drives processes, such as behavioural avoidance of places that might trigger a panic attack, cognitive attempts to control thinking to avoid thoughts spiralling out of control, and thought suppression to eliminate intrusions. Unfortunately, these processes, which are motivated by an attempt to avoid a feared possible self, actually serve to maintain and reinforce the disorder, thus blocking recovery.

Self-discrepancies

Higgins (1987) suggests that people have an 'actual' self (self-concept, self-schema), an 'ideal' self (beliefs about one's aspirations), and an 'ought' self (beliefs about duties and responsibilities). Ideal and ought selves are by definition hypothetical constructs in the individual's imagination. To date, images of ideal and ought selves have not been investigated, but this may be a fruitful line of enquiry because these different selves can be discrepant and different types of discrepancies are associated with different emotions. Higgins and colleagues (Higgins, 1987; Higgins, Bond, Klein, & Strauman, 1986; Higgins, Klein, & Strauman, 1985) found that actual–ideal discrepancies signify the absence of positive outcomes, which are associated with negative emotions, such as dejection (disappointment, dissatisfaction, sadness). In contrast, actual–ought discrepancies signify the presence of negative outcomes, which are associated with different negative emotions, such as agitation (fear, threat, restlessness). The feelings associated with each discrepancy are triggered when mismatches (discrepancies) between different selves are detected (Strauman & Higgins, 1987; cf. Gramzow, Sedikides, Panter, & Insko, 2000). Of most relevance to the clinical domain are Strauman's (1989, 1992) findings that depressed and dysphoric individuals experience actual–ideal discrepancies, whereas socially phobic and anxious individuals experience actual–ought discrepancies (cf. Scott & O'Hara, 1993). In addition, priming these discrepancies increases feelings of dejection among depressed individuals, and agitation among socially phobic individuals (Strauman, 1989). More recent research has found that people with generalised social phobia or dysthymia report higher actual–ought discrepancies than healthy controls, whereas people with a diagnosis of anxiety and depression report high levels of both actual–ought and actual–ideal discrepancies (Weilage & Hope, 1999).

Self-concept clarity

The extent to which different aspects of the self are dependent on each other, and are clearly defined, internally consistent, and temporally stable, is represented by a construct termed *self-concept clarity* by Campbell (1990). Low self-concept clarity is associated with low self-esteem, high neuroticism, high depression, negative affectivity, low private and public self-consciousness, and high levels of anxiety (Butzer & Kuiper, 2006; Campbell, 1990; Campbell *et al.*, 1996), as well as overprotective parental bonding (Perry, Silvera, Neilands, Rosenvinge, & Hanssen, 2008) and poor decision-making strategies (Setterlund & Niedenthal, 1993).

Campbell (1990) proposed that people with low self-concept clarity 'should be more dependent on, susceptible to, and influenced by external self-relevant stimuli' (p. 539). This may account for why the outcome of social events impacts on feelings of self-worth in people with social phobia to a greater extent than in non-anxious individuals or those with other anxiety disorders (Gilboa-Schechtman, Franklin, & Foa, 2000). A related point is that socially phobic individuals showed less certainty or clarity with regard to whether they possessed negative personality characteristics or lacked positive characteristics, compared to non-clinical controls (Wilson & Rapee, 2006).

Large discrepancies between the self in different roles, between actual and ideal selves, or between current and past selves might all interfere with the clarity with which an individual views himself or herself. It is easy to see how clinical disorders might contribute to self-discrepancies as described above. Disorders in which individuals experience frequent swings of mood could contribute to lower self-concept clarity, as the individual may experience the self very differently when depressed, anxious, or panicking compared to normal mood states. Also, an individual whose sense of self is ruptured through trauma might find it harder to have a clear sense of self compared to those for whom change has been more gradual and is more congruent with past experiences.

Self-organisation and self-complexity

The discussion so far has focused on the content of the self-concept. It should be clear to the reader by now that the construction and maintenance of the individual's self-concept draws on an extensive range of information including schematic knowledge, memory, and affective and behavioural information. In this section, we are going to move away from the content of the self-concept to the way in which knowledge about the self is organised. Showers (1992) proposed two different types of self-organisation: compartmentalised and integrative. In compartmentalised self-organisation, positive and negative self-aspects, roles, or schematic beliefs about the self are organised in separate knowledge structures, such that each structure contains largely positive or largely negative information about the self. For example, an individual whose self-knowledge is organised in a compartmentalised way may define him- or herself in the role of 'public speaker' as 'stupid, boring, inferior, and inarticulate', but describe him- or herself in the role of romantic partner as 'loving, supportive, warm, and caring'. In this type of self-organisation, there is no overlap between the attributes that are used to describe these two different roles or aspects of the self. By comparison, the definitions of different roles or self-aspects in an individual whose self-knowledge is organised in an integrated way will contain a mixture of negative and positive self-beliefs. For instance, an individual whose self-knowledge is organised in an integrated way may describe himself as 'warm, supportive, kind, lazy, and thoughtless' in his role as a friend, and use some of the same descriptors to characterise his role as 'son' or 'father'. An interesting question is whether images of the self are more likely to be associated with a compartmentalised than with an integrated type of self-organisation, given that it might be easier to represent an unambiguous collection of either positive or negative qualities in an image. If this did occur, then a compartmentalised view of self might contribute to the maintenance of the disorder, because compartmentalised self-organisation can make an individual extremely vulnerable to extreme mood swings in response to social stress (Showers, 1992).

Integrative organisation may be preferable to compartmentalised organisation, because an integrated self-organisation structure could incorporate positive information that buffers the negative information. One potential mechanism underlying the success of cognitive therapy could be that therapy helps individuals to shift from a more negatively compartmentalised self-organisation to a more integrated organisation. This suggestion is consistent with Brewin's (2006) retrieval competition account, according to which positive and negative self-representations compete, and therapy changes the frequency with which positive representations are accessed rather than the content of negative self-representations. Type of self-organisation might influence the retrieval routes, and thus make certain representations more accessible.

The self-organisation model described above does not take account of the complexity of an individual's self-organisation. Self-complexity has been defined by Linville (1985, 1987) as the number of different self-aspects that an individual uses to describe him- or herself and the degree of overlap between them. Linville argues that a 'simple' self-concept is characterised by a smaller number of self-aspects and also by more overlap between the attributes that describe each aspect. She suggests that individuals with simpler self-concepts are potentially more vulnerable to emotional distress if the same negative attributes occur in a number of self-aspects. For example, a person who sees him- or herself as a 'failure' in a number of different self-aspects will be more vulnerable to dysphoric mood than a person for whom failure is associated with only one self-aspect.

A more 'complex' self-concept is potentially protective because negative information is more likely to be encapsulated within a single role or a smaller number of roles. Thus, a more complex self-concept, which consists of many differentiated or independent self-aspects, can prevent the impact of a negative event in one self-aspect from 'spilling over' into other self-aspects, thereby minimising distress.

Summary

In this section, we have examined ways in which information about the self is stored and represented. The self-concept can be construed as the output of a number of self-schemas. The idea of a working self-concept is useful in that it represents the dynamic nature of the self, and also allows us to see how the experience of self can vary according to time and context. In anxiety disorders, for example, the self is frequently experienced as vulnerable. For some individuals, a vulnerable working self-concept may be limited to specific situations (e.g. giving a speech for someone who is socially anxious), but for others a vulnerable working self-concept may be repeatedly constructed, so that the perception of the self as vulnerable may become all-pervasive. Indeed, in panic disorder, the fear of having a panic attack and the experience of apparently uncued attacks often create pervasive feelings of vulnerability that the individual responds to by increasing avoidance.

The self-concept is not limited to actual selves, and this part of the chapter has looked at the ways in which individuals construct possible selves that are both hoped for and feared. The existence of multiple actual and hypothetical selves means that there can be discrepancies between different self-representations, and the perception of these discrepancies can influence both feelings and behaviour. Multiple representations of self also create the problem of having to maintain a sense of consistency and continuity, and the idea of self-concept clarity describes the end point of this task. Greater self-concept clarity seems to be associated with a more functional view of self. The structure of the self is important, as well as the content, because the structural organisation of the self can influence what information is retrieved and the final output (i.e. the experience of self) is likely to be a complex interaction between structure and content.

Part 2: Continuity and change: The self over time

The self does not simply exist at a given moment in time. The self contains knowledge of current self-representations and self-definitions, and also a sense of the growth and development of the self over time (Sedikides, Wildschut, Gaertner, Routledge, & Arndt, 2008; Skowronski, Walker, & Betz, 2003). As a result, most researchers on the self agree that the self-concept and autobiographical memory are inextricably linked (Conway & Pleydell-Pearce, 2000; Nelson & Fivush, 2004). The development of an Axis I disorder may produce a rupture between the self that existed before the disorder developed and the self that exists after. As we discussed earlier, this can happen dramatically in cases of PTSD, where an individual may feel that the old self has died, and memories of the traumatic experience are often taken as evidence for the existence of the new self that has emerged. However, there are many more subtle ways in which this can occur. For example, in anxiety disorders, the experience of vulnerability discussed above and the resulting restrictions that often ensue may conflict with a self that was previously experienced as confident and adventurous. The symptoms of depersonalisation or derealisation that can occur in states of extremely high anxiety will result in an individual having a very different experience of self when anxious than when in a normal mood state. This experience may raise questions about whether the person is 'going mad' or is 'normal' and, again, memories of situations in which these experiences have occurred are experienced as potential threats that initiate behaviours, such as 'checking whether things feel real' or 'checking that I can control my thoughts'.

This part of the chapter will start by discussing autobiographical memory and how it is related to self-concept and will go on to look at temporal comparison and temporal self-appraisal, which are processes through which people try to make sense of the changes that occur in the self over time. The final section will provide a brief review of existential theories of the self. Time is finite for all humans and, according to existential theories, this poses a fundamental question of meaning. Believing that the self is of worth provides one way to create meaning.

Autobiographical memories

Autobiographical memories are events that are recalled from one's past. According to Conway and Pleydell-Pearce (2000), these memories are located within a self-memory system that contains an autobiographical knowledge base and current self-relevant goals. Furthermore, these authors suggest that the self-memory system regulates access to autobiographical knowledge by shaping the cues necessary to activate autobiographical memory structures, and, ultimately, specific memories.

Several lines of research indicate that memories for autobiographical events are affected by a variety of psychological disorders. According to Klein, German, Cosmides, and Gabriel (2004), autobiographical memory is a mental state that is normally the result of self-reflection, self-agency, self-ownership, and personal temporality (i.e. personal 'mental time travel'), all of which translate into an autobiographical experience. However, in the clinical domain there is a breakdown in these components, resulting in disrupted autobiographical memories. This is particularly true for people with amnesia, autism, frontal lobe pathology, and schizophrenia. In a similar vein, Williams *et al.* (2007) suggested that patients with depression and PTSD experience a disruption in how autobiographical events are recalled, because these individuals summarise categories of events when they recall autobiographical events rather than a single memory. This over-general memory is associated with poor problem-solving skills and difficulty in imagining future events, both of which may contribute to the maintenance of the disorders.

Another line of research indicates that people with psychological disorders experience different levels of affective intensity associated with autobiographical memories. In particular, Walker, Skowronski, and their colleagues (Ritchie *et al.*, 2006; Walker, Skowronski, Gibbons, Vogl, & Thompson, 2003a; Walker, Skowronski, & Thompson, 2003b) have found that affect for negative autobiographical events fades faster than affect associated with positive autobiographical events, a phenomenon called the fading affect bias (FAB). Crucially, however, the FAB is smaller in people with dysphoria (Walker *et al.*, 2003a), because affect associated with pleasant events fades faster than affect associated with unpleasant events in dysphoric individuals. Furthermore, the FAB is larger for atypical events and smaller for events that are important to the self or are perceived as being caused by the self (Ritchie *et al.*, 2006). Thus, for example, people with social anxiety/social phobia may be less likely to experience the FAB, because they are likely to consider negative social interactions as highly important to the self. Likewise, for an individual with bulimia nervosa, previous episodes of bingeing are likely to be remembered with high levels of affect that fade slowly compared to meals that were eaten without bingeing. Finally, the FAB increases when people engage in more frequent social interactions (Skowronski, Gibbons, Vogl, & Walker, 2004; Skowronski & Walker, 2004). Presumably, more frequent social interaction reduces the salience of each specific occasion but, as people with social anxiety/social phobia avoid social interactions, they have fewer opportunities for the FAB to develop and, therefore, continue to experience significantly intense negative affect that takes longer to fade when recalling negative social occasions.

Temporal comparison and temporal self-appraisal

The theory of temporal comparison (Albert, 1977), in which people compare themselves at different points in time, is related to autobiographical memory because it describes the way that people maintain their identity by relating different temporal selves to a core sense of self. In general, people are motivated to enhance the self (Sedikides & Gregg, 2003, 2008), and one way they do so is by recalling the past and making predictions about the future in a manner that makes the self look favourable. This process is known as temporal self-appraisal (Ross & Wilson, 2000). People usually recall their past selves as more negative or mixed than their current self, and they view their future selves as more positive (Newby-Clark & Ross, 2003; Ross & Buehler, 2004; Ross & Wilson, 2000). This provides a way to enhance the self, because it allows the individual to perceive the self as improving over time (Ross & Wilson, 2003; Wilson & Ross, 2000, 2001). Furthermore, McFarland and Alvaro (2000) have found that the perception of personal growth over time can help people cope with traumatic events (for a review of research on posttraumatic growth, see Zoellner & Maercker, 2006).

The degree to which people enhance or derogate their past selves depends on their perception of the psychological distance between the current and the past self. It also depends on whether the attribute that they are comparing across time is seen as important to the self. For example, people derogate psychologically distant selves if the self-attribute is important to the current self, but enhance a psychologically distant self if the self-attribute is unimportant to the current self (Ross & Wilson, 2000). However, if individuals see themselves as declining on an important attribute over time, they are likely to experience depression and lower self-esteem. For example, this can occur when unemployed individuals focus on periods in their life when they were employed. People are also likely to indicate that negative events from their past are more distant than positive events that occurred at the same time (Ross & Wilson, 2002). Crucially, Ross and Wilson (2002) have found that this distancing bias is stronger among people with high self-esteem than people with low self-esteem. Given that people who suffer from anxiety or depression frequently have low self-esteem (Tennen & Affleck, 1993; Wood & Lockwood, 1999; see Roberts, 2006, for a review), Ross and Wilson's research seems to suggest that these people are less likely to exhibit the distancing bias. However, this idea has not been directly tested.

Another body of research indicates that current self-views influence how people recall their past (Cameron, Wilson, & Ross, 2004; Karniol & Ross, 1996; Wilson & Ross, 2003). People generally recall their past as being consistent with their present. This suggests that people with negative self-views are likely to recall their past and present as more negative than people with more positive self-views. Thus, people with anxiety or depression are likely to recall their past and present as more negative than healthy individuals, and this perception may create feelings of hopelessness and increase their belief that they cannot cope. According to James, Reichelt, Freeston, and Barton (2007), memories are integrally bound into one's current self-perception in the form of schemas that incorporate representations of past experiences, which are multi-level representations that include sensory features as well as cognitions and can be stored and retrieved as coherent units. These schematic representations, together with perceptions of the past as negative and the absence of the distancing bias, may interact with each other and contribute to the persistent negative view of self often experienced by depressed and anxious patients.

Existential theories

Existential theories of the self may be relevant to a variety of psychological disorders. Terror Management Theory (TMT; Greenberg, Solomon, & Pyszczynski, 1997) highlights the importance of having meaning in one's life and believing that the self is of worth, as these beliefs serve to alleviate the ultimate terror, which is the realisation that one will cease to exist at some point in the future. Meaning is often provided through cultural beliefs, whereas feelings of self-worth (i.e. self-esteem) are derived from the notion that one is living up to the standards imposed by the culture. A threat to these beliefs or to self-esteem can lead to the engagement of various defences, such as harming those that threaten our beliefs and rewarding or clinging to people who support our views.

In support of TMT, many studies have found that, when mortality is made salient, people respond positively to individuals who uphold cultural values and negatively to those who threaten those values or cling to close others who may offer protection and comfort (Arndt, Greenberg, Schimel, Pyszczynski, & Solomon, 2002; Florian, Mikulincer, & Hirschberger, 2002; Rosenblatt, Greenberg, Solomon, Pyszczynski, & Lyon, 1989). Furthermore, manipulated or trait high self-esteem can decrease anxiety and cultural worldview defences (Greenberg et al., 1992; Harmon-Jones, Simon, Greenberg, & Pyszczynski, 1997; Pyszczynski, Greenberg, Solomon, Arndt, & Schimel, 2004). However, in some cases, traumatic or near-death experiences can be life-affirming, as these experiences can help to strengthen the belief that one's life is meaningful (Davis & McKearney, 2003; Janoff-Bulman & Yopyk, 2004; Martin, Campbell, & Henry, 2004).

Near-death experiences are likely to have a negative impact on people suffering from a variety of psychological disorders. Some research suggests that people with psychological disorders are more likely to engage in psychological defences when their mortality is made salient. For example, Simon and colleagues (Simon, Arndt, Greenberg, Pyszczynski, & Solomon, 1998; Simon, Greenberg, Harmon-Jones, & Solomon, 1996) found that depressed persons are highly motivated to engage in defences when reminded of their own death. More recently, Strachan *et al.* (2007) have found that mortality salience increases phobic and compulsive behaviours in spider phobics and in people with obsessive-compulsive and social anxiety tendencies. According to these authors, anxiety disorders are the result of unsuccessful or dysfunctional attempts to cope with death anxiety, although people may not be consciously aware of their death anxiety. However, Solomon, Greenberg, and Pyszczynski (1991) suggest that it will be useful for therapists to help strengthen their clients' cultural anxiety buffers (e.g. positive self-beliefs, cultural values or beliefs) rather than making clients aware of their death anxiety, because the latter may lead to more feelings of terror and dread.

Summary

The self exists at a specific time and also as a series of past selves and of potential future selves. The fundamental link between autobiographical memory and self is disrupted in disorders such as depression and PTSD, where the phenomenon of over-general memory (OGM) serves as a potential maintaining factor, because it may be easier to use generic memories to substantiate dysfunctional views of self. For example, generic memories of failure to achieve desired results provide an apparent data bank for a depressed person who believes 'I'm a failure'. By comparison, retrieval of specific, episodic memories of failure might have helped him or her to contextualise the memory in such a way that it becomes explicable in terms of a particular set of circumstances rather than by a global and stable attribution to the self. OGM is not the only process that is disrupted in clinical disorders. The FAB is reversed in dysphoric individuals, who are more likely to forget the affect associated with positive than with negative events, unlike healthy individuals. In fact, the increased accessibility of negative affect, particularly to events that are the most salient to the self, might contribute to OGM because the increased availability of negative affect might lead to a blurring across a number of specific events to create a more generic memory of 'failure'.

The process of temporal comparison is one way in which healthy individuals enhance positive feelings about themselves, by seeing their current selves as 'better' in some way than their past selves. Again, disruptions to this process could contribute to the maintenance of clinical problems. For example, if the distancing bias is compromised in anxious or depressed individuals, they are much more likely to see a negative event in the past as having continued significance to their present selves compared to individuals who see the event and the self associated with that event as temporally distant. If the event is a relationship that has broken down, a depressed person may blame himself or herself and see himself or herself as a failure. This perception, together with the lack of psychological distance, might contaminate a current relationship because the person experiences both OGM ('all my relationships end in disaster') and a lack of psychological distance (fusion between past and present self rather than past self as distinct from present self). This lack of psychological distance is also inherent in the idea that schemas themselves may be connected sets of stored representations from the past that include sensory as well as cognitive information.

According to existential theories of self, high self-esteem and identification with core cultural values provide one way for individuals to create meaning in their lives. Conversely, low self-esteem, which is common across a range of disorders, interferes with people's ability to create adaptive defences against the strategies to cope with the fear of death and leads them to use cognitive, emotional, and behavioural avoidance.

Part 3: Maintaining self-representations

Self-regulation and self-evaluation are fundamental processes that allow people to reflect on and to monitor who they are, what they wish to become, and what they want to avoid becoming. In many clinical disorders, self-evaluation is harsh and uncompromising and may display characteristic thinking errors, such as black and white thinking, personalisation, and blame. The links between the ideas discussed earlier in the chapter and self-evaluation can be easily illustrated. In social phobia, for example, individuals often have extremely idealised and unrealistic expectations about how they should perform in social situations to be accepted (Clark & Wells, 1995). These beliefs may form part of an ideal self that the individual aspires to, but the gulf between this ideal and the actual self creates a major discrepancy. Reflections on this discrepancy may trigger further negative thinking about the self and cue the individual to recall memories of past failures. The high rate of co-morbidity between social phobia and depression may, in part, result from this kind of self-processing.

In this part of the chapter, we are going to start by looking at various social psychological theories about the motives that drive self-evaluation. These theories have focused primarily on healthy individuals. However, at least one of the motives (self-verification) is highly applicable to negative self-views in clinical disorders, because it explains why individuals seek to perpetuate negative self-representations even though they cause distress. We will also look at regulatory focus, which provides a way of understanding links between self-concept and whether individuals adopt approach or avoidance strategies to pursue desired goals or to avoid undesirable outcomes. Although this theory has not been tested on clinical populations, it does have a potentially useful application in the clinical field. Finally, we will cover the more familiar area of self-affirmation and self-compassion and look at recent ways that self-compassion has been used in therapy (for a full description of self-compassion, see Chapter 9).

Self-evaluation motives

Self-evaluation is driven by a number of contrasting motives, but these share common aims, which are to (a) search for or receive certain kinds of information about the self, and (b) interpret, appraise, and filter such information. Social psychologists have proposed four key motives (Sedikides & Strube, 1997; Taylor, Neter, & Wayment, 1995). The first is the self-enhancement motive, which describes the desire to receive positive information and to reject negative information about the self. The second is the self-verification motive, which describes the search for consistency within the self. The third is the self-assessment motive and describes the search for accurate information about the self. The fourth is the self-improvement motive and describes the search for information that will lead to self-improvement. These self-evaluation motives are most likely to be activated when the individual thinks about past or future failures or threats, because these types of events elicit information about personal standards that one may or may not easily meet.

There is an abundance of research suggesting that people solicit positive, consistent, accurate and improving information from other people or behave in a manner that is consistent with the self-enhancement, self-verification, self-assessment, and self-improvement perspectives. For example, people engage in self-enhancement by being unrealistically optimistic about their own future (Taylor & Brown, 1988). They may engage in self-verification by favouring individuals who provide evaluations of them that are consistent with their own self-view (Swann, Stein-Seroussi, & Giesler, 1992). People engage in self-assessment by preferring tasks that provide high amounts of diagnostic feedback over tasks that provide small amounts of diagnostic feedback, because the former tasks help to provide accurate information about their ability in a specific domain (Trope, 1980). Finally, people are more likely to recall negative feedback on important traits that are modifiable than negative feedback on important traits that cannot be modified, which suggests that this feedback may be used for self-improvement purposes (Green, Pinter, & Sedikides, 2005).

Several lines of research in social psychology have pitted the different self-motives against one another to determine which motive is the most important. For example, Sedikides (1993) compared the self-assessment, self-enhancement, and self-verification motives and found that people prefer and choose self-enhancing information the most. This is especially true of people with high explicit self-esteem, but not necessarily true for people with low implicit self-esteem (Bosson, Brown, Zeigler-Hill, & Swann, 2003). These findings are echoed by the fact that people interpret ambiguous feedback as positive when feedback follows success on a task (Moore, 1979). Sedikides and Strube (1997) argue that self-enhancement is the primary motive because the self-verification, self-assessment, and self-improvement motives all ultimately have self-enhancing effects after they have satisfied their own function. This point is consistent with Trope and Pomerantz's (1998) finding that the self-relevance of a goal increases interest in positive feedback after failure, whereas the self-relevance of a goal increases interest in negative feedback after success. Once the motive to self-enhance has been met, such as completing a task successfully, people are likely to be more receptive to negative feedback, as it may provide information on how one can improve (i.e. do even better in the future). However, if the motive to self-enhance has not been met, such as failing to complete a task, people are going to be focused on ways to enhance the self, and receiving positive feedback is one way to enhance the self. Sedikides' point is also consistent with Gervey, Igou, and Trope's (2005) finding that positive mood increases interest in negative feedback when this information is used for self-assessment and self-improvement purposes.

However, additional research suggests that the issue of motive importance is not always clear-cut. For example, Swann, Griffin, Predmore, and Gaines (1987) found that affective responses to feedback are driven by the self-enhancement motive, whereas cognitive responses to feedback are driven by the self-verification motive. This is consistent with Dauenheimer, Stahlberg, Spreemann, and Sedikides' (2002) finding that affective responses to feedback decrease positive affect when a trait (e.g. assertiveness) is regarded as unmodifiable. However, cognitive responses to feedback are driven by the self-verification motive when assertiveness is regarded as unmodifiable, but driven by the self-enhancement motive when assertiveness is regarded as modifiable. Behavioural responses to feedback are driven by the self-assessment motive. Other research suggests that both self-enhancement and self-verification are primary motives because self-enhancement operates at the global level of self-views, whereas self-verification operates at the level of specific strengths and weaknesses (Neff & Karney, 2002).

There is a limited amount of research on these self-evaluation motives in clinical populations. Of most interest to the clinical domain is Dykman's and Swann's research on self-verification among individuals with depression or low self-esteem. This research has found that the self-enhancement motive is less pronounced in those individuals (Dykman, Abramson, Alloy, & Hartlage, 1989; Giesler & Swann, 1999; Swann, Wenzlaff, Krull, & Pelham, 1992). Self-verification may be a more important driver in people with clinical disorders, because clinical observation supports the idea that patients routinely seek out information that is consistent with negative self-views. Information used for self-verification and self-assessment may be drawn from faulty information processing in which individuals selectively attend to threat or misinterpret ambiguous or neutral information in a negatively biased way. The interactions between these different cognitive biases might lead individuals to believe that they are drawing on accurate and consistent information about the self, when in fact this information is the product of distortions in other areas of information processing. To date, as far as we are aware, no research has looked at the effects of positive and negative images of self on these self-evaluation processes.

There is a pressing need to examine these four self-evaluation motives in clinical populations. Self-enhancement is clearly disrupted in a number of disorders. While individuals may retain the desire to receive positive information about the self, this information does not always reduce anxiety and in a disorder such as social phobia may increase expectations about what is required in future social interactions, thus leading to increased anxiety (Wallace & Alden, 1997). Self-verification can reinforce negative self-beliefs rather than positive self-representations in clinical populations. Self-assessment may drive the desire to seek accurate information about the self, but this information may be distorted. In eating disorders, body dysmorphic disorder (BDD), and social phobia, the information that the individual seeks may be represented in the form of an image. These images are not usually realistic pictures of what other people see (e.g. over-estimation of body size in eating disorders, significant distortions of body parts in BDD). However, images may feel realistic and may be accepted without question as accurate representations of reality.

Self-improvement is clearly relevant to the clinical population, who seek to live up to their ideal or ought selves, but believe that they typically fail to do so. According to Bentall, Kinderman, and Kaney (1994), individuals with paranoia try to protect themselves from the negative beliefs that they hold about themselves by attributing blame to other people for negative events rather than attributing blame to themselves. Although the evidence for Bentall *et al.*'s theory is mixed, the theory itself provides a clear illustration of an attempt to self-enhance that has unintended negative consequences, that is, the attributions of blame to other people can result in a hostile suspicious attitude that forms the basis for the development of paranoid beliefs and can result in social isolation. Furthermore, this strategy of blaming other people leads to the belief that others perceive the self negatively, which, as described in the section on sociometer theory, ultimately decreases self-esteem (Bentall, Corcoran, Howard, Blackwood, & Kinderman, 2001; Kaney & Bentall, 1989; Leary, Haupt, Strausser, & Chokel, 1998).

Regulatory focus

According to regulatory focus theory (Higgins, 1997; Higgins & Spiegel, 2004), people can regulate their behaviour to pursue favourable outcomes or avoid unfavourable outcomes. Thus, people engage in promotion or prevention strategies, respectively. Individuals with a promotion-focus strategy concentrate on obtaining success and advancement. They are likely to engage in approach behaviours. In contrast, individuals with a prevention-focus strategy concentrate on avoiding failure and obtaining security. They are likely to engage in avoidance behaviours and prefer vigilant goal pursuit.

Furthermore, promotion-focused individuals are most inspired by positive role models who highlight achievement strategies, whereas prevention-focussed individuals are most inspired by negative role models who highlight strategies for avoiding failure (Lockwood, Jordan, & Kunda, 2002).

Although there has been no direct research on regulatory focus in people suffering from psychological disorders, there is some evidence to suggest that regulatory focus can be affected by self-esteem and also that failures of a particular strategy can lead to certain mood states. For example, high self-esteem people have a promotion-focus orientation, whereas low self-esteem people have an avoidance (prevention)-focus orientation (Baumeister, Tice, & Hutton, 1989; McGregor, Gailliot, Vasquez, & Nash, 2007). Furthermore, people feel disappointment and dejection when promotion-focus strategies fail, but they feel agitation and anger when prevention strategies fail (Leung & Lam, 2003). However, adopting a promotion (rather than prevention)-focus strategy is less likely to lead to negative emotions when the strategy fails. Finally, highly rejection-sensitive individuals who are generally successful in preventing negative outcomes (i.e. adopting prevention-focus strategies) engage in self-silencing to prevent rejection; however, when they perceive that they are rejected, they express passive hostility (withdrawing love and support), but inhibit more active forms of hostility (Ayduk, May, Downey, & Higgins, 2003).

Self-affirmation and self-compassion

Next, we will discuss self-affirmation and self-compassion, two processes that have different aims. Self-affirmation is about increasing the positivity of the self, especially after a threat to self-integrity, whereas self-compassion is about accepting the self as it is. Steele and colleagues coined the term 'self-affirmation' after discovering that affirming an important value could reduce cognitive dissonance (psychological inconsistency between cognitions and behaviours; Steele & Liu, 1981, 1983). In classic cognitive dissonance fashion, people normally change their attitudes to be consistent with their behaviour. However, Steele and Liu (1981, 1983) found that affirming an important value eliminated the need to change the attitude to be consistent with the behaviour. Affirming an important value is the most common self-affirmation method, although other instances include receiving positive feedback, visualising a positive personal experience, or thinking of an intimate relationship (Fein & Spencer, 1997; Kumashiro & Sedikides, 2005; Steele, Spencer, & Lynch, 1993; see McQueen & Klein, 2006, for a review). Furthermore, people engage in self-affirmation after a threat, usually by emphasising positive qualities in a domain separate from the threat (Tesser, 2000).

Steele (1988) suggests that self-affirmation processes are activated when the self is threatened, which is consistent with the self-enhancement motive (i.e. people are motivated to maintain high self-esteem). Affirmations can be used to mitigate the effects of low self-esteem in some circumstances. For example, Spencer, Fein, and Lomore (2001) found that people with low self-esteem anticipate poor performance on a task when they expect immediate feedback, but these performance expectations disappear after a self-affirmation exercise. Other research relevant to the clinical domain suggests that a self-affirmation manipulation reduces rumination about a frustrated goal (Koole, Smeets, van Knippenberg, & Dijksterhuis, 1999) and thoughts about social rejection (Schimel, Arndt, Banko, & Cook, 2004) and increases implicit self-esteem and positive mood (Koole *et al.*, 1999). Further research is needed to establish whether and when self-affirmations could be usefully implemented in a clinical setting. Some of the imagery techniques described in the next chapter (for example, imaginal rehearsal, where a person visualises him or herself achieving a successful outcome in a feared situation) might implicitly contain an element of self-affirmation, but this has not been tested directly.

In contrast, self-compassion is concerned with accepting oneself for one's faults and misgivings as part of the common human experience. Self-compassion has been conceptualised as consisting of three key components: self-kindness (adopting an understanding toward the self), common humanity (perceiving a negative experience as part of larger human experience), and mindfulness (awareness of the present moment and balancing positive and negative feelings; Neff, 2003a). Rather than focusing on maintaining positive evaluations of the self, self-compassion focuses on adopting a compassionate and kind attitude toward the self. Thus, self-compassion is less likely to be associated with inflated positive views of the self.

Self-compassionate attitudes are associated with positive mental health. For example, self-compassionate people are less likely to be self-critical, anxious, depressed, or neurotic, and are more likely to exhibit greater life satisfaction, and feel socially connected, happy, and optimistic (Gilbert & Irons, 2004; Neff, 2003b; Neff, Rude, & Kirkpatrick, 2007). Furthermore, other research suggests that a self-compassionate attitude can have beneficial effects on mental health. Specifically, adopting a self-compassionate attitude undermines self-criticism, reduces emotional disturbances, facilitates self-acceptance, and buffers the effects of anxiety and negative self-feelings (Gilbert & Procter, 2006; Leary, Tate, Adams, Allen, & Hancock, 2007; Neff, Kirkpatrick, & Rude, 2007). These latter findings suggest that training people who are depressed or self-critical to adopt a more self-compassionate attitude can be a useful tool for therapy. In fact, Gilbert and colleagues (Gilbert & Irons, 2004; Gilbert & Procter, 2006) and Lee (2005) have successfully used self-compassionate training as a part of therapy sessions (see Chapter 9 for a discussion of imagery and self-compassion in depression). Furthermore, Shapiro and colleagues (Shapiro, Astin, Bishop, & Cordova, 2005; Shapiro, Brown, & Biegel, 2007) showed that mindfulness, which is one component of self-compassion in some formulations, can decrease anxiety, rumination, and stress and increase self-compassion in health care professionals. However, one should note that self-critics can have difficulties generating self-compassionate images (Gilbert, Baldwin, Irons, Baccus, & Palmer, 2006). Nevertheless, inducing self-compassion in people with negative self-views should be easier than simply increasing self-esteem, because people with low self-esteem may be motivated to maintain a negative view of themselves (Swann, 1996).

Summary

At the beginning of this chapter, we talked about the way in which the self is unique, given that it can simultaneously be both subject ('I') and object ('me'). The process of self-evaluation neatly illustrates this distinction, because the individual has both a self that can be observed, monitored, and judged (the object or the 'me') and a self that does the judging (the subject or the 'I'). We introduced four self-evaluation motives and discussed how these motives might operate differently in clinical compared to healthy populations. We speculated that, for people with clinical disorders, self-enhancement is inactive or operates differently, whereas self-assessment operates similarly but is influenced by other processes (e.g. self-images are distorted and maintained in part by attentional and interpretative biases).

The theory of regulatory focus was developed in the field of social psychology and suggests that promotion and prevention strategies are linked to self-goals. Paradoxically, a prevention strategy is more likely to produce negative affect when it fails than a promotion-focused strategy. This may well lead to a vicious cycle in which the individuals try to protect themselves but then experience negative affect. In order to alleviate this affect, they may work harder to use the avoidance strategy, but again, if this does not work, it will result in intensification of negative affect. A frequent aim of cognitive therapy is to help individuals move from avoidant to approach behaviours, and this could be reconceptualised within the theory of regulatory focus as a move from prevention to promotion strategies.

Finally, we examined self-affirmation and self-compassion. Therapists are well aware of the limited efficacy of a simplistic self-affirmation strategy (e.g. positive self-statements). Interestingly, self-affirmation works best when individuals utilise indirect methods of self-affirmation, such as affirming an important value or imagining a positive experience, rather than affirming the self on the aspect that was threatened. These two different methods of self-affirmation may work through different routes. The former might have similarities to self-compassion in that affirming an important value might reinforce the sense of being part of a community of people who share this value rather than being an isolated individual. The latter might work more directly on the self by helping the individual to access a more positive working self-concept. In social phobia, holding a positive image in mind reduces social anxiety, improves self and other perceptions of performance, and increases the accessibility of positive autobiographical memories (Stopa

& Jenkins, 2007). Self-compassion is dealt with more fully in Chapter 9, but it seems to be an important means of accepting the self and it can provide a secure foundation for mental well-being. In therapy, creating visual images that represent a compassionate self can be an important method of alleviating distress.

Part 4: The self as agent

Earlier in the chapter, we discussed how self-beliefs are organised into systematic structures (schemas) that form the basis of an individual's self-concept. There is, however, another set of self-beliefs that determine the degree to which an individual perceives himself or herself as an effective agent capable of achieving desired goals and outcomes. These beliefs are captured in Bandura's (1977) concept of self-efficacy. High self-efficacy is associated with better mental health and outcomes than low self-efficacy, although it is not clear whether low self-efficacy is a cause or consequence of psychological disorders. Prolonged anxiety and avoidance have a direct impact on the self, and one aim of therapy is often to help individuals develop higher self-efficacy through tackling fears and avoided situations. Another way of understanding the self as agent is through Deci's (1980) theory of self-determination, which derives from social rather than clinical psychology. Self-determination describes the different ways in which humans strive to get their needs met. The sections below provide brief descriptions of self-efficacy and self-determination and discuss the impact that each theory can have on psychological health and well-being.

Self-efficacy

Self-efficacy theory was introduced by Bandura (1977). He proposed that self-efficacy is the belief that one is capable of performing a specific behaviour and achieving certain goals. People become fearful if they believe that they are incapable of coping with aversive events or stimuli. These self-efficacy beliefs are derived mostly from performance and vicarious experiences, but also from verbal persuasion and physiological reactions (Maddux, 1991). Furthermore, Bandura's (1977) self-efficacy model indicates that the following cognitive processes are important in predicting whether people will persist in actions when they encounter obstacles and what behaviours they will perform: (a) self-efficacy expectancies (beliefs about ability to perform the necessary behaviours), (b) outcome expectancies (beliefs that a certain outcome will follow a specific behaviour), and (c) outcome value (subjective value placed on an expected outcome).

Several additional lines of research by Bandura and colleagues have examined the psychological benefits of high self-efficacy. For example, people with low self-efficacy are more likely to suffer from anxiety disorders (generalised anxiety, social anxiety, PTSD; Bandura, 1991; Leary & Atherton, 1986; Solomon, Benbenishty, & Mikulincer, 1991), distress, and depression (Bandura, Pastorelli, Barbaranelli, & Caprara, 1999) than people high in self-efficacy. In contrast, people high in self-efficacy beliefs are healthier, more effective, and more successful in general than people low in self-efficacy (Bandura, 1997). Furthermore, a lack of self-efficacy is associated with avoidance behaviour, which leads to the person never coping with the aversive event or stimuli (Bandura, 1983). However, increasing self-efficacy beliefs either through desensitisation to threatening stimuli or through a mastery thinking task can lead to more approach behaviour and better coping skills in snake phobics and agoraphobics (Bandura & Adams, 1977; Bandura, Adams, Hardy, & Howells, 1980). In fact, mastery exercises are effective in treating anxiety disorders, depression, and eating disorders (see Bandura, 1997, for a review). Thus, one way to exercise control over anxiety is to induce beliefs about behavioural coping efficacy and efficacy in controlling dysfunctional thoughts (Bandura, 1988). Indeed, self-efficacy beliefs regarding the ability to cope with traumatic events increase the likelihood of post-traumatic recovery (Benight & Bandura, 2004).

Self-determination

Self-determination, a theory of human motivation, was proposed by Deci (1980; Deci & Ryan, 1980, 2000). Motivation arises from the drive to grow and through the requirement to meet specific needs, such as competence, relatedness, and autonomy. If these needs are met, people are likely to be intrinsically motivated and self-determined. That is, people engage in behaviours because they value the activity. However, if one focuses primarily on meeting the need of relatedness, one can become focused on pleasing others. If this is the case, people are likely to be extrinsically motivated. That is, people engage in behaviours that will please others. People with a relatedness focus are more likely to use self-presentation tactics (i.e. present themselves in a favourable way to attract others) than people who have met the need of autonomy (Lewis & Neighbors, 2005). Beck's (see Clark & Beck, 1991) concepts of autonomy and sociotropy, which he argues are personality styles that can confer vulnerability to depression, link well to these ideas of intrinsic and extrinsic motivation.

Self-determination has been associated with a variety of psychological outcomes in the clinical domain. In particular, people experience better psychological well-being if they are intrinsically motivated (i.e. if their needs for autonomy, competency, and relatedness have been met). Specifically, if competence and relatedness needs are met, people are likely to have positive true self-esteem (self-esteem that is solid and stable), positive internal working models (of the self and others) and attachment security, be satisfied with life, and experience positive emotions, but are less likely to have an eating disorder or to experience anxiety, depression, or physical illness symptoms (La Guardia, Ryan, Couchman, & Deci, 2000; Reis, Sheldon, Gable, Roscoe, & Ryan, 2000; Sheldon, Ryan, Deci, & Kasser, 2004). Furthermore, people perform better on tasks if they are intrinsically rather than extrinsically motivated (Bierma, 2005).

Several lines of research have discussed adopting an attitude of self-determination or becoming intrinsically motivated as a tool for therapy. For example, this approach has been used in patients suffering from depression, eating disorders, obsessive-compulsive disorder, and posttraumatic stress (Sheldon, Williams, & Joiner, 2003; Vansteenkiste, Soenens, & Vandereycken, 2005). In one study, self-determination in schizophrenic patients was dependent on community nurses educating their clients about the illness, fostering self-reliance, and developing a reciprocal relationship (McCann & Clark, 2004).

Summary

Self-efficacy has been extensively studied in the clinical field and behavioural techniques, such as systematic desensitisation, are well-established means of increasing self-efficacy through the reduction of fear and through overcoming avoidance. The specific effects of cognitive therapy on self-efficacy are less well known. Although one component of self-efficacy is the beliefs that individuals hold about their ability to perform the necessary behaviours, it is unlikely that trying to tackle these beliefs at a purely cognitive level would be effective. However, behavioural experiments that are designed to tackle beliefs about low self-efficacy and give individuals the direct experience of dealing with a feared or difficult situation are ideally suited to raising self-efficacy.

There is a substantial body of evidence that demonstrates that imagery can directly improve self-efficacy and performance in sporting activities (Beauchamp, Bray, & Albinson, 2002; Cumming, Nordin, Horton, & Reynolds, 2006). However, we do not know whether more recent interventions, such as imagery rescripting (e.g. Holmes, Arntz, & Smucker, 2007; and see Chapter 3), also have an impact on self-efficacy. In imagery rescripting, the individual re-experiences a situation in which he or she previously felt overwhelmed in a way that allows the imagined self to have control over and to direct the outcome of the event. It also allows the individual to contextualise views of the self that might underpin low self-efficacy. For example, a child who was unable to prevent her father from physically attacking her mother might see herself as useless and ineffective and feel helpless. Imagery rescripting can allow the adult to see why these beliefs about the self developed and to distinguish between the child and the adult, which may help to modify self-efficacy beliefs. In some cases, individuals bring their adult selves into the image to change the outcome, but in other cases, they use an external agent (e.g. another adult family member, a policeman, or the therapist). We do not know whether using the self is better at increasing self-efficacy or not. It is possible that using another person is equally effective because the act of creating the image, drawing on other resources, and changing the outcome could create a sense of the self as an active agent rather than a passive recipient. In other words, the process, as well as changing the content of the image, may have an impact on self-efficacy. To date, as far as the authors are aware, none of the areas described above have been tested directly.

Self-determination is important as well as self-efficacy because it helps us to understand why people adopt different strategies in order to meet their needs and why some strategies are more effective than others. The idea that intrinsic motivation is linked to better psychological health suggests that further work is required on how to foster intrinsic motivation in therapy.

Part 5: Self-awareness and self-consciousness

Self-focused attention describes a state in which one is aware of self-referent information that can have an impact on current self-concept. This information can include thoughts, feelings, body state information, memories, attitudes, and beliefs. Self-focused attention is not in itself a pathological process, but it can become problematic if it is excessive, rigid and prolonged because it interferes with the individual's ability to process external information. Self-focused attention occurs across a range of disorders, and, in general, the more severe the pathology, the greater is the degree of self-focus (Woodruff-Borden, Brothers, & Lister, 2001).

Ingram (1990) proposes a model of self-focused attention in which he argues that the process of self-focused attention is the same across all disorders, but the content reflects the schemas that are specific to the particular disorder. Current accounts of self-focused attention rely heavily on earlier theories of self-awareness and self-consciousness, and these are described in more detail below. Negative thought content increases self-focused attention and also generates negative affect. If the focus of attention is on negative images of the self, this is likely to have an even more powerful effect because of the amount of information that images can contain as well as their more powerful emotional impact.

Self-awareness and self-consciousness

Self-awareness refers to the notion that one is aware that one exists independently of others and that one has independent thoughts and can engage in behaviours independently of others. The theory of objective self-awareness was proposed by Duval and Wickland (1972). According to this theory, focusing inwardly on the self invokes a comparison of the self against a standard. In this context, a standard is defined as some kind of internal representation of what constitutes the right attitude or behaviour. If there is a discrepancy between the self and the standard, then negative affect should follow. This negative affect would prompt the person to restore consistency by changing actions, attitudes, or traits or by avoiding the self-focused stimuli, particularly for people with low self-esteem (Sedikides, 1992). Subsequently, Silvia and Duval (2001) summarised a series of research studies on non-clinical participants which suggest that, when the self is discrepant from a standard, people make attributions for the cause of the discrepancy and assess whether the discrepancy can be easily reduced. If the discrepancy can be easily reduced, people will attribute failure to the self and try to change the self. If the discrepancy cannot be easily reduced, people will attribute failure to an external cause. Furthermore, when the discrepancy is due to the standard, people are likely to change the standard.

The consequences of failure to meet an expected or desired standard can be clearly illustrated with reference to socially phobic patients. Many patients have unrealistic expectations about performance together with extremely dysfunctional beliefs about the consequences of showing anxiety (e.g. if they see me blushing, they will assume I'm incompetent). At the same time, current models of social phobia (Clark & Wells, 1995; Rapee & Heimberg, 1997) suggest that patients often create a visual representation or image of themselves in social situations. If a patient imagines the self as small, red-faced, quivering, and sweating, and at the same time believes that the only acceptable standard of social performance is to be confident, witty, and fluent at all times, then the discrepancy between the self and the standard is simply too great to resolve. According to the theory though, patients should either attribute failure externally or alternatively reduce the standard, and yet what actually happens is that patients generally attribute failure to the self and the standard remains unmodified. Why does this happen? First of all, many patients will avoid the feared situation as a means of resolving the conflict. A second possibility is that the presence of the distorted visual image of the self provides such compelling evidence that the 'fault' lies with the self that this overrides the normal tendency to attribute failure to an external cause. Consistent with this explanation, George and Stopa (2008) found that a high socially anxious group was more likely to attribute success in a conversation to their partners and failure to themselves than a low socially anxious group, who did the opposite. In therapy, the target is to help the patient to create a more veridical image of how he or she actually comes across as well as to modify the standard. (See Chapter 4 for a more detailed discussion of imagery in social phobia and how it can be used in treatment.)

Self-awareness has been implicated in a number of other psychological disorders. For example, heightened self-awareness is associated with depression (Chen, Mechanic, & Hansell, 1998; Schmitt, 1983; Schwartz, 2001). Pyszczynski and Greenberg (1987) suggest that depression is the result of the loss of self-worth when the discrepancy between actual and desired states cannot be resolved. Self-focus leads to negative affect, self-derogation, further negative outcomes, and a depressive self-focusing style. Other research suggests that self-awareness promotes anxiety (agoraphobia, general anxiety, social anxiety and test anxiety; Bogels & Lamers, 2002; Bogels & Mansell, 2004; Gibbons, 1991). However, the literature is not completely consistent and there are some studies that show the opposite, namely that low self-awareness is indicative of anxiety and depression (Bekker & Belt, 2006). Nevertheless, the association with heightened self-awareness and clinical disorders is likely to be due to the fact that self-awareness increases awareness of bodily states, impairs task performances due to decreased attention, disrupts coping skills, increases avoidant behaviours, and activates relevant self-schemas (see Wells & Matthews, 1994, for a review).

In addition, knowing how self-awareness and self-evaluations interact can have implications for therapy. Based on findings from his experience-sampling study, Figurski (1992) has drawn several conclusions on how to tailor therapy sessions in patients suffering from depression. Figurski found that private self-awareness is associated with negative affect if people hold negative beliefs about themselves. Making private self-awareness salient in patients with negative self-beliefs can then lead to resistance to change, as a means of avoiding negative feelings about the self. This is problematic, because the process of identifying and challenging negative self-beliefs inevitably induces attention to the self. Thus, other strategies, such as attentional training or mindfulness, might mitigate the effects of private self-awareness and help to facilitate therapy.

Self-consciousness describes a state of being self-aware. Public and private self-consciousness refer to dispositional states (traits) in which the individual is either aware of the self as it is viewed by others (public) or aware of his or her inner self and feelings (private). Private and public self-consciousness can be measured by scales developed by Fenigstein, Scheier, and Buss (1975), which have generated a good deal of research. For example, poor health during childhood is an antecedent of private self-consciousness, whereas harsh parenting (excessive achievement demands, parental rejection or overprotection; Klonsky, Dutton, & Liebel, 1990) is an antecedent of public self-consciousness. These studies suggest that early experience not only influences the contents of belief systems, but also influences the type of processing that individuals engage in.

Of most relevance to the clinical domain are the correlations between public and private self-consciousness and various psychological disorders. Several lines of research suggest that public self-consciousness is associated with shyness, social anxiety, or blushing (Bogels, Alberts, & de Jong, 1996; Bruch, Gorsky, Collins, & Berger, 1989; Cheek & Buss, 1981; see Spurr & Stopa, 2002, for a review), although some research suggests that social anxiety is associated with private self-consciousness (Panayiotou, 2005) and that private self-focused attention leads to an increase in reporting negative daily events (Nezlek, 2002). In general, public self-consciousness is more critical in triggering social anxiety. However, both private and public self-consciousness are associated with blushing and social anxiety (Edelmann, 1990; Monfries & Kafer, 1994) and with depression and paranoia (Kuiper, Olinger, & Swallow, 1987; von Gemmingen, Sullivan, & Pomerantz, 2003).

Summary

Self-focused attention, or self-awareness, is important in the maintenance of a number of emotional disorders. There is an overlap between some of the theories presented here and those that were described earlier in the chapter. In particular, Duval and Wicklund's (1972) argument that self-awareness invokes the comparison of the self with a standard has parallels with Higgins' (1987) theory of self-discrepancy. The standard of comparison could easily be either an 'ideal' or an 'ought' self. We have suggested ways in which dysfunctional images of the self might interfere with the operation of self-awareness, so that, instead of changing the standard when the discrepancy between self and standard is large, the individual attributes failure to the self. Self-consciousness, particularly public self-consciousness, has well-established associations with a range of psychopathological states, especially social anxiety. Self-consciousness is at the core of Clark and Wells' (1995) model of social phobia, and, for many socially phobic individuals, there is an integral link between self-consciousness and distorted mental self-images that are hypothesised to have a causal role in the disorder (Hirsch, Mathews, Clark, Williams, & Morrison, 2006).

Part 6: The self through interactions with others

The self does not develop in isolation; instead it develops and changes in a nexus of social connections. In early childhood the social context predominantly comprises the family. In later childhood and adolescence, the peer group gains prominence as the social group against which the self is measured. In adulthood, there are myriad social worlds in which the self must operate and against which the individual judges the worth and efficacy of the self.

In this part of the chapter, we will start by looking at attachment theory, which describes the ways in which early experiences influence the development of beliefs about the self and others and how these beliefs can influence responding and self-esteem later in life. Next, we will consider a form of self-regulation known as social comparison, in which individuals try to maintain self-esteem by comparing themselves with other people. Finally, we will examine the fundamental human need to belong and discuss the impact of failing to meet this need on self-esteem and related self processes.

Attachment theory and relational schemas

There is an enduring fascination with the notion that children's early experiences with their parents leave a permanent stamp on their lives. This idea is the centrepiece of Bowlby's (1973, 1977, 1980) seminal theory about attachment processes. Bowlby suggested that early attachment experiences (e.g. parental care) influence the development of internal working models, which are crucial variables in subsequent social behaviour throughout the lifespan. These internal working models are complex schemas that include feelings of self-worth and self-acceptance (model of self) and beliefs about the availability and responsiveness of attachment figures, such as primary caregivers and significant others (model of others; Bowlby, 1973, 1977, 1980). In general, if a child receives sensitive and responsive care, then he or she will develop a view of the self as worthy and a view of others as reliable and predictable (i.e. positive internal working models). However, if a child receives inconsistent care, rejection, or neglect, he or she may develop a view of the self as unworthy and a view of others as unreliable (i.e. negative internal working models). These models of early attachment experiences will be carried forward in life and influence expectations for other attachment figures and for people in the world in general.

In fact, Hazan and Shaver (1987; cf. Bartholomew & Horowitz, 1991) have conceptualised adult romantic relationships in terms of internal working models and relational schemas (evaluations of the self and others in a relationship context; Baldwin, 1995). Bartholomew and Horowitz's (1991) measure can be used to assess four different attachment styles in adult relationships: secure, preoccupied, fearful, and dismissing. Securely attached people have a positive model of the self and of others in their relationships. People with a preoccupied attachment style have a negative model of self and a positive model of others in their relationships. Fearfully attached people have a negative model of self and of others in their relationships. People with a dismissive attachment style have a positive model of self and a negative model of others in their relationships. Thus, people with any kind of negative internal working model (i.e. preoccupied, fearful or dismissing attachment style) are conceptualised as insecurely attached.

There have been several relevant studies on the relations between internal working models/attachment styles and psychopathology. For example, people who possess a positive attachment self-model report higher self-esteem and self-acceptance (Bartholomew & Horowitz, 1991; Luke, Maio, & Carnelley, 2004; Murray, Holmes, Griffin, Bellavia, & Rose, 2001). Also, a positive attachment self-model is negatively associated with depression and social anxiety (Carnelley, Pietromonaco, & Jaffe, 1994; Darcy, Davila, & Beck, 2005). In addition, an insecure attachment style is positively linked with anxiety disorders, antisocial disorders, borderline personality disorder, bipolar disorder, conduct disorder, depression, narcissistic personality, obsessive-compulsive disorder, schizophrenia, and substance abuse (Bohlin, Hagekull, & Rydell, 2000; Eng, Heimberg, Hart, Schneier, & Liebowitz, 2001; Mickelson, Kessler, & Shaver, 1997; see Dozier, Stovall, & Albus, 1999, for a review).

Another line of research has examined the effect of priming attachment security and relationship partners. Priming involves making attachment relationships salient at a conscious or unconscious level through reading a script that describes a close relationship or visualising an attachment figure. In particular, Carnelley and Rowe (2007) showed that priming attachment security increases positive self-views relative to a neutral prime, whereas Baldwin and colleagues (Baldwin, 1994; Baldwin, Carrell, & Lopez, 1990) have found that priming a critical significant other leads to negative self-evaluation. Attachment priming can have a direct clinical impact; for example, Mikulincer, Shaver, and Horesh (2006) found that priming a secure attachment lowered the accessibility of trauma-related thoughts in people with PTSD symptoms.

Finally, other research has examined how people with low self-esteem and social anxiety react to and interact with relationship partners and people in general. For example, people with low self-esteem are more likely to feel more positive about themselves and their relationships and respond positively to a partner's compliment when they are encouraged to describe the meaning and significance of the compliment (Marigold, Holmes, & Ross, 2007). Also, giving people with social anxiety a negative appraisal of their social interaction with another person increases the likelihood that they will elicit negative responses from other people relative to when they are given a positive appraisal (Alden & Bieling, 1998). Similarly, people with social anxiety who are highly self-conscious and receive a computer tone paired with thoughts of social rejection expect to receive, and actually do receive, more negative evaluations from other people (Baldwin & Main, 2001).

Social comparison and self-evaluation maintenance

Attachment theory describes some of the ways in which individuals form models of themselves and other people and how these models exert an effect on self-perception and behaviour. The relationship of self to others can be conceptualised in more direct terms, and Festinger's (1954) theory of social comparison proposes that people make direct comparisons between themselves and others in order to regulate self-esteem. Festinger argued that individuals are motivated to define their abilities and opinions accurately, and, when there is a lack of objective evidence available, people compare themselves to others. There are various types of comparison: In downward social comparison, people compare themselves to others worse off than themselves; in lateral social comparison, people compare themselves to others who are neither worse off nor better off than themselves; and in upward social comparison, people compare themselves to others who are better off than themselves. In general, upward social comparisons produce a decrease in self-esteem, whereas downward social comparisons produce an increase in self-esteem. However, the effect of social comparisons on self-esteem is generally moderated by the importance of the task to the self, and by the degree of closeness to the person who is the comparator (Beach & Tesser, 2000; Tesser & Campbell, 1982). In particular, people feel worse when they are outperformed by someone who is close to them on an attribute or task that is important to the self. By comparison, they feel better when they are outperformed by someone close to them on an attribute or task that is not important to the self. This process is known as self-evaluation maintenance and is a means of maintaining high self-esteem.

There is some evidence that people with low self-esteem, high self-criticism, or low self-concept clarity engage and react to social comparisons in particular ways. For example, negative self-feelings, a component of low self-esteem, are antecedents of the social comparison process (Stiles & Kaplan, 2004). Furthermore, people with low self-esteem feel particularly anxious after they engage in social comparisons (Biaggio, Crano, & Crano, 1986). Finally, individuals with high self-criticism or low self-esteem are more likely to engage in social comparisons when comparisons are unfavourable, which serves to maintain their negative beliefs about themselves (Butzer & Kuiper, 2006; Santor & Yazbek, 2006; Sturman & Mongrain, 2005).

Low self-esteem is implicated in numerous psychological disorders (Tennen & Affleck, 1993; Wood & Lockwood, 1999; see Roberts, 2006, for a review). However, there is an even more direct link between the different types of social comparisons described above and psychological disorders. People with depression and dysphoria are more likely to use social comparison as a means of regulating the self, and they are particularly likely to use upward social comparisons (Bazner, Brömer, Hammelstein, & Meyer, 2006; Butzer & Kuiper, 2006; Wood & Lockwood, 1999), although they also engage in downward social comparisons when negative affect is made salient and this downward social comparison improves their mood (Gibbons, 1986). Furthermore, depressed and dysphoric individuals tend to make their most frequent social comparisons following poor performances on a task (Swallow & Kuiper, 1992).

Depressed individuals, who frequently use social comparison, experience negative affect when they are confronted with a high-effort target (Buunk & Brenninkmeijer, 2001). In other words, when people are depressed they are more likely to use social comparison. In particular, they are more likely to choose upward social comparison, and therefore to experience a reduction in self-esteem. Furthermore, they are likely to experience negative affect when faced with a high-effort target, presumably because they judge themselves as less adequate than other people.

There is also some research on the dimensions (e.g. academic/professional and social skills) that people with depression are likely to choose in order to make social comparisons. Giordano, Wood, and Michela (2000) showed that dysphoric individuals make social comparisons in domains that are congruent with their personality. Specifically, dysphoric participants with an autonomous personality made social comparisons in achievement domains, whereas dypshoric participants with a sociotropic personality made social comparisons in interpersonal relations. Furthermore, Thwaites and Dagnan (2004) found that the link between depression and social comparison on a particular dimension, such as social skills, sporting ability, physical attractiveness, leadership ability, common sense, emotionality stability, sense of humour, intelligence, artistic/musical ability, and discipline, is moderated by the perceived importance of that dimension in attracting the interest of others.

There has also been some research on social comparison among people suffering from other psychological disorders. For example, people with social phobia are more likely to make upward than downward social comparisons and to exhibit greater changes in affect following social comparison (Antony, Rowa, Liss, Swallow, & Swinson, 2005). In addition, anxiety is associated generally with an increase in social comparison, and in particular with upward social comparisons (Butzer & Kuiper, 2006). Finally, Heilbrun, Diller, and Dodson (1986) found that reactive paranoid schizophrenics minimise the possession of a particular trait (e.g. hostility, untrustworthiness) in themselves by distorting this trait in people with whom they make social comparisons. This projection of a trait might be a defensive mechanism in reactive paranoid schizophrenics that helps to contribute to the development of delusions.

Need to belong, sociometer, and looking-glass self

People have a fundamental need to belong or feel included. This is evidenced by the notion that people form social bonds and resist the break-up of these bonds (Baumeister & Leary, 1995). This motive is so universal that people who have a negative internal working model of others react favourably (i.e. they feel better about themselves) when they learn that they are accepted by others (Carvallo & Gabriel, 2006). In fact, when people are thwarted from meeting their need to belong, there are disruptions in intelligent thought and self-regulation (Baumeister & DeWall, 2005). In particular, when socially excluded people perform poorly on intelligence tests, they have impaired recall memory, difficulties processing information in a logical way, regulating healthy eating and drinking behaviours, and paying attention in a dichotic listening task, and fail to persist on difficult tasks. Furthermore, when people are excluded from important groups, they feel anxious, engage in antisocial behaviours, and selectively remember socially relevant stimuli (Baumeister & Tice, 1990; Blackhart, Baumeister, & Twenge, 2006; Gardner, Pickett, & Brewer, 2000). Therefore, people are likely to engage in a variety of behaviours, such as being attentive and accurately decoding social cues (Pickett, Gardner, & Knowles, 2004) and regulating their behaviour to be consistent with that of others around them (Vohs & Ciarocco, 2004), as a means of fulfilling their need to belong.

Acting as a sociometer, self-esteem is one way in which the individual monitors whether the need to belong has been met (Leary & Baumeister, 2000). Self-esteem decreases when exclusionary cues, such as rejection, are present, which alert the individual to the fact that the need to belong is not being met. Indeed, several lines of research have provided evidence that low self-esteem and negative affect are the result of being rejected or disregarded by others, whereas high self-esteem is the result of being accepted by others (Leary et al., 1998; Leary, Tambor, Terdal, & Downs, 1995; Srivastava & Beer, 2005).

This notion that self-esteem is the outcome of social acceptance or rejection is consistent with Cooley's (1964) looking-glass self theory. According to Cooley, feelings and beliefs about the self emanate from how a person imagines that other people judge the self based on how the individual appears to others. If an individual believes that others' negative evaluations of him or her are based on an imagined negative presentation of the self, then he or she is likely to have negative feelings and beliefs about the self. It is easy to see how a negative vicious circle can develop in many clinical disorders between the individual's beliefs about others' negative judgements and a negative internal representation of self.

People with social anxiety likely fail to have their need to belong met. They have lower self-esteem than people without social anxiety (Roberts, 2006) and they feel that others will evaluate them negatively or reject them (Clark & Wells, 1995; Rapee & Heimberg, 1997). This fear of exclusion is likely to be a key source of their anxiety, which is consistent with Baumeister and Tice's (1990) finding that actual exclusion leads to feelings of anxiety. Furthermore, they remain hypervigilant for exclusionary cues in the environment (Clark & Wells, 1995; Rapee & Heimberg, 1997). Cognitive biases, such as negative interpretation of ambiguous cues, make them resistant to possible acceptance cues in the environment, thus increasing the perceived frequency of negative events and outcomes of significance for the self.

Summary

It is impossible to understand the self without reference to the social world and to other people. Attachment theory provides us with a framework for understanding the critical role that early relationships and experiences play in developing a sense of self, an appreciation of the individual's value and worth, and their place in the world. Attachment theory has been influential in the development of both theories and treatments of personality disorders (Kellogg & Young, 2006). The concepts derived from attachment theory are being increasingly applied to other disorders, such as social anxiety (Vertue, 2003) and depression (Shaw & Dallos, 2005). There is an overlap between concepts described in attachment theory and some of the ideas discussed earlier in the chapter. For example, the internal working models in attachment theory could be described as a set of schematic beliefs about the self accompanied by the memories and affect attached to those beliefs. Images of the self that we have suggested might represent working self-concepts could equally well represent an internal working model.

Attachment theory envisages the relationship between self and others as complex and in some cases indirect, or mediated through internal models that influence thinking and behaviour. In social comparison theory, we covered a much simpler method of regulating self-esteem through direct comparison with other people. Although this process can be used to maintain high self-esteem, it is much more likely to reinforce negative views of self when upward rather than downward comparison is used. The need to belong is a basic human need and the perception of social exclusion has deleterious consequences. The internal models that individuals develop are likely to influence the type of social comparison that they engage in as well as their beliefs about other people and their own acceptability, which will in turn influence the strategies that they use in order to meet the need to belong to a social group.

Conclusions

Advances in the understanding and treatment of clinical disorders have been critically dependent on delineating specific cognitive and behavioural processes that are thought to maintain particular disorders, and then isolating and testing these processes to see how they operate and how they can be changed. There have been two recent developments to this approach. First, in the combined cognitive processes hypothesis, Hirsch, Clark, and Mathews (2006) have argued that the interactions between different cognitive biases, such as imagery and interpretation (Hirsch et al., 2006), or imagery and autobiographical memory (Stopa & Jenkins, 2007), need to be examined. Second, in the transdiagnostic approach (Harvey, Watkins, Mansell, & Shafran, 2004), proponents have argued that we should examine cognitive biases, such as attention, rumination, and interpretation bias, across rather than within disorders, because many of these processes are not unique to a specific disorder. To date, this careful delineation and testing of processes has generally not included the self.

In this chapter, we have tried to show that a person's view of self is the end result of a set of processes. We started by examining theories about self-concept. To date, clinical applications of models of self have largely relied on the concept of self-schemas, which can sometimes be conceptualised as somewhat fixed and static. However, the self is a dynamic entity and the idea of a 'working self-concept' goes some way towards capturing the idea of the self being formed and re-formed using both knowledge stored in the form of self-schemas and the various processes outlined in the chapter. Any understanding of the self must also take into account the human capacity to imagine hypothetical selves, and we have described a number of theories that look at differences between ideal and actual selves, and at self-discrepancies. For healthy individuals, the ability to imagine alternative possible selves may serve an important function in providing goals that they can aim towards, and in regulating behaviour, and beliefs and views about self. However, for individuals suffering from certain clinical problems, such as social phobia, eating disorders, and body dysmorphic disorder to name but a few, possible selves that are idealised and unrealistic may be just as crippling as the disturbed and dysfunctional actual-self representations that are frequently reported. If we, as clinicians, had a better understanding of the function of possible selves in non-clinical populations and of the processes that operate to form and maintain these possible selves, then we might be in a better position to target effective treatment that helps individuals with clinical disorders to construct and generate possible selves that facilitate rather than inhibit goal attainment and affective stability.

We hope that it will be clear after reading this chapter that it is important to look not only at the content of self-representations, but also at the way that information is stored, and at the various processes that link content and structure. We have provided a brief overview of current theories that describe self-organisation, but it is clear that self-organisation has been largely neglected by clinical researchers even though one might suppose that self-organisation could play a critical role in determining what information about the self is retrieved. Some aspects of self-processing, such as self-awareness and self-consciousness, are much better understood, although our methods for changing them are still in their infancy. Other aspects of self-processing, such as the self-evaluation motives, have been extensively studied in non-clinical populations, but hardly examined in people with disorders. This seems to us to be a major omission in the field, because if these processes are critical pathways to maintaining a stable sense of self and high self-esteem, we, as clinicians and researchers, need to know how and why this process breaks down when individuals develop clinical disorders and then how to restore these processes effectively.

One possible explanation for why some individuals find it harder to maintain a healthy sense of self may lie in their relationship to other people and critically in their relationship history. Clinically, individuals who have longer term, more intractable, and more complex difficulties often describe childhood experiences of emotional and physical neglect or abuse or a history of sexual abuse. Attachment theory provides one way to model the impact of these early experiences and to explain why such early relationships could continue to affect individuals later in life. Even less severe disruptions in relationships may produce an insecure attachment that could influence the individual's sense of self. The discovery that attachment priming can be beneficial and can reduce symptoms in some clinical populations is an exciting development and opens up interesting possibilities for future research.

Finally, we have looked at the stability of the self both across situations and across time and considered how individuals respond to situational demands for different types of self-presentation and yet at the same time retain a sense of continuity about who they are. This continuity can be ruptured by trauma, for example, and the processes outlined in this chapter for maintaining continuity and flexibility in normal circumstances may help us to gain a better understanding of how ruptures to the self occur, and most importantly how to help people repair them.

We have provided a brief overview of theories about the content of self-knowledge and how it is represented, about self-organisation and about a range of self-processes. In order for them to be most useful clinically, we, as clinicians and researchers, need to know how these self-related processes interact with each other, and also how they interact with other well-documented cognitive biases in order to gain a theoretically complete understanding of emotional disorders. We hope that by bringing work on the self together in this chapter, we will stimulate researchers to tackle self-processing with the same rigour that has been applied to other areas of psychopathology.

Acknowledgements

Preparation of this chapter was supported by a Wellcome Trust Grant (WT079794MF). We would like to thank Glenn Waller and Constantine Sedikides for their extremely helpful comments on earlier versions of this chapter.

References

Albert, S. (1977). Temporal comparison theory. *Psychological Review*, *84*, 485–503.

Alden, L.E., & Bieling, P. (1998). Interpersonal consequences of the pursuit of safety. *Behaviour Research and Therapy*, *36*, 53–64.

American Psychiatric Association (2000). *Diagnostic and statistical manual of mental disorders* (4th Text Revision ed.). Washington, DC: American Psychiatric Association.

Antony, M.M., Rowa, K., Liss, A., Swallow, S.R., & Swinson, R.P. (2005). Social comparison processes in social phobia. *Behavior Therapy*, *36*, 65–75.

Arndt, J., Greenberg, J., Schimel, J., Pyszczynski, T., & Solomon, S. (2002). To belong or not to belong, that is the question: Terror management and identification with gender and ethnicity. *Journal of Personality and Social Psychology*, *83*, 26–43.

Ayduk, O., May, D., Downey, G., & Higgins, E.T. (2003). Tactical differences in coping with rejection sensitivity: The role of prevention pride. *Personality and Social Psychology Bulletin*, *29*, 435–448.

Baldwin, M.W. (1994). Primed relational schemas as a source of self-evaluative reactions. *Journal of Social and Clinical Psychology*, *13*, 380–403.

Baldwin, M.W. (1995). Relational schemas and cognition in close relationships. *Journal of Social and Personal Relationships, 12*, 547–552.

Baldwin, M.W., Carrell, S.E., & Lopez, D.F. (1990). Priming relationship schemas: My advisor and the Pope are watching me from the back of my mind. *Journal of Experimental Social Psychology, 26*, 435–454.

Baldwin, M.W., & Main, K.J. (2001). Social anxiety and the cued activation of relational knowledge. *Personality and Social Psychology Bulletin, 27*, 1637–1641.

Bandura, A. (1977). Self-efficacy: Toward a unifying theory of behavioral change. *Psychological Review, 84*, 191–215.

Bandura, A. (1983). Self-efficacy determinants of anticipated fears and calamities. *Journal of Personality and Social Psychology, 45*, 464–469.

Bandura, A. (1988). Self-efficacy conception of anxiety. *Anxiety Research, 1*, 77–98.

Bandura, A. (1991). Self-efficacy conception of anxiety. In R. Schwarzer & R.A. Wicklund (Eds.), *Anxiety and self-focused attention* (pp. 89–110). Amsterdam: Harwood Academic Publishers.

Bandura, A. (1997). *Self-efficacy: The exercise of control*. New York: W H Freeman.

Bandura, A., & Adams, N.E. (1977). Analysis of self-efficacy theory of behavioral change. *Cognitive Therapy and Research, 1*, 287–310.

Bandura, A., Adams, N.E., Hardy, A.B., & Howells, G.N. (1980). Tests of the generality of self-efficacy theory. *Cognitive Therapy and Research, 4*, 39–66.

Bandura, A., Pastorelli, C., Barbaranelli, C., & Caprara, G.V. (1999). Self-efficacy pathways to childhood depression. *Journal of Personality and Social Psychology, 76*, 258–269.

Bargh, J.A., & Tota, M.E. (1988). Context-dependent automatic processing in depression: Accessibility of negative constructs with regard to self but not others. *Journal of Personality and Social Psychology, 54*, 925–939.

Bartholomew, K., & Horowitz, L.M. (1991). Attachment styles among young adults: A test of a four-category model. *Journal of Personality and Social Psychology, 61*, 226–244.

Baumeister, R.F., & DeWall, C.N. (2005). The inner dimension of social exclusion: Intelligent thought and self-regulation among rejected persons. In K.D.Williams, J.P. Forgas, & W. von Hippel (Eds.), *The social outcast: Ostracism, social exclusion, rejection and bullying* (pp. 53–73). New York: Psychology Press.

Baumeister, R.F., & Leary, M.R. (1995). The need to belong: Desire for interpersonal attachments as a fundamental human motivation. *Psychological Bulletin, 117*, 497–529.

Baumeister, R.F., & Tice, D.M. (1990). Anxiety and social exclusion. *Journal of Social and Clinical Psychology, 9*, 165–195.

Baumeister, R.F., Tice, D.M., & Hutton, D.G. (1989). Self-presentational motivations and personality differences in self-esteem. *Journal of Personality, 57*, 547–579.

Bazner, E., Brömer, P., Hammelstein, P., & Meyer, T.D. (2006). Current and former depression and their relationship to the effects of social comparison processes. Results of an internet based study. *Journal of Affective Disorders, 93*, 97–103.

Beach, S.R., & Tesser, A. (2000). Self-evaluation maintenance and evolution: Some speculative notes. In J. Suls & L. Wheeler (Eds.), *Handbook of social comparison: Theory and research* (pp. 123–140). Dordrecht, The Netherlands: Kluwer Academic Publishers.

Beauchamp, M.R., Bray, S.R., & Albinson, J.G. (2002). Pre-competition imagery, self-efficacy and performance in collegiate golfers. *Journal of Sports Sciences, 20,* 697–705.

Beck, A.T., Rush, J.T., Shaw, B.F., & Emery, G. (1979). *Cognitive therapy of depression.* New York: Guilford Press.

Bekker, M.H.J., & Belt, U. (2006). The role of autonomy-connectedness in depression and anxiety. *Depression and Anxiety, 23,* 274–280.

Benight, C.C., & Bandura, A. (2004). Social cognitive theory of posttraumatic recovery: The role of perceived self-efficacy. *Behaviour Research and Therapy, 42,* 1129–1148.

Bentall, R., Corcoran, R., Howard, R., Blackwood, N., & Kinderman, P. (2001). Persecutory delusions: A review and theoretical integration. *Clinical Psychology Review, 21,* 1143–1192.

Bentall, R., Kinderman, P., & Kaney, S. (1994). The self, attributional processes and abnormal beliefs: Towards a model of persecutory delusions. *Behaviour Research and Therapy, 32,* 331–341.

Biaggio, A., Crano, S.L., & Crano, W.D. (1986). Relationships between self-concept and state-trait anxiety under different conditions of social comparison. In C.D. Spielberger & R. Diaz-Guerrero (Eds.), *Cross-cultural anxiety* (pp. 11–20). New York: Harper & Row.

Bierma, J.R. (2005). Evidence-based remotivation: An application of self-determination theory in mental health, substance abuse, and developmental disabilities. In J.A. Dyer & M.L. Stotts (Eds.), *Handbook of remotivation therapy* (pp. 43–54). Binghamton, NY: Haworth Clinical Practice Press.

Blackhart, G.C., Baumeister, R.F., & Twenge, J.M. (2006). Rejection's impact on self-defeating, prosocial, antisocial, and self-regulatory behaviors. In K.D. Vohs & E.J. Finkel (Eds.), *Self and relationships: Connecting intrapersonal and interpersonal processes* (pp. 237–253). New York: Guilford Press.

Bogels, S.M., Alberts, M., & de Jong, P.J. (1996). Self-consciousness, self-focused attention, blushing propensity and fear of blushing. *Personality and Social Psychology Bulletin, 21,* 573–581.

Bogels, S.M., & Lamers, C.T.J. (2002). The causal role of self-awareness in blushing-anxious, socially-anxious and social phobics individuals. *Behaviour Research and Therapy, 40,* 1367–1384.

Bogels, S.M., & Mansell, W. (2004). Attention processes in the maintenance and treatment of social phobia: Hypervigilance, avoidance and self-focused attention. *Clinical Psychology Review, 24,* 827–856.

Bohlin, G., Hagekull, B., & Rydell, A.-M. (2000). Attachment and social functioning: A longitudinal study from infancy to middle childhood. *Social Development, 9,* 24–39.

Bosson, J.K., Brown, R.P., Zeigler-Hill, V., & Swann, W.B.J. (2003). Self-enhancement tendencies among people with high explicit self-esteem: The moderating role of implicit self-esteem. *Self and Identity, 2,* 169–187.

Bowlby, J. (1973). *Attachment and loss (Vol 2: Separation).* New York: Basic Books.

Bowlby, J. (1977). The making and breaking of affectional bonds I. Aetiology and psychopathology in light of attachment theory. *British Journal of Psychiatry, 130,* 201–210.

Bowlby, J. (1980). *Attachment and loss (Vol. 3: Loss, sadness and depression)*. London: Hogarth Press.

Brewin, C.R. (2006). Understanding cognitive behaviour therapy: A retrieval competition account. *Behaviour Research and Therapy*, *44*, 765–784.

Bruch, M.A., Gorsky, J.M., Collins, T.M., & Berger, P.A. (1989). Shyness and sociability reexamined: A multicomponent analysis. *Journal of Personality and Social Psychology*, *57*, 904–915.

Butzer, B., & Kuiper, N.A. (2006). Relationships between the frequency of social comparisons and self-concept clarity, intolerance of uncertainty, anxiety, and depression. *Personality and Individual Differences*, *41*, 167–176.

Buunk, B.P., & Brenninkmeijer, V. (2001). When individuals dislike exposure to an actively coping role model: Mood change as related to depression and social comparison orientation. *European Journal of Social Psychology*, *31*, 537–548.

Cameron, J.J., Wilson, A.E., & Ross, M. (2004). Autobiographical memory and self-assessment. In D.R. Beike, J.M. Lampinen, & D.A. Behrend (Eds.), *The self and memory* (pp. 207–226). New York: Psychology Press.

Campbell, J.L. (1990). Self-esteem and clarity of the self-concept. *Journal of Personality and Social Psychology*, *59*, 538–549.

Campbell, J.L., Trapnell, P.D., Heine, S.J., Katz, I.M., Lavallee, L.F., & Lehman, D.R. (1996). Self-concept clarity: Measurement, personality correlates and cultural boundaries. *Journal of Personality and Social Psychology*, *70*, 141–156.

Carnelley, K.B., Pietromonaco, P.R., & Jaffe, K. (1994). Depression, working models, and relationship functioning. *Journal of Personality and Social Psychology*, *66*, 127–140.

Carnelley, K.B., & Rowe, A.C. (2007) Repeated priming of attachment security influences later views of self and relationships. *Personal Relationships*, *14*, 307–320.

Carvallo, M., & Gabriel, S. (2006). No man is an island: The need to belong and dismissing avoidant attachment style. *Personality and Social Psychology Bulletin*, *32*, 697–709.

Cheek, J.M., & Buss, A.H. (1981). Shyness and sociability. *Journal of Personality and Social Psychology*, *41*, 330–339.

Chen, H., Mechanic, D., & Hansell, S. (1998). A longitudinal study of self-awareness and depressed mood in adolescence. *Journal of Youth and Adolescence*, *27*, 719–734.

Clark, D.A., & Beck, A.T. (1991). Personality-factors in dysphoria – a psychometric refinement of Beck Sociotropy-Autonomy Scale. *Journal of Psychopathology and Behavioral Assessment*, *13*, 369–388.

Clark, D.M., & Wells, A. (1995). A cognitive model of social phobia. In R.G. Heimberg, M.R. Liebowitz, D.A. Hope, & F.R. Schneier (Eds.), *Social phobia: Diagnosis, assessment, and treatment* (pp. 69–93). New York: Guilford Press.

Conway, M.A., & Pleydell-Pearce, C.W. (2000). The construction of autobiographical memories in the self-memory system. *Psychological Review*, *107*, 261–288.

Cooley, C.H. (1964). *Human nature and social order*. New York: Schocken Books.

Cumming, J., Nordin, S.M., Horton, R., & Reynolds, S. (2006). Examining the direction of imagery and self-talk on dart-throwing performance and self efficacy. *Sport Psychologist*, *20*, 257–274.

Darcy, K., Davila, J., & Beck, G. (2005). Is social anxiety associated with both interpersonal avoidance and interpersonal dependence? *Cognitive Therapy and Research*, *29*, 171–186.

Dauenheimer, D.G., Stahlberg, D., Spreemann, S., & Sedikides, C. (2002). Self-enhancement, self-verification, or self-assessment? The intricate role of trait modifiability in the self-evaluation process. *Revue Internationale de Psychologie Sociale, 15*, 89–112.

Davis, C.G., & McKearney, J.M. (2003). How do people grow from their experience with trauma or loss? *Journal of Social and Clinical Psychology, 22*, 477–492.

Deci, E.L. (1980). *The psychology of self-determination*. Lexington, MA: Heath.

Deci, E.L., & Ryan, R.M. (1980). The empirical exploration of intrinsic motivational processes. *Advances in Experimental Social Psychology, 13*, 39–80.

Deci, E.L., & Ryan, R.M. (2000). The 'what' and 'why' of goal pursuits: Human needs and the self-determination of behavior. *Psychological Inquiry, 11*, 227–268.

Dozier, M., Stovall, K.C., & Albus, K.E. (1999). Attachment and psychopathology in adulthood. In J. Cassidy & P.R. Shaver (Eds.), *Handbook of attachment: Theory, research and clinical applications* (pp. 497–519). New York: Guilford Press.

Duval, S., & Wicklund, R.A. (1972). *A theory of objective self awareness*. Oxford, UK: Academic Press.

Dykman, B.M., Abramson, L.Y., Alloy, L.B., & Hartlage, S. (1989). Processing of ambiguous and unambiguous feedback by depressed and nondepressed college students: Schematic biases and their implications for depressive realism. *Journal of Personality and Social Psychology, 56*, 434–445.

Edelmann, R.J. (1990). Chronic blushing, self-consciousness, and social anxiety. *Journal of Psychopathology and Behavioral Assessment, 12*, 119–127.

Eng, W., Heimberg, R.G., Hart, T.A., Schneier, F.R., & Liebowitz, M.R. (2001). Attachment in individuals with social anxiety disorder: The relationship among adult attachment styles, social anxiety and depression. *Emotion, 1*, 365–380.

Fein, S., & Spencer, S.J. (1997). Prejudice as self-image maintenance: Affirming the self through derogating others. *Journal of Personality and Social Psychology, 73*, 31–44.

Fenigstein, A., Scheier, M.F., & Buss, A.H. (1975). Public and private self-consciousness: Assessment and theory. *Journal of Consulting and Clinical Psychology, 43*, 522–527.

Festinger, L. (1954). A theory of social comparison processes. *Human Relations, 7*, 117–140.

Figurski, T.J. (1992). Everyday self-awareness: Implications for self-esteem, depression, and resistance to therapy. In M.W. deVries (Ed.), *The experience of psychopathology: Investigating mental disorders in their natural settings* (pp. 304–313). New York: Cambridge University Press.

Fleury, J., Sedikides, C., & Donovan, K.D. (2002). Possible health selves of older African Americans: Toward increasing the effectiveness of health promotion efforts. *Topics in Geriatric Rehabilitation, 18*, 52–58.

Florian, V., Mikulincer, M., & Hirschberger, G. (2002). The anxiety-buffering function of close relationships: Evidence that relationship commitment acts as a terror management mechanism. *Journal of Personality and Social Psychology, 82*, 527–542.

Gardner, W.L., Pickett, C.L., & Brewer, M.B. (2000). Social exclusion and selective memory: How the need to belong influences memory for social events. *Personality and Social Psychology Bulletin, 26*, 486–496.

George, L., & Stopa, L. (2008). Private and public self-awareness in social anxiety. *Journal of Behavior Therapy and Experimental Psychiatry, 39*, 57–72.

Gervey, B., Igou, E.R., & Trope, Y. (2005). Positive mood and future-oriented self-evaluation. *Motivation and Emotion, 29*, 269–296.

Gibbons, F.X. (1986). Social comparison and depression: Company's effect on misery. *Journal of Personality and Social Psychology, 51*, 140–148.

Gibbons, F.X. (1991). Self-evaluation and self-perception: The role of attention in the experience of anxiety. In R. Schwarzer & R.A. Wicklund (Eds.), *Anxiety and self-focused attention* (pp. 15–25). Amsterdam: Harwood Academic Publishers.

Giesler, R.B., & Swann, W.B.J. (1999). Striving for confirmation: The role of self-verification in depression. In T. Joiner & J. Coyne (Eds.), *The interactional nature of depression: Advances in interpersonal approaches* (pp. 189–217). Washington, DC: American Psychological Association.

Gilbert, P., Baldwin, M.W., Irons, C., Baccus, J.R., & Palmer, M. (2006). Self-criticism and self-warmth: An imagery study exploring their relation to depression. *Journal of Cognitive Psychotherapy, 20*, 183–200.

Gilbert, P., & Irons, C. (2004). A pilot exploration of the use of compassionate images in a group of self-critical people. *Memory, 12*, 507–516.

Gilbert, P., & Procter, S. (2006). Compassionate mind training for people with high shame and self-criticism: Overview and pilot study of a group therapy approach. *Clinical Psychology and Psychotherapy, 13*, 353–379.

Gilboa-Schectman, E., Franklin, M.E., & Foa, E.B. (2000). Anticipated reactions to social events: Differences among individuals with generalized social phobia, obsessive compulsive disorder, and nonanxious controls. *Cognitive Therapy and Research, 24*, 731–746.

Giordano, C., Wood, J.V., & Michela, J.L. (2000). Depressive personality styles, dysphoria, and social comparisons in everyday life. *Journal of Personality and Social Psychology, 79*, 438–451.

Gramzow, R.H., Sedikides, C., Panter, A.T., & Insko, C.A. (2000). Aspects of self-regulation and self-structure as predictors of perceived emotional distress. *Personality and Social Psychology Bulletin, 26*, 188–206.

Green, J.D., Pinter, B., & Sedikides, C. (2005). Mnemic neglect and self-threat: Trait modifiability moderates self-protection. *European Journal of Social Psychology, 335*, 225–235.

Greenberg, J., Solomon, S., & Pyszczynski, T. (1997). Terror management theory of self-esteem and cultural worldviews: Empirical assessments and conceptual refinements. *Advances in Experimental Social Psychology, 29*, 61–139.

Greenberg, J., Solomon, S., Pyszczynski, T., Rosenblatt, A., Burling, J., Lyon, D., et al. (1992). Why do people need self-esteem? Converging evidence that self-esteem serves an anxiety-buffering function. *Journal of Personality and Social Psychology, 63*, 913–922.

Harmon-Jones, E., Simon, L., Greenberg, J., & Pyszczynski, T. (1997). Terror management theory and self-esteem: Evidence that increased self-esteem reduced mortality salience effects. *Journal of Personality and Social Psychology, 72*, 24–36.

Harvey, A., Watkins, E., Mansell, W., & Shafran, R. (2004). *Cognitive behavioural processes across psychological disorders: A transdiagnostic approach to research and treatment.* Oxford: Oxford University Press.

Hazan, C., & Shaver, P. (1987). Romantic love conceptualized as an attachment process. *Journal of Personality and Social Psychology*, *52*, 511–524.

Heilbrun, A.B., Diller, R.S., & Dodson, V.S. (1986). Defensive projection and paranoid delusions. *Journal of Psychiatric Research*, *20*, 161–173.

Higgins, E.T. (1987). Self-discrepancy: A theory relating self and affect. *Psychological Review*, *94*, 319–340.

Higgins, E.T. (1997). Beyond pleasure and pain. *American Psychologist*, *52*, 1280–1300.

Higgins, E.T., Bond, R.N., Klein, R., & Strauman, T. (1986). Self-discrepancies and emotional vulnerability: How magnitude, accessibility, and type of discrepancy influence affect. *Journal of Personality and Social Psychology*, *51*, 5–15.

Higgins, E.T., Klein, R., & Strauman, T. (1985). Self-concept discrepancy theory: A psychological model for distinguishing among different aspects of depression and anxiety. *Social Cognition*, *31*, 51–76.

Higgins, E.T., & Spiegel, S. (2004). Promotion and prevention strategies for self-regulation: A motivated cognition perspective. In R.F. Baumeister & K.D. Vohs (Eds.), *Handbook of self-regulation: Research, theory, and applications* (pp. 171–187). New York: Guilford Press.

Hirsch, C.R., Clark, D.M., & Mathews, A. (2006). Imagery and interpretations in social phobia: Support for the combined cognitive biases hypothesis. *Behavior Therapy*, *37*, 223–236.

Hirsch, C.R., Mathews, A., Clark, D.M., Williams, R., & Morrison, J.A. (2006). The causal role of negative imagery in social anxiety: A test in confident public speakers. *Journal of Behavior Therapy and Experimental Psychiatry*, *37*, 159–170.

Holmes, E.A., Arntz, A., & Smucker, M.R. (2007). Imagery rescripting in cognitive behaviour therapy: Images, treatment techniques and outcomes. *Journal of Behavior Therapy and Experimental Psychiatry*, *38*, 297–305.

Ingram, R.E. (1990). Self-focused attention in clinical disorders – review and a conceptual-model. *Psychological Bulletin*, *107*, 156–176.

James, I.A., Reichelt, F.K., Freeston, M.H., & Barton, S.B. (2007). Schemas as memories: Implications for treatment. *Journal of Cognitive Psychotherapy*, *21*, 51–57.

James, W. (1890). *The principles of psychology*. New York: Cosimo.

Janoff-Bulman, R., & Yopyk, D.J. (2004). Random outcomes and valued commitments: Existential dilemmas and the paradox of meaning. In J.J. Griffin, S.L. Koole, & T. Pyszczynski (Eds.), *Handbook of experimental existential psychology* (pp. 122–138). New York: Guilford Press.

Kaney, S., & Bentall, R. (1989). Persecutory delusions and attributional style. *British Journal of Medical Psychology*, *62*, 191–198.

Karniol, R., & Ross, M. (1996). The motivational impact of temporal focus: Thinking about the future and the past. *Annual Review of Psychology*, *47*, 593–620.

Kellogg, S.H., & Young, J.E. (2006). Schema therapy for borderline personality disorder. *Journal of Clinical Psychology*, *62*, 445–458.

Kircher, T., & David, A.E. (2003). *The self in neuroscience and psychiatry*. Cambridge, UK: Cambridge University Press.

Klein, S.B., German, T.P., Cosmides, L., & Gabriel, R. (2004). A theory of autobiographical memory: Necessary components and disorders resulting from their loss. *Social Cognition*, *22*, 460–490.

Klonsky, B.G., Dutton, D.L., & Liebel, C.N. (1990). Developmental antecedents of private self-consciousness, public self-consciousness and social anxiety. *Genetic, Social, and General Psychology Monographs, 116*, 273–297.

Koole, S.L., Smeets, K., van Knippenberg, A., & Dijksterhuis, A. (1999). The cessation of rumination through self-affirmation. *Journal of Personality and Social Psychology, 77*, 111–125.

Kowalski, R.M., & Leary, M.R.E. (2004). *The interface of social and clinical psychology.* New York: Psychology Press.

Kuiper, N.A., Olinger, L.J., & Swallow, S.R. (1987). Dysfunctional attitudes, mild depression, views of self, self-consciousness, and social perceptions. *Motivation and Emotion, 11*, 379–401.

Kumashiro, M., & Sedikides, C. (2005). Taking on board liability-focused feedback: Close positive relationships as a self-bolstering resource. *Psychological Science, 16*, 732–739.

La Guardia, J.G., Ryan, R.M., Couchman, C.E., & Deci, E.L. (2000). Within-person variation in security of attachment: A self-determination theory perspective on attachment, need fulfillment, and well-being. *Journal of Personality and Social Psychology, 79*, 367–384.

Layden, M.A. (2000). *Cognitive therapy using imagery techniques.* Workshop, London.

Leary, M.R., & Atherton, S.C. (1986). Self-efficacy, social anxiety, and inhibition in social encounters. *Journal of Social and Clinical Psychology, 4*, 258–267.

Leary, M.R., & Baumeister, R.F. (2000). The nature and function of self-esteem: Sociometer theory. *Advances in Experimental Social Psychology, 32*, 1–62.

Leary, M.R., Haupt, A.L., Strausser, K.S., & Chokel, J.T. (1998). Calibrating the sociometer: The relationship between interpersonal appraisals and the state self-esteem. *Journal of Personality and Social Psychology, 74*, 1290–1299.

Leary, M.R., Tambor, E.S., Terdal, S.K., & Downs, D.L. (1995). Self-esteem as an interpersonal monitor: The sociometer hypothesis. *Journal of Personality and Social Psychology, 68*, 518–530.

Leary, M.R., Tate, E.B., Adams, C.E., Allen, A.B., & Hancock, J. (2007). Self-compassion and reactions to unpleasant self-relevant events: The implications of treating oneself kindly. *Journal of Personality and Social Psychology, 92*, 887–904.

Lee, D.A. (2005). The perfect nurturer: A model to develop a compassionate mind within the context of cognitive therapy. In P. Gilbert (Ed.), *Compassion: Conceptualisations, research and use in psychotherapy* (pp. 326–351). New York: Routledge.

Leung, C.M., & Lam, S.F. (2003). The effects of regulatory focus on teachers' classroom management strategies and emotional consequences. *Contemporary Educational Psychology, 28*, 114–125.

Lewis, M.A., & Neighbors, C. (2005). Self-determination and the use of self-presentation strategies. *Journal of Social Psychology, 145*, 469–489.

Linville, P.W. (1985). Self-complexity and affective extremity: Don't put all of your eggs in one basket. *Social Cognition, 3*, 94–120.

Linville, P.W. (1987). Self-complexity as a cognitive buffer against stress-related illness and depression. *Journal of Personality and Social Psychology, 52*, 633–676.

Lockwood, P., Jordan, C.H., & Kunda, Z. (2002). Motivation by positive or negative role models: Regulatory focus determines who will best inspire us. *Journal of Personality and Social Psychology, 83*, 854–864.

Luke, M.A., Maio, G.R., & Carnelley, K.B. (2004). Attachment models of the self and others: Relations with self-esteem, humanity-esteem, and parental treatment. *Personal Relationships*, *11*, 281–303.

Maddux, J.E. (1991). Self-efficacy. In C.R. Snyder & D.R. Forsyth (Eds.), *Handbook of social and clinical psychology: The health perspective* (pp. 57–78). Oxford, UK: Pergamon Press.

Marigold, D.C., Holmes, J.G., & Ross, M. (2007). More than words: Reframing compliments from romantic partners fosters security in low self-esteem individuals. *Journal of Personality and Social Psychology*, *92*, 232–248.

Markus, H. (1977). Self-schemata and processing information about the self. *Journal of Personality and Social Psychology*, *35*, 63–78.

Markus, H., & Nurius, P. (1986). Possible selves. *American Psychologist*, *41*, 954–969.

Markus, H., & Nurius, P. (1987). Possible selves: The interface between motivation and the self-concept. In K.Yardley & T. Honess (Eds.), *Self and identity: Psychosocial perspectives* (pp. 157–172). Oxford, UK: Wiley.

Markus, H., & Ruvolo, A. (1989). Possible selves: Personalized representations of goals. In L.A. Pervin (Ed.), *Goal concepts in personality and social psychology* (pp. 211–241). Hillsdale, NJ: Lawrence Erlbaum Associates, Inc.

Markus, H., & Wurf, E. (1987). The dynamic self-concept: A social psychological perspective. *Annual Review of Psychology*, *38*, 299–337.

Martin, L.L., Campbell, W.K., & Henry, C.D. (2004). The roar of awakening: Mortality acknowledgement as a call to authentic living. In J. Greenberg, S.L. Koole, & T. Pyszczynski (Eds.), *Handbook of experimental existential psychology* (pp. 431–448). New York: Guilford Press.

McCann, T.V., & Clark, E. (2004). Advancing self-determination with young adults who have schizophrenia. *Journal of Psychiatric and Mental Health Nursing*, *11*, 12–20.

McFarland, C., & Alvaro, C. (2000). The impact of motivation on temporal comparisons: Coping with traumatic events by perceiving personal growth. *Journal of Personality and Social Psychology*, *79*, 327–343.

McGregor, I., Gailliot, M.T., Vasquez, N.A., & Nash, K.A. (2007). Ideological and personal zeal reactions to threat among people with high self-esteem: Motivated promotion focus. *Personality and Social Psychology Bulletin*, *33*, 1587–1599.

McQueen, A., & Klein, W.M.P. (2006). Experimental manipulations of self-affirmation: A systematic review. *Self and Identity*, *5*, 289–354.

Mickelson, K.D., Kessler, R.C., & Shaver, P.R. (1997). Adult attachment in a nationally represenative sample. *Journal of Personality and Social Psychology*, *73*, 1092–1106.

Mikulincer, M., Shaver, P.R., & Horesh, N. (2006). Attachment bases of emotion regulation and postraumatic adjustment. In D.K. Snyder, J.A. Simpson, & J.N. Hughes (Eds.), *Emotion regulation in families: Pathways to dysfunction and health* (pp. 77–99). Washington, DC: American Psychological Association.

Monfries, M.M., & Kafer, N.F. (1994). Private self-consciousness and fear of negative evaluation. *Journal of Psychology: Interdisciplinary and Applied*, *128*, 447–454.

Moore, B.S. (1979). Generalization of feedback about performance. *Cognitive Therapy and Research*, *3*, 371–380.

Murray, S.L., Holmes, J.G., Griffin, D.W., Bellavia, G., & Rose, P. (2001). The mismeasure of love: How self-doubt contaminates relationship beliefs. *Personality and Social Psychology Bulletin*, *27*, 423–436.

Neff, K.D. (2003a). Self-compassion: An alternative conceptualization of a healthy attitude toward oneself. *Self and Identity*, *2*, 85–101.

Neff, K.D. (2003b). The development and validation of a scale to measure self-compassion. *Self and Identity*, *2*, 223–250.

Neff, K.D., Kirkpatrick, K.L., & Rude, S.S. (2007). Self-compassion and its link to adaptive psychological functioning. *Journal of Research in Personality*, *41*, 139–154.

Neff, K.D., Rude, S.S., & Kirkpatrick, K.L. (2007). An examination of self-compassion in relation to positive psychological functioning and personality traits. *Journal of Research in Personality*, *41*, 908–916.

Neff, L.A., & Karney, B.R. (2002). Self-evaluation motives in close relationships: A model of global enhancement and specific verification. In P. Noller & J.A. Feeney (Eds.), *Understanding marriage: Developments in the study of couple interaction* (pp. 32–58). New York: Cambridge University Press.

Nelson, K.D., & Fivush, R. (2004). The emergence of autobiographical memory: A social cultural developmental theory. *Psychological Review*, *111*, 486–511.

Newby-Clark, I.R., & Ross, M. (2003). Conceiving the past and future. *Personality and Social Psychology Bulletin*, *29*, 807–818.

Nezlek, J.B. (2002). Day-to-day relationships between self-awareness, daily events, and anxiety. *Journal of Personality*, *70*, 249–275.

Panayiotou, G. (2005). Chronic self-consciousness and its effects on cognitive performance, physiology, and self-reported anxiety. *Representative Research in Social Psychology*, *28*, 21–34.

Perry, J.A., Silvera, T.H., Neilands, T.B., Rosenvinge, J.H., & Hanssen, T.H.A. (2008). study of the relationship between parental bonding, self-concept and eating disturbances in Norwegian and American college populations. *Eating Behaviors*, *9*, 13–24.

Pickett, C.L., Gardner, W.L., & Knowles, M. (2004). Getting a cue: The need to belong and enhanced sensitivity to social cues. *Personality and Social Psychology Bulletin*, *30*, 1095–1107.

Pyszczynski, T., & Greenberg, J. (1987). Self-regulatory perseveration and the depressive self-focusing style: A self-awareness theory of reactive depression. *Psychological Bulletin*, *102*, 122–138.

Pyszczynski, T., Greenberg, J., Solomon, S., Arndt, J., & Schimel, J. (2004). Why do people need self-esteem? A theoretical and empirical review. *Psychological Bulletin*, *130*, 435–468.

Rapee, R.M., & Heimberg, R.G. (1997). A cognitive-behavioral model of anxiety in social phobia. *Behavior Research and Therapy*, *35*, 741–756.

Reis, H.T., Sheldon, K.M., Gable, S.L., Roscoe, J., & Ryan, R.M. (2000). Daily well-being: The role of autonomy, competence, and relatedness. *Personality and Social Psychology Bulletin*, *26*, 419–435.

Ritchie, T.D., Skowronski, J.J., Wood, S.E., Walker, W.R., Vogl, R.J., & Gibbons, J.A. (2006). Event self-importance, event rehearsal, and the fading affect bias in autobiographical memory. *Self and Identity*, *5*, 172–195.

Roberts, J.E. (2006). Self-esteem from a clinical perspective. In M.H. Kernis (Ed.), *Self-esteem issues and answers: A sourcebook for current perspectvives* (pp. 298–305). Hove, UK: Psychology Press.

Rosenblatt, A., Greenberg, J., Solomon, S., Pyszczynski, T., & Lyon, D. (1989). Evidence for terror management theory. 1. The effects of mortality salience on reactions to those who violate or uphold cultural-values. *Journal of Personality and Social Psychology*, *57*, 681–690.

Ross, M., & Buehler, R. (2004). Identity through time: Constructing personal pasts and futures. In M.B. Brewer & M. Hewstone (Eds.), *Self and social identity* (pp. 25–51). Malden, MA: Blackwell Publishing.

Ross, M., & Wilson, A.E. (2000). Constructing and apprasing past selves. In D.L. Schacter & E. Scarry (Eds.), *Memory, brain, and belief* (pp. 231–258). Cambridge, MA: Harvard University Press.

Ross, M., & Wilson, A.E. (2002). It feels like yesterday: Self-esteem, valence of personal past experiences, and judgments of subjective distance. *Journal of Personality and Social Psychology*, *82*, 792–803.

Ross, M., & Wilson, A.E. (2003). Autobiographical memory and conceptions of self: Getting better all the time. *Current Directions in Psychological Science*, *12*, 66–69.

Ruvolo, A.P., & Markus, H.R. (1992). Possible selves and performance: The power of self-relevant imagery. *Social Cognition*, *10*, 95–124.

Santor, D.A., & Yazbek, A.A. (2006). Soliciting unfavourable social comparison: Effects of self-criticism. *Personality and Individual Differences*, *40*, 545–556.

Schimel, J., Arndt, J., Banko, K.M., & Cook, A. (2004). Not all self-affirmations were created equal: The cognitive and social benefit of affirming the intrinsic (vs extrinsic) self. *Social Cognition*, *22*, 75–99.

Schmitt, J.P. (1983). Focus of attention in the treatment of depression. *Psychotherapy: Theory, Research and Practice*, *20*, 457–463.

Schwartz, R.C. (2001). Self-awareness in schizophrenia: Its relationship to depressive symptomatology and broad psychiatric impairments. *Journal of Nervous and Mental Disease*, *189*, 401–403.

Scott, L., & O'Hara, M.W. (1993). Self-discrepancies in clinically anxious and depressed university students. *Journal of Abnormal Psychology*, *102*, 282–287.

Sedikides, C. (1992). Attentional effects on mood are moderated by chronic self-conception valence. *Personality and Social Psychology Bulletin*, *18*, 580–584.

Sedikides, C. (1993). Assessment, enhancement, and verification determinants of the self-evaluation process. *Journal of Personality and Social Psychology*, *65*, 317–338.

Sedikides, C. (1995). Central and peripheral self-conceptions are differentially influenced by mood: Tests of the differential sensitivity hypothesis. *Journal of Personality and Social Psychology*, *69*, 759–777.

Sedikides, C., & Gregg, A. (2003). Portraits of the self. In M.A. Hoog & J. Cooper (Eds.), *Sage handbook of social psychology* (pp. 110–138). London: Sage Publications.

Sedikides, C., & Gregg, A. (2008). Self-enhancement: Food for thought. *Perspectives on Psychological Science*, *3*, 102–116.

Sedikides, C., & Strube, M.J. (1997). Self evaluation: To thine own self be good, to thine own self be sure, to thine own self be true, and to thine own self be better. *Advances in Experimental Social Psychology*, *29*, 209–269.

Sedikides, C., Wildschut, T., Gaertner, L., Routledge, C., & Arndt, J. (2008). Nostalgia as enabler of self-continuity. In F. Sani (Ed.), *Self-continuity: Individual and collective perspectives* (pp. 227–239). New York: Psychology Press.

Setterlund, M.B., & Niedenthal, P.M. (1993). 'Who am I? Why am I here?' Self-esteem, self-clarity, and prototype matching. *Journal of Personality and Social Psychology*, *65*, 769–780.

Shapiro, S.L., Astin, J.A., Bishop, S.R., & Cordova, M. (2005). Mindfulness-based stress reduction for health care professionals: Results from a randomized trial. *International Journal of Stress Management*, *12*, 164–176.

Shapiro, S.L., Brown, K.W., & Biegel, G.M. (2007). Teaching self-care to caregivers: Effects of mindfulness-based stress reduction on the mental health of therapists in training. *Training and Education in Professional Psychology*, *1*, 105–115.

Shaw, S.K., & Dallos, R. (2005). Attachment and adolescent depression: The impact of early attachment experiences. *Attachment and Human Development*, *7*, 409–424.

Sheldon, K.M., Ryan, R.M., Deci, E.L., & Kasser, T. (2004). The independent effects of goal contents and motives on well-being: It's both what you pursue and why you pursue it. *Personality and Social Psychology Bulletin*, *40*, 475–486.

Sheldon, K.M., Williams, G., & Joiner, T. (2003). *Self-determination theory in the clinic: Motivating physical and mental health*. New Haven, CT: Yale University Press.

Sherman, D.A.K.N.L.D., & Steele, C.M. (2000). Do messages about health risks threaten the self? Increasing the acceptance of threatening health messages via self-affirmation. *Personality and Social Psychology Bulletin*, *26*, 1046–1058.

Showers, C.J. (1992). Compartmentalization of positive and negative self-knowledge: Keeping bad apples out of the bunch. *Journal of Personality and Social Psychology*, *62*, 1036–1049.

Silvia, P.J., & Duval, T.S. (2001). Objective self-awareness theory: Recent progress and enduring problems. *Personality and Social Psychology Review*, *5*, 230–241.

Simon, L., Arndt, J., Greenberg, J., Pyszczynski, T., & Solomon, S. (1998). Terror management and meaning: Evidence that the opportunity to defend the worldview in response to mortality salience increases the meaningfulness of life in the mildly depressed. *Journal of Personality*, *66*, 359–382.

Simon, L., Greenberg, J., Harmon-Jones, E., & Solomon, S. (1996). Mild depression, mortality salience, and defense of the worldview: Evidence of intensified terror management in the mildly depressed. *Personality and Social Psychology Bulletin*, *22*, 81–90.

Skowronski, J.J., Gibbons, J.A., Vogl, R.J., & Walker, W.R. (2004). The effect of social distance on intensity of affect provoked by autobiographical memories. *Self and Identity*, *3*, 285–309.

Skowronski, J.J., & Walker, W.R. (2004). How describing autobiographical events can affect autobiographical memories. *Social Cognition*, *22*, 555–590.

Skowronski, J.J., Walker, W.R., & Betz, A.L. (2003). Ordering our world: An examination of time in autobiographical memory. *Memory*, *11*, 247–260.

Solomon, S., Greenberg, J., & Pyszczynski, T. (1991). Terror management theory of self-esteem. In C.R. Snyder & D.R. Forsyth (Eds.), *Handbook of social and clinical psychology* (pp. 21–40). Elmsford, NY: Pergamon Press.

Solomon, Z., Benbenishty, R., & Mikulincer, M. (1991). The contribution of wartime, prewar and postwar factors in self-efficacy: A longitudinal study of combat stress reaction. *Journal of Traumatic Stress*, *4*, 345–361.

Spencer, S.J., Fein, S., & Lomore, C.D. (2001). Maintaining one's self-image vis-a-vis others: The role of self-affirmation in the social evaluation of the self. *Motivation and Emotion*, *25*, 41–65.

Spurr, J.M., & Stopa, L. (2002). Self-focused attention in social phobia and social anxiety. *Clinical Psychology Review, 22*, 947–975.

Srivastava, S., & Beer, J.S. (2005). How self-evaluations relate to being liked by others: Integrating sociometer and attachment perspectives. *Journal of Personality and Social Psychology, 89*, 966–977.

Steele, C.M. (1988). The psychology of self-affirmation: Sustaining the integrity of the self. In L. Berkowitz (Ed.), *Advances in experimental social psychology (Vol. 21): Social psychological studies of the self: Perspectives and programs* (pp. 261–302). San Diego, CA: Academic Press.

Steele, C.M., & Liu, T.J. (1981). Making the dissonance act in reflective of self: Dissonance avoidance and the expectancy of a value-affirming response. *Personality and Social Psychology Bulletin, 7*, 393–397.

Steele, C.M., & Liu, T.J. (1983). Dissonance processes as self-affirmation. *Journal of Personality and Social Psychology, 45*, 5–19.

Steele, C.M., Spencer, S.J., & Lynch, M. (1993). Self-image resilience and dissonance: The role of affirmational resources. *Journal of Personality and Social Psychology, 64*, 885–896.

Stiles, B.L., & Kaplan, H.B. (2004). Adverse social comparison processes and negative self-feelings: A test of alternative models. *Social Behavior and Personality, 32*, 31–44.

Stopa, L., & Jenkins, A. (2007). Images of the self in social anxiety: Effects on the retrieval of autobiographical memories. *Journal of Behavior Therapy and Experimental Psychiatry, 38*, 459–473.

Strachan, E., Schimel, J., Arndt, J., Williams, T., Solomon, S., Pyszczynski, T. *et al.* (2007). Terror mismanagement: Evidence that mortality salience exacerbates phobic and compulsive behaviors. *Personality and Social Psychology Bulletin, 33*, 1137–1151.

Strauman, T.J. (1989). Self-discrepancies in clinical depression and social phobia: Cognitive structures that underlie emotional disorders? *Journal of Abnormal Psychology, 98*, 14–22.

Strauman, T.J. (1992). Self-guides, autobiographical memory, and anxiety and dysphoria: Toward a cognitive model of vulnerability to emotional distress. *Journal of Abnormal Psychology, 101*, 87–92.

Strauman, T.J., & Higgins, E.T. (1987). Automatic activation of self-discrepancies and emotional syndromes: When cognitive structures influence affect. *Journal of Personality and Social Psychology, 53*, 1004–1014.

Sturman, E.D., & Mongrain, M. (2005). Self-criticism and major depression: An evolutionary perspective. *British Journal of Clinical Psychology, 44*, 505–519.

Swallow, S.R., & Kuiper, N.A. (1992). Mild depression and frequency of social comparison behavior. *Journal of Social and Clinical Psychology, 11*, 167–180.

Swann, W.B. (1996). *Self traps: The elusive quest for higher self-esteem.* New York: Freeman.

Swann, W.B., Griffin, J.J., Predmore, S.C., & Gaines, B. (1987). The cognitive-affective crossfire: When self-consistency confronts self-enhancement. *Journal of Personality and Social Psychology, 52*, 881–889.

Swann, W.B., Stein-Seroussi, A., & Giesler, R.B. (1992). Why people self-verify. *Journal of Personality and Social Psychology, 62*, 392–401.

Swann, W.B., Wenzlaff, R.M., Krull, D.S., & Pelham, B.W. (1992). Allure of negative feedback: Self-verification strivings among depressed persons. *Journal of Abnormal Psychology, 101*, 293–306.

Taylor, S.E., & Brown, J. (1988). Illusion and well-being: A social psychological perspective on mental health. *Psychological Bulletin, 103*, 193–210.

Taylor, S.E., Neter, E., & Wayment, H.A. (1995). Self-evaluation processes. *Personality and Social Psychology Bulletin, 21*, 1278–1287.

Tennen, H., & Affleck, G. (1993). The puzzles of self-esteem: A clinical perspective. In R.F. Baumeister (Ed.), *Self-esteem: The puzzle of low self-regard* (pp. 241–262). New York: Plenum.

Tesser, A. (2000). On the confluence of self-esteem maintenance mechanisms. *Personality and Social Psychology Review, 4*, 290–299.

Tesser, A., & Campbell, J.L. (1982). Self-evaluation maintenance and the perception of friends and strangers. *Journal of Personality, 50*, 261–279.

Thwaites, R., & Dagnan, D. (2004). Moderating variables in the relationship between social comparison and depression: An evolutionary perspective. *Psychology and Psychotherapy: Theory, Research and Practice, 77*, 309–323.

Trope, Y. (1980). Self-assessment, self-enhancement, and task preference. *Journal of Experimental Social Psychology, 16*, 116–129.

Trope, Y., & Pomerantz, E.M. (1998). Resolving conflicts among self-evaluative motives: Positive experiences as a resource for overcoming defensiveness. *Motivaton and Emotion, 22*, 53–72.

Vansteenkiste, M., Soenens, B., & Vandereycken, W. (2005). Motivation to change in eating disorder patients: A conceptual clarification on the basis of self-determination theory. *International Journal of Eating Disorders, 37*, 207–219.

Vertue, F.M. (2001). Internal working models, the regulation of others' emotions and social anxiety: An integrative, socio-developmental model. *Australian Journal of Psychology, 53*, 130.

Vertue, F.M. (2003). From adaptive emotion to dysfunction: An attachment perspective on social anxiety disorder. *Personality and Social Psychology Review, 7*, 170–191.

Vohs, K.D., & Ciarocco, N.J. (2004). Interpersonal functioning requires self-regulation. In R.F. Baumeister & K.D. Vohs (Eds.), *Handbook of self-regulation: Research, theory, and applications* (pp. 392–407). New York: Guilford Press.

von Gemmingen, M.J., Sullivan, B.F., & Pomerantz, A.M. (2003). Investigating the relationships between boredom proneness, paranoia, and self-consciousness. *Personality and Individual Differences, 34*, 907–919.

Walker, W.R., Skowronski, J.J., Gibbons, J.A., Vogl, R.J., & Thompson, C.P. (2003a). On the emotions that accompany autobiographical memories: Dysphoria disrupts the fading affect bias. *Cognition and Emotion, 17*, 703–723.

Walker, W.R., Skowronski, J.J., & Thompson, C.P. (2003b). Life is pleasant – and memory helps to keep it that way! *Review of General Psychology, 72*, 203–210.

Wallace, S.T., & Alden, L.E. (1997). Social phobia and positive social events: The price of success. *Journal of Abnormal Psychology, 106*, 416–424.

Weilage, M., & Hope, D.A. (1999). Self-discrepancy in social phobia and dysthymia. *Cognitive Therapy and Research, 23*, 637–650.

Wells, A. (1997). *Cognitive therapy of anxiety disorders: A practice manual and conceptual guide*. Chichester, UK: Wiley.

Wells, A., & Matthews, G. (1994). *Attention and emotion: A clinical perspective*. Hove, UK: Psychology Press.

Williams, J.M., Barnhofer, T., Crane, C., Herman, D., Raes, F., Watkins, E., *et al.* (2007). Autobiographical memory specificity and emotional disorder. *Psychological Bulletin, 133*, 122–148.

Wilson, A.E., & Ross, M. (2000). The frequency of temporal-self and social comparisons in people's personal appraisals. *Journal of Personality and Social Psychology, 78*, 928–942.

Wilson, A.E., & Ross, M. (2001). From chump to champ: People's appraisals of their earlier and present selves. *Journal of Personality and Social Psychology, 80*, 572–584.

Wilson, A.E., & Ross, M. (2003). The identity function of autobiographical memory: Time is on our side. *Memory, 11*, 137–149.

Wilson, J.K., & Rapee, R.M. (2006). Self-concept certainty in social phobia. *Behaviour Research and Therapy, 44*, 113–136.

Wood, J.V., & Lockwood, P. (1999). Social comparisons in dysphoric and low self-esteem people. In R. Kowlaski & M.R. Leary (Eds.), *The social psychology of emotional and behavioral problems: Interface of social and clinical psychology* (pp. 97–135). Washington, DC: American Psychological Association.

Woodruff-Borden, J., Brothers, A.J., & Lister, S.C. (2001). Self-focused attention: Commonalities across psychopathologies and predictors. *Behavioural and Cognitive Psychotherapy, 29*, 169–178.

Young, J. (1999). *Cognitive therapy for personality disorders: A schema-focused approach*. Sarasota, FL: Professional Resource Press.

Young, J.E., Klosko, J.S., & Weishaar, M.E. (2003). *Schema therapy: A practitioner's guide*. New York: Guilford Press.

Zoellner, T., & Maercker, A. (2006). Posttraumatic growth in clinical psychology – a critical review and introduction of a two component model. *Clinical Psychology Review, 26*, 626–653.

Chapter 3

How to use imagery in cognitive-behavioural therapy

Lusia Stopa

The first chapter of this book provided a definition of imagery, discussed why imagery is important in psychopathology, and proposed that there are important links between imagery and self-representations. The second chapter described theories of the self and illustrated some of the ways in which images can represent the self in psychological disorders. This chapter focuses specifically on how imagery is currently used in cognitive-behavioural therapy (CBT). I am using the term CBT in its widest possible sense to cover the family of therapies that have been developed over the past 30 years. The importance of imagery has been recognised in cognitive therapy from the start, but early conceptualisations saw images as functional equivalents of thoughts (e.g. Beck, Rush, Shaw, & Emery, 1979) that could be tackled using the same cognitive therapy techniques, such as thought challenging. In the early days of cognitive therapy, there was no attempt to focus on the unique qualities of images or to develop specific interventions for them.

The picture now is far more complex and varied. Imagery is acknowledged as an important topic in its own right, although Hackmann and Holmes (2004) point out that there is still a need to integrate what we know about imagery from experimental cognitive psychology and from our knowledge of the role of imagery in psychopathology. For example, Holmes and Mathews (2005; Holmes, Mathews, Dalgleish, & Mackintosh, 2006; Holmes, Mathews, Mackintosh, & Dalgleish, 2008) demonstrated that imagery has a more powerful impact on emotion than verbal processing of the same material. The implication of these findings is that we need to pay more attention to imagery in assessment and to the use of the kind of imagery techniques discussed in this chapter in treatment.

The main focus of this book is on the relationship between emotional imagery and the self. That relationship is more apparent in some disorders than in others. Distorted self-images may have both a causal and a maintaining role in disorders where the visible self is associated with self-worth, such as eating disorders or body dysmorphic disorder; or in disorders where the self-conscious emotions predominate, such as social phobia. So, for example, if a woman with an eating disorder sees herself in her mind's eye as disgustingly fat and ugly, and this image is associated with her core beliefs about herself as being unacceptable and worthless, the constant repetition of this image may be a powerful driver of the disorder. Likewise, the man with social phobia who pictures himself dripping with sweat and bright red while he tries to hold a conversation with a new acquaintance will fear social interaction because his image of himself represents a feared self that he does not wish others to see, as well as a belief that he will be rejected or humiliated if other people do see this self.

As well as these very specific images of self, in many disorders there are images of fearful situations, which range from vivid memories of traumatic situations to images of a feared object such as a snake or a spider. Although the self may not be directly represented in these images, the individual's beliefs about the meaning and consequences of these feared images often have negative consequences for the self. So for example, the person with PTSD who has constant intrusive images of the trauma may fear that he or she is going mad, or losing control. As we have seen in Chapter 2, there is a need for consistency and clarity about the self and a fear of madness, or loss of control, represents a direct threat to the integrity of the self, which may lead to the person adopting dysfunctional strategies in order to protect the self. The increased recognition and understanding of the role that images play in creating and maintaining psychopathology has been accompanied by developments in methods and techniques for working with images.

I have divided the material in this chapter into three sections. The first section looks at the use of imagery in assessment; the second and third sections focus on treatment. The first treatment section looks at imagery techniques that are used to complement or facilitate traditional CBT techniques, and at the use of imagery to overcome roadblocks in therapy. The third and final section looks at imagery techniques that are used as an intervention in their own right, albeit within a CBT framework. To some extent these divisions are arbitrary because assessment can, and often does, go on throughout therapy rather than being a one-off session at the beginning, particularly with clients who have more complex or intractable difficulties. The second and third sections both have an explicit focus on intervention, but the boundary between them should be thought of as fuzzy rather than absolute. These divisions are intended to have heuristic value in organising and making sense of the material rather than providing absolute categorical distinctions.

Imagery in and for assessment

A basic distinction can be made between establishing the presence of imagery in assessment and using imagery to facilitate assessment. At its simplest, the therapist needs to know whether the client is experiencing any images, and whether and how these images are contributing to the client's emotional problems. Beck *et al.* (1979) advocated assessing for images in their book on depression, and defined cognition as 'either a thought or an image' (p. 147). Therapists can use straightforward questions that ask directly about images: for example, 'What went through your mind when you noticed your heart racing and started to feel anxious? Did you have any thoughts, did you have any images?' If a client reports an image, the therapist can ask him or her to describe it, and can then explore the impact of the image on the client's feelings, physiology, and behaviour, in much the same way as the exploration that follows on from identifying negative automatic thoughts. Clients can also be asked to report images on thought records, as well as verbal thoughts. As images are very powerful encoders of meaning and can be associated with high levels of affect, it is helpful if their investigation is a routine part of the therapy assessment.

Imagery assessment with Axis I disorders

Current models of disorders can be used as a guide to suggest what particular types of images therapists should be on the look-out for. In social phobia, distorted images of the self are common, in which the individual looks ridiculous or foolish or absurd and these images convey important meanings about the potential humiliation of the social self (see for example: Hackmann, Clark, & McManus, 2000; Hirsch, Clark, Mathews, & Williams, 2003). By comparison, individuals with panic disorder or health anxiety might be more likely to have images of the self that point to an impending physical catastrophe and consequent disintegration of the physical self. Images are not only visual; they can be somatic, auditory, gustatory or olfactory. Assessment for images should include awareness of the different possible modalities; for example in PTSD, the image of a particular smell or sound that is associated with the trauma can be a potent trigger for emotional responding.

The relationship between images and verbal material is also important. In some disorders, images serve to amplify and intensify verbal meanings; for example, a man who is experiencing panic attacks and fears that he will have a heart attack might see an image of himself being resuscitated and this image is likely to intensify the emotional impact of the feared catastrophe. In cases like this, the meaning of the disorder can be explored verbally, and the ways in which the image intensifies and amplifies the emotion can be demonstrated. In other disorders, the relationship might be quite different, and one form of processing might serve as a mask to the other. Borkovec's model of generalised anxiety disorder (GAD: e.g. Ruscio & Borkovec, 2006) suggests that worry, which is seen as the cardinal feature of GAD, is a form of avoidance. In this model, worry is used to block or avoid highly distressing visual images that create intense anxiety.

Assessment handbooks and practice guides (e.g. Hawton, Salkovskis, Kirk, & Clark, 1989; Wells, 1997) recommend asking clients to give a detailed description of a recent distressing episode to help identify triggers and maintaining factors. Of course, any description of a past event involves first recalling that event and then describing it. We tend to take for granted that people will be able to do this, but when we ask them to describe what happened, we rarely ask about how the memory is constructed. For some people at least, recalling the situation will involve imagistic components even if the whole event is not imaged. As such, this assessment procedure constitutes an implicit imagery task. This may help to explain why some people have difficulty recalling a specific instance of a feared situation. We know that there are individual differences in people's ability to image and maybe poor imagers have more difficulty with this task than others. On the other hand, some people might want to avoid recalling a difficult situation precisely because they are very good at creating images and the recall process may create high levels of anxiety because it is accompanied by vivid images of the situation. At the moment these comments are purely speculative as there is no evidence to refute or corroborate them. However, it might be useful to ask people whether they had an image of the situation while recalling it and what effect this had on them during assessment. Hirsch and Holmes (2007) provide a useful description of the types of images to look for in anxiety disorders.

Imagery assessment with personality disorders

So far I have looked at ways to identify images in assessment and considered the various roles that images can have in maintaining Axis I disorders. The treatments of personality disorders (Axis II disorders) that have been developed in recent years, such as schema-focused therapy (e.g. Young, 1999a) and dialectical behaviour therapy (Linehan, 1993), have an explicit focus on the use of imagery in treatment. In schema-focused therapy, imagery also has an explicit role in assessment to help the therapist identify maladaptive schemas and to understand the context in which these schemas have developed. Young (1999a) argues that imagery is the best way of getting at the affective content of schemas. Verbal methods such as interviews and questionnaires (e.g. Young's Schema Questionnaire, www.schematherapy.com/id54.htm) are effective methods of eliciting the cognitive content of early maladaptive schemas, but are less effective at eliciting the emotional content of the schema.

Young (1999a) describes two different methods for eliciting schemas in assessment and the interested reader should consult his book for more detailed information. In one technique, the therapist asks the patient to shut his or her eyes and report spontaneous images that come to mind. In the other technique, the therapist asks the patient to imagine a situation that he or she believes will trigger the schema based on previous information gained from interview and self-report. In many cases this may be a situation that involves a key relationship with a parent or spouse, for example. If the therapist focuses on an early life experience, Young (1999b) suggests that he or she asks the patient questions such as 'What are you thinking, what are you feeling, what is your parent thinking and feeling?', which allows the therapist to see the dynamic in the relationship. The patient can also be asked what he or she would like the parent to say, or to do, differently. Young suggests that if therapists use this exercise, they should then ask the patient to switch to a current life situation that feels the same, so that links can be made between the past and the present. At the end of the session, therapists should leave enough time to debrief the patient on what has happened during the imagery session, label the schemas, and discuss how the information gained fits with the current case conceptualisation.

In personality disorders, images can sometimes contain contradictory meanings (Layden, 2000), and it is important to assess all the meanings contained by a particular image. Layden stresses the need to use content-free questions when assessing stored images so as not to implant meanings. She suggests questions such as 'Do you see a picture? Are you seeing something? Is something flashing through your mind? In the image, where are you? Is there anyone else there? What are you doing, saying, thinking, feeling?' Layden links imagery work specifically with the self and conceptualises the aim of treatment for people with personality disorders as the search for them to become the self that they were meant to be. She argues that because many of the dysfunctional views of self relate to early experiences of abuse and/or neglect, critical meanings about the self are often encoded pre-verbally and therefore contain sensory and perceptual rather than verbal information. Imagery can provide a route to accessing and changing the meaning of these stored experiences.

Patients with personality disorders may experience high levels of distress and arousal when they are doing imagery exercises. There are a number of ways to help patients to reduce distress and arousal following an imagery exercise. These include having an imagined 'safe place' to return to following an imagery exercise, or even during the exercise if the patient feels too overwhelmed to continue. Patients can also be encouraged to use grounding objects to help distinguish between the reality present in the image and the actual reality of sitting in the therapist's room. Grounding objects are often used to help patients to cope with dissociation (e.g. Kennerley, 1996) and can consist of a small object that has some meaning to the patient, and that is a concrete reminder of being in the 'here and now'; for example, a grounding object for one patient might be a smooth pebble found on a trip to the beach, whereas for another it might be a soft toy. If the therapist thinks that the patient is likely to experience high levels of affective distress during an imagery exercise, then he or she needs to establish methods of coping with that distress before doing the imagery exercise. Young (1999b) recommends beginning the imagery for assessment exercise, for patients with personality disorders, by visualising a safe place and then ending the exercise by returning to the safe place. An example of using imagery to create a safe place is given below.

Imagery exercise to create a 'safe place'

THERAPIST: I'd like you to close your eyes and imagine a place where you feel completely safe and comfortable. It can be anywhere you want and it can be a real place that you have actually been to or it can be somewhere imaginary. Just spend a little time imagining somewhere where you feel safe and protected and calm. (*Pause*) When you're ready I'd like you to describe where you are to me.

PATIENT: I'm in my Grandma's house. That's a good place to be. I always felt safe there even when my mum and dad were having their worst rows.

THERAPIST: Whereabouts in your Grandma's house are you?

PATIENT: I'm sitting in the kitchen.

THERAPIST: What are you doing?

PATIENT: I'm sitting in the big chair next to the fire.

THERAPIST: Is your Grandma in there with you?

PATIENT: Yes, she's baking.

THERAPIST: Can you smell what she's baking?

PATIENT: Mmm yes, it smells great. She's made a cake and it's cooking and I can smell the cake and it smells sort of homely and nice and safe.

THERAPIST: Is your Grandma talking to you?

PATIENT: No she's singing, she always used to sing a lot and I'm just listening to her, thinking about the glass of milk and the slice of cake she's going to give me when it's ready and it'll still be warm and really yummy . . . And I've got Harris her cat on my lap and he's sort of wheezing . . . he's kind of old and he sleeps a lot.

THERAPIST: And how are you feeling while you sit in your Grandma's kitchen with Harris asleep on your lap and your Grandma singing and the cake is baking?

PATIENT: I feel really (*pause*) I don't know, I do feel safe but it's more than that . . . I feel really looked after, loved I suppose 'cos I know my Grandma's always there for me . . . but it's more than that really . . . it's a kind of warm inside feeling that I don't really have anywhere else . . .

The therapist can continue to expand the image, focusing on sensory details and asking the patient to get in touch with the feeling of safety and of being protected. Once that has been accomplished, the therapist can ask the patient to spend a few more minutes in the safe place and remind the patient that it is a place to which he or she can always return. After doing this exercise, it is always useful to ask the patient for his or her view on it and to find out if any problems were encountered. Patients, particularly those who are not used to the experience of being nurtured, can often find it a surprisingly powerful experience and if you are planning to use imagery to look at difficult and distressing experiences, starting off by creating a safe place in imagery can provide the patient with confidence in the method as well as the knowledge that he or she can create a powerful refuge in the imagination (see also Chapter 9 for a discussion of compassionate mind imagery).

Difficulty in accessing images

Some patients with personality disorders or with a complex history of problems, and particularly those with a trauma history, may find it difficult to access images (although many others are flooded with images). For those who do have problems accessing images, this may be due to individual differences in ability to image that make the task inherently more difficult for some people. For these people, you can give practice in forming images by asking them to imagine a concrete object such as a piece of furniture, or you can use an abstract shape, such as a blue triangle, and then ask the person to transform the shape into a green oval. Layden (2000) has a useful exercise in which she asks people to walk around their childhood home until they get to where the food is kept, and to describe what they see on the journey. As well as assessing imagery ability, this exercise also provides the therapist with information about the affective tone of the person's childhood world. However, difficulties with accessing images may be related to avoidance rather than to poor visualisation abilities. This is more challenging to work with, but there are a number of possibilities. These include educating the patient about the value of the imagery work; using imagery for relaxation; and teaching emotion regulation strategies before embarking on imagery work. The therapist can also discuss whether the patient would feel more able to tolerate the imagery with his or her eyes open.

From assessment to treatment

The use of imagery in assessment ranges from simply asking patients to notice and monitor images to the more complex procedures that are used to investigate schematic beliefs about the self. The use of images to investigate self-schemas and procedures such as creating a safe place in imagery can also be used in treatment, and indeed are more likely to be used as part of an intervention in Axis I disorders, where assessment is not usually as prolonged as it can be when working with Axis II disorders.

Imagery techniques that are used to complement or facilitate traditional CBT

In the next section, I am going to focus on how imagery is used in therapy as an intervention technique rather than as an assessment technique. However, it is important to remember that therapy can move in and out of assessment and intervention, so that these are not necessarily discrete and encapsulated phases. I am going to discuss a number of different techniques and uses of imagery in this section. Table 3.1 shows which techniques will be discussed in each of the following sections.

First, I will look at imaginal exposure to specific stimuli. Prolonged exposure and imaginal reliving for trauma processing will be covered in the third section of this chapter because these are major components of treatment and can be used as a treatment in and of themselves, whereas imaginal exposure is usually used as a prelude to *in vivo* exposure or because *in vivo* exposure is not feasible. Second, I will look at imaginal rehearsal, which is sometimes known as covert modelling. While there is considerable overlap between imaginal exposure and imaginal rehearsal, I am conceptualising imaginal exposure as exposure to a discrete stimulus such as a snake or a spider, and imaginal rehearsal as a sequence of imagined events in which the person constructs a new behavioural repertoire and practises this repertoire in the imagination. Of course, these distinctions are rather artificial because a therapist might want to use both, or to integrate the two techniques. However, for the purposes of helping a reader who is unfamiliar with imagery techniques, I thought it would be useful to distinguish between them. Third, I will look at guided imagery, which has been used in a number of ways including self-soothing (Esplen & Garfinkel, 1998) and to manage pain, psychological distress, insomnia and other conditions (see Sheikh, 2002, for a review). In the fourth section, I will contrast guided imagery with Socratic imagery and illustrate the similarities and differences between the two approaches. The fifth and final part of this section will consider the various

Table 3.1 Imagery techniques covered in this chapter

Section	Imagery technique	Brief description
This section	Imaginal exposure	Exposure to feared stimulus in the imagination
	Imaginal rehearsal	Imagining a sequence of events
	Guided imagery	Following an imagery script
	Socratic imagery	Using Socratic questioning to elicit patient's images and explore meaning
	Imagery to overcome roadblocks in therapy	Using imagery to supplement a traditional CBT technique
Imagery techniques that can be used as an intervention	Prolonged exposure	Exposure to the memory of an event or sequence of events, typically exposure to a traumatic memory
	Imagery rescripting	Modifying an image that represents a memory to change the meaning associated with the memory

ways in which imagery techniques can be used to deal with roadblocks in therapy.

A useful typology for understanding imagery techniques is presented in Holmes, Arntz, and Smucker's (2007) article on imagery rescripting. They divide imagery techniques into those that directly address negative images, such as imaginal exposure, and those that promote positive images, such as compassionate mind imagery (see Chapter 9). Some techniques, such as imagery rescripting, can be used both to transform negative images and to promote positive images. Holmes *et al.* also make a useful distinction between direct and indirect techniques for modifying images. All the techniques discussed in this chapter are direct techniques that focus on creating, holding, and manipulating images in the mind. Indirect techniques include, for example, mindfulness-based cognitive therapy and image-based positive interpretation bias training.

Imaginal exposure

Exposure to feared stimuli and feared situations has been an essential component of behaviour therapy (Marks, 1987) since its inception and remains a key constituent of cognitive-behavioural treatments for the anxiety disorders. Exposure can take two forms: *in vivo* and imaginal exposure. *In vivo* exposure describes a situation where the individual is faced with the actual feared stimulus or situation: for example, spending time in proximity to a snake or a spider, or going into feared social situations. *In vivo* exposure can also include exposure to feared bodily sensations, such as a racing heart, and can be helpful in panic disorder and health anxiety. Imaginal exposure refers to exposure in the imagination and has typically been used when the client cannot tolerate *in vivo* exposure or when the feared stimulus is difficult to obtain.

In early forms of CBT, cognitive restructuring was used alongside behavioural exposure; for example, Butler, Cullington, Munby, Amies, and Gelder's (1984) study found that cognitive restructuring with exposure was better than exposure alone for social phobia. Since its first use there has been a debate over the mechanisms that underlie change in exposure (see Mineka & Oehlberg, 2008, for a review). More traditional views of extinction and habituation were superseded by arguments about the role of exposure in effecting cognitive change, although the debate ranges from arguments about the ability of a stimulus to predict change at the behavioural end of the spectrum to arguments about change in higher order beliefs at the more cognitive end of the spectrum: see Salkovskis, Hackmann, Wells, Gelder, and Clark (2007) for a discussion of cognitive change versus habituation in the treatment of panic disorder.

The way in which exposure is used in CBT has also shifted and increasingly exposure is used not so much to bring about habituation or extinction as to test out beliefs (see Bennett-Levy *et al.*'s [2004] excellent book on behavioural experiments for more detail). The function of exposure in a therapy pro- gramme is critical because it will affect how the therapist uses it and what sort of change he or she is looking for. In traditional behavioural programmes of treatment, exposure (both *in vivo* and imaginal) is continued until the indi- vidual experiences a significant reduction in anxiety measured in subjective units of distress (SUDs: Wolpe, 1990). However, when exposure is used in a behavioural experiment, the key unit of change is not so much the perceived reduction in anxiety as the change in belief, although the theory predicts that reductions in belief should be accompanied by reductions in anxiety.

Let us move on now to the actual technique and look at how to conduct imaginal exposure. For purposes of illustration, let's consider how imaginal exposure could be used to treat a straightforward case of spider phobia (see also Hunt & Fenton, 2007, who compared imaginal exposure and imagery rescripting for snake fears). After I have described the basic technique, I will discuss the differences between using it in this way and the use of imaginal exposure as part of a behavioural experiment.

Jane is a 31-year-old woman who is terrified of spiders. She has been frightened of spiders ever since she was a small child and avoids any contact with them. She doesn't even like talking about them and her whole family refers to spiders as 'Henrys' rather than using the word 'spider'. She could not tolerate the thought of starting treatment with *in vivo* exposure, but was willing to try imaginal exposure as a prelude to *in vivo* exposure. Jane had been taught to use a SUDs scale of 0 to 10, where 0 represented no anxiety at all and 10 was labelled as 'the most anxiety you have ever felt'. The following script illustrates how to conduct imaginal exposure.

THERAPIST: OK Jane, we're going to start the exposure in a moment, but before we do can you tell me how anxious you're feeling right now?

JANE: Oh, around 5 I think. I'm feeling pretty nervous but I know it's not a real (*pause*) er, spider.

THERAPIST: Right, can you close your eyes and sit comfortably. Now I'd like you to try to imagine a medium-sized black spider in a jar with the lid firmly closed. (*Pause for a few seconds*) Can you do that? What can you see?

JANE: Yes I've got an image of it; it's about this big (*makes a circle with her fingers to show the therapist*). It's in a big jar and it's sitting at the bottom. The lid's on top and it's got sellotape and a big thick rubber band round it.

THERAPIST: OK, how anxious are you feeling right now?

JANE: About 7 or 8.

THERAPIST: Now I want you to really focus on the spider. I want you to describe it to me and tell me what it looks like, what colour it is, whether you can see its legs or not, how long its legs are, what it's doing, and if it's moving at all.

JANE: Er it's just a black blob, the jar is quite a long way away so I can't see it properly. It's just like a ball of fluff or something.

THERAPIST: We need to get a bit closer to the spider so that you can see it properly. You could try zooming in on it the way you can with a camera. Do you know what I mean?

JANE: Yes.

THERAPIST: Are you willing to give that a try?

JANE: Yes, OK. Right, I can see it more clearly now. It's a browny black colour, ugh it's all mottled, yuk it's disgusting. I can see its legs. Oh help, it's moving them. Its legs are about two or three centimetres long, it looks really evil, like it's out to get me.

THERAPIST: How anxious are you feeling right now?

JANE: Oh it's gone up to a 9. I'm feeling really panicky now, I really don't like it.

THERAPIST: You're doing really well, can you stick with it? Do you remember we discussed how important it is to stay with it when you are feeling this frightened?

JANE: OK, I'm amazed that it is making me so scared because part of me knows that it is only in my mind and can't hurt me.

THERAPIST: Can you keep focusing on the image of the spider? What's it doing now?

This process can continue until the client's SUDs reduce significantly. It is neither essential nor likely that anxiety will reduce to zero, but anxiety should reduce by several points; in this case it is important for the patient's anxiety to drop below 5 before terminating the exposure session. In this brief extract, I have illustrated imaginal exposure as it is traditionally used in behaviour therapy. However, this approach can easily be incorporated into CBT; for example, the therapist could ask Jane 'What's going through your mind right now?' when she says 'yuk' and expresses disgust. The creation of the image may help the therapist to identify relevant negative thoughts about the spider ('It's going to bite me') or about Jane's ability to cope ('I'll die if it gets out of that jar'). At the end of the exposure session the therapist can help Jane to evaluate her reactions and make explicit any new learning that has taken place. The session could be used as a behavioural experiment; for example, Jane is highly avoidant of spiders and may believe that she will go mad or lose control if she lets herself think about them for too long. In this case the imaginal exposure is set up to test out those beliefs rather than simply to monitor how anxious she is. It is still important to record anxiety ratings so that the she can see that her anxiety reduces over time rather than spiralling out of control, which is what she fears will happen.

This extract also illustrates another important feature of imagery, that is, our ability to manipulate imagery. In this case the therapist asked Jane to zoom in; patients who have distressing images that they cannot control may find it helpful initially to be able to zoom in and out. This procedure can achieve two key aims. First, the patient realises that she has some control over the disturbing images, which challenges the belief that these images are totally uncontrollable. Second, the intensity of the emotions that are experienced will probably vary so that the stimulus is more frightening when she zooms in and less frightening when she zooms out. These changes in intensity of affect can be used in the case conceptualisation to illustrate the importance of imagery in maintaining the fears. There are a number of other techniques for manipulating imagery, such as: fading out; moving around the image; making objects, people, or the self grow larger or smaller. The ability to manipulate the internal contents of consciousness imaginatively may be one reason why imagery is such a potentially powerful tool. Imagery can provide symbolic representations of the self, the world, and other people. It can create imagined worlds and also reconstruct memories of past experiences. The ability to manipulate these symbolic representations may be one way in which we can change them and thus lessen their power over the emotions.

I have discussed imaginal exposure as exposure to a single discrete stimulus; however, this technique can be used to imagine a sequence of events and then it is more commonly labelled 'imaginal rehearsal'.

Imaginal rehearsal

Imaginal rehearsal or covert modelling is a procedure in which some kind of future performance is imagined in detail. This procedure has been widely used in sports psychology to help athletes achieve optimal performance in challenging situations.

The function of imagery in these situations is twofold: first to rehearse being confident and in control in a difficult situation, and second to regulate arousal levels (Gregg & Hall, 2006). There are two types of imaginal rehearsal: one aimed at mastery and the other aimed at coping. Sports psychology is more likely to use mastery imagery because the aim is to help the sportsman or woman to achieve the highest standard of performance possible. In mastery imagery, the individual imagines a 'perfect performance' and focuses only on positive aspects of the performance and not on any potential negative outcomes. By comparison, coping imagery is generally more appropriate for work with emotional disorders.

Imaginal rehearsal has been used to help individuals cope with feared situations such as dental fears (Mathews & Rezin, 1977). In this case the procedure involves identifying the client's usual response, and then discussing alternative ways of responding. Once the therapist has helped the client to identify specific alternative behaviours, the future situation can then be imagined in detail and rehearsed in the imagination. The procedure may also involve using relaxing imagery to calm arousal levels and positive self-talk to facilitate coping. In the following example, an anxious probationer teacher prepares for an appraisal with her head of department. In the first phase, the therapist identifies the client's key anxieties, which are her fears that the head of department will judge her performance as below the required standard and will think that she is incompetent and not fit for the profession. Discussion of objective measures has shown that the teacher is a perfectionist and that she usually accomplishes tasks to a high standard. The therapist and client have run through the imagined scenario in order to identify key cognitions and to see what the client imagines will happen in this interview. The teacher describes herself as sitting in a very small chair and looking up at the head of department, who sits behind an impressively large desk. Her anxiety rises sharply when she enters the room and seems to escalate so that she notices herself feeling breathless and describes her heart as racing and fluttering alternately. She sees herself as tongue-tied and unable to defend herself when her head of department tells her that he is very disappointed in her performance.

After a detailed discussion of this imagined scenario, the therapist and client focus on how she would like to behave and respond during the interview. They identify the negative thoughts that are running through the client's mind ('I'm incompetent . . . a failure . . . he's going to get rid of me'), assess how realistic these are, and formulate more realistic responses. Then they replay the imagery scenario and the client imagines herself getting anxious, but being able to cope with the interview.

THERAPIST: When you're ready I'd like you to shut your eyes and then start to imagine that you are about to go into your head of department's office. Try to imagine the situation in as much detail as possible.

CLIENT: I'm standing outside the office door and I'm feeling very nervous but I'm telling myself that Jeff is a nice guy and that if there were major problems he would have told me at my last review. I take a deep breath and knock on the door.

THERAPIST: What do you see when you open the door?

CLIENT: Jeff's sitting behind his desk and he smiles at me and says come in. I walk through the door and I'm feeling very nervous but I smile back at him and I stand up straight and smile back. I tell myself that I can manage this, even if there are negative things it can't be all bad. I sit down and make sure that I sit up straight and breathe slowly and calmly.

THERAPIST: What happens next?

CLIENT: Jeff says that we're going to review how I've got on as this is the end of my probationer year but that first he'd like me to tell him how I think I've done.

The client then continues to work through the situation using the problems that she has identified previously with the therapist and the solutions that they have generated together. Once the client has created an imaginal script for the event, she can practise it on a daily basis in order to control her anxiety and prepare for the forthcoming interview. The therapist can ask her to stop at any time during the rehearsal, and either freeze the frame, for example if she is having particular difficulty with something, or rewind to an earlier part in order to explore the negative appraisals driving her anxiety or to help her to develop more adaptive responses. As mentioned above, it is not usually helpful to imagine 'perfect' performance, which is probably unobtainable, so it is preferable to imagine some negative content and rehearse how to cope with this. On the other hand it is equally important to identify catastrophic appraisals of the situation and to replace these with more realistic possibilities.

As we will see later in the chapter, imaginal rehearsal has a lot in common with imagery rescripting. However, in imagery rescripting, the problem-solving and transformation are done within the imagery itself and the therapist's role is to help the client to generate her own responses, whereas the procedure in imaginal rehearsal is much more of a collaborative effort between the therapist and the client and more work is done prior to the imaging work to establish a repertoire of available responses. This work might, for example, include identifying and challenging negative thoughts and role-playing alternative behavioural responses. Another important difference is that imagery rescripting can be much more creative and draw on imagined and imaginary figures, e.g. a dead parent, an imaginary superhero, who can enter the image to perform a particular function, whereas imaginal rehearsal in preparation for forthcoming encounters in real life is more likely to stick to fairly realistic imagined scenarios.

Imaginal rehearsal has also been used extensively to treat idiopathic nightmares (i.e. nightmares that are not part of posttraumatic stress disorder or other anxiety disorders). Indeed, according to Spoormaker, Schredl, and van den Bout (2006), imaginal rehearsal is the treatment of choice for idiopathic nightmares, although they do point out that no randomised controlled trials have been conducted to date. When treating nightmares the procedure is slightly different because the rehearsal focuses on changing the content of the nightmare in some way and, as dreams can be extremely bizarre and not at all realistic, imagery rehearsal of an alternative meaning or content may draw on similar content. As such, imagery rehearsal used to treat nightmares is probably even closer to the technique of imagery rescripting.

Guided imagery

Guided imagery is sometimes used as a synonym for imaginal rehearsal in the literature on imagery. However, I am using it here to describe a procedure where the therapist deliberately guides the client through an imagery exercise in order to achieve a specific end. Guided imagery has been used to achieve a number of ends including relaxation and self-soothing, managing psychological distress, pain management, insomnia, tackling addictions such as smoking, weight reduction, managing nausea from medical interventions such as chemotherapy, and dealing with complicated grief (e.g. Cohen & Fried, 2007; Dyregov, 2006; Fried, 1987; Hall, Hall, Stradling, & Young, 2006; Lewandowski, Good, & Draucker, 2005; Menzies, Taylor, & Bourguignon, 2006; Overholser, 1991). In guided imagery the therapist can use or adapt an existing script (see Sheikh, 2002, for a number of examples of scripts), or alternatively the therapist can devise an individual script for a patient.

In guided imagery, scripts range from the concrete and specific to the more abstract. At the 'concrete' end of the spectrum, for example, Achterberg, Dossey, Kolkmeier, and Sheikh (2003) provide a script for weight management that starts with imagining light energising the self, but then focuses on imagining a new body size and shape followed by mentally planning the foods that the person wants to eat. Next the script focuses on the sensations of fullness that are linked to cessation of eating, and this is followed by imagining the self eating in a favourite restaurant and at home. The final section of the script concentrates on imagining an exercise routine and reinforces the images of the new body weight and shape. At the other end of the spectrum, imagery scripts are more abstract and focus on qualities such as healing energy and light, These scripts may be linked to a particular philosophy or view of life and are perhaps closer to self-hypnosis than the more structured scripts that resemble covert rehearsal. While there is an extensive literature on guided imagery, the evidence base is variable and the evidence is mixed in terms of rigour and quality. For example, a randomised control trial of guided imagery to enhance self-comforting in bulimia demonstrated significant reductions in both bingeing and purging as well as improvements in attitudes towards eating and body weight (Esplen, Garfinkel, Olmsted, Gallop, & Kennedy, 1998), whereas two recent systematic reviews of guided imagery for patients with cancer and nonulcer dyspepsia both found that results were equivocal and criticised the poor methodology of many of the studies (Roffe, Schmidt, & Ernst, 2005; Soo, Forman, Delaney, & Moayyedi, 2004).

Guided imagery versus Socratic imagery

As we have already seen, guided imagery follows a specific format in that the therapist either uses a pre-existing script or develops an individualised script for a particular patient. Either way the therapist is determining – 'guiding' – the patient's responses. Socratic imagery describes a contrasting open-ended process that is analogous to the Socratic questioning that is used with verbal dialogue in CBT. Smucker and Dancu (1999) in their book on imagery rescripting, which we will cover later in the chapter, argue that Socratic imagery is linked to the idea that self-directed imagery is likely to be more empowering than imagery that is suggested or directed by the therapist.

In Socratic imagery the therapist can use open-ended questions such as

'What can you see? ... Can you see anything? ... Can you describe the image/picture/sound/smell to me? ... Where are you in the image? ... Who else is in the image? ... What are you doing/saying/thinking? ... What are other people doing/saying/thinking? ... How do you feel in the image? ...' The Socratic procedure uses content-free questions in order to elicit the patient's own images, whereas the guided imagery procedure suggests and directs in order to achieve a particular end. Socratic imagery can be more powerful because it allows the patient to explore emotions and meanings and to discover resolutions for conflicts and difficulties. However, it can be more challenging for the therapist, especially novices, because it is harder to know where you are going in a session as the material is being generated by the patient. Socratic imagery can be used to explore the meaning of a particular image, or to help the patient discover what he or she needs to do in order to transform the meaning of an image during imagery rescripting.

Imagery to overcome roadblocks in therapy

One of cognitive therapy's strengths is the use of empirically validated therapies. However, even in well-validated therapies, things do not always go according to plan. Despite the impressive evidence base, there are still many lacunae in our knowledge and the establishment of an evidence base for working with complex cases and personality disorders is at an early stage. To put it plainly, therapy and therapists can often get stuck; one example is the patient who learns how to challenge his or her thoughts but still says 'I know that I'm not a failure but I still *feel* as if I am'. In other cases, what appeared to be a straightforward case of an anxiety problem may reveal difficulties in defining the self; the patient may complain of not knowing who she is, or of feeling no continuity between her sense of self at different times. These are difficult problems for which we do not yet have clear and effective techniques. However, imagery can be used to tackle difficulties like this (see for example Chapter 9 on adopting a compassionate stance towards the self, and Chapter 7 for ideas on working with a poor sense of self).

A good example of using imagery to overcome difficulties in therapy is provided in a paper by Mountford and Waller (2006). They present a case study to illustrate using imagery to overcome the restrictive mode in eating disorders. In this context, the restrictive mode refers to a schema mode (see Beck & Clark, 1997), in which individuals define the self in terms of over-valued ideas about weight, shape and body size, use emotional suppression as the principal method of emotion regulation, and engage in behaviours such as restricting food intake, exercise and body checking. The restrictive mode interferes with treatment for two reasons: first, because there are a number of positive reinforcers in the early stages, such as losing weight and providing a sense of control; second, because the restrictive mode is integrated into the person's sense of self and therefore the demands of treatment seem to directly challenge fundamental beliefs about the self and what is right for the individual.

Mountford and Waller (2006) present a case in which they supplemented traditional CBT for eating disorders with imagery work that was designed to tackle the restrictive mode. This was done by personifying the mode (described as the patient's 'anorexia') and initially asking the patient to draw a picture of the anorexia and then to build on this work to create an image of the anorexia. Traditional cognitive techniques such as behavioural experiments, diary-keeping, and challenging beliefs expressed by the mode were interwoven with the imagery work. The authors stress that a distinctive feature of this work is precisely this use of imagery as a technique to increase the effectiveness of CBT therapy, rather than as a stand-alone technique, and they report success with this approach in a series of nine out of ten cases.

This is a novel and interesting approach to eating disorders that can be adapted for use with other types of problems. However, Mountford and Waller (2006) point to some cautions when experimenting with work of this type. Their patients were highly motivated and they speculate about whether it would be effective with less well-motivated patients. They also caution against the use of such an approach with patients who have severe abuse histories, with whom a more gradual approach that focuses on engagement and trust might be necessary. In terms of eating disorders, clinicians also need to be aware of the effects of starvation, which intensify the rigidity of thinking patterns that can act as a significant block to working with the eating disorders.

Imagery techniques that can be used as an intervention

In the previous section, we looked at a range of imagery techniques that have generally been used as part of a wider therapeutic intervention. The imagery techniques in the following section can be used in this way as well, but they have also been used as interventions in their own right. All of them are embedded within a basic CBT approach and to a greater or lesser extent draw on various CBT techniques to complement the approach. As such, then, the difference between these techniques and those in the previous section could be conceptualised in terms of whether the imagery procedures constitute the prime focus of therapy or not. In this section we will look at prolonged exposure to aid trauma processing (Foa, Rothbaum, Riggs, & Murdock, 1991), imagery rescripting (Smucker & Dancu, 1999), and compassionate mind training (Gilbert, 2005; Lee, 2005). Imagery rescripting and compassionate mind training both offer powerful illustrations of the theme of this book because both explicitly address the theme of the self via imagery. This will be discussed in more detail in the relevant sections below.

Prolonged exposure

Over the past 10 to 15 years there has been increasing recognition of the need for specific trauma-focused therapies within CBT. Prolonged exposure (PE) is one of the first of this family of CBT therapies. PE was developed by Edna Foa (Foa, Rothbaum, Riggs, & Murdock, 1991) and incorporates both imaginal and *in vivo* exposure to the trauma and to trauma cues. The theoretical underpinning of PE is based on the idea that the fear network must be activated and corrective information incorporated for successful emotional processing to take place. PE typically comprises nine 90-minute sessions. There are four components to the treatment (Resick, Nishith, Weaver, Astin, & Feuer, 2002): psycho-education and rationale for the treatment, breathing retraining, imaginal exposure to the trauma memory, and *in vivo* exposure to aspects of the trauma situation (e.g. revisiting the place where the trauma occurred) and to trauma triggers (e.g. sights, sounds or smells that trigger flashbacks and/or high arousal). Hembree, Rauch, and Foa (2003) stress the importance of developing a strong therapeutic alliance and providing a convincing rationale, as well as ensuring good self-care for the therapist while delivering PE.

In the imaginal exposure sessions, patients are asked to imagine the trauma scene in the first person in order to promote full engagement with the trauma memory. They are asked to imagine the trauma in as much detail as possible, focusing on all the sensory details as well as on the emotions that they experienced and the thoughts either that occurred during the trauma or that occur while they are reliving the trauma. Both of these types of thoughts are important and may be linked to differences in emotional responding; for example, a patient who was held at gunpoint during a robbery and thought 'I'm going to die' experienced intense fear and anxiety and these emotions comprise part of the trauma memory. When the patient experiences flashbacks that trigger the same levels of fear, he thinks 'I'm going mad' and 'I'm a weak person to feel so frightened now that it's all over'. These appraisals of the symptoms lead to feelings of shame. The imaginal exposure to the trauma is repeated during the session, depending on the length of the person's narrative, and the session is taped so that the patient can listen to the exposure every day between sessions along with periods of *in vivo* exposure. Ratings of distress are taken every 10 minutes during exposure using 0–100 SUDs (subjective units of distress).

In the following example, the therapist is doing a session of PE with a patient (Martin) who was involved in a motor vehicle accident in which he was seriously injured and one of the other drivers was killed. This is Martin's second session of imaginal exposure, so he knows what to expect and has started to provide a more detailed description of the trauma than in the first session.

THERAPIST: OK, in a minute I'm going to ask you to shut your eyes and go through the accident in detail but before we start can you rate how anxious you're feeling on the 0 to 100 scale?

MARTIN: Um about 60 I guess. I'm not looking forward to doing this again.

THERAPIST: Are you clear about why we're going through it again?

MARTIN: Yes, I know I need to do it, but I don't enjoy it. I know that I need to stop avoiding thinking about it and kind of look at it all and then it should be a bit easier.

THERAPIST: Yes, that's right, are you ready to go ahead now?

MARTIN: Yes, fine.

THERAPIST: OK, I'd like you to shut your eyes and then start to relive what happened to you in the accident in as much detail as possible. Remember to talk in the present tense, so 'I am driving down the road' and try to describe everything that you can see, any sounds or smells and how you're feeling and what is going through your mind.

MARTIN: (*Shuts his eyes*) I'm driving down the road to see my sister. It's a sunny day and I drive round the bend at XXXX and I'm dazzled for a moment, I can't see anything just for a moment and then as I blink, I'm thinking 'Oh that sun's bright' and suddenly there's a car coming towards me on my side of the carriageway . . . I just feel stunned for a moment . . . I can't feel anything, I feel numb just for a moment . . . it's as if everything has just stopped, I'm kind of frozen in time staring . . . as if I'm just suspended . . . it's such a horrible feeling . . . as if I'm hanging in a space between life and death and I just feel nothingness . . . then I was terrified . . .

THERAPIST: I am terrified.

MARTIN: I am terrified. I can see this car . . . it's bright red and it's hurtling towards me . . . (*starts breathing rapidly and whole body tenses up*) it's heading straight for me, Christ I'm going to die . . . my heart is racing . . . I'm so frightened . . . I feel so completely alone. . . . My whole body feels as if it's going to explode, everything is going so fast and I just know that this is it . . . I've slammed the brakes on but I know it's no good so I swerve. I just think if it hits me that's it I'll be dead. I yank the steering wheel . . . I can feel the car pull, I'm still going too fast. . . . There's a horrible scrape, it's so loud and it . . . he's hit me and my car bounces . . . it literally bounces up into the air, I can feel the car as it lifts off the ground . . . (*pauses*)

THERAPIST: How anxious are you feeling right now?

MARTIN: 95 I think, maybe 100. It's awful.

THERAPIST: You're doing really well, can you carry on?

MARTIN: Then the car hit the bank. I was . . .

THERAPIST: I am . . .

MARTIN: Yes, sorry, I am in the car and I am alive and I can't believe it but the car is kind of embedded in the bank and then just as I start to think thank God I'm not dead, I see smoke coming out of the engine and it starts all over again . . . I've got to get out . . . I've got to get out . . . but I can't move my legs and I just start to scream and it's as if someone else is screaming . . . I can hear this awful noise and I know it's me and yet it's not me and I can't stop . . .

The patient continues with the exposure and the therapist repeats the exposure until the SUDs ratings are significantly reduced. After the exposure session, the therapist discusses the exposure experience, and assigns the homework.

PE is effective in the treatment of PTSD following a diverse range of traumatic experiences such as rape, including complex PTSD following multiple assaults (Foa et al., 1991; Resick et al., 2002; Resick, Nishith, & Griffin, 2003; Nishith, Nixon, & Resick, 2005) and terrorist attacks (Marshall & Suh, 2003). While PE is demonstrably effective in treating PTSD, it is an emotionally demanding treatment, and has a significant failure rate including dropouts and patients who fail to improve or whose symptoms are exacerbated (Grunert, Smucker, Weis, & Rusch, 2003). In a pilot study that compared PE with eye movement desensitisation and reprocessing (EMDR), Ironson, Freund, Strauss, and Williams (2002) found that although both treatments were effective for patients who completed treatment, EMDR was better tolerated than PE and patients receiving EMDR reported significant symptom reductions earlier in therapy.

At the moment there are no clear predictors that allow us to identify who is most likely to benefit from PE and who is most likely to drop out. Van Minnen, Arntz, and Keijsers (2002) examined a range of possible predictors including demographic and personality variables, use of alcohol and drugs, and a range of symptoms including anxiety, depression, shame, guilt and anger. The only stable predictor was that patients who had more PTSD symptoms at pre-treatment also had more PTSD symptoms at post-treatment and follow-up.

In general, exposure-based therapies have been used successfully to bring about a reduction in fear and anxiety. While anxiety is a characteristic feature of PTSD, there are also a number of other emotions that are common such as guilt, shame and anger. In many cases, especially when PTSD results from Type II trauma such as child sexual abuse, there are fundamental shifts to the individual's view of self so that the self is perceived as bad, shameful and fundamentally flawed or damaged. Exposure of the traditional kind is unlikely to be helpful for emotions such as shame (Grey, Young, & Holmes, 2002) and some kind of cognitive restructuring or compassionate mind training (Lee, 2005) is more likely to be beneficial.

Grey et al. (2002) suggest that therapy needs to target cognitive restructuring within imaginal reliving on peri-traumatic 'hotspots'. Hotspots are those memories of the traumatic experience where distress is at its highest and that often contain distinctive and important meanings about the nature of the trauma and its impact on the self. Grey et al. argue that this approach can significantly improve the treatment of PTSD and help to explain why PE is not always successful because exposure *per se* does not necessarily target the meanings that are embedded in certain memories, and in particular exposure alone for images and memories that are associated with emotions such as shame is likely to be ineffective (for a more detailed discussion see Chapter 6).

Imagery restructuring and reprocessing therapy (IRRT; Smucker & Dancu, 1999) was developed originally to treat victims of child sexual abuse. Smucker and Dancu argued that exposure to the fear memories alone may not be sufficient to alter the meanings attached to those memories and that therapy needs to target these meanings directly. IRRT is a therapy that combines imaginal exposure to the traumatic memories with imagery rescripting where imagery is used to transform the memories in the imagination. Imagery rescripting is described below: For a full description of imagery rescripting in IRRT, see Smucker and Dancu's (1999) book, *Cognitive-behavioral treatment for adult survivors of childhood trauma: Imagery rescripting and reprocessing*.

Imagery rescripting

Imagery rescripting describes a set of related procedures that are directed at changing the memory of a distressing or traumatic event. Holmes *et al.* (2007) define imagery rescripting techniques in terms of two categories: those that transform an existing negative image into a more benign image, and those that create a new positive image. In this section of the chapter, I am focusing on the use of imagery rescripting to transform negative images. Here, the core of the technique is its focus on changing a person's memory in his or her imagination through the use of imagery. This can be done in a number of ways, which can include imagining a different ending to the event or bringing an adult into a memory of childhood abuse, which might involve bringing the adult self into the memory or bringing a trusted adult at the time of the abuse into the memory to protect the vulnerable child, or it might involve punishing the perpetrator of the distressing or traumatic event. There can also be transformations of either the victim or the perpetrator, such as making a child grow bigger and turn into an adult, or shrinking a perpetrator such as a school bully or making him or her look ridiculous in some way.

Imagery rescripting differs from prolonged exposure in that it is an explicit attempt to change the nature and thus the meaning of the memory within the imagery process itself. It also differs critically from guided exposure in that the patient generates the solution himself or herself. Smucker and Dancu (1999) refer to this as Socratic imagery, which they describe as analogous to Socratic questioning in so far as the therapist's role is to help the client discover his or her own resolution rather than suggesting or prescribing an alternative scenario or attempting to rescue the client. There are some exceptions to this; for example, when clients with personality disorders are completely unable to generate an alternative scenario or to access a protective figure, then it may be necessary for the therapist to suggest a person who can take on this role, which may in some cases be the therapist. Nevertheless, even in cases like these, the therapist usually aims to move from this more directive approach to a facilitative approach in which modification of the images is being led by the client.

Imagery rescripting is a relatively new technique and therefore to date there is only a limited evidence base. However, the current evidence is promising and indicates that imagery rescripting is effective for a range of conditions including PTSD following child sexual abuse (Smucker & Niederee, 1995); PTSD following industrial accidents (detailed report of two cases: Grunert et al., 2003); bulimia nervosa (single case report: Ohanian, 2002); intrusive images (Rusch, Grunert, Mendelsohn, & Smucker, 2000); social phobia (Wild, Hackmann, & Clark, 2007, 2008); and snake fear (Hunt & Fenton, 2007). Imagery rescripting is an important part of schema-focused therapy and Waller, Kennerley, and Ohanian (2007) describe it as 'one of the most powerful techniques within schema-focused therapy' (p. 165), but to date there are no studies that look specifically at the effect of the imagery component of the therapy. A more recent development that is linked to imagery rescripting is compassionate mind training in which the focus of the imagery work is to help the client to discover and use a 'perfect nurturer' (Lee, 2005), and to change meanings and views of the self by adopting a more compassionate stance towards the self, which is described in more detail in Chapter 9.

There are a number of different descriptions of methods of imagery rescripting in the literature. Most of these are descriptions of imagery modification procedures within other therapies such as schema-focused cognitive therapy (SFCT). However, there are a couple of exceptions to this. First, there is a comprehensive description of the protocol in Smucker and Dancu's (1999) book on IRRT. IRRT follows a specific structure. In the first session after assessment, there is a mastery imagery phase in which the patient imagines the childhood trauma and then introduces the adult self (or other competent adult) into the memory. In the next phase of the imagery, the adult learns to nurture the child. Smucker and Dancu point out that this phase should be given the neutral title of 'adult–child' phase as victims of sexual abuse often have extremely negative views of their child selves initially and the intervention is less likely to be successful if the therapist indicates that nurturing the child is the aim of this phase. Smucker and Dancu recommend allowing two hours for the first rescripting session and 90 minutes thereafter. Sessions 1–5 follow the same basic structure, i.e. mastery imagery followed by adult–child imagery, but later sessions focus exclusively on the adult–child imagery. Following imagery rescripting, patient and therapist discuss what happened during the rescripting session and the patient's reactions to it. Smucker and Dancu also discuss ways of managing risk and keeping the patient safe through the treatment and homework exercises that allow the patient to build on and consolidate the imagery work, e.g. writing a letter to the perpetrator.

This protocol has been further developed by Arntz and Weertman (1999), who modified the original protocol because they found that many patients had difficulties integrating the new information provided by introducing the adult perspective into the imagery. They also wanted to expand the use of the protocol so that it could be applied to a range of interpersonal issues that arise in the treatment of personality disorders and complex difficulties. In Arntz and Weertman's protocol, they added a third phase in which the patient takes the perspective of the child and again responds to the imagined adult self in the memory. In Arntz and Weertman's experience, although the adult self (or other protective adult) did usually stop the abuse, the patient often experienced difficulty in successfully nurturing the child or changing the dysfunctional beliefs about the self that developed as a result of these early experiences. In the third phase, the child is instructed to ask the adult for what he or she feels that he or she needs, and Arntz and Weertman argue that this additional phase both helps to integrate the new information more success-fully and helps the patient to make the transition between knowing that what was done to him or her was wrong and starting to feel it. This shift from knowing to feeling is captured in Barnard and Teasdale's (1991) interacting cognitive sub-systems model, where it would represent a transfer of informa-tion from the propositional meaning system to the implicational meaning system.

The development of imagery rescripting followed two parallel paths as discussed above, namely as an approach to treating PTSD following trauma, particularly Type II traumas, and at the same time as a treatment that was aimed at modifying the deeply held schematic beliefs that often characterise individuals with personality disorders. Of course there is convergence between these two streams because of the recognition of the high frequency of abuse histories in the personality disorders. However, more recently there has been an interest in applying imagery rescripting to other Axis I disorders such as social phobia (Wild *et al.*, 2007) and snake fears (Hunt & Fenton, 2007) with extremely promising results.

In order to illustrate imagery rescripting with anxiety disorder, a brief example is given below of a socially phobic patient, Bernadette, who was very worried about losing control of her bladder when she was away from the house. Part of the way through therapy, she disclosed that her stepmother had shut her in a wardrobe on several occasions as a punishment when she was a child. On two of these occasions at least she had been shut in the wardrobe for what had seemed like an extremely long time. She had needed to go to the toilet and had been unable to hold it and had wet herself. When she was let out of the wardrobe, her stepmother had got very angry with her for wetting herself and Bernadette had felt extremely ashamed and humiliated.

THERAPIST: I'm going to ask you to imagine being locked in the wardrobe again and then we'll ask someone to come in and help you. Is that OK?

BERNADETTE: Yes, fine.

THERAPIST: OK, shut your eyes and let yourself imagine being in the wardrobe again. When you have a clear image I'd like you to describe it to me. I'd like you to describe it in the present tense as if you were there right now, so you'll say 'I am sitting in the wardrobe . . .'.

(*Pause*)

BERNADETTE: (*In a very small voice*) I'm sitting in the wardrobe again. I don't know what I've done but Patty's very angry with me (*she sobs*). I'm really frightened.

THERAPIST: What can you see?

BERNADETTE: It's dark, she's locked the door so I know I can't get out . . . I . . . I'm feeling really panicky. I can't see anything . . . there's a little crack of light through the edges of the door but I can't make anything out clearly and I feel as if I can't breathe properly (*her voice gets higher and more panicky*). I've really got to get out. I have to go to the toilet so I shout 'Patty' but nothing happens (*she curls up on her chair*).

THERAPIST: What's happening now?

BERNADETTE: (*In a tiny voice, barely audible*) I've wet myself. It's all warm to begin with but now my legs are getting cold and I can smell it. Oh God she's going to kill me.

THERAPIST: OK Bernadette, can you imagine your adult self as you are now coming into the picture?

(*Pause*)

BERNADETTE: I'll try . . . yes I can sort of get a picture of me.

THERAPIST: Where are you in the room?

BERNADETTE: I'm right over by the door.

THERAPIST: Where is the wardrobe?

BERNADETTE: In the corner on the wall opposite the door.

THERAPIST: What can you see while you are standing by the door?

BERNADETTE: Well I can see the wardrobe and I know that she's in there and that she's frightened but I feel quite shaky too and I don't know what to do.

THERAPIST: What would you like to do?

(*Pause*)

BERNADETTE: Well, I'd like to let her out.

THERAPIST: Why don't you try to do that?

BERNADETTE: OK, I'll give it a try.

(*Pause*)

THERAPIST: What's happening now?

BERNADETTE: I'm walking over to the wardrobe and I can smell the pee – it's kind of disgusting – I sort of want to open the door and let her out because I feel sorry for her but I know she's going to be a real mess and she's going to stink of pee and it's kind of disgusting.

THERAPIST: What will happen if you leave her in the wardrobe?

BERNADETTE: Oh no, I can't do that. I know I've got to let her out but I just have to get my courage up a bit . . . OK, I'm opening the door . . . My God she's so little . . . how could she have put her in that wardrobe? . . .

In this extract, Bernadette relives the experience of being locked in the wardrobe and wetting herself. When she enters the memory with her adult self, she has mixed feelings about the child in the wardrobe – she is frightened so she may be reliving some of the experiences of the child; she feels sorry for her, but she also finds her disgusting so it could be hard for her adult self to start nurturing the child at this point. However, at the same time, she has a strong sense of how wrong it is for the child to be locked in a wardrobe so she knows that she has to let her out. At the end of the imagery rescripting session the therapist can explore all the different meanings and feelings that have come up during the imagery work and build on any shifts in belief or perceptions that have occurred by using more traditional cognitive methods. This can then lay the groundwork for the next session of imagery rescripting.

Conclusions

We have seen in this chapter that there are a number of imagery methods and techniques that are currently being used in cognitive therapy either as an aid to more traditional approaches or as a more substantial treatment component in themselves. The experience that many patients and therapists have of working directly with imagery is that it is a very powerful technique for both revealing meaning and effecting change. In particular, imagery methods seem to achieve change in the implicational meaning system more quickly than traditional verbal methods. However, some of the most successful treatment approaches at the moment may involve a skilful interweaving between the newer imagery methods described here and the more familiar traditional methods of CBT. In the subsequent chapters, each of which focuses on a particular disorder, there are many examples of how to achieve this successful interweaving, and illustrations of its effectiveness in therapy.

References

Achterberg, J., Dossey, B., Kolkmeier, L., & Sheikh, A.A. (2003). Use of imagery in the treatment of cardiovascular disorders. In A.A. Sheikh (Ed.), *The role of imagination in health* (pp. 99–122). Amityville, NY: Baywood.

Arntz, A., & Weertman, A. (1999). Treatment of childhood memories: Theory and practice. *Behaviour Research and Therapy*, *37*, 715–740.

Barnard, P.J., & Teasdale, J.D. (1991). Interacting cognitive subsystems – a systemic approach to cognitive-affective interaction and change. *Cognition and Emotion, 5*, 1–39.

Beck, A.T., & Clark, D.A. (1997). An information processing model of anxiety: Automatic and strategic processes. *Behaviour Research and Therapy, 35*, 49–58.

Beck, A.T., Rush, J.T., Shaw, B.F., & Emery, G. (1979). *Cognitive therapy of depression*. New York: Guilford Press.

Bennett-Levy, J., Butler, G., Fennell, M., Hackmann, A., Mueller, M., & Westbrook, D. (2004). *Oxford guide to behavioural experiments in cognitive therapy*. Oxford, UK: Oxford University Press.

Butler, G., Cullington, A., Munby, M., Amies, P., & Gelder, M. (1984). Exposure and anxiety management in the treatment of social phobia. *Journal of Consulting and Clinical Psychology, 52*, 642–650.

Cohen, M., & Fried, G. (2007). Comparing relaxation training and cognitive-behavioral group therapy for women with breast cancer. *Research on Social Work Practice, 17*, 313–323.

Dyregov, A. (2006). Complicated grief: Theory and treatment. *Tidsskrift for Norsk Psykologforening, 43*, 779–786.

Esplen, M.J., & Garfinkel, P.E. (1998). Guided imagery treatment to promote self-soothing in bulimia nervosa. *Journal of Psychotherapy Practice and Research, 7*, 102–118.

Esplen, M.J., Garfinkel, P.E., Olmsted, M., Gallop, R.M., & Kennedy, S. (1998). A randomized controlled trial of guided imagery in bulimia nervosa. *Psychological Medicine, 28*, 1347–1357.

Foa, E.B., Rothbaum, B.O., Riggs, D.S., & Murdock, T.B. (1991). Treatment of posttraumatic-stress-disorder in rape victims – a comparison between cognitive behavioral-procedures and counseling. *Journal of Consulting and Clinical Psychology, 59*, 715–723.

Fried, R. (1987). Relaxation with biofeedback-assisted imagery: The importance of breathing rate as an index of hyperarousal. *Applied Psychology and Biofeedback, 12*, 273–279.

Gilbert, P. (Ed.) (2005). *Compassion: Conceptualisations, research and use in psychotherapy*. Hove, UK: Routledge.

Gregg, M., & Hall, C. (2006). Measurement of motivational imagery abilities in sport. *Journal of Sports Sciences, 24*, 961–971.

Grey, N., Young, K., & Holmes, E. (2002). Empirically grounded clinical interventions section: Cognitive restructuring within reliving: A treatment for peritraumatic emotional 'hotspots' in posttraumatic stress disorder. *Behavioural and Cognitive Psychotherapy, 30*, 37–56.

Grunert, B.K., Smucker, M.R., Weis, J.M., & Rusch, M.D. (2003). When prolonged exposure fails: Adding an imagery-based cognitive restructuring component in the treatment of industrial accident victims suffering from PTSD. *Cognitive and Behavioral Practice, 10*, 333–346.

Hackmann, A., Clark, D.M., & McManus, F. (2000). Recurrent images and early memories in social phobia. *Behaviour Research and Therapy, 38*, 601–610.

Hackmann, A., & Holmes, E. (2004). Reflecting on imagery: A clinical perspective and overview of the special issue of *Memory* on mental imagery and memory in psychopathology. *Memory, 12*, 389–402.

Hall, E., Hall, C., Stradling, P., & Young, D. (2006). *Guided imagery: Creative interventions in counselling.* London: Sage.

Hawton, K., Salkovskis, P., Kirk, J., & Clark, D.M. (1989). *Cognitive behaviour therapy for psychiatric problems: A practical guide.* Oxford, UK: Oxford University Press.

Hembree, E.A., Rauch, S.A.M., & Foa, E.B. (2003). Beyond the manual: The insider's guide to prolonged exposure therapy for PTSD. *Cognitive and Behavioral Practice, 10*, 22–30.

Hirsch, C.R., Clark, D.M., Mathews, A., & Williams, R. (2003). Self-images play a causal role in social phobia. *Behaviour Research and Therapy, 41*, 909–921.

Hirsch, C., & Holmes, E.A. (2007). Mental imagery in anxiety disorders. *Psychiatry, 6*, 161–165.

Holmes, E.A., Arntz, A., & Smucker, M.R. (2007). Imagery rescripting in cognitive behaviour therapy: Images, treatment techniques and outcomes. *Journal of Behavior Therapy and Experimental Psychiatry, 38*, 297–305.

Holmes, E.A., & Mathews, A. (2005). Mental imagery and emotion: A special relationship? *Emotion, 5*, 489–497.

Holmes, E.A., Mathews, A., Dalgleish, T., & Mackintosh, B. (2006). Positive interpretation training: Effects of mental imagery versus verbal training on positive mood. *Behavior Therapy, 37*, 237–247.

Holmes, E.A., Mathews, A., Mackintosh, B., & Dalgleish, T. (2008). The effect of mental imagery on emotion assessed using picture-word cues. *Emotion, 8*, 395–409.

Hunt, M., & Fenton, M. (2007). Imagery rescripting versus in vivo exposure in the treatment of snake fear. *Journal of Behavior Therapy and Experimental Psychiatry, 38*, 329–344.

Ironson, G., Freund, B., Strauss, J.L., & Williams, J. (2002). Comparison of two treatments for traumatic stress: A community-based study of EMDR and prolonged exposure. *Journal of Clinical Psychology, 58*, 113–128.

Kennerley, H. (1996). Cognitive therapy of dissociative symptoms associated with trauma. *British Journal of Clinical Psychology, 35*, 325–340.

Layden, M.A. (2000). *Cognitive therapy using imagery techniques.* Workshop presented in London.

Lee, D.A. (2005). The perfect nurturer: A model to develop a compassionate mind within the context of cognitive therapy. In P. Gilbert (Ed.), *Compassion: Conceptualisations, research and use in psychotherapy* (pp. 326–351). New York: Routledge.

Lewandowski, W., Good, M., & Draucker, C. (2005). Changes in the meaning of pain with the use of guided imagery. *Pain Management Nursing, 6*, 58–67.

Linehan, M.M. (1993). *Cognitive-behavioural treatment of borderline personality disorder.* New York: Guilford Press.

Marks, I.M. (1987). *Fears, phobias and rituals: Panic, anxiety, and their disorders.* New York: Oxford University Press.

Marshall, R.D., & Suh, E.J. (2003). Contextualizing trauma: Using evidence-based treatments in a multicultural community after 9/11. *Psychiatric Quarterly, 74*, 401–420.

Mathews, A., & Rezin, V. (1977). Treatment of dental fears by imaginal flooding and rehearsal of coping behavior. *Behaviour Research and Therapy, 15*, 321–328.

Menzies, V., Taylor, A.G., & Bourguignon, C. (2006). Effects of guided imagery on outcomes of pain, functional status, and self-efficacy in persons diagnosed with fibromyalgia. *Journal of Alternative and Complementary Medicine, 12,* 23–30.

Mineka, S., & Oehlberg, K. (2008). The relevance of recent developments in classical conditioning to understanding the etiology and maintenance of anxiety disorders. *Acta Psychologica, 127,* 567–580.

Mountford, V., & Waller, G. (2006). Using imagery in cognitive-behavioral treatment for eating disorders: Tackling the restrictive mode. *International Journal of Eating Disorders, 39,* 533–543.

Nishith, P., Nixon, R.D., & Resick, P.A. (2005). Resolution of trauma-related guilt following treatment of PTSD in female rape victims: A result of cognitive processing therapy targeting comorbid depression? *Journal of Affective Disorders, 86,* 259–265.

Ohanian, V. (2002). Imagery rescripting within cognitive behavior therapy for bulimia nervosa: An illustrative case report. *International Journal of Eating Disorders, 31,* 352–357.

Overholser, J.C. (1991). The use of guided imagery in psychotherapy: Modules for use with passive relaxation training. *Journal of Contemporary Psychotherapy, 21,* 159–172.

Resick, P.A., Nishith, P., & Griffin, M.G. (2003). How well does cognitive-behavioral therapy treat symptoms of complex PTSD? An examination of child sexual abuse survivors within a clinical trial. *CNS Spectrums, 8,* 351–355.

Resick, P.A., Nishith, P., Weaver, T.L., Astin, M.C., & Feuer, C.A. (2002). A comparison of cognitive-processing therapy with prolonged exposure and a waiting condition for the treatment of chronic posttraumatic stress disorder in female rape victims. *Journal of Consulting and Clinical Psychology, 70,* 867–879.

Roffe, L., Schmidt, K., & Ernst, E. (2005). A systematic review of guided imagery as an adjuvant cancer therapy. *Psycho-Oncology, 14,* 607–617.

Rusch, M.D., Grunert, B.K., Mendelsohn, R.A., & Smucker, M.R. (2000). Imagery rescripting for recurrent, distressing images. *Cognitive and Behavioral Practice, 7,* 173–182.

Ruscio, A.M., & Borkovec, T.D. (2004). Experience and appraisal of worry among high worriers with and without generalized anxiety disorder. *Behaviour Research and Therapy, 42,* 1469–1482.

Salkovskis, P.M., Hackmann, A., Wells, A., Gelder, M.G., & Clark, D.M. (2007). Belief disconfirmation versus habituation approaches to situational exposure in panic disorder with agoraphobia: A pilot study. *Behaviour Research and Therapy, 45,* 877–885.

Sheikh, A.A. (2002). *Handbook of therapeutic imagery techniques.* Amityville, NY: Baywood.

Smucker, M.R., & Dancu, C.V. (1999). *Cognitive-behavioral treatment for adult survivors of childhood trauma: Imagery rescripting and reprocessing.* Northvale, NJ: Jason Aronson.

Smucker, M.R., & Niederee, J. (1995). Treating incest-related PTSD and pathogenic schemas through imaginal exposure and rescripting. *Cognitive and Behavioral Practice, 2,* 63–92.

Soo, S., Forman, D., Delaney, B.C., & Moayyedi, P. (2004). A systematic review of psychological therapies for nonulcer dyspepsia. *American Journal of Gastro-enterology, 99,* 1817–1822.

Spoormaker, V.I., Schredl, M., & van den Bout, J. (2006). Nightmares: From anxiety symptom to steep disorder. *Sleep Medicine Reviews, 10,* 19–31.

Van Minnen, A., Arntz, A., & Keijsers, G.P. (2002). Prolonged exposure in patients with chronic PTSD: Predictors of treatment outcome and dropout. *Behaviour Research and Therapy, 40,* 439–457.

Waller, G., Kennerley, H., & Ohanian, V. (2007). Schema-focused cognitive-behavioural therapy for eating disorders. In L.P. Riser, P.L. du Toit, D.J. Stein, & J.E. Young (Eds.), *Cognitive schemas and core beliefs in psychological problems: A scientist-practitioner guide.* Washington, DC: American Psychological Association.

Wells, A. (1997). *Cognitive therapy of anxiety disorders: A practice manual and conceptual guide.* Chichester, UK: Wiley.

Wild, J., Hackmann, A., & Clark, D.M. (2007). When the present visits the past: Updating traumatic memories in social phobia. *Journal of Behavior Therapy and Experimental Psychiatry, 38,* 386–401.

Wild, J., Hackmann, A., & Clark, D.M. (2008). Rescripting early memories linked to negative images in social phobia: A pilot study. *Behavior Therapy, 39,* 47–56.

Wolpe, J. (1990). *The practice of behavior therapy* (4th ed.). New York: Pergamon.

Wolpe, J. (1997). Thirty years of behavior therapy. *Behavior Therapy, 28,* 633–635.

Young, J. (1999a). *Cognitive therapy for personality disorders: A schema-focused approach.* Sarasota, FL: Professional Resource Exchange.

Young, J. (1999b). *Introduction to schema-focused cognitive therapy with personality disorders.* Workshop presented at Cape Cod, MA.

Chapter 4

Imagery and the self in social phobia

Jennifer Wild

Social phobia is a common and enduring anxiety disorder in which imagery plays a prominent role. People with social phobia are afraid they will come across as inadequate to other people and consequently avoid social and performance situations, such as chatting to a colleague on a coffee break, speaking up in a meeting or giving a presentation in class. They worry they will show signs of anxiety, such as blushing, sweating, or trembling, or that they will do something that will cause others to think less of them, such as saying something silly or boring. They typically have images of their fears unfolding while in these situations and are convinced that others will see them as they appear in their images, leading to negative evaluation, criticism, or rejection. Yet they rarely receive criticism in social situations. This point has puzzled clinicians and researchers who have sought to understand why social anxiety persists in the absence of negative feedback from others.

One of the key factors that explains the persistence of social anxiety is mental imagery: the pictures that socially phobic individuals generate in their mind's eye when in feared social situations. These are typically distorted pictures of how they are coming across to others. For example, a person who worries about sweating may have an image of sweat droplets forming on their forehead when talking to a colleague. These self-images are problematic because sufferers believe they are an accurate reflection of how they appear to other people. Therefore, they think that they come across much worse than they actually do. Like flashbacks in posttraumatic stress disorder, the images take sufferers' attention away from what is happening in the present, preventing them from noticing what is actually unfolding, that is, that their worst fears are not happening and that they are not receiving negative feedback. Thus, they do not learn that they come across as acceptable and do not update their negative self-images with more realistic pictures of how they do come across. The consequence is that their social anxiety persists. One of the key components to successfully treating social anxiety, therefore, is to help sufferers view themselves in a more realistic and positive fashion and to replace their negative self-imagery with realistic self-imagery. This chapter will review the origins of negative self-imagery in social phobia, the consequences of holding negative self-images, and how to address the imagery therapeutically.

Content of imagery

The spontaneous imagery that social phobia patients experience tends to be focused on the self, to be negative and distorted, to be seen from the observer perspective; and it mostly involves the visual modality. Hackmann, Surawy, and Clark (1998) conducted one of the first studies of imagery in social phobia. They asked patients with social phobia and non-anxious controls to recall a recent social situation in which they had felt anxious. They were then asked whether an image had passed through their minds at the moment they were most anxious. Socially phobic individuals were significantly more likely than controls to report experiencing images when anxious in social situations. Their images were significantly more negative and more likely to involve seeing themselves from an observer perspective, that is, as if they could see themselves from an external point of view. Their images tended to depict their worst fears unfolding before their eyes. For example, one participant in the study feared that she would blush and people would think she was odd. She described her image as a camera zooming in on a horrible, red, panicky face, looking really put-on-the-spot and nervous. Another participant feared that he would sweat and people would then think he was inept. He described his image as seeing himself looking uncomfortable, drenched in beads of sweat with a red face and a worried look of wanting to get out. Almost all the images participants described consisted of vivid visual representations of the self, in which the self was seen as distorted and anxious-looking.

Hackmann, Clark, and McManus (2000) administered a semi-structured interview to explore further the nature of spontaneous imagery in patients with social phobia. They discovered that patients' negative images predominantly involved the visual modality, but could also involve bodily sensations and sounds. Thus, patients with a fear of stuttering may have an image of their face looking frightened with their lips moving repetitively (visual component). They may hear incomprehensible sounds being repeated from their lips (auditory component) and have a bodily sensation of butterflies in their tummy (physiological component). The negative images were also linked in theme and content to earlier adverse social events, such as being bullied at school. These events clustered around the onset of their social anxiety. As episodic events can be stored in memory as images (Conway, 2001), it is likely that memory images of adverse social events influence the content of subsequent negative self-imagery in social phobia. This is discussed in the next section.

Origins of the imagery

The negative self-images common to patients with social phobia have their roots in early socially traumatic events. Hackmann *et al.* (2000) were the first to discover this link. They interviewed patients with social phobia and asked them to recall an image that recurred across social situations. They then asked patients when they first remembered experiencing the sort of sensations, emotions and thoughts reflected in their image. Most patients identified a memory, such as being bullied for blushing at school, that occurred around the onset of their social anxiety. The memories and images were linked in theme and content. For example, one participant in the study had a recurring image of seeing herself as looking stupid with a very red face and a closed posture. In her memory, she was in a classroom, being harshly criticised by a teacher for a stupid answer and looking very red with a closed body posture. The content of the image and the memory were similar, as was the theme: being criticised for getting something wrong. Individuals with social anxiety often cite the content of their negative imagery and memories as evidence for their negative self-beliefs.

Coupled with negative interpretations made at the time, these events are laid down in memory and form the basis of subsequent negative imagery. The memories include sensory details, such as feeling flushed in the face, and the negative meanings of the event, such as 'I'll be rejected if I blush' or 'I'll be criticised if I say something stupid'. Such interpretations can become more negative over time (e.g. Brendle & Wenzle, 2004). Further, with memory being a process of continuous reconstruction as the person recalls and considers the situation (Coles, Turk, & Heimberg, 2002), it is possible that more negative interpretations are assimilated into the memory image of the original event and then remembered as actually happening. This is in keeping with Hertel, Brozovich, Joormann, and Gotlib (2008), who found that patients with social phobia provide negative interpretations of ambiguous hypothetical social scenarios and remember their interpretations as actually happening when recalling these scenarios.

The process of post-event processing or rumination, in which patients dwell on their negative perception of their social performance after a social situation, may also contribute to negative interpretations becoming progressively more negative over time. Hirsch, Clark, and Mathews (2006a) suggest that during post-event processing, negative information is assimilated into the image memory. Further, they suggest that the incorporated interpretations are not spontaneously re-evaluated but tend to remain in a relatively encapsulated and unchanging form. This would explain the very negative quality of 'encapsulated beliefs', the beliefs that capture the meaning of patients' negative imagery, self-concept, and early memory, which are likely to have become more negative since the original event. Wild, Hackmann, and Clark (2007, 2008) investigated the outcome of updating the meaning of the early socially traumatic event linked to negative imagery in social phobia. They found that updating the meaning of the memory through cognitive restructuring and imagery rescripting led to significant clinical improvement. Examples of encapsulated beliefs reported in their studies include: 'I'm an outsider and always will be because I'm odd and different and weak; people will reject me or laugh at me if I am myself' and 'I am an anxious and weird person; people will see this and reject me'. They also found that sometimes the event had not unfolded the way participants had originally thought and this was discovered when the patient and therapist relived the early experience. This is consistent with the suggestion of Hirsch *et al.* (2006a) that the patient interpreted the earlier event in a catastrophic way and that the stored memory contained elements of the catastrophic interpretation. For other patients, the early rejection actually did happen but they were no longer rejected as adults. In fact, all patients were no longer rejected as adults and yet their image encapsulated a much earlier self-impression and recurred in different social situations. This suggests that it was likely triggered by social cues that matched the original event in some way and failed to be updated in the light of later, more benign experiences (Hackmann *et al.*, 2000).

In essence, the negative image in the present is an extracted fragment of the past socially traumatic event. Negative interpretations and social cues linked to the memory maintain the individual's negative image and self-concept. Conway and Pleydell-Pearce (2000) suggest that there is a feedback loop between working self-concept and memory. Working self-concept is an individual's self-concept, which includes feared or desired possible selves that they might become (Markus & Ruvolo, 1989). Activation of a particular self-concept may increase the chance of retrieving memories consistent with the self-concept. The retrieved memories reinforce the negative self-concept, and both fail to get updated.

Why negative imagery persists

Patients with social phobia fail to update their spontaneous negative imagery because of two processes that are involved in the maintenance of social anxiety: self-focused attention and negative interpretation bias.

Self-focused attention

Self-focused attention refers to one's attention being absorbed in a detailed monitoring of oneself rather than with what is unfolding in the external environment. Cognitive models of social phobia (Clark & Wells, 1995; Rapee & Heimberg, 1997) suggest that when patients with social phobia fear negative evaluation, they become excessively self-focused. They shift their attention to a detailed monitoring of themselves, notice internal sensations and signs of anxiety, and assess whether or not their fears are unfolding. This, unsurprisingly, increases their anxiety (e.g. Woody, 1996). Self-focused attention prevents individuals with social phobia from noticing that they are not receiving negative feedback and that their worst fears are not unfolding, and hence prevents them from gaining information that could update their negative self-imagery. Clark (1999) suggests that after an early traumatic social experience, a mental model of the patient's observable, social self is laid down and is reactivated in subsequent social encounters. Self-focused attention in social situations prevents this model from being updated (Clark, 1999).

Negative interpretation bias

Negative interpretation bias refers to the tendency to interpret ambiguous information in a negative direction. In relation to social anxiety, it refers to interpreting ambiguous social information negatively. For example, if an individual smiles at another person, it could be because the person who is smiling is being friendly and likes the other person (positive interpretation), or it could be because he or she thinks that the other person is foolish and the smile is derisive (negative interpretation) (Hirsch et al., 2006a). A large body of research shows that patients with social phobia evidence a cognitive bias to underestimate how well they perform to a greater extent than non-anxious controls (Alden & Wallace, 1995; Rapee & Lim, 1992; Stopa & Clark, 1993). When presented with written scenarios of ambiguous social events, they make negative interpretations afterwards (e.g., Amir, Foa, & Coles, 1998; Stopa & Clark, 2000). With respect to online processing, research has focused on comprehension tasks of ambiguous and non-ambiguous texts of social scenarios. Non-anxious people show a positive interpretation bias in response to ambiguous social information, whereas patients with social phobia do not (see Hirsch & Clark, 2004, for a review).

In relation to imagery, inducing a negative interpretation bias appears to make subsequent self-imagery negative. Hirsch, Mathews, and Clark (2007) trained volunteers to have a negative or benign interpretation bias. To do this, they had participants read scenarios depicting ambiguous social situations, such as 'At a dinner party, you are introduced to someone new and chat to them for quite a while. When you telephone them the next week to suggest meeting again, they reply that it would be . . . .' The ambiguity was resolved at the end of each scenario, consistently in a negative (e.g. 'They reply that it would be pointless') or in a benign way (e.g. 'They reply that it would be great'). After the training phase, participants listened to new descriptions of ambiguous social scenarios. They were asked to imagine themselves in each situation, to describe their images aloud, and to rate how pleasant or unpleasant it would be for them in the imagined situation. Those participants who had been trained to have a negative interpretation bias reported more negative self-images than those who had been trained to have a benign bias.

Assessors, who did not know which bias participants had been trained to have, rated the images of the negative-trained group as being less pleasant than those of the benign trained group. After completing the imagery task, participants rated how anxious they would feel in a to-be-anticipated stressful social situation (leading a seminar) and how well they thought they would perform. Participants trained to develop a more negative interpretation bias rated their anticipated anxiety in this stressful social situation as greater, and their expected social performance as poorer, than participants trained to develop a more benign interpretation bias. Hirsch *et al.* (2007) suggest that the induced negative interpretation bias influenced the content of imagery and increased anticipatory anxiety and expectations of poor social performance.

Thus, when in a feared social situation, patients with social phobia are less likely to notice when others respond favourably to them because they are self-focused and because they are inclined to miss making positive interpretations of ambiguous social information. They are less likely to believe that they have come across well and more likely to leave thinking they came across in line with their negative self-image, which possibly prevents them from updating their perception of themselves.

Why negative imagery maintains social anxiety

Negative imagery influences emotional inferences

Negative self-imagery blocks positive interpretation bias. This may explain why people with social phobia fail to interpret ambiguous social information in a positive direction. Hirsch, Mathews, Clark, Williams, and Morrison (2003b) asked low socially anxious participants to hold a negative self-image in mind or just to imagine themselves in the given situation while reading texts of being interviewed for a job. At critical points in the text, participants were required to respond as quickly as possible to word or non-word probes, deciding whether the target word formed a word or non-word (lexical decision). The word probes matched positive (non-threatening) or negative (threatening) interpretations. An example of a text participants would have seen is as follows: 'As the interviewer asks the first question you realise that all your preparation was useful (forgotten).' Parentheses indicate the word probe of a negative interpretation. Participants also completed a baseline task in which another set of word probes were presented at different points when there could be only one possible inference. An example of a text in the baseline task is: 'If it is important to remember a particular detail, then it is annoying if it is (forgotten).' Parentheses indicate the word probe inference. Participants who held a negative image had greater differences in response times between the ambiguous and baseline contexts for non-threatening word probes, whereas participants in the control condition had much smaller differences. As larger differences in response times between these two contexts indicate that any inferences made were less marked, the findings suggest that non-anxious individuals who held a negative image were not making benign inferences. They also reported higher levels of state anxiety. The authors concluded that when non-anxious people are required to hold a negative self-image in mind, it blocks their normal positive inferential bias. Negative self-imagery may work in a similar way in people with social phobia, accounting for their lack of a positive inferential bias.

While negative self-imagery blocks positive interpretation bias in non-anxious people, the converse has also been found with positive self-imagery in high-anxious people. That is, positive self-imagery appears to block negative interpretation bias in high-anxious individuals. Hirsch, Clark, Williams, Morrison, and Mathews (2005) trained participants with high social anxiety to hold a benign self-image in mind, adopting the perspective of a confident interviewee, while reading texts of job descriptions and performing lexical decisions similar to the study described above. Participants showed increased lexical decision response times to words consistent with a threatening interpretation, suggesting that positive imagery blocks access to threatening interpretations of ambiguous social situations.

Further, negative self-imagery leads to more negative interpretations about one's actual social performance. Hirsch, Mathews, Clark, Williams, and Morrison (2006b) asked participants who were very confident about public speaking to produce an image of themselves before giving a speech of performing extremely well or extremely badly. Participants then gave a speech without any requirement to hold a particular image in mind during the speech. Participants who had previously generated a negative self-image reported feeling significantly more anxious during their speech than did those allocated to the positive self-image condition. They had more negative thoughts and believed that they had performed less well. Thus, negative imagery led to more anxiety and more negative interpretations of performance than positive imagery.

Inferential bias and negative self-imagery interact

Indeed, inferential bias and negative self-imagery are two cognitive biases that directly influence each other. Hirsch *et al.* (2006a) put forward a combined cognitive biases account which postulates that these two processes interact in the maintenance of social anxiety. In the research reviewed above, negative self-imagery had negative consequences. It led to increased anxiety, negative interpretations of social performance, and an exaggerated view of oneself as coming across poorly compared to assessors. Negative interpretative bias also had negative consequences on imagery. Individuals in whom a negative interpretation bias had been induced went on to generate more negative self-imagery about ambiguous social situations, and reported more anticipatory anxiety and more negative expectations of social performance than those trained to have a benign bias. Thus, the detrimental impact of negative self-imagery is enhanced by negative interpretations of social performance and the detrimental impact of negative interpretations (or lack of positive inferences) is enhanced when they are incorporated within self-images (Hirsch *et al.*, 2006a).

Negative self-imagery inhibits retrieval of positive memories

Negative self-imagery may maintain social anxiety by inhibiting retrieval of positive past memories, which are likely to be incongruent with patients' fears of how they come across. Stopa and Jenkins (2007) had high socially anxious individuals give a speech while holding a positive or negative self-image in mind. Afterwards participants had to retrieve negative and positive memories from their past. Participants retrieved positive memories more slowly when they had held a negative image in mind compared to when they had held a positive image in mind, suggesting that negative self-images inhibit the retrieval of positive memories. They also retrieved negative memories more quickly when they had held a negative image in mind. Thus, negative self-imagery facilitates retrieval of negative memories and as such may maintain social anxiety as these are more likely to be consistent with patients' feared outcomes, making it more difficult for them to disconfirm their fears when they have a negative image in mind.

Negative self-imagery increases anxiety and contaminates social performance

Four studies have manipulated negative self-imagery in individuals with social phobia or high social anxiety to determine whether it has a role in maintaining the disorder. Hirsch, Clark, Mathews, and Williams (2003a) asked patients with social phobia to have a conversation with a stranger while holding a negative image of themselves or a less negative (control) image. The negative image led participants to feel more anxious. Further, an assessor, who did not know which image participants held in mind, rated their anxiety as more evident and their behaviour as less positive in the negative imagery condition. Thus, negative self-imagery increased anxiety and undermined effective social performance.

Vassilopoulos (2005) conducted a similar study with high and low socially anxious volunteers. Participants gave a speech in front of a camera. Half of each group held a negative observer perspective image in mind during the speech, while the other half held a positive image of themselves. The high-anxious group perceived more bodily sensations, rated specific aspects of their performance more poorly, and believed their self-image to be a more accurate reflection of how they came across when they held a negative image in mind.

Hirsch, Meynen, and Clark (2004) had high socially anxious individuals have two conversations with a conversational partner. During one conversation they held a negative self-image in mind and during the other they held a less negative (control) image in mind. When holding the negative image in mind, the socially anxious volunteers felt more anxious. They also reported using more safety behaviours and believed they came across more poorly compared to ratings the conversational partners made. Their partners rated them as performing more poorly in the negative imagery condition. The study replicated the earlier finding that negative self-imagery leads patients with social phobia to feel and look more anxious. In addition, it suggested that negative self-images motivate patients to use safety behaviours which can, in turn, contaminate the social interaction.

Stopa and Jenkins (2007) investigated the effect of holding a negative or positive image in mind on retrieving memories in participants with high social anxiety. Part of the study involved participants giving a speech holding a negative or positive image in mind. The results of this manipulation showed that when participants held a negative self-image in mind, they were more anxious, predicted worse performance, rated actual performance as worse and rated a range of behaviours during the speech as worse compared to when they gave a speech holding a positive image. An independent rater also judged their performance as worse in the negative compared to the positive image condition. In the negative imagery condition, there was close correspondence between participants' predicted and actual ratings, whereas in the positive image condition, participants made better predictions than in the negative condition and more favourable judgements of how they actually performed.

Patients believe negative imagery is true

Patients with social phobia believe their negative imagery is true, that is, they believe it to be an accurate reflection of how they appear to others (e.g. Vassilopoulos, 2005) and this is likely to make it feel more real than a benign image. Further, rehearsal of negative imagery is likely to make it feel more familiar and this could be associated with making it seem believable. Lang (1977, 1979) suggests that the physiological, emotional, and behavioural responses activated in imagery are similar to what is activated in real scenarios and Epstein (1994) suggests that imagery is akin to having a real experience. This is likely to be a key reason why patients believe that their negative imagery is a true reflection of who they are and how they come across to others. It is also likely to be one reason why therapeutic interventions that utilise imagery (e.g. imagery rescripting) are effective.

Negative self-imagery increases self-focused attention

Negative imagery most likely increases self-focused attention, a key maintaining factor of social anxiety, which refers to intense self-monitoring and evaluation (see Spurr & Stopa, 2002, for a review). When patients with social phobia are self-focused, they become more aware of internal information, such as negative thoughts, negative imagery and signs of anxiety. When they are more attentive to this information, they are less likely to notice what is unfolding in a social situation (i.e. that they are not receiving negative feedback), less likely to respond as well as they could, and more likely to believe they are coming across similarly to how they appear in their distorted self-images.

How to address imagery in social phobia

Several CBT programmes for social phobia (e.g. Clark & Wells, 1995; Clark et al., 2003; Heimberg & Becker, 2002; Rapee & Sanderson, 1998) include techniques for correcting distorted self-images. The techniques include: video feedback, audio feedback, surveys of others people's observations, behavioural experiments and imagery rescripting.

Video and audio feedback

Video feedback is a powerful therapeutic technique that helps patients to see themselves as others objectively see them and, in so doing, aims to update their distorted self-image. Cognitive therapy programmes (e.g. Clark et al., 2003) that use video feedback have patients engage in social situations in therapy (for example, talking to a stranger, such as a colleague of the therapist) while their performance is videotaped. Afterwards, patients watch their performance with their therapist, who first takes them through a series of questions (cognitive preparation) to ensure they watch the video as objectively as possible. Research (Harvey, Clark, Ehlers, & Rapee, 1999) suggests that cognitive preparation enhances the effects of video feedback. It involves asking patients to (1) predict in detail what they will see in detail on the video, (2) form an image of themselves in the recorded social task, and (3) watch the video as though they were watching a stranger (Harvey et al., 1999). It is thought that without cognitive preparation prior to viewing the video, patients may recall images of how they felt they came across and these could become confused with the actual contents of the video (Clark & Wells, 1995). Clinical reports from patients receiving cognitive therapy for social phobia suggest that video feedback changes their self-imagery. This has not yet been confirmed empirically through mediation analysis of trials of cognitive therapy for social phobia.

Audio feedback is used in the same way as video feedback, but to help correct clients' distorted perceptions of how they think they sound to other people (Hirsch & Clark, 2007). This is particularly useful for patients with social phobia who have a distorted belief about their voice quavering when they speak to others.

Surveys

When surveys are used in CBT for social phobia to update negative imagery, they are intended to gain objective information about how others perceive the patient. The aim is to highlight the discrepancy between the patient's subjective image and the actual impression they give others. Surveys are often used in conjunction with a patient's video recorded performance in a social task in therapy, or photographs of the same. For example, surveys were used with one of the author's patients who had a fear of blushing and believed that when she felt anxious her face turned scarlet red and expanded so that it was much bigger than other people's. The author photographed the patient conversing with a group of others in a therapy session. She then asked the patient to imagine how she came across and to rate how red her face turned and how much bigger it was than other people's. She showed the photograph to the patient, asking what she noticed. The patient was surprised that how she felt and imagined she appeared in her image was much different to how she actually looked in the photograph. She also noticed that she looked similar to other people. The author then showed the photograph to five colleagues, asking them to fill out a short survey with two sections. The first was an open-ended question asking them to write down what they noticed in the photograph, specifically what stood out. It was assumed that if the patient's face was much bigger than other people's and scarlet red, then respondents would notice this and write it down in this section. The second part of the survey asked respondents to rate how red the patient was and how much bigger her face was compared to other people's in the photograph. The results of the survey were given to the patient. They indicated that how others see them is much different to how they feel they appear (i.e. their negative image) and more in line with how they think they look when they objectively watch a video recording of themselves or look at a photograph. Objective feedback from others helps to show the patient that others do not perceive them in the way they fear, and that perhaps the image they carry of themselves is distorted. This allows the opportunity to update their self-image.

Behavioural experiments

Behavioural experiments help to disconfirm patients' beliefs about how they come across and in this sense help to update their image of how they appear to other people. For example, one patient the author treated feared that he would stutter when he spoke to his boss in their weekly meeting. In his image of how he thought he would come across, he saw himself with his lips flapping about but no words coming out and he believed this was what others saw. The behavioural experiment asked him to predict the likelihood that he would stutter in his next weekly meeting. He was also asked to indicate how his boss would behave when he stuttered. The patient indicated that his boss would lean forward, frown, and ask him to repeat himself. He was convinced that this would happen. The patient left the therapy session and had his meeting with his boss a few days later. He was instructed to focus his attention externally in the experiment so that he could gather a lot of information about how his boss responded to him, rather than focusing on himself, which he agreed with his therapist would increase the amount of information he would take in about his boss's behaviour. It would also make him feel less nervous. After his meeting, he completed the outcome section of the behavioural experiment, that is, he wrote down what actually happened. He was to note how his boss responded to him and whether or not he leaned forward, frowned, and asked him to repeat himself, as he had predicted. The patient noted that he did stutter, but not as much as he appeared to in his image. He also noted that his boss did not react in the way he thought he would if he noticed him stuttering. He concluded that how he looks is different to how he feels and that there was a possibility that he did not come across as someone with flapping lips with no words coming out. Experiments like this helped to update his distorted image of himself. Behavioural experiments set up in a similar fashion can help to disconfirm patients' distorted images of how they come across, encouraging them to update their self-images.

Imagery rescripting

Imagery rescripting is a therapeutic procedure in which patients revisit unpleasant past events with an adult perspective (see Chapter 3 for a further description of imagery rescripting). The aim is to update the meaning of these events, so they no longer colour the way in which patients view themselves and the present. The procedure has been used in CBT programmes for borderline personality disorder (Giesen-Bloo et al., 2006), and for post-traumatic stress disorder arising from childhood sexual abuse (Smucker & Neiderdee, 1995). In social phobia, imagery rescripting has been used to update the early memories linked to negative imagery. Two studies (Wild et al., 2007, 2008) show that it is an effective technique leading to clinical improvement in social phobia. The technique reduces the distress and vividness of the early aversive social memory as well as patients' negative imagery in the present. It also significantly reduces the meaning of the encapsulated belief, that is, the distorted belief that captures the meaning of the aversive memory and the negative self-image.

The way in which imagery rescripting has been used with patients with social phobia and in which effectiveness has been demonstrated is described in Wild *et al.* (2007) with clinical examples, and in Wild *et al.* (2008) as compared to a control session. The procedure builds on Arntz and Weertman's (1999) procedure in which patients revisit their memory in three stages. It differs in that it first involves cognitive restructuring of the encapsulated belief that lasts about 45 minutes. During this phase, the therapist and patient work together to challenge the meaning of the early event and its implications for the present. The example referred to in Wild *et al.* (2008) describes a patient who had been bullied and who interpreted the event as meaning 'I'm an outsider and always will be because I'm different and weak; people will reject me or laugh at me if I am myself'. During the cognitive restructuring phase, the patient was encouraged to come up with alternative ways of seeing the event, which included thinking of all the reasons why children bully other children and what this says about the bullies, rather than the patient. The patient was also encouraged to think of examples in which he was not rejected then or now. In essence, the therapist helped the patient to distinguish between what happened when he was a young child and what happens now as an adult in order to help him to see the event as a time-limited experience without implications for the present or future. The aim was to generate an adult perspective that the patient would then incorporate in the rescripting phase.

During imagery rescripting, patients imagined they were the age at which the event occurred and relived it as if it were happening again. Then they relived the memory at their current age, watching what happens to their younger self, and intervened if they wished, often conveying to the younger self the alternative perspective they had come up with in the cognitive restructuring phase. Finally, they relived it from the perspective of their younger self with their adult self in the room with them, intervening as before. This time the younger self was also asked what else he might need to happen in order to feel better, and the image then incorporated this material too. The younger self often requested extra nurturing and compassion at this point.

Imagery rescripting has many components and likely works as a result of the combination of the components: repeated evocation of the socially traumatic memory, cognitive restructuring, inserting new information derived from cognitive restructuring into the memory with an imagery exercise, and introducing a compassionate perspective, all of which may help the patient to reappraise the original event (Wild *et al.*, 2008). Further, imagery rescripting likely makes positive representations of the self more accessible, possibly inhibiting more negative and dysfunctional views of the self.

Inducing positive interpretation bias

Finally, it appears that inducing a positive interpretation bias may shift negative self-imagery. Hirsch *et al.* (2007) had non-anxious participants complete a positive or negative interpretation training phase and then a self-imagery exercise. Participants read texts on a computer screen that were initially ambiguous but were resolved by the final word to give a negative or positive interpretation. An example of a text used in their study was: 'At a dinner party, you are introduced to someone new and chat to them for quite a while. When you telephone them the next week to suggest meeting again, they reply that it would be pointless (great).' The positive interpretation is in parentheses. Participants were randomly allocated to the positive or negative interpretation condition in which they read 100 texts with meanings to match positive or negative meanings as appropriate. After reading the texts, they were asked to generate a mental image of themselves while listening to a short ambiguous social scenario. They then completed an anticipation task in which they had to imagine they were about to lead a seminar on a topic they were only a little familiar with. Participants' self-images were more positive after they had received the positive interpretation training. Further, participants in the positive interpretation condition rated their anticipated anxiety as lower and their expected social performance as better when anticipating leading a seminar compared to participants in the negative interpretation training task. Although this study was completed with non-anxious people, it suggests that it may be possible to generate more positive imagery in high socially anxious individuals by inducing a positive interpretation bias. Future research will need to explore this possibility in samples of socially anxious individuals.

What about positive self-imagery?

Few studies have looked at the effect of positive imagery on modifying negative imagery or on treating symptoms of social anxiety. This is surprising given the wealth of literature in other areas of psychology on the benefits of positive imagery. Studies in sports psychology, for example, consistently demonstrate that positive imagery quickly improves performance (e.g., Woolfolk, Parrish, & Murphy, 1985) and in health psychology, studies demonstrate that positive coping imagery has real physiological benefits, reducing pain and the stress hormone, cortisol (e.g. Manyande et al., 1995). With regard to social anxiety, positive imagery reduces anxiety and improves performance. As described above, Stopa and Jenkins (2007) and Vassilopoulos (2005) found that when high socially anxious participants held a positive self-image in mind while giving a speech, they felt less anxious and performed better than when they held a negative image in mind. Hirsch et al. (2003a) found that when patients with social phobia held a neutral image in mind as compared to a negative image, they too felt less anxious and performed better while having a conversation with a stranger. Hirsch et al. (2005) found that when individuals who were high in interview anxiety read job interview descriptions and held a positive image in mind of someone who is confident in job interviews, they had slower responses to words consistent with a threatening interpretation, suggesting that positive imagery reduced access to threatening interpretations of ambiguous social situations.

Future research needs to investigate the stability of the effects of positive self-imagery over time in socially anxious individuals and to determine to what extent negative imagery can simply be replaced by positive imagery or to what extent it must be addressed in the methods described above in order to sustain long-lasting change.

Conclusion

This chapter has reviewed negative self-imagery in social anxiety. We have seen that negative imagery is a key maintaining factor in the persistence of social phobia. Patients with social phobia typically have distorted, negative images of their worst fears unfolding while in social situations. The negative self-images have their roots in early socially aversive events, such as being bullied or humiliated at school. Coupled with negative interpretations made at the time, the events are laid down in memory and remembered as a memory image. The image is likely rehearsed during post-event processing and kept alive in situations that bear similar social cues to the original event. As patients with social phobia are more inclined to interpret social situations negatively and to endure them in a self-focused state, they fail to update their images because they do not notice that they come across as acceptable and that as adults they are not rejected.

Addressing negative self-imagery is a key component of CBT programmes for social phobia and is done through video and audio feedback, surveys, behavioural experiments, and imagery rescripting. This chapter also discussed the potential role of positive self-imagery in alleviating symptoms of social anxiety. Future research needs to determine the longer term outcome of using positive imagery to replace negative imagery in patients with social phobia and whether it is more effectively used in conjunction with other techniques to produce long-lasting therapeutic change.

References

Alden, L.E., & Wallace, S.T. (1995). Social phobia and social appraisal in successful and unsuccessful social interactions. *Behaviour Research and Therapy, 33*, 497–505.

Amir, N., Foa, E.B., & Coles, M.E. (1995). Negative interpretation bias in social phobia. *Behaviour Research and Therapy, 36*, 945–957.

Arntz, A., & Weertman, A. (1999). Treatment of childhood memories: Theory and practice. *Behaviour Research and Therapy, 37*, 715–740.

Brendle, J.R., & Wenzel, A. (2004). Differentiating between memory and interpretation biases in socially anxious and non-anxious individuals. *Behaviour Research and Therapy, 42*, 155–171.

Clark, D.M. (1999). Anxiety disorders: Why they persist and how to treat them. *Behaviour Research and Therapy*, *37*, S5–S27.

Clark, D.M., Ehlers, A., McManus, F., Hackmann, A., Fennell, M.J.V., Campbell, H., Flower, T., Davenport, C., & Louis, B. (2003). Cognitive therapy vs fluoxetine in generalized social phobia: A randomized controlled trial. *Journal of Consulting and Clinical Psychology*, *71*, 1058–1067.

Clark, D.M., & Wells, A. (1995). A cognitive model of social phobia. In R. Heimberg, M. Liebowitz, D.A. Hope, & F.R. Schneier (Eds.), *Social phobia: Diagnosis, assessment and treatment* (pp. 69–93). New York: Guilford Press.

Coles, M.E., Turk, C.L., & Heimberg, R.G. (2002). The role of memory perspective in social phobia: Immediate and delayed memories for role-played situations. *Behavioural and Cognitive Psychotherapy*, *30*, 415–425.

Conway, M.A. (2001). Sensory-perceptual episodic memory and its context: Auto-biographical memory. *Philosophical Transactions of the Royal Society of London B: Biological Sciences*, *356*, 1375–1384.

Conway, M.A., & Pleydell-Pearce, C.W. (2000). The construction of autobiographical memories in the self-memory system. *Psychological Review*, *107*, 261–268.

Epstein, S. (1994). Integration of the cognitive and the psychodynamic unconscious. *American Psychologist*, *49*, 709–724.

Giesen-Bloo, J., van Dyck, R., Spinhoven, P., van Tilburg, W., Dirksen, C., van Asselt, T., Nadort, M., & Arntz, A. (2006). Outpatient psychotherapy for borderline personality disorder: A randomized clinical trial of schema focused therapy versus transference focused psychotherapy. *Archives of General Psychiatry*, *63*, 649–658.

Hackmann, A., Clark, D.M., & McManus, F. (2000). Recurrent images and early memories in social phobia. *Behaviour Research and Therapy*, *38*, 601–610.

Hackmann, A., Surawy, C., & Clark, D.M. (1998). Seeing yourself through others' eyes: A study of spontaneously occurring images in social phobia. *Behavioural and Cognitive Psychotherapy*, *26*, 3–12.

Harvey, A.G., Clark, D.M., Ehlers, A., & Rapee, R.M. (1999). Social anxiety and self-impression: Cognitive preparation enhances the beneficial effects of video feedback following a stressful social task. *Behaviour Research and Therapy*, *38*, 1183–1192.

Heimberg, R.G., & Becker, R.E. (2002). *Cognitive-behavioral group therapy for social phobia: Basic mechanisms and clinical strategies*. New York: Guilford Press.

Hertel, P.T., Brozovich, F., Joormann, J., & Gotlib, I.H. (2008). Biases in interpret-ation and memory in generalized social phobia. *Journal of Abnormal Psychology*, *117*, 278–288.

Hirsch, C.R., & Clark, D.M. (2004). Information-processing bias in social phobia. *Clinical Psychology Review*, *24*, 728–731.

Hirsch, C.R., & Clark, D.M. (2007). Imagery special issue: Underestimation of auditory performance in social phobia and the use of audio feedback. *Journal of Behavior Therapy and Experimental Psychiatry*, *38*, 447–458.

Hirsch, C.R., Clark, D.M., & Mathews, A. (2006a). Imagery and interpretations in social phobia: Support for the combined cognitive biases hypothesis. *Behavior Therapy*, *37*, 223–236.

Hirsch, C.R., Clark, D.M., Mathews, A., & Williams, R. (2003a). Self-images play a causal role in social phobia. *Behaviour Research and Therapy*, *41*, 909–921.

Hirsch, C.R., Clark, D.M., Williams, R., Morrison, J.A., & Mathews, A. (2005).

Interview anxiety: Taking the perspective of a confident other changes inferential processing. *Behavioural and Cognitive Psychotherapy, 33*, 1–12.

Hirsch, C.R., Mathews, A., & Clark, D.M. (2007). Inducing an interpretation bias changes self-imagery: A preliminary investigation. *Behaviour Research and Therapy, 45*, 2173–2181.

Hirsch, C.R., Mathews, A., Clark, D.M., Williams, R., & Morrison, J.A. (2003b). Negative self-imagery blocks inferences. *Behaviour Research and Therapy, 41*, 1383–1396.

Hirsch, C.R., Mathews, A., Clark, D.M., Williams, R., & Morrison, J.A. (2006b). The causal role of negative imagery in social anxiety: A test in confident public speakers. *Journal of Behavior Therapy and Experimental Psychiatry, 37*, 159–170.

Hirsch, C.R., Meynen, T., & Clark, D.M. (2004). Negative self-imagery in social anxiety contaminates social interactions. *Memory, 12*, 496–506.

Lang, P.J. (1977). Imagery in therapy: An information processing analysis of fear. *Behaviour Therapy, 8*, 862–886.

Lang, P.J. (1979). A bio-informational theory of emotional imagery. *Psychophysiology, 16*, 495–512.

Manyande, A., Berg, S., Gettins, D., Stanford, S.C., Mazhero, S., Marks, D.F., & Salmon, P. (1995). Preoperative rehearsal of active coping imagery influences subjective and hormonal responses to abdominal surgery. *Psychosomatic Medicine, 57*, 2, 177–182.

Markus, H., & Ruvolo, A. (1989). Possible selves: Personalized representations of goals. In L.A. Pervin (Ed.), *Goal concepts in personality and social psychology* (pp. 211–242). Hillsdale, NJ: Lawrence Erlbaum Associates, Inc.

Rapee, R.M., & Heimberg, R.G. (1997). A cognitive-behavioral model of anxiety in social phobia. *Behaviour Research and Therapy, 35*, 741–756.

Rapee, R.M., & Lim, L. (1992). The discrepancy between self and observer ratings of performance in social phobics. *Journal of Abnormal Psychology, 101*, 728–731.

Rapee, R.M., & Sanderson, W.C. (1998). *Social phobia: Clinical application of evidence-based psychotherapy.* Northvale, NJ: Aronson.

Smucker, M.R., & Neiderdee, J. (1995). Treating incest-related PTSD and pathogenic schemas through imaginal exposure and rescripting. *Cognitive and Behavioral Practice, 2*, 63–93.

Spurr, J., & Stopa, L. (2002). Self-focused attention in social phobia and social anxiety. *Clinical Psychology Review, 22*, 947–975.

Stopa, L., & Clark, D.M. (1993). Cognitive processes in social phobia. *Behaviour Research and Therapy, 31*, 255–267.

Stopa, L., & Clark, D.M. (2000). Social phobia and the interpretation of social events. *Behaviour Research and Therapy, 38*, 273–283.

Stopa, L., & Jenkins, A. (2007). Images of the self in social anxiety: Effects on the retrieval of autobiographical memories. *Journal of Behavior Therapy and Experimental Psychiatry, 38*, 459–473.

Vassilopoulos, S. (2005). Social anxiety and the effects of engaging in mental imagery. *Cognitive Therapy and Research, 29*, 261–277.

Wild, J., Hackmann, A., & Clark, D.M. (2007). When the present visits the past: Updating traumatic memories in social phobia. *Journal of Behavior Therapy and Experimental Psychiatry, 38*, 386–401.

Wild, J., Hackmann, A., & Clark, D.M. (2008). Rescripting early memories linked to negative images in social phobia: A pilot study. *Behavior Therapy*, *39*, 47–56.

Woody, S.R. (1996). Effects of focus of attention on anxiety levels and social performance of individuals with social phobia. *Journal of Abnormal Psychology*, *105*, 61–69.

Woolfolk, R.L., Parrish, M.W., & Murphy, S.M. (1985). The effects of positive and negative imagery on motor skill performance. *Cognitive Therapy and Research*, *9*, 335–341.

Chapter 5

Agoraphobia
Imagery and the threatened self

Ann Hackmann, Samantha Day, and Emily A. Holmes

At the heart of cognitive models of anxiety lies the idea that dysfunctional anxiety results from distorted appraisals of danger inherent in certain situations. Such appraisals are often described as if they were verbal-type thoughts. However, Beck (1976) stressed that meanings that account for the strength of the emotion aroused are accessible through imagery (i.e. images and memories) as well as verbal thoughts. Recently there has been a surge of interest in the topic, and speculation that imagery may play an important role across psychological disorders. For overviews see Holmes and Hackmann (2004) and Holmes, Arntz, and Smucker (2007). In particular, it has been proposed that imagery has a stronger impact on emotion than verbal cognitions (Holmes & Mathews, 2005), and is therefore worthy of more research attention. This chapter explores imagery and memories in agoraphobia.

It has been suggested that imagery can play a role in the maintenance of anxiety disorders such as social phobia (Clark & Wells, 1995; Hackmann, Surawy, & Clark, 1998), obsessive-compulsive disorder (de Silva, 1986), and health anxiety (Wells & Hackmann, 1993). Images have also been shown to be useful in uncovering memories of events that occurred around the time of onset, the meanings of which may encapsulate core beliefs. For reviews see Hackmann and Holmes (2004) and Hirsch and Holmes (2007). In this chapter we present further findings from a study on images and early memories in agoraphobia initially reported in Day, Holmes, and Hackmann (2004), and their implications for our understanding of the threatened or damaged view of the self in this disorder (see also Conway & Holmes, 2005, for a discussion of intrusions as autobiographical memory in distress). The earlier paper looked at quantitative data, while this study looks more closely at content and themes, using qualitative methods to examine how agoraphobics view themselves in relation to the world and other people. The themes uncovered include not only fears of mental or physical catastrophe, but also social humiliation, intimidation, lack of protection from others, and a negative view of the self and the world. We discuss this in relation to the wider literature on the sense of self in agoraphobia.

The concept of agoraphobia

In DSM-IV (American Psychiatric Association, 1994) agoraphobia is not included as a codeable disorder. Instead it is defined in relationship to panic attacks, or panic-like symptoms. Agoraphobia is defined as anxiety about being in situations from which escape would be difficult or embarrassing, or in which help might not be available, in the event of a panic attack or panic-like symptoms. Typical situations feared by people with agoraphobia may involve being alone or among strangers, in crowded places, on public transport, or far from home. Such situations are avoided, or cause great anxiety, and the person with agoraphobia is usually relieved by the presence of a trusted companion. The symptoms must not be better accounted for by another disorder (such as social phobia, or posttraumatic stress disorder).

In Clark's (1986) model it is suggested that people suffering from panic disorder have a relatively enduring tendency to misinterpret bodily sensations as signalling an imminent physical or mental catastrophe, such as a heart attack, fainting or going crazy. Panic attacks are thought to result from this type of catastrophic misinterpretation (Clark, 1986, 1988). However, a number of studies indicate that individuals who suffer from agoraphobia appear to have extra concerns, concerning the interpersonal consequences of having panic attacks or more limited symptom attacks in particular situations. This raises the possibility that we need to pay more attention to perceived personal cost, coping and rescue factors when considering the 'threat appraisal model' as applied to agoraphobia. It was suggested by Beck, Emery, and Greenberg (1985) that anxiety is proportional to the estimated probability of an event and how awful it would be, moderated by the person's estimate of possible coping and rescue factors, i.e. how they perceive themselves, the world and other people.

Interpersonal concerns in agoraphobia have been investigated by Hoffart, Hackmann, and Sexton (2006). A questionnaire was devised using the format for the Agoraphobic Cognitions Questionnaire (Chambless, Caputo, Bright, & Gallagher, 1984), adapted by Clark, but looking at a different range of cognitions. The original version asked patients to rate the frequency with which they had thoughts about experiencing an imminent physical or mental catastrophe, and (in Clark's version) how strongly they believed this when feeling anxious. In the new questionnaire, Hoffart, Hackmann, and Sexton (2006) enquired about how frequently and how strongly patients with moderate to severe agoraphobia believed that if they became anxious there would be unfortunate interpersonal consequences. With the final selection of questionnaire items three new factors emerged: patients strongly endorsed fears that (if they experienced panic symptoms) they might be neglected and not offered help; be negatively evaluated by others; or be trapped and separated from safe persons and places. Patients described fears that they might never get back to safe persons or places, and images of the self being abandoned and neglected or isolated. For example, several people feared that they might be locked up in a hospital, or lost for ever, and had vivid images of such eventualities. These results are consistent with Day *et al.* (2004). Hoffart *et al.* plan to test the hypothesis that greater degrees of agoraphobic avoidance are correlated with more interpersonal fears of this nature. This hypothesis arises on the basis of clinical experience, but also with reference to the wider literature on agoraphobia.

Some years ago Clum and Knowles (1991) posed the question of why some individuals with panic disorder suffer from agoraphobia, while in others there is either mild agoraphobic avoidance or none. This question has been raised many times. It does not appear to be the case that agoraphobia is associated with more severe panic disorder, or that the panic disorder develops first and agoraphobia appears at a later stage (Salkovskis & Hackmann, 1997). However, many studies that compare panic disorder with or without agoraphobia indicate that the personal history and/or personality of those with more severe agoraphobia may be different from those who are not so agoraphobic. Patients with greater agoraphobic avoidance have been shown to be more likely to have dependent or avoidant personality traits, and to be less assertive, with lower self-esteem and lower perceived levels of self-sufficiency. They often have social-evaluative concerns, and are more likely to be depressed and have a history of separation anxiety or school refusal predating the agoraphobia. Finally, they are also more likely to come from families where other individuals have suffered from separation anxiety and/or school refusal. For a review see Hackmann (1998).

Thus it appears likely that attachment issues play an important part in agoraphobia. Parenting has been implicated by Farvelli, Webb, Ambonetti, Fonnesu, and Sessarego (1985), who found that people with agoraphobia had experienced separation from their mothers or parental divorce more often than a control group with no psychiatric disorder. Brown and Harris (1993) found that patients with panic disorder were more likely to have experienced early loss of a caregiver, or extremely inadequate caregiving compared to people with no psychiatric disorder. Chambless, Gillis, Tran, and Skeketee (1996) found that patients with agoraphobia or obsessive-compulsive disorder described their parents as unloving and controlling, and that those who engaged in more avoidant behaviour reported that their mothers had been neglectful. For a fuller discussion of attachment issues see Chapter 2.

In line with the findings from the studies summarised above are the results presented by Day *et al.* (2004). This study examined images and early memories in agoraphobia, and provided evidence of many cases in which there were apparent links between recurrent images warning of imminent physical or mental catastrophes (and their interpersonal consequences such as separation, humiliation or lack of protection) and distressing memories of similar actual events in the past. In a number of cases people were surprised that they had not considered these links before. In some instances, insight into the origins of their fear may have had the effect of motivating patients to try deliberately to discriminate between the past and the present, as there was a significant drop in avoidance scores when the follow-up data were subsequently collected.

The finding that patients had recurrent images of potential feared events, and that these in turn had similar content to earlier upsetting experiences, accords with similar findings in other disorders. For example, Hackmann *et al.* (1998) investigated images in social phobia, and demonstrated that patients described negative, distorted images of themselves, seen from an observer perspective (i.e. as if seen through the eyes of another person) when they were anxious in social situations. A second study (Hackmann, Clark, & McManus, 2000) demonstrated that such images were recurrent (patients reported having the same image again and again). They were also associated with memories of having been bullied, rejected or humiliated in events that frequently clustered around the date of onset, as previously reported at an assessment interview.

Hackmann (2004) has speculated that the common finding across disorders of recurrent images with content echoing disturbing past experience may be a manifestation of similar memory mechanisms to those thought to underpin the nature of trauma memory in PTSD. Ehlers and Clark (2000) postulate that intrusive images in PTSD are sensory fragments of memory of the traumatic event, often entering awareness without information concerning their proper time-code or original context. They also carry meanings from the original event, which have never been updated. Ehlers and Clark further suggest that one aim of therapy is to elaborate and contextualise these fragments of memory in order to update their meanings, and provide them with a time-code, so that they can find their proper place in the autobiographical memory base. This results in them being less easily triggered, and less likely to lead to safety behaviours (including avoidance) that perpetuate the problem. This is consistent with other cognitive models of PTSD: see Brewin and Holmes (2003) for a review.

If recurrent images in agoraphobia have roots in upsetting memories, the meanings of which are negative and distorted and have not been updated, this has potential therapeutic implications for the treatment of the disorder. Conway, Meares, and Standart (2004) have speculated that traumatic memories (and the images derived from them) have powerful effects on the self, and that this might be because such images are derived from the person's goals, and represent states of the world to be avoided. They encapsulate beliefs about the self, other people and the world, triggering emotion and avoidance behaviour that can then maintain the negative beliefs.

The study reported here carefully examined the themes present in the recurrent imagery of people with agoraphobia, and whether similar themes emerge in linked memories associated with the images. The differences between this study and previous studies examining imagery in anxiety disorders include the use of a content analysis approach (Smith, 2000) to analyse the themes in a more rigorous way, and the addition of a control group to explore whether the emerging themes are specific to those with agoraphobia. These additions offer promising extra value, as there has been so little research in this area. Since we are attempting to explore meanings about the self in agoraphobia, and their origins in past distressing experiences, qualitative methods may complement findings from more quantitative studies.

Method

Core parts of the method and the Imagery Interview are described in Day *et al.* (2004). They are repeated here for clarity. The Imagery Interview is available from the chapter authors.

Participants

Twenty patients with agoraphobia (15 females and 5 males) and 20 matched non-symptomatic controls participated in the study. The participants with agoraphobia were currently on waiting lists or had just begun therapy in four different outpatient psychology departments in a large city. Diagnosis was made by the General Practitioner (GP) or clinician responsible for their care and checked against DSM-IV criteria (American Psychiatric Association, 1994). In the sample, three participants also fulfilled criteria for PTSD, and one participant for obsessive-compulsive disorder. The mean age of the participants with agoraphobia was 48.9 years (SD = 16.3) and the mean number of years they reported experiencing agoraphobic fears was 14.5 (SD = 16.3). The mean age for the onset of agoraphobia was 34.5 years (SD = 11.6). The control group consisted of 20 people matched for age and sex who were contacted through local hairdressers.

The *Imagery Interview* designed specifically for agoraphobic images was substantially modified from the one used by Hackmann *et al.* (2000) in their study on social phobia. To summarise the modifications, we added a preliminary imaginal relaxation situation, in order to familiarise all participants with evoking and discussing their mental imagery. A set of typical agoraphobic feared scenarios was constructed from the Fear Questionnaire (Marks & Mathews, 1979) to trigger imagery if the participant did not report a spontaneous, recurrent image, by providing example situations in which imagery might occur. An anagram task was used to provide a break between the imagery and the memory questions, and to act as a cognitive distraction task so the description of the memory was not contaminated by the description just given about the image (MacLeod, Williams, & Bekerian, 1991). For further details of the procedure see Day *et al.* (2004). The use of such an interview has proved a useful tool, providing a window on the inner world of participants, and its idiosyncratic features. Administration of the interview took approximately 30 minutes and the questions were asked in a fixed order. Some of the questions require a rating scale (detailed in Day *et al.*, 2004) that the interviewer displayed at the relevant times.

At the section of the interview probing agoraphobic images, participants were asked whether they had any fleeting, recurrent mental images when they were in agoraphobic situations. If so, they were asked to bring a typical recurrent image to mind. If a participant could not recall such an image, one of the typically 'agoraphobic' scenarios could be read to the participant to encourage the generation of an image. All the agoraphobic participants and none of the controls reported and recalled a spontaneous recurrent image. All the controls were able to generate an image when prompted by the therapist, with the use of the scripted scenarios.

Once participants indicated that they had an image in mind, they were asked a series of questions about the sensory aspects, physical sensations, cognitions and emotions that were present in the image. After gaining a description of the image, participants were asked about the events that led up to the events in the image, how they were feeling in the image, whether the image made them want to do anything, and what the worst thing about the image was. The meaning was assessed by asking what the image meant 'about you, about other people, and about the world'.

Next, participants were asked when in their lives they had first experienced the sort of emotions, thoughts, and sensations reflected in the image. Participants were then asked whether they could recall a particular memory that seemed closely linked to the image. Before a description and further information about the memory were requested, the participant was asked to engage in an anagram task for five minutes, as a distracter task, to minimise conflation of material from the previously reported image with that in the associated memory that was to be separately described.

At the section of the interview probing associated memories in detail, they were asked to evoke the memory they had identified before the distraction task. As with the recalled spontaneous images and the evoked images, once participants had a memory in mind they were asked a series of questions about the sensory characteristics, cognitions, physical sensations, and emotions that were present in the memory. The experimenter enquired about the worst thing about the memory, and asked what the memory told the participant about themselves, other people and the world.

All participants with agoraphobia were interviewed individually in their homes. The control participants were interviewed individually at home, or in a room at the university. The questions in the Imagery Interview were read out to each participant, and the experimenter recorded the response. For further details see Day *et al.* (2004).

Method of analysis

All the agoraphobic participants and none of the controls reported spontaneous, recurrent images. The control participants were all able to evoke an image in response to one of the scenarios. The data acquired were analysed using a content analysis approach (Smith, 2000). The themes of the data were elicited using both *a priori* methods (specifying categories from other research) and an empirical method (new categories emerging from the data). The transcripts were read and a list covering the emergent themes was compiled. Closely related themes from this list were grouped together under appropriate higher order themes. This resulted in an organised summary list of themes. A coding frame (Smith, 2000) was devised, which consisted of a list of the themes, and a definition of each theme. Details of the results of this analysis, and examples of each theme, are provided below.

A second marker reviewed the transcripts and the coding frame, to provide a check on validity. The interviewer went through all the transcripts and coded whether or not a particular theme was present in the transcript. Each theme could only be coded once in each transcript. The second marker also coded all the transcripts with the coding frame to provide inter-rater reliability as to whether the theme was present or absent in each transcript. Queries or differences between the two coders were discussed to reach a consensus. Inter-rater reliability was calculated using Cohen's Kappa (1960).

There is an assumption that content analysis is an interactive process in which the researcher's own beliefs and understandings also play a part as the researcher engages in a process of interpretative activity in order to make sense of the participant's subjective world (Smith, 2000). It is therefore important for the researcher to acknowledge pre-existing values, assumptions and beliefs that may affect the interpretation of data, and to attempt to 'bracket' these in order to take as objective an approach as possible when trying to understand the meaning of participants' accounts (Elliott, Fischer, & Rennie, 1999). In the present case there was an assumption that the imagery would have the themes that had emerged from similar past research in panic disorder, such as isolation, panic, entrapment and loss of control (Cook, Melamed, Cuthbert, McNeil, & Lang, 1988; Marks, 1969) and preliminary agoraphobic studies that suggested the imagery might involve a range of physical or mental catastrophes, together with untoward interpersonal consequences (Hackmann & Suraway, personal communication).

Results

The study reported in Day *et al.* (2004) and discussed in further detail here had three main aims.

1   It aimed to explore the themes in (a) images and (b) associated memories

reported by patients with agoraphobia and controls in 'agoraphobic' situations.

2   The themes in the images and memories of people with agoraphobia were compared with those in the sample of matched, non-clinical, control participants.

3   The similarity between themes in the images and memories of the agoraphobic group was considered, and this was repeated for a control group of people from a similar background, but who were not suffering from agoraphobia.

This exploratory study was carried out because we were interested in the interpersonal themes and views of the self that might emerge from a study of images and memories in agoraphobia, in addition to catastrophic misinterpretations of bodily sensations typical of panic disorder. We speculated that there might be themes to do with separation, isolation, humiliation and abandonment, in view of the wider literature about the sense of self in agoraphobia.

Here we present the results of this study, and highlight how the various themes link to the individual's sense of self in agoraphobia.

Themes that emerged from the data in the imagery and associated memories

The themes, definitions and examples that emerged from the transcripts of the image and associated memories are illustrated below. The themes of the images and the memories could be split into six main sections: sense of impending doom (i.e. a physical or mental catastrophe); panic and dissociation; emotions (primary and complex); underestimating resources to cope with situation; need to escape from the situation; and meanings (about self, others and the world) of the situation. These main headings have been subdivided into themes that are related to the main overarching themes, and are presented in Table 5.1. A more detailed description of these themes is presented below.

Sense of impending doom

This theme relates to the anticipation or actual occurrence of a physical catastrophe, where the perceived consequence is actual harm or death. Examples include 'crossing road, pass out in the middle', 'hit my head on the door knob, knocked out', 'I have stopped breathing' and 'I pass out and do not wake up'. Most of the situations relate to a situation where the participant is stuck somewhere: in public transport, in a supermarket, by people not letting them escape or by illness. Table 5.2 shows the physical catastrophes present in the imagery and memories of the agoraphobic group. An actual physical catastrophe was reported in 19/20 of these memories. Thus the

Table 5.1 Themes present in the transcripts

Main overarching theme	Subdivisions in main theme
Sense of impending doom	Anticipation of or actual mental catastrophe
	Anticipation of or actual physical catastrophe
Panic and dissociation	Amplification, distortion of senses
	Physical panic symptoms
	Disorientation
	Frozen
Emotions: primary	Fear
	Anger
	Depression
Emotions: complex	Overwhelmed
	Social humiliation and shame
	Intimidation
	Loneliness
Lack of resources to cope	Inability to protect self
	Lack of protection
	Use of alcohol by others
Needing to escape	Wanting to hide
	Wanting to return home
	Wanting to disappear
	Entrapment
Meaning of situation	Negative view of self
	Negative view of others
	Negative view of world

catastrophes pictured in the memories often reflect times when the physical integrity of the self was actually threatened in the past.

Anticipation of, or actual mental catastrophe

This theme relates to the anticipation or actual feeling of losing control, either physically or mentally (e.g. going 'crazy'). This could be in terms of

Table 5.2 Physical catastrophes cited by the agoraphobic group (*n* = 20)

Physical catastrophes	Imagery frequencies	Memory frequencies
Getting stuck somewhere: no escape	14	15
Passing out/collapsing/drowning	2	2
Physical attack	2	2
Getting run over	1	0
Not being able to protect children	1	0
None	0	0

losing control due to panic or anger. Examples within the transcripts include 'feeling out of control', 'losing control' and 'having no control'. Such a sense of loss of control has important implications for the sense of self as an effective agent.

Panic and dissociation

Amplification/distortion of senses

This theme relates to people feeling as if their senses are being amplified, such as noises seeming to be louder, or senses being distorted, such as not being able to make things out clearly. Examples of amplification include 'lots of noise', 'all things are in extreme' and 'talking loudly'. Examples of distortion include 'blurred faces', 'just see faces' and 'can see myself and other people from lots of different angles'.

Disorientation/unreality/changes to sense of time

This theme relates to the person experiencing a sense of confusion, disorientation or unreality due to the experience. Examples relate to the person not being sure what is going on, such as 'didn't know what was happening', 'disorientated', 'confused whether real or not' and 'losing sense of direction'.

Some participants spoke about a change in time in terms of a speeding up, slowing down or a general awareness of time. Examples include 'seemed like hours', 'takes seconds' and 'felt really afraid for half an hour'.

Physical panic symptoms

This theme relates to physical sensations of panic that are experienced by the person. Examples from the people with agoraphobia include 'couldn't breathe', 'heart pounding', 'all kinds of alarming sensations coming', 'feeling really hot' and 'look completely white'. Compared to the agoraphobic group, the control group spoke about milder symptoms of anxiety rather than panic, for example 'anxious', 'sweating', 'heart beating fast' and 'blushing'.

Immobility/frozen

This theme refers to the feeling of not being able to move, like being frozen to the spot. This could either be the person, or things that are happening around the person. Examples of this in the transcripts include 'unable to move', 'stranded in a supermarket', 'have to be on the floor and wait till someone gets me up' and 'not moving, like stuck monsters'.

Although this section focuses on panic and dissociation, many of the things that people reported could have a major impact on their sense of self.

For example, sensory distortions such as lots of noise or blurring could contribute to a feeling of either being insubstantial and not really there (which would also link to dissociative feelings) or feeling overwhelmed or stuck, which could in turn link up with attachment issues such as feeling small, abandoned, helpless or lost.

Emotions

Using Ekman's (1999) distinction between primary and secondary emotions, where primary emotions are viewed as a direct response to overwhelming circumstances and secondary emotions arise from more elaborate appraisals made after the event, this section has been split into these two categories. The primary emotions include emotions such as fear, anger, and depression, and the secondary emotions include loneliness, being overwhelmed, being trapped, shame and social humiliation, being misunderstood, and intimidation.

Primary emotions

Fear emotions

Fear emotions relate to the feelings of terror and fright that accompany the perception of threat. Examples of this include 'frightened', 'scared', 'so distressed', 'absolutely terrified', 'inner dread' and 'this is not panic but terror'.

Anger and frustration

Participants spoke about anger or feelings to express anger to describe how they felt in their images and their related memories. Examples of these feelings include 'feeling cross', 'being irritated' and 'angry'.

Depressive cognitions: Resignation, sadness, hopelessness

This theme relates to depression cognitions spoken about by the participants in terms of their imagery and related memories. Examples of these cognitions include 'resignation', 'hopeless' and 'sadness'.

Complex emotions

Loneliness

Participants spoke about a sense of being alone and isolated. This includes being forced to be alone, or being unwanted. Extracts from this theme include 'no one to tell, no one to listen', 'living in a family that mostly ignored ... me', 'being on my own', 'I am alone', 'sitting there aged five, alone', 'separate',

'I am on my own' and 'my mother did not love me'. Again there is a potential link to attachment models (see Chapter 2).

Overwhelmed

This theme refers to a feeling of being overwhelmed, physically or emotionally. The definition includes being overpowered, being surrounded, or a sense of things looming in. Examples of being overwhelmed include 'people over me', 'everything crowding in on me', 'carriages closing in around', 'as go further into the shop, everything closes in', 'other cars surrounding the car I am in' and 'overpowered'.

Shame and social humiliation

This theme refers to the situation of being humiliated, embarrassed or shown up in front of other people. This includes the worry and fear of being the cause of negative attention. Examples of this theme include 'tail between my legs', 'making a fool of self', 'I look ridiculous, I am embarrassing', 'I have been made to look a fool', 'humiliated', 'judging me, laughing at me', 'feeling so uncomfortable in front of other people' and 'will I panic and look silly?'.

Being misunderstood

This theme relates to other people not understanding what is happening, and the person not feeling understood. Examples of this theme include 'some people are scared of me, don't understand what is happening', 'people thinking I am mad, they do not understand what it is like' and 'anger at people who do not understand'.

Intimidation/lack of assertiveness

Some participants spoke about feeling weak or wanting to do things but not being able to. This theme has been termed feeling intimidation or lacking in assertiveness. Examples of this theme include 'couldn't say nothing to no one, seen as weakness', 'I should have hit harder', 'I was stifled', 'when I was young, not allowed to say things' and 'couldn't look round at other people'.

Interestingly, the emotions reported here go far beyond the fear of bodily sensations which is central to our understanding of panic disorder. Many secondary emotions are described, which could impact on or interact with the person's subjectively experienced sense of self. These may include the sense of loneliness because one fears being misunderstood or ignored by others when in trouble, and also the sense of being ineffectual because one feels weak, overwhelmed and unable to be assertive. In turn these ideas could trigger depression and anger.

Underestimating/lack of resources to cope in situation

This section of themes relates to the participants feeling as if they have a lack of resources to cope.

Lack/inability to protect self

This theme relates to an inability of a person to protect himself or herself. Examples include 'weak', 'powerless', 'vulnerable', 'how am I going to cope with everything?', 'there to be abused' and 'helpless'.

Others not being protective/help not available

This theme relates to a lack of protection from those around the person who needs protecting, for example by carers. Again, attachment issues seem important. Examples of this include 'as a child, had to look after self', 'I was brought up by an abusive mother', 'Mum running out the house, leaving us there', 'no one there for me', 'parents did not realise seriousness of situation' and 'no one to help'. Also included in this theme is the use of alcohol by other people in a negative way. Examples include 'Dad came in drunk, been drinking all night', 'my father used to come in drunk', 'Mum and Dad used to go out to the pub' and 'my father was an alcoholic'.

Themes of inability to protect the self, and help not being available, echo those reported in the previous section and give some insight into why certain situations might be particularly likely to be avoided by people with agoraphobia.

Plan to deal with the situation

These themes relate to how people try to deal with what is perceived as a negative situation.

Needing to escape

This theme relates to the general sense of needing to escape from the situation. Examples in the transcripts include 'need to escape', 'get away', 'need to get out', 'wanted out', 'want to run', and 'let me out'.

Wanting to hide

This theme relates to wanting to hide the symptoms of anxiety. Examples within the transcripts include 'trying not to let other people see', and 'trying to hide'.

Wanting to return home

This theme relates to the desire to be at home, or in a safe place. Examples include 'wanting to get home', 'trying to get home', 'want people to disappear so can crawl home', 'needed to be at home alone' and 'get out, back to somewhere where can shut self in'.

Wanting to disappear

'Wanting to disappear' refers to the desire to become invisible. Examples in the transcripts include 'want to jump out of body', 'try and hide self', and 'yes, must find a ditch to die'.

Entrapment

This specifically refers to the feeling of being trapped in a situation, not being able to get away. Examples include 'I couldn't climb out', 'I am stuck in the middle', 'I am trapped', 'people are not letting me escape', 'banging at the door, wanting to get out' and 'door shuts, oh my god, I am trapped'.

Meaning of situation

This section of themes refers to the meaning the participants give to the situation.

Negative view of self

This theme represents low self-esteem and a negative view of self. Examples include 'unlovable', 'not good enough', 'am nothing', 'useless, weak and valueless' and 'pathetic, coward'. This negative view of the self may be partly a response to earlier experiences, in which patients had been ignored, abused, misunderstood or humiliated by caregivers, and had felt lonely and vulnerable, as well as enduring actual catastrophic events in some cases, without emotional support.

Negative view of other people

This theme refers to having a negative view of other people. This includes other people being seen as 'dangerous', 'some are ignorant', 'nasty, moody', 'don't want to know' and 'not in a hurry to help'.

Negative view of the world

This theme represents participants having a negative view of the world. Examples of this theme include the world being 'full of obstacles', 'horrible place to be', 'pretty shitty', 'dangerous', 'hateful, I don't want to be here' and 'hate it – feel so sorry for younger generation'.

Comparison of the frequency of themes in the imagery and the associated memories between the two groups

For a summary of the results see Table 5.3. It can be seen that within the fear imagery, the agoraphobic group were significantly more likely than the control group to describe the anticipation or the actual occurrence of a physical or mental catastrophe. Individuals in the agoraphobic group were also more likely to have amplified or distorted senses, and to feel disoriented or experience changes in time perception. Further significant themes that were highlighted in the agoraphobic group in the image were fear cognitions, being socially humiliated, feeling intimidated, and a lack of protection by others. The agoraphobic participants were more likely to want to 'disappear' to deal with the situation: a manifestation of the perceived extreme threat to the self. The imagery of the agoraphobic group was also significantly different to that of the control group in terms of the negative meaning given to the self, others and the world. For example, one patient believed she was weak, and others were horrible. In her image people's faces were coming towards her, telling her off. She associated this with her violent, abusive parents. Another patient believed she was fearful, powerless, and child-like while others were powerful. Her image was of being stranded in a supermarket, unable to breathe or move, unable to surface. Her memories were of being bullied for being small, and of nearly drowning in the sea, with her parents not realising she was in serious trouble.

With reference to the themes in the memories, the agoraphobic group recalled significantly more real physical or mental catastrophes. An actual physical catastrophe was reported in 19/20 of these memories. The memories included significantly more themes of being fearful and angry; also not being able to protect the self, a lack of protection by others, and feeling trapped. In addition they were more likely to report the use of alcohol by others. The agoraphobic group, in the memories, took a significantly more negative view of the self.

Similarities between images and memories

A further interesting finding was the similarity in the themes in the images and memories of the agoraphobic group. The most common themes in the upsetting memories were those of an actual physical catastrophe, panic

Table 5.3 Frequency count of the themes in the data

Themes in agoraphobic transcripts compared to controls	Imagery		Memory	
	Frequency in imagery of agoraphobics	Frequency in imagery of controls	Frequency in memory of agoraphobics	Frequency in memory of controls
Catastrophe				
Mental catastrophe	7**	1	6	2
Physical catastrophe	20****	1	19****	4
Panic and dissociation				
Amplification/senses	10**	4	3	2
Disorientation	8***	1	4	2
Panic symptoms	18	14	13	10
Immobility/frozen	3	1	3	1
Negative emotions				
Fear emotions	16***	8	15*	9
Anger	4	4	5*	1
Depression cognitions	4	1	4	4
Loneliness	4	3	4	3
Overwhelmed	9	6	5	2
Social humiliation	12****	2	8	4
Being misunderstood	3	0	1	0
Intimidation	7****	0	5	2
Lack of help and resources to cope				
Inability to protect self	6	2	5*	1
Lack of protection	10***	2	13***	4
Use of alcohol by others	0	0	6***	0
Needing to escape				
Wanting to hide	0	0	3	1
Wanting to disappear	8***	1	1	2
Wanting to return home	4	4	3	2
Entrapment	7	5	9***	1
Negative views				
Negative view/of self	13****	2	11****	1
Negative view/of others	12***	3	9	5
Negative view/of world	13****	3	6	5

****p < .001; ***p < .01; **p < .05; *p < .1 (trend).*

symptoms, fear emotions, lack of protection from others, and a negative view of the self. Each of these themes was also present in more than half of the images of the agoraphobic sample, and each of these themes was significantly more common in the agoraphobic sample than in the control sample.

Panic symptoms were the most commonly reported theme in the images and memories of the control sample, along with fear emotions. However, physical catastrophes and the more interpersonal aspects of a negative view of the self, lack of protection from others, social humiliation, intimidation and inability to protect the self were much less commonly represented, making comparison of frequencies difficult.

Discussion

Themes in the agoraphobic imagery related to the literature

All the people with agoraphobia reported an imagined physical catastrophe occurring in their imagery. Further themes of panic and dissociation, other primary and complex emotions, a lack of ability to cope with the situation and negative meanings about the self, the world and other people were common.

The theme of a potential impending catastrophe in those with agoraphobia has been highlighted in much of the literature (e.g. from Westphal, 1871, to DSM-IV, American Psychiatric Association, 1994). In the imagery tran- scripts in this study, the data suggest that the panic symptoms and the fear of an impending catastrophe are interrelated, with 90% of the people with agoraphobia talking about both an imminent catastrophe and panic, which is an understandable link, as a physical catastrophe represents a threat to the self as a whole. The participants also described other dangers that might prevent their escape, such as being run over, not being able to pass people, or being attacked. As seen with recent studies into PTSD (Grey & Holmes, 2008; Grey, Holmes, & Brewin, 2001; Holmes, Grey, & Young, 2005) fear was not the only emotion, but humiliation, intimidation, and the sense of not being protected also featured.

The themes that emerged in the panic and dissociation category from the agoraphobic imagery support the vicious cycle model of panic (Clark, 1988). In the imagery described by the sample, themes concerning the symptoms of panic such as amplification and distortion of senses, disorientation and fear all emerged as significant differences compared to the control group. Eighty-five per cent of the agoraphobic group spoke about panic symp- toms being part of their fear imagery, and scores on the Body Sensations Questionnaire (Chambless et al., 1984) showed that the group were signifi- cantly more frightened by these sensations than the control group. Other symptoms of panic that emerged were sensory distortion, disorientation and changes in the sense of time, which have been reported in other studies (McNab, 1993). These experiences are aspects of losing a coherent sense of the self in a stable environment.

The emotions that emerged as significant themes from the agoraphobic transcripts compared to the control group were fear, shame, humiliation, intimidation and the desire to disappear. The fear cognitions seem related to the panic sensations, and the fear of the imagined impending catastrophe. The social evaluative concerns of shame and social humiliation have been reported by other researchers (see Hackmann, 1998, for a review). The theme of intimidation relating to the feeling of being surrounded, or a sense of things looming in, seems to relate to the experience of panic and the fear of not being able to escape or cope.

Thirty per cent of the people with agoraphobia spoke about feeling as if they did not have the resources to cope with the situation. This theme seems to relate to the threat appraisal model (Beck *et al.*, 1985), which argues that individuals implicitly calculate the strength of the threat based on the 'cost' of the disaster compared to their coping resources.

The negative appraisals given by the agoraphobic group to the self, others and the world suggest how the anxiety is maintained, as the self is judged to be ineffectual, others critical and unhelpful, and the world dangerous. The imagery illustrates how people with agoraphobia feel that an overwhelming catastrophe will occur, they will not be able to deal with it, no one will help, and escape may not be possible.

Themes in the associated memories related to the literature

The significant themes in the associated memories of the agoraphobic patients included an actual physical catastrophe; emotions of fear, anger and entrapment; needing to escape; not being able to protect the self; feeling a lack of protection by others; and a negative view of self.

All participants in the agoraphobic group described traumatic memories that they associated with their agoraphobic imagery. The catastrophic events included being abused by parents, almost drowning, thinking a plane would crash, and being attacked. These events were accompanied by feelings of fear and anger, and a desire to escape. In the traumatic situation, the agoraphobic group were more likely to recall feelings of being unable to protect themselves and not getting help from other people around. The result of the memory of the traumatic situation was often a negative appraisal of the self.

Hackmann (1998) speculates that since research (e.g. Chambless & Goldstein, 1982; Hoffart, 1995) has shown that people with agoraphobia often believe that they will find it difficult to cope in the world when alone, this may be due to early experiences that have laid the foundation for such beliefs. The themes of anger, early memories of abuse and neglect, other people not helping, and not being able to protect the self that emerged from the transcripts of the associated memories do seem to support this view. This also accords with the assertion that negative, self-defining moments in a person's life can support avoidance later, as the person strives to prevent the distressing memories from being triggered (Conway *et al.*, 2004). When the images (with their input from associated memories) are triggered they reflect an internal model in which the self is lonely, abandoned and vulnerable, and others are uncaring and unwilling to be protective. This working model may reflect early attachment patterns.

From a cognitive perspective, it could be hypothesised that the people with agoraphobia may hold negative core beliefs concerning helplessness and/or unlovability (Beck, 1995) that developed in childhood. This may have led to intermediate beliefs, rules and assumptions, such as 'I am helpless: If I am in danger, I will not be able to protect myself' and 'I am unlovable: If I am in danger other people would not help me'. As a result of such beliefs, certain situations where escape has been difficult in the past (such as those recalled in the memories of those with agoraphobia) are avoided or approached with anticipatory anxiety. This would make a panic attack more likely, and avoidance and safety behaviour could maintain the fear.

In their study of socially anxious participants, Hackmann *et al.* (2000) suggested that the close similarity between their imagery and associated memories could indicate that early unpleasant social experiences may lead to the development of a negative, observer perspective image that is activated in social situations. In this study and that of Day *et al.* (2004) it can be seen that the recurrent images (seen in this case from a fluctuating field/observer perspective) may also reflect input from memory of traumatic experiences with similar themes. It is possible that early negative memories could be maintaining the fear in situations with similar meanings, via disturbing imagery. Recurrent images warn not only of physical danger, but of damage to the emotional security of the self, since the self is seen as lonely, vulnerable, unlovable, helpless and unlikely to get help from other people *in extremis*.

Although the early memories recalled by the agoraphobic group did not cluster round the time that the agoraphobia developed, it could be speculated that this type of memory has contributed to the onset and maintenance of the disorder by the powerful influence that the image (with similar themes to the memory) could have in certain situations. It could be that critical events that occurred around the onset of agoraphobia may have had similar meanings or sensory characteristics to the earlier traumatic experiences, which may activate the disorder of agoraphobia, as seen in delayed onset PTSD (Buckley, Blanchard, & Hickling, 1996). A case example has been given by Hackmann (2004) in which the patient's memory was of hospitalisation aged three, appraised as abandonment by unloving parents. The agoraphobia was triggered when (as an adult) the patient was threatened with hospital admission for a back complaint. He became hypervigilant for any bodily sensations that could result in a mental or physical catastrophe leading to hospital admission. The image that always drove avoidance was one of collapsing, being taken to hospital, and kept there indefinitely against his will.

It would have been useful if an account of events around the time of the onset of agoraphobia had been elicited from the participants so that this hypothesis could be more carefully explored. As many of the agoraphobic memories focused on near-death experiences such as drowning, falling, or suffocating, it could be hypothesised that a later experience, such as a situation evoking a similar reaction, could lead to a tendency to misinterpret anxiety symptoms such as dizziness, breathlessness or heart pounding as being likely to have catastrophic consequences.

Although the memories of the agoraphobic group were rated as being more distressing (Day *et al.*, 2004), 95% of the control group also recalled negative experiences. This finding suggests that it is not a negative event *per se* that can lay down the foundations of a fear template that may be activated later in life, but the meaning that was given to the event at the time, and subsequently. It can be seen that significantly more negative ideas about the self were associated with the memories in those with agoraphobia than in the control group. This supports the view of cognitive therapy that it is not the situation that causes negative emotion but the views that are taken of it (Beck, 1976). The findings also suggest that the meaning of a traumatic experience may not be updated unless the memory is carefully reappraised (Grey, Young, & Holmes, 2002).

Treatment implications

This study has limitations due to the small size of the sample, although the numbers are comparable to other studies of imagery in anxiety disorders (Hackmann *et al.*, 2000; Wells & Hackmann, 1993). The findings have some interesting clinical implications. They suggest that when formulating a case and planning treatment, it may be important to consider various aspects of threat appraisal, and that these should include the person's view of the self. In this context recurrent, spontaneous images are worth exploring in agoraphobia, as they appear to be frequently reported and often seem to have roots in past history. Their contents are rich in meanings not only about the feared catastrophes, but also about the person's view of their ability to cope, and their perception that they are not the sort of person who is likely to be helped or protected by others. There may be some therapeutic benefit simply from evoking the images and any associated memories, as this provides an opportunity for cognitive reappraisal, which may lead to decreased avoidance and a shift in self-view (Day *et al.*, 2004).

During treatment it may be important to consider a range of behavioural experiments, looking not only at the causes and consequences of the physical symptoms but also at the possible interpersonal implications (see Hackmann chapter in Bennett-Levy *et al.*, 2004). In this way core beliefs and assumptions about the self, the world and other people can be tackled, alongside the more usual work on the catastrophic misinterpretation of bodily sensations, and their imagined consequences. A common fear is that if the patient were to collapse in public, passers-by might laugh or jeer, or the patient might be totally ignored. A favourite behavioural experiment involves the therapist accompanying the patient to a public place, and then pretending to faint, so that the patient can observe what really happens. Typically the therapist is offered appropriate help. The patient is usually much relieved, and may even be persuaded to repeat the experiment themselves, in a different location. In this way an image can be compared with reality, and a new schema can be under construction, where the self is seen as less vulnerable and more worthy of kind attention.

Since the beliefs encapsulated in the images and memories often appear to have the status of core beliefs (e.g. 'I am helpless/unlovable; others are unkind/hostile'), other schema change methods may also be appropriate. A promising avenue lies in attempting to rescript the early memories of people with agoraphobia, using techniques such as those described by Arntz and Weertman (1999) and Hackmann (2004). Preliminary studies suggest that updating and rescripting upsetting memories in people with social phobia has a significant effect on various measures of social anxiety, at least in the short term (Wild, Hackmann, & Clark, 2007, 2008). Good results have also been obtained with rescripting in patients with depression and disturbing intrusive memories (Wheatley *et al.*, 2007). Patients received between five and nine sessions of treatment that targeted only the intrusive memories, and improvement was maintained at follow-up (Wheatley & Hackmann, 2007). For a review of imagery rescripting techniques see Holmes *et al.* (2007) and Chapter 3 of this book.

Finally, it would be interesting to explore images of patients with panic disorder with lower levels of avoidance. The hypothesis would be that (in line with other research on personality characteristics in these two groups) the images in this group might be less likely to portray interpersonal aspects of the panic situation, and might be less vivid, less distressing, and less likely to be linked to early memories.

Conclusion

This piece of work looked at distressing images and memories in patients with agoraphobia and matched controls. As in the study by Day *et al.* (2004), supported by results from the questionnaire measure developed by Hoffart *et al.* (2006), agoraphobic patients were shown to be anxious about situations in which they feared they might be neglected, humiliated, or separated from safe people or places if they suddenly became ill. Further more careful questioning revealed that there was also a theme of self-blame for this, with patients describing themselves as weak, ineffectual, powerless, incapable of asserting themselves, or just plain unlovable. These findings accord well with the wider literature, where there are findings in studies comparing panic patients with and without severe agoraphobia, which have provided evidence for more separation anxiety, depression, dependency and low self-esteem, and less self-sufficiency or assertiveness in the more agoraphobic group (see Hackmann, 1998).

The reported memories linked to the panic images give some insight as to what kind of childhood experiences set the scene for this. For many patients, childhood seems to have been a lonely experience, with separation or abuse, commonly with scant opportunities to express feelings or have them acknowledged or validated. The main implication for treatment is that this method of enquiry provides a clear focus for exploring material that should be included in the formulation and treatment plan.

Acknowledgements

The data are from Samantha Day's D.Clin.Psych. thesis at University College, London, supervised by Emily Holmes and Peter Scragg. Chris Barker, Pasco Fearon and Agnes van Minnen provided helpful discussion and statistical advice. We would also like to thank the clinical psychologists who helped recruit participants for this study, especially John Cape and Peter Butcher.

References

American Psychiatric Association (1994). *Diagnostic and statistical manual of mental disorders* (4th ed.). Washington, DC: APA.

Arntz, A., & Weertman, A. (1999). Treatment of childhood memories: Theory and practice. *Behaviour Research and Therapy*, 37, 715–740.

Beck, A.T. (1976). *Cognitive therapy and the emotional disorders*. New York: International Universities Press.

Beck, A.T., Emery, G., & Greenberg, R. (1985). *Anxiety disorders and phobias: A cognitive perspective*. New York: Guilford Press.

Beck, J.S. (1995). *Basics and beyond*. New York: Guilford Press.

Bennett-Levy, J., Butler, G., Fennell, M.J.V., Hackmann, A., Mueller, M., & Westbrook, D. (Eds.) (2004). *Oxford guide to behavioural experiments in cognitive therapy*. Oxford, UK: Oxford University Press.

Brewin, C.R., & Holmes, E.A. (2003). Psychological theories of posttraumatic stress disorder. *Clinical Psychology Review*, 23(3), 339–376.

Brown, G.W., & Harris, T.O. (1993). Aetiology of anxiety and depressive disorders in an inner city population: 1. Early adversity. *Psychological Medicine*, 23, 143–154.

Buckley, T.C., Blanchard, E.B., & Hickling, E.J. (1996). A prospective examination of delayed onset PTSD secondary to motor vehicle accidents. *Journal of Abnormal Psychology*, 105(4), 617–625.

Chambless, D.L., Caputo, G.C., Bright, P., & Gallagher, R. (1984). Assessment of fear of fear in agoraphobics: The Body Sensations Questionnaire and the Agoraphobic Cognitions Questionnaire. *Journal of Consulting and Clinical Psychology*, 52, 1090–1097.

Chambless, D.L., Gillis, M.M., Tran, G.Q., & Skeketee, G.S. (1996). Parental bonding reports of clients with obsessive compulsive disorder and agoraphobia. *Clinical Psychology and Psychotherapy*, 3, 77–85.

Chambless, D.L., & Goldstein, A.J. (1982). *Agoraphobia: Multiple perspectives on theory and treatment*. New York: Wiley.

Clark, D.M. (1986). A cognitive approach to panic. *Behaviour Research and Therapy*, 24, 461–470.

Clark, D.M. (1988). A cognitive model of panic attacks. In S. Rachman & J.D. Maser (Eds.), *Panic: Psychological perspectives* (pp.71–89). Hillsdale, NJ: Lawrence Erlbaum Associates, Inc.

Clark, D.M., & Wells, A. (1995). A cognitive model of social phobia. In R. Heimberg, M. Liebowitz, D.A. Hope, & F.R. Schneiser (Eds.), *Social phobia: Diagnosis, assessment and treatment* (pp. 69–93). New York: Guilford Press.

Clum, G.A., & Knowles, S.L. (1991). Why do some people with panic disorder become avoidant? A review. *Clinical Psychology Review, 11*, 295–313.

Cohen, J. (1960). A coefficient of agreement for nominal scales. *Educational and Psychological Measurement, 20*, 37–46.

Conway, M.A., & Holmes, E.A. (2005). Autobiographical memory and the working self. In N.R. Braisby & A.R.H. Gellatly (Eds.), *Cognitive psychology* (pp. 507–538). Oxford, UK: Oxford University Press.

Conway, M., Meares, K., & Standart, S. (2004). Images and goals. *Memory, 12*(4), 525–531 [Special Issue on Mental Imagery and Memory in Psychopathology].

Cook, E.W., Melamed, B.G., Cuthbert, B.N., McNeil, D.W., & Lang, P.J. (1988). Emotional imagery and the differential diagnosis of anxiety. *Journal of Consulting and Clinical Psychology, 56*, 734–740.

Day, S., Holmes, E.A., & Hackmann, A. (2004). Occurrence of imagery and its links to memory in agoraphobia. *Memory, 12*(4), 416–427 [Special Issue on Mental Imagery and Memory in Psychopathology].

de Silva, P. (1986). Obsessional-compulsive imagery. *Behaviour Research and Therapy, 24*, 333–350.

Ehlers, A., & Clark, D.M. (2000) A cognitive model of posttraumatic stress disorder. *Behaviour Research and Therapy, 38*, 319–345.

Ekman, P. (1999). Basic emotions. In T. Dalgleish & M. Power (Eds.), *Handbook of cognition and emotion* (pp. 45–60). Chichester, UK: Wiley.

Elliot, R., Fischer, C.T., & Rennie, D.L. (1999) Evolving guidelines for publication of qualitative research studies in psychology and related fields. *British Journal of Clinical Psychology, 38*(3), 215–229.

Farvelli, C., Webb, T., Ambonetti, A., Fonnesu, F., & Sessarego, A. (1985). Prevalence of traumatic early life events in 31 agoraphobic patients with panic attacks. *American Journal of Psychiatry, 142*, 1493–1494.

Grey, N., & Holmes, E.A. (2007). 'Hotspots' in trauma memories in the treatment of posttraumatic stress disorder: A replication. *Memory, 16*, 788–796.

Grey, N., Holmes, E.A., & Brewin, C.R. (2001). It is not only fear: Peritraumatic hotspots in posttraumatic stress disorder. *Behavioural and Cognitive Psychotherapy, 29*(3), 367–372.

Grey, N., Young, K.A.D., & Holmes, E.A. (2002). Cognitive restructuring within reliving: A treatment for peritraumatic 'hotspots' in posttraumatic stress disorder. *Behavioural and Cognitive Psychotherapy, 30*(1), 37–56.

Hackmann, A. (1998). Cognitive therapy with panic and agoraphobia: Working with complex cases. In N. Tarrier, A. Wells, & G. Haddock (Eds.), *Treating complex cases: The cognitive behavioural therapy approach* (pp. 27–43). Chichester, UK: Wiley.

Hackmann, A. (2004). Compassionate imagery in the treatment of early memories in Axis I disorders. In P. Gilbert (Ed.), *Compassion: Conceptualisations, research and use in psychotherapy* (pp. 352–368). London: Routledge.

Hackmann, A., Clark, D.M., & McManus, F. (2000). Recurrent images and early memories in social phobia. *Behaviour Research and Therapy, 38*, 601–610.

Hackmann, A., & Holmes, E.A. (2004). Reflecting on imagery: A clinical perspective and overview of the Special Issue on Mental Imagery and Memory in Psychopathology. *Memory, 12*(4), 389–402 [Special Issue].

Hackmann, A., Suraway, C., & Clark, D.M. (1998). Seeing yourself through others' eyes: A study of spontaneously occurring images in social phobia. *Behavioural and Cognitive Psychotherapy, 26*, 3–12.

Hirsch, C., & Holmes, E.A. (2007). Mental imagery in anxiety disorders. *Psychiatry, 6*(4), 161–165.

Hoffart, A. (1995). Cognitive mediators of situational fear in agoraphobia. *Journal of Behavior Therapy and Experimental Psychiatry, 26*, 313–320.

Hoffart, A., Hackmann, A., & Sexton, H. (2006). Interpersonal fears among patients with panic disorder with agoraphobia. *Behavioural and Cognitive Psychotherapy, 34*, 359–363.

Holmes, E.A., Arntz, A., & Smucker, M.R. (2007). Imagery rescripting in cognitive behaviour therapy: Images, treatment techniques and outcomes. *Journal of Behaviour Therapy and Experimental Psychiatry, 38*(4), 297–305.

Holmes, E.A., Grey, N., & Young, K.A.D. (2005). Intrusive images and 'hotspots' of trauma memories in posttraumatic stress disorder: An exploratory investigation of emotions and cognitive themes. *Journal of Behavior Therapy and Experimental Psychiatry, 36*(1), 3–17.

Holmes, E.A., & Hackmann, A. (Eds.) (2004). Mental imagery and memory in psychopathology. *Memory, 12*(4) [Special Issue].

Holmes, E.A., & Mathews, A. (2005). Mental imagery and emotion: A special relationship? *Emotion, 5*(4), 489–497.

MacLeod, A.K., Williams, J.M., & Bekerian, D.A. (1991). Worry is reasonable: The role of explanations in pessimism about future personal events. *Journal of Abnormal Psychology, 100*(4), 478–486.

Marks, I.M. (1969). *Fears and phobias*. New York: Academic Press.

Marks, I.M., & Mathews, A.M. (1979). Brief standard self-rating for phobic patients. *Behaviour Research and Therapy, 17*, 263–267.

McNab, B. (1993). *Perceptions of phobias and phobics: The quest for control*. London: Academic Press.

Salkovskis, P.M., & Hackmann, A. (1997). Agoraphobia. In G.C.L. Davey (Ed.), *Phobias: A handbook of theory, research and treatment* (pp. 27–61). Chichester, UK: Wiley.

Smith, C.P. (2000). Content analysis and narrative analysis. In H.T. Reis & C.M. Judd (Eds.), *Handbook of research methods in social and personality psychology* (pp. 313–335). Cambridge, UK: Cambridge University Press.

Wells, A., & Hackmann, A. (1993). Imagery and core beliefs in health anxiety: Content and origins. *Behavioural and Cognitive Psychotherapy, 21*, 265–273.

Westphal, C.F.O. (1871). Die Agoraphobia, eine neuropathische Erscheinung. *Archiv für Psychiatrie und Nerven Krankheiten, 3*, 138–161 & 219–221.

Wheatley, J., Brewin, C., Patel, T., Hackmann, A., Wells, A., Fisher, P., & Myers, S. (2007) 'I'll believe it when I can see it': Imagery rescripting of intrusive sensory memories in depression. *Journal of Behavior Therapy and Experimental Psychiatry, 38*(4), 371–385.

Wheatley, J., & Hackmann, A. (2007). *Imagery rescripting in Axis I disorders.* Workshop presented at the World Congress of Cognitive Therapy, Barcelona, Spain.

Wild, J., Hackmann, A., & Clark, D.M. (2007). When perspective visits the past: Updating memories in social phobia. *Journal of Behavior Therapy and Experimental Psychiatry, 38*(4), 386–401.

Wild, J., Hackmann, A., & Clark, D.M. (2008). Rescripting early memories linked to negative images in social phobia: A pilot study. *Behavior Therapy, 39,* 47–56.

Chapter 6

Imagery and psychological threat to the self in PTSD

Nick Grey

Posttraumatic stress disorder (PTSD) is a pattern of distressing symptoms that may follow experiencing a traumatic event. Such events include natural disasters, physical and sexual assaults, road traffic accidents, other accidents, and terrorist attacks. The formal diagnostic criteria for PTSD are that the person has 'experienced, witnessed, or was confronted with an event or events that involved actual or threatened death or serious injury, or a threat to the physical integrity of self or others' and the person's 'response involved intense fear, helplessness, or horror' (Diagnostic and Statistical Manual IV, American Psychiatric Association, 1994). Furthermore, the person must have at least one symptom of re-experiencing such as intrusions, nightmares and flashbacks; at least three symptoms of avoidance and emotional numbing; and at least two symptoms of hyperarousal, such as hypervigilance and an exaggerated startle response.

PTSD is unusual in that the presence of images, in the form of intrusions, flashbacks and nightmares, is among the diagnostic criteria and these are the hallmark symptoms of the problem. Most commonly these take the form of visual imagery, but they can also include other somatosensory information (Hackmann, Ehlers, Speckens, & Clark, 2004). Examples of such images include 'feeling like I'm thrown around in the car', 'being rushed down the corridor', 'seeing the gun', 'seeing men in balaclavas', 'the impact and pain', 'sound of glass shattering and screaming', and 'seeing and smelling smoke' (Grey & Holmes, 2008). Despite the importance of intrusions, there has been relatively little detailed scientific investigation of the nature of these images until recently. Previously an assumption was made that the images experienced in PTSD were frightening replays of the original incident. While this is very often true, the images in PTSD are considerably more varied than this and the meanings associated with such images are idiosyncratic. This has implications for addressing such images in therapy and for the overall treatment of PTSD. Frightening replays of events may be associated with physical threat to the self, such as 'I'm going to be paralysed' or 'I'm going to die', but other meanings may also be associated with images, such as 'I'm useless' or 'it's my fault', which may be better conceptualised as a psychological threat to the self (Conway & Pleydell-Pearce, 2000; Ehlers & Clark, 2000). It is on these latter meanings that this chapter and book are focused.

This chapter will draw on recent cognitive formulations of PTSD and phenomenological research to examine the varied nature of spontaneous posttraumatic images in PTSD. It will then describe a clinical typology of such images and categories of psychological threat to the self in images in PTSD. Numerous clinical examples of these are described together with possible therapeutic strategies that can be used to address the associated meanings. The focus is on adult-onset PTSD from a small number of traumatic events rather than on those people who have experienced multiple and prolonged traumatic events in childhood (see Chapter 7 for a discussion of imagery and childhood trauma). Many people who meet criteria for personality disorders may also meet criteria for PTSD.

Theoretical background

Cognitive models of PTSD

There are a number of recent psychological models of PTSD (Brewin, 2003; Brewin, Dalgleish, & Joseph, 1996; Ehlers & Clark, 2000; Foa & Rothbaum, 1998). Each addresses key elements of PTSD including alterations in memory functioning and specific appraisals during and following the traumatic events. Ehlers and Clark's (2000) model (Figure 6.1) offers clear guidelines for therapy and has increasing empirical evidence to support it both from randomised controlled trials (Ehlers *et al.*, 2003; Ehlers, Clark, Hackmann, McManus, & Fennell, 2005) and from dissemination studies (Duffy, Gillespie, & Clark, 2007; Gillespie, Duffy, Hackmann, & Clark, 2002).

Ehlers and Clark (2000) suggested that PTSD becomes persistent when traumatic information is processed in a way that leads to a sense of serious *current* threat. Due to high levels of arousal at the time of the trauma, the trauma memory is poorly elaborated and not well integrated with context such as time, place, and autobiographical memories, and can be unintentionally triggered by a wide range of low-level cues (Conway & Pleydell-Pearce, 2000; Ehlers & Clark, 2000; Ehlers *et al.*, 2009). In particular there is no 'time-code' on the memory that tells the individual that the event occurred in the past. Thus, when the memory intrudes, it feels as if the event is actually happening again to some degree. The persistence of the sense of current threat, and hence PTSD, arises from not only the nature of the trauma memory but also from the negative interpretations of the symptoms experienced (e.g. 'I'm going mad'), the event itself (e.g. 'It's my fault'), and its sequelae (e.g. 'I should have got over it by now'; 'others don't care about me'). Change in these appraisals and in the nature of the trauma memory is prevented by a variety of cognitive and behavioural strategies, such as avoiding thoughts, feelings, places or other reminders of the event, suppression of intrusive

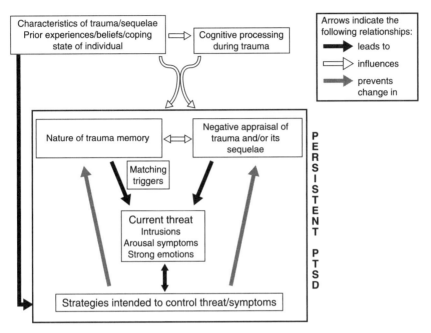

Figure 6.1 Cognitive model of PTSD. From Ehlers, A., and Clark, D. M. (2000), 'A cognitive model of posttraumatic stress', *Behaviour Research and Therapy*, *38*, 319–345. © Elsevier. Reproduced with permission.

memories, rumination about certain aspects of the event or its sequelae, and other avoidant/numbing strategies such as alcohol and drug use (see Figure 6.1).

Psychological threat to the self in PTSD

Foa and Rothbaum (1998) proposed that two basic dysfunctional cognitions mediate the development of PTSD: the world is *completely* dangerous and one's self is *totally* incompetent. Broadly speaking these cognitions map onto ongoing threat, encompassing both physical and psychological threat as conceptualised by Ehlers and Clark (2000). Believing that one is incompetent is a psychological threat to the self. Ehlers and Clark (2000) broaden the concept of psychological threat to include not only beliefs such as 'I am incompetent' but also beliefs such as 'I am unacceptable' and 'I am helpless'. They also include negative appraisals of the traumatic stress symptoms themselves (e.g. 'my reactions mean I am going crazy') and beliefs about the permanent nature of the negative impact of the trauma ('I have permanently changed for the worse') as psychological threats to the self. In related developments, Lee, Scragg, and Turner (2001) outlined clinical models for guilt-based and shame-based PTSD presentations, which also focus on psychological threat to the self, although the authors did not originally describe it in this manner.

In order to better assess and research the role of appraisals following traumatic events, a number of scales have been validated. These include the World Assumptions Scale (WAS; Janoff-Bulman, 1992), which measures perceived self-worth and benevolence of the interpersonal world, and the Personal Beliefs and Reactions Scale (PBRS; Resick & Schnicke, 1993), which was developed for use with people who experienced rape and measures a number of cognitive themes, including beliefs about safety, trust, power, esteem and self-blame. However, the more recently developed Posttraumatic Cognitions Inventory (PTCI; Foa, Ehlers, Clark, Tolin, & Orsillo, 1999) shows better internal consistency and specificity in identifying individuals with and without PTSD in a traumatised sample than either the WAS or the PBRS. The PTCI is a 36-item inventory which factors into three subscales: negative cognitions about the self (e.g. 'I am a weak person', 'I can't rely on myself'), negative cognitions about the world (e.g. 'people can't be trusted', 'I have to be on guard all the time'), and self-blame (e.g. 'the event happened to me because of the way I acted', 'the event happened to me because of the sort of person I am'). Each item is answered on a seven-point scale from 'totally disagree' to 'totally agree'.

A series of studies using the PTCI and other idiosyncratic appraisal measures have provided evidence in support of the importance of the role of cognitive variables in PTSD. Excessively negative appraisals of the traumatic event were related to persistent PTSD in people who had been assaulted (Dunmore, Clark, & Ehlers, 1999). Negative appraisals of initial PTSD symptoms predicted persistent PTSD in people involved in road traffic accidents (Ehlers, Mayou, & Bryant, 1998). Perceived permanent change, a sense of alienation, and 'mental defeat' impeded recovery from rape, physical assault and political imprisonment (Dunmore et al., 1999; Ehlers et al., 1998; Ehlers, Maercker, & Boos, 2000). Other cross-sectional and retrospective studies have similarly shown a relationship between posttraumatic appraisal and PTSD (Clohessy & Ehlers, 1999; Steil & Ehlers, 2000).

More recently prospective studies have investigated the role of appraisals in the development and persistence of PTSD. Negative beliefs about the self and the world were predictive of later PTSD severity in both accident survivors (Ehring, Ehlers, & Glucksman, 2006; O'Donnell, Elliott, Wolfgang, & Creamer, 2007) and assault survivors (Dunmore, Clark, & Ehlers, 2001; Halligan, Michael, Clark, & Ehlers, 2003; Kleim, Ehlers, & Glucksman, 2007). Kleim et al. (2007) found that the most important cognitive factor at two weeks posttrauma in predicting PTSD status six months later in over 200 assault survivors was 'mental defeat'. Mental defeat is 'the perceived loss of all autonomy, a state of giving up in one's own mind all efforts to retain one's identity as a human being with a will of one's own' (p. 45, Ehlers et al., 2000).

Hence it is perhaps a cognitive factor very clearly related to 'psychological threat to the self'.

Intrusive images in PTSD

An image can be defined as 'a mental representation that occurs without the need for external sensory input' (Stopa, Chapter 3, this volume). There is a strong relationship between images and autobiographical memory (Conway, 2005; Conway & Pleydell-Pearce, 2000; Conway, Meares, & Standart, 2004). Mental images may reflect goals that form part of the 'active self' (Conway *et al.*, 2004), where goals are processes that are not usually accessed directly or consciously but through their representations such as images (see also Chapters 1 and 2 for further discussion).

Intrusive trauma memories should be distinguished from other non-memory cognitions that may also be experienced as intrusive (Ehlers, Hackmann, & Michael, 2004). These non-memory intrusions include rumination and dwelling on aspects of the traumatic event ('what could I have done differently?') or its consequences ('I'll never drive/work again'), and also other thoughts and images that involve further cognitive processing or elaboration of the original situation (e.g. images of the self as lonely and sad in the future). Such non-trauma memory intrusions are common in both PTSD and depression (Reynolds & Brewin, 1999).

The characteristics of intrusive memories are very important in accounting for PTSD severity. A recent cross-sectional clinical study investigated intrusive images in PTSD and in traumatised and non-traumatised depressed patients (Birrer, Michael, & Munsch, 2007). Intrusive images of PTSD patients had a more 'here-and-now quality' (also referred to as 'nowness'), and were perceived more visually than those of both depressed groups. There was a lot of similarity concerning other image qualities, including, importantly, distress associated with the images. In addition, Michael, Ehlers, Halligan, and Clark (2005) showed in both a cross-sectional study and a subsequent longitudinal study that PTSD severity at six months was predicted by initial intrusion frequency and distress, lack of context and nowness. Nowness, distress and lack of context predicted 43% variance in PTSD severity compared to 9% that was predicted by intrusion frequency.

The types of images that occur in other psychological disorders may also be present in PTSD, especially given that comorbidity is the rule rather than the exception for people with PTSD. Others chapters in this volume address particular images that may be seen in such disorders. However, people with PTSD additionally have peritraumatic memories and associated intrusive images. This chapter focuses on these PTSD-specific trauma memory images rather than the total range of possible images.

Content of images in PTSD

A distinction may be made between imagery that arises directly from the traumatic event itself (i.e. peritraumatically) and imagery that is associated with later appraisals. These secondary images are those that did not occur at the time of the trauma but are linked to preoccupations/appraisals of the trauma and its sequelae, e.g. violent dreams and images of killing an assailant, or seeing images of the deceased in traumatic bereavement. While traditionally peritraumatic imagery in PTSD is assumed to be a replica reliving of the traumatic event, it is sometimes noted that the images reported by patients do not exactly match their experience. Hence a further clinical distinction may be made between veridical and non-veridical images. Non-veridical images include out-of-body experiences (dissociation), composite images, worst-case scenarios (Merckelbach, Muris, Horselenberg, & Rassin, 1998), and reconstructed images. A clinical typology of spontaneous imagery in PTSD is shown in Table 6.1.

Veridical images

- *Classic flashbacks:* This is the most common imagery seen, in which the person relives what happened to them at the time of the trauma, or very shortly before (Ehlers *et al.*, 2002). These images may have a range of meanings, relating to both physical and psychological threat.
- *Other autobiographical images:* Memories that do not form part of the traumatic memory structure itself can also be associated with psychological threat related to the traumatic event and to PTSD symptoms.

> After a road traffic accident a woman had images of her brother come into her mind together with images of the accident itself. Her brother had had an extensive psychiatric history and had killed himself some years previously. The meaning for her was that she was 'becoming like her brother' and would 'go mad', and possibly kill herself.

Table 6.1 Spontaneous imagery in PTSD

	'Veridical' images	*Non-veridical images*
Peritraumatic	'Classic' flashback	Depersonalisation Composite Worst-case scenario
Secondary	'Normal' autobiographical image	Reconstructed image Specific appraisal as image

Non-veridical images

- *Composite images:* These are images formed from a combination of events, which may share similar sensory features, or share meanings. These can be seen in people who have experienced repeated traumatic events, such as domestic violence, childhood abuse, torture, working in emergency or armed services, and living in a war zone. Particular features of the traumas such as emotions, physiology and meanings/thoughts may overlap and therefore a number of representations in memory may be activated by suitable triggers (and also may be seen where past traumatic memories are activated by a more recent event).

  A man who had experienced repeated episodes of torture while imprisoned had repeated intrusive images of the torturer's face and hearing his voice. This did not come from a single specific memory, but was a composite of his experiences with this torturer. The image of the face was associated with fear and shame, particularly relating to what had happened in the torture and the appraisal that he had been defeated as he gave up information about his political colleagues.

- *Worst-case scenario:* Images of what might be about to happen can occur peritraumatically, or images of what could have happened can occur as a later appraisal.

  A woman was trapped in a burning carriage in a rail crash. While still on the train she had an image of her clothes burnt to her skin and then being on an operating table with medics having to pick off bits of clothes and skin. Even though she experienced no serious physical injuries or burns she continued to experience this image for years after the incident.

- *Depersonalisation:* Images occur in which one sees oneself from outside the self, watching the event from an observer perspective (cf. social phobia, see Chapter 4 in this volume).

  A woman who was raped experienced much of the event by seeing herself from above, in an out-of-body experience. The moment before this dissociation she had the thought that she was 'ruined as a person'. This observer perspective image was one of most distressing symptoms, as it continued to mean for her that she was 'ruined as a person'.

- *'Reconstructed':* Some people report little conscious recollection of the trauma due to psychogenic amnesia, or organic factors such as head injury or alcohol/drug use (including drug-facilitated assaults). However, they may still report some memories relating to the event. These may be fragments of memory that are likely to be veridical flashbacks. Alternatively, some people may encode aspects of traumatic events that are not consciously recalled, and implicit memory processes can lead to physiological reactivity on exposure to internal or external cues that symbolise or resemble an aspect of the event.

> A nightclub doorman was assaulted at work and reported no memory for the event itself, and the hospital records reported a loss of consciousness. He demonstrated increased arousal to situations such as pubs and nightclubs, even from media coverage. He also experienced frightening images of the assault from an observer perspective from reading and hearing the witness reports of the assault.

There may be encoding of events perceived as traumatic after resolution of posttraumatic amnesia.

> A man who had a motorcycle accident had intrusive images of the wreckage of his bike even though he had no memory of the accident itself. On further questioning the 'traumatic event' for him was in fact being shown a photo of this scene in hospital at which point he felt horrified and thought, 'I could have died'.

Other reconstructed images may be best conceptualised as secondary appraisals in which the person may or may not have PTSD.

> A woman whose son had been stabbed to death experienced images of seeing the event even though she was not present. The key part of the image was seeing a hand come viciously down on her son meaning to her that he must have suffered. Strictly speaking she did not meet criteria for PTSD but had a complicated grief reaction and low mood.

Warning signal hypothesis

Ehlers *et al.* (2002) investigated the function of intrusive images in four studies in a sample of over 300 trauma-exposed people who were asked to describe the quality and content of their typical intrusive memories. Visual intrusions were the most common, and comprised 70% to 97% of the intrusions across the studies. There were no consistent differences across the studies in the qualities endorsed by participants with and without PTSD. Ehlers *et al.* (2002) went on to suggest that the intrusive memories often appeared to consist of moments *before* the traumatic event happened, or shortly *before* the moments that had the largest emotional impact. They suggested that these intrusions can be understood as stimuli that had acquired the status of warning signals: stimuli that if encountered again would indicate impending danger, and hence produce a sense of serious *current* threat. Although not explicitly discussed in Ehlers *et al.* (2002), the warning signal could indicate both physical and psychological threat. Ehlers *et al.* (2002) did not provide any data as to the proportion of intrusions that met the warning signal criteria or how the 'worst moments' of the trauma were judged (i.e. by participant or by researcher).

More empirical support for the warning signal hypothesis comes from Hackmann *et al.* (2004). Prior to treatment for chronic PTSD, 22 patients were asked in detail about the quality and content of their intrusions. They had a mean of 2.2 intrusive memories (range 1 to 4). Again visual qualities were the most common (79% across all intrusions) and taste/smell the least common (15%). Most intrusions had at least two sensory qualities. Patients also described their worst moment during the trauma to the interviewer, and were then asked to classify whether the intrusion was about something that happened before, during, or after the worst moment. The most common category of the content of intrusions was a stimulus signalling a moment when the meaning became more traumatic, and the second most common category was a stimulus signalling trauma onset. These results provide support for the warning signal hypothesis most clearly for those stimuli that preceded the onset of the trauma as the time course of events can be unambiguously established. As Hackmann *et al.* (2004) note, it is more difficult to establish temporal relationships unambiguously during the course of the traumatic event, which raises the question as to whether stimuli that signalled a moment when the meaning of the event became more traumatic should also be understood as a warning signal. However, the interviews indicated that even if the intrusions represented the worst moments of the trauma they often appeared to comprise re-experiencing of sensory stimuli that signalled the onset of the moment rather than sensory stimuli from later in the moment.

The emotions and meanings associated with the intrusive images were not reported in either of the above studies, and hence the relative rates of images with physical threat to self and images with psychological threat to self are unknown.

Psychological threat in imagery

Holmes, Grey, and Young (2005) examined the intrusive images and worst moments of the trauma memories ('hotspots') of 32 people with PTSD receiving cognitive-behavioural therapy. For each of the hotspots the clinician also identified the associated emotions and thoughts/meanings. The patients were also asked if any of the intrusive images matched any of the hotspots. The mean number of intrusive images reported was four and mean number of hotspots was six. Seventy-seven per cent of intrusions matched a hotspot. The verbatim emotion words and cognitions used were coded with good inter-rater reliability into broader categories. The most common emotion in the hotspots was fear, but overall only 42% of the emotions in these worst moments were fear, helplessness or horror – the diagnostic emotions of PTSD. For those hotspots that were also intrusive images this rose slightly to 54%. For the cognitions, 21 distinct categories were further grouped into seven overarching themes. Two themes related to direct threat to physical integrity: 'general threat of injury and death' (e.g. 'I will die/be injured') and 'uncertain threat' (e.g. 'what's going to happen?'). Five themes better related to a psychological threat to one's sense of self: 'control and reasoning', 'consequences of trauma', 'abandonment', 'esteem', and 'cognitive avoidance'. The most common themes were 'control and reasoning', 'general threat' and 'uncertain threat'. Overall 36% of the cognitions related to physical threat and 64% to psychological threat to one's sense of self.

Examples of images that corresponded to hotspots associated more with psychological threat to the self than physical threat to the self are given below.

Control and reasoning

This common cognitive theme includes a number of categories.

- *Defeat:* hopelessness, giving up, and images of mental defeat.

  A man had images of his jail cell in which he was tortured. The meaning for him was 'I can't do anything, I wish I was dead' and he felt helpless.

- *Planning:* planning one's own actions during a trauma.

  A man in a rail crash had images of one of the other passengers in pain and asking for help. He had the thought that he should try to help her but could not work out how to get over to her before being led away himself by the emergency services.

- *Interpersonal reasoning:* including trying to work out others' motives or intentions.

  A man had images of the face of the other driver in an accident, and hearing the driver say, 'it's one of those things'. His thought was that 'he doesn't care – I want to kill him'.

  Another man also had images of the other driver in an accident. He thought 'why has he done this to me?' He believed the other driver had deliberately run him off the road as his face was expressionless with shock, but he perceived it as being 'cold like a murderer'.

- *Consequences of trauma*

  A man had images of seeing a gun following an incident in which he was facing two gunmen and thought he was about to be shot.

In addition to the fear of dying he also felt very sad at the time of the incident and when seeing the image of the gun. The meaning for him was that he wouldn't see his son again and see him grow up.

A man had images of sliding towards a bus while on his motor-bike. He had the thought that he was losing everything and that 'life is crap'.

- *Abandonment and isolation*

    A woman had images of lying on a hospital trolley after a road traffic accident. She had the thought 'I'm out of sight and they've forgotten about me', although in fact hospital staff were helping her but were away for a few moments.

    The man who slid on his motorbike towards the bus also had images of lying in the road. He thought that he was 'all alone' and felt scared and detached from the world.

- *Esteem*

    A woman had images of her attacker towering above her after a physical assault. The meaning for her was that she was a bad person for the attack to have happened to her.

    A man had images of sitting tied up after an armed robbery. He thought that he was to blame that the men had got into the shop and felt very guilty about the loss of the money and goods, and the fact that his staff were frightened during the event.

In a further study of 42 people with PTSD at a different outpatient clinic, Grey and Holmes (2008) replicated the results of Holmes *et al.* (2005). People seeking treatment for PTSD almost always have a number of very distressing moments (hotspots) in the trauma memory rather than a single moment. Only about half of the emotions in these worst moments are the 'standard' PTSD emotions of fear, helplessness and horror. Moreover, half the mean-ings associated with these hotspots are related to psychological threat to the self rather than to physical threat. This high level of emotions other than fear is also consistent with a recent study by Speckens, Ehlers, Hackmann, Ruths, and Clark (2007). In a sample of 31 people receiving cognitive therapy for PTSD the emotion most commonly associated with the most prominent intrusive memory was anger. The next most common emotions were 'anxiety', 'helplessness' and 'sadness'.

An individual's report of hotspots may vary depending on the retention interval since trauma (Marshall & Schell, 2002). It may be that soon after the trauma, patients recall and report fear more, and that over time, during which there is further cognitive elaboration of the intrusions, other emotions emerge and become associated with specific moments. Consistent with this suggestion, Speckens *et al.* (2007) reported that the emotions of anger and sadness were reported by patients to be stronger during their intrusive experiences as compared to during the trauma itself. The opposite pattern was observed for anxiety and helplessness.

There are methodological differences between these hotspot studies and the warning signal studies. The hotspot studies were focused mainly on worst moments of the traumatic memory identified during the first reliving as part of treatment, with possible variance in data collection between clinicians. Grey and Holmes (2008) only asked for the main intrusive image. The intrusion studies focused on the qualities of intrusive phenomena themselves in a specific research interview, only asked patients to identify a single worst moment, and did not focus specifically on the meaning of these moments (Hackmann *et al.*, 2004). These studies have clinical implications. As the intrusions themselves may have a particular function as a warning signal of the onset of trauma or the moment when the meaning of the trauma changes for the worst (Ehlers *et al.*, 2002; Hackmann *et al.*, 2004), patients can be educated about this and explanations found for particular triggers of flashbacks and intrusive images. The meanings associated with the worst moments of the trauma memory are not restricted to a threat to one's physical integrity, but are equally likely to be related to a threat to one's sense of self (Grey & Holmes, 2008; Holmes *et al.*, 2005). Hence therapy should also be directed towards addressing these meanings (Ehlers *et al.*, 2009).

Treatment

Cognitive therapy for PTSD

There is compelling evidence that trauma-focused cognitive-behavioural therapy is a highly effective treatment for PTSD (National Institute for Health and Clinical Excellence, 2005). More specifically, the treatment derived from the Ehlers and Clark (2000) cognitive model for PTSD has among the largest effect sizes in the field and has been shown to be effective both in randomised controlled trials (Ehlers *et al.*, 2003, 2005) and in effectiveness studies (Duffy *et al.*, 2007; Gillespie *et al.*, 2002). The main principle of the treatment is to help the individual process the trauma in such a way that it no longer is associated with a sense of serious current threat. This is done in three main ways.

- It reduces re-experiencing by elaboration of the trauma memory and discrimination of triggers, and by integration of the memory within existing autobiographical memory.
- It addresses the negative appraisals of the event and its sequelae.
- It changes the avoidant/numbing strategies that prevent processing of the memory and reassessment of appraisals.

A wide range of both general and PTSD-specific cognitive-behavioural interventions can be used to achieve such changes (Ehlers & Clark, 2000; Ehlers *et al.*, 2005, 2009; Mueller, Hackmann, & Croft, 2004).

Updating trauma memories with imaginal reliving

Imaginal reliving is in essence a method of working with imagery (see Chapter 3). This method has a number of functions, which may be seen as 'processing' the memory. Overall it allows for reconstruction of fragments and elaboration of the memory. Within a cognitive framework it allows access to meanings that are contained within the trauma memory and that may not be ordinarily accessed during more general discussion. Other complementary approaches that are not discussed here include constructing a written narrative, *in vivo* exposure, and working on discrimination of triggers (see Ehlers *et al.*, 2009).

While imaginal reliving is a very successful treatment for PTSD, it is a frightening prospect for people and a clear rationale must be provided. Socratically presented metaphors are useful and can be elaborated to account for the particular circumstances of each client. Two examples are provided below (from Grey, 2007).

> The memory can be compared to a duvet cover that has just been stuffed into a linen cupboard and it keeps making the door pop open. What needs to happen is for you to take out the duvet, fold it up properly, make space for it in the cupboard and then put the duvet back in so that the door doesn't pop open.

> Processing the memory is like it going down a conveyor belt before being stored away with normal memories in a filing cabinet. Those memories in the filing cabinet you have more control over and can bring them out when you want to. At the moment every time the memory comes back onto the conveyor belt, when it pops into your mind, you just push it off not allowing it to be fully processed.

Before starting reliving, the moment that the event started or 'became traumatic' for the client should be ascertained and also when they felt safer again. It may continue to be traumatic during time in hospital or while getting to a place of safety. The person is asked to describe the event from shortly before the agreed start in as realistic a way as possible. They are asked to close their eyes, imagine the events clearly, and talk in the first person and present tense. They are encouraged to provide information on all senses and also on the emotions and thoughts experienced (Foa & Rothbaum, 1998).

During the first reliving it is usually best to allow the patient to describe the whole event without much questioning or interruption, while still being attentive, supportive and encouraging. If people do not give much detail, cue in information with occasional questions such as: *What can you see, hear, and smell? What are you feeling?* They can be helped to remain in the present tense by repeating any statements in the past tense in the present tense: '*I was walking down the street*' to '*so, you* are *walking down the street*'.

During or after the reliving, ratings (0–100%) of distress and vividness of the imagery should be taken as a guide. After the reliving, a number of questions should be asked such as: *How did you find that? How did it compare to what you predicted? Were there any changes or differences to how you remembered it before? Did anything surprising come up? Were you holding back at all? What were the worst moments?* For homework, the person is asked to listen to the tape of the reliving each day if possible, rating the distress each time, and any other information they think is significant (Grey, 2007).

A number of authors have highlighted the need to focus on the moments of highest emotion experienced during the traumatic event, referred to as 'hotspots' (Ehlers & Clark, 2000; Foa & Rothbaum, 1998; Grey, Holmes, & Brewin, 2001; Grey, Young, & Holmes, 2002; Richards & Lovell, 1999). Treatment failures with the use of reliving alone may be a result of not directly addressing peritraumatic appraisals. Equally, cognitive therapy in a non-reliving session is very helpful for posttraumatic negative appraisals, but it is unlikely to affect the emotions and cognitions experienced peritraumatically, as those structures are only accessed during reliving. Thus, there is a need to address the meanings attached to these hotspots explicitly and to use this information to 'update' the traumatic memory during reliving, including the information that the event occurred in the past – providing a 'time-tag' for the memory.

The cognitive restructuring of these hotspots follows the outline given below.

- Initial reliving.
- Identify peritraumatic hotspots during reliving: Ask 'what were the worst moments?' and observe any indicators of affect change and ask about those moments.
- Identify the associated cognitions/meanings (*What was going through your mind at that moment? What does that mean to you?*).
- Outside reliving, discuss these meanings and use cognitive restructuring to address distortions in the appraisals. Such restructuring may be verbal or involve imagery manipulations. This may take some sessions in the case of particular self-evaluations such as 'I'm weak' and 'I'm to blame'.
- Discuss the fact that these new meanings are needed to help update the trauma memory, and rehearse the specific cognitive reappraisals (including imagery manipulations) and at which points during the reliving they will be introduced.
- Begin reliving again, either of the whole event or focusing only on one particular hotspot.

- Ask the client to hold the hotspot vividly in mind and prompt the person to bring the 'new' (and rehearsed) information into their mind in order to update the previous meaning. This can be done either verbally or with an image that conveys the new meaning.

Whether additional cognitive restructuring techniques used within reliving/ exposure procedures increase the effectiveness of treatments, particularly for appraisals linked to psychological threat that may be associated with emotions such as anger, sadness, guilt and shame, should be addressed in future research.

Working with images in PTSD

There are many imagery techniques that can be used within cognitive therapy (Hackmann, 1998; Chapter 3 of this volume). A key maxim is 'accessing the memory [image] is not in itself curative unless the key cognitive distortions are identified and altered' (Edwards, 1990, p. 46). Imagery rescripting has been described as a specific treatment for PTSD, in which the main focus is changing (aspects of) the images experienced (Smucker & Dancu, 1999). Imagery rescripting has also been used with those people whose PTSD symptoms are related to childhood experiences (Arntz & Weertman, 1999). Such rescripting procedures are helpful and broadly consistent with cognitive therapy for PTSD (Ehlers *et al.*, 2009). For those people experiencing high levels of shame, often in the context of longstanding negative self-beliefs, Lee (2005) describes a possible approach to develop compassionate imagery: encouraging warmth to oneself and decreasing self-criticism (see also Chapter 9 by Paul Gilbert).

Detailed assessment of the distressing images is important. First it is important to ascertain whether in fact the images occur in the context of PTSD, and hence represent a disrupted, unprocessed or contextualised trauma memory, or whether they are simply secondary images that represent appraisals within other difficulties. Second, it is important to ask specifically what happened during the traumatic event and whether the images are in fact reliving those events. Furthermore, the therapist should ask whether any images came into the person's mind during the trauma. The images experienced should be matched to moments of the trauma (or very shortly before). If the image is not a veridical replay of the trauma, is the image peritraumatic or a later appraisal or reconstruction? The key questions from a cognitive therapy perspective are: *What are the worst/most distressing parts of the image and what does this image mean to you?* In addition, appraisals concerning the fact that one is having such images should be elicited, i.e. metacognitive beliefs such as 'these images show I am going mad'. It can also be helpful to ask about the person's previous imagery ability or tendency to have mental images. If they have rarely had images before, they may be more likely to appraise their presence negatively now. If they predominantly 'thought in images' before, they may have already developed strategies for 'working with them'.

Imagery may be a more powerful way to update a trauma memory than verbal techniques, as the meanings in PTSD are often stored in imaginal form. The images are fragments of trauma memory that lack the context of one's full autobiographical memory. An aim of treatment is to provide this fuller context to allow changes in meaning and hence facilitate emotional change. This context may develop spontaneously from reliving, as the entire traumatic memory is brought into consciousness, rather than being avoided or suppressed as previously. It allows the person to 'run on past the worst point' rather than 'being stuck' at that worst moment of the image. In addition, this context can be provided from other imagery techniques (Ehlers *et al.*, 2009; Hackmann, 1998; see Chapter 3). For example, if a person feared during the traumatic event that they would never see their children again, they can bring in an image of their children as they are now into their mind at that point of the reliving.

Another use of imagery is to try to gain a new perspective on the event. If someone is inappropriately guilty about what they did or didn't do, it can be helpful for them to run through the event from an observer perspective in imagery, and then be asked whether or not that person could have done anything different, and who is truly responsible? Actions *not* taken can be explored in imagery. For example, a man who thought he should have fought back against his attackers vividly imagined in the session what would have occurred if he had done so. He realised that things would have probably been very much worse for him if the level of violence had escalated. Changing beliefs that imagery is uncontrollable or means one is going mad may be achieved by manipulating the nature of the image. Techniques include asking the patient to imagine the image on a screen and making the image change size or nature.

The overall cognitive therapy approach is an interweaving of discussion, imaginal reliving, and imaginal manipulation in order to address the meanings associated with the images that are experienced. The overall outline is as follows.

- Identify images – most frequent and distressing intrusions.
- Identify meanings – from broadly discussing the images, but also through reliving as other important aspects of the images may then emerge as the trauma memory is more fully accessed.
- Use cognitive restructuring for meaning in a variety of ways through verbal discussion and imagery techniques. Identify how the image may change/has changed in order to reflect a change in meaning.
- Engage in new imagery repeatedly if necessary to reinforce new meanings.

Effect of treatment on intrusive images

There is some research investigating the effects of treatment, including imaginal reliving, on the intrusive images experienced by people with PTSD. Overall, changes in intrusive image frequency, distress, vividness, and 'now-ness' were gradual (Hackmann *et al.*, 2004; Speckens, Ehlers, Hackmann, & Clark, 2006). Poorer outcome was associated with greater initial PTSD sever-ity, greater anger, greater 'nowness' and more negative interpretations of symptoms (Speckens *et al.*, 2006). As the emotions and meanings associated with the intrusive images were not reported, it is unclear whether particular meanings and emotions (say, physical vs. psychological threat) are more or less likely to change over the course of this treatment. In addition these studies were unable to identify specifically the effect of imaginal reliving from other usual treatment techniques such as normalisation and verbal cognitive restructuring.

Case examples of working with images of psychological threat in PTSD

The specific imagery interventions described here are for illustrative purposes rather than being a full account of the treatment strategies necessary in cogni-tive therapy for PTSD (Ehlers *et al.*, 2009). These cases focus on *psychological threat* to self rather than physical threat, although physical threat is also a major part of the treatment of PTSD.

Working with an image associated with isolation and abandonment

Mary had an image of looking out through her car windscreen. She had been in a road traffic accident in which her car had burst a tyre and slid out of control. Initially she thought that she was going to die, and as she came to a halt at the side of the road, she saw another car and could see the driver's face as he just drove past without stopping. She had the thought 'he's just leaving me, no one's helping, I'm all alone'. One of her most prominent PTSD symp-toms was feeling detached from others, even her husband and children who had been very supportive of her.

The image was devoid of the later context, which was that another driver and a pedestrian came to her aid, that an ambulance had taken her to hos-pital for prompt medical care, and that her family had met her very soon after at the hospital. The image was updated by providing the fuller context of her 'abandonment'. Mary relived the accident in imagery and at the moment when she was looking out of the windscreen at the other driver and felt abandoned, she brought into her mind the image of her family attending her bedside. She thus had in her mind the image of both the driver's face and the faces of her family, framed by the windscreen. She then fast-forwarded to the moments when others came to her aid. She reported that these imagery man-oeuvres reduced her feelings of abandonment and isolation, but increased her anger with the behaviour of the other driver. Following this session she car-ried a photo of her family with her, which she looked at if she had the image of the windscreen and driver. This allowed her to better engage with her family at home, and decreased her feelings of detachment. Further interventions addressing the anger towards the other driver were then employed.

Working with an image associated with guilt and self-blame

A 45-year-old man was left tied up after an armed robbery in his jeweller's shop. During the robbery, he and his staff had been threatened and felt afraid. He felt guilty and thought that he was to blame for having let the two men into the shop. He had seen the men outside the shop and thought they 'looked dodgy'. He believed that he should have known that they were going to rob the shop, and should have locked the door and called the police. Through discussion he agreed that he was judging himself with hindsight, but he still felt guilty. He was directed to describe the incident in imagery as if he were an observer above the situation. From this he was better able to see the actions that he, his staff and the robbers took as they unfolded. After this imagery exercise, he was asked whether the man in the image (i.e. himself) had acted sensibly, whether he was to blame, and whether there was anything he could have done to prevent the event. He was also asked whether, from this perspective, he thought that 'the man' (i.e. himself) would have done some-thing to prevent the event if he had been able to do so. Having seen the event from this alternative perspective, he was better able to accept that there was nothing he could have done to prevent the robbery and that he was not to blame.

Working with images associated with shame, including using art

Hannah was a 29-year-old nurse with a two-year-old child. Aged 19, Hannah had been on holiday abroad and had experienced a cannabis-induced psych-osis. This caused her to believe that 'people were out to kill her'. In order to 'maintain her dignity and sense of control', she felt she had no option but to try to kill herself first. She jumped off a very high bridge across a motorway into the path of oncoming traffic. She suffered extensive injuries including multiple fractures and internal damage. As she lay on the road, she believed she was dying. In the hospital emergency room, a hospital porter sexually abused her as she was taken to and from x-rays and other investigations. She made a good physical recovery and had no previous or further history of psychotic episodes.

The intrusive images that Hannah experienced, together with the associ-ated meanings, were: standing at the top of the bridge – 'I'm going to be killed, I must be bad if they want me dead'; lying on road and being put on stretcher – 'it's my fault, I'm a bad person'; sexual abuse at hospital – 'my body responded, which is disgusting and makes me a bad person'; and blood suddenly coming out of her mouth in hospital – 'I'm going to die'. In addition she had posttraumatic appraisals of a similar theme: 'it's my fault, I'm a bad person, I shouldn't have been taking drugs'. She rated her level of shame at 90%.

Following imaginal reliving, Hannah reported that although the imagery was vivid she felt detached from any emotion. This had also been a strategy that she had adopted more generally since the event. If she allowed herself to experience any emotion, it often triggered the intrusive memories of the trauma, and served to reinforce her belief that she was a bad person. Hannah also brought into therapy drawings that she had done very soon after the event in order to cope with the feelings she was experiencing at that time. These drawings illustrated her feelings of shame and guilt, and indicated that she was seeing herself as a bad person. She had not drawn anything related to the sexual abuse, as it was simply too disgusting and shameful.

As she could not access the emotion through imaginal reliving, Hannah was asked to draw the hotspots of her experience and also to draw an overall representation of being a bad person (see Figure 6.2). She brought these to the next session and reported that while drawing, she had experienced the emotions more strongly than in imaginal reliving. She also said that she had felt a little better about the moments of sexual abuse as it became clearer to her that it was not her fault, and that even though her body had responded physically this did not make her a bad person. She rated her overall shame at 70%.

However, these drawings and the associated emotional experience also increased the shame that Hannah felt between sessions. She thought she was 'a failure for being so stupid' and that it was shameful and disgusting that she let herself 'get to that state'. The context of Hannah's drug use was discussed. Hannah reported that she had felt inferior to others at her private school as she was singled out by other pupils for being on a scholarship and teased about various things including her accent. In addition, she had had no contact with her father throughout her childhood as her parents were estranged. She reported feeling his loss keenly. As a teenager she had really enjoyed dance music and clubbing, and during this time she had fallen in love with a man who started using recreational drugs himself and supplied them to Hannah. She greatly enjoyed recreational drug use. The drugs also made her physically thinner, for which she received compliments, which was the first time she could remember being praised. Some time later, a close friend was killed in a road traffic accident. She used drugs to cope with her grief at that time. Two months later she went on an enjoyable holiday, including using recreational drugs. Soon after the holiday her personal relationship broke up and she was feeling low in mood. In order to try to feel better again, she went

Figure 6.2 Hannah's representation of shame felt at the start of therapy.

on holiday with a friend during which she had the psychotic experience. This discussion helped to place the traumatic experiences in context rather than it being an isolated event, as it had seemed when she was purely experiencing the intrusive images and trying to avoid thinking about the circumstances of the trauma. She rated her level of shame at 50% after this discussion.

Following this, the sessions focused on identifying Hannah's qualities and strengths and on how she tries to build her young son's confidence in himself. In order to better emotionally experience the changed meanings, Hannah did a further drawing to attempt to feel compassion for herself generally and at the moment on the bridge (see Figure 6.3; Lee, 2005). She reported that she no longer regarded herself as disgusting and shameful, but as having been unwell at the time. She rated her shame at 10%. At the end of treatment, following further consolidation of these new meanings, she rated her shame

Figure 6.3 Hannah's representation of compassion towards herself at the end of therapy.

at 0% and no longer had intrusive images of the experience. This was maintained at one-year follow-up. This case demonstrates how images can be used and manipulated to enhance change in meanings through the use of drawings rather than imaginal reliving. (See also Chapter 7 for a discussion of the use of drawing in trauma work.)

Working with a composite image associated with feeling weak and helpless

Ann was a 50-year-old woman, who had the repeated image of the face of her abusive ex-husband 'popping into her mind'. She felt afraid and defeated whenever she had this image; she thought that 'I'm weak and helpless', as she had at the time of the assaults; and 'he's still controlling me', as an appraisal of the image itself. He had physically and sexually assaulted her in their home on a large number of occasions. The image was not of any specific incident but was conceptualised as a composite image from the many incidents. The incidents shared the similar features of fear, his face, physical pain, and details of the house in which the assaults occurred. Verbal cognitive restructuring techniques concerning whether she was in fact weak then or now led to only partial improvement. She had moved house, her ex-husband was now in prison, convicted of other offences, and she did not feel at any actual risk from him. Imagery rescripting to help her feel less weak and helpless was attempted (Smucker & Dancu, 1999).

THERAPIST: Can you describe his face to me please?

ANN: He has short dark, but greying, hair, is in his early forties, with a deep tan. He is wearing a gold chain around his neck . . . He is looking right at me.

THERAPIST: Is he saying anything?

ANN: He's saying, 'You'll do what I tell you'.

THERAPIST: Keeping this image in mind, how are you feeling?

ANN: Scared and helpless.

THERAPIST: Scared and helpless. What does this image mean to you?

ANN: I can't do anything to stop him. I'm tiny compared to him. He's still controlling me. I'm just weak and helpless.

THERAPIST: What do you need to do to feel less weak and helpless?

ANN: I have to control his face.

THERAPIST: Try to do that in the image. Do what you need to feel less weak and helpless?

(*Pause*)

THERAPIST: What's happening now?

ANN: There are police coming into the picture to arrest him.

THERAPIST: Aha . . . and now . . .

ANN: He's talking to the police. They are going away again. It's just like it always happened.

THERAPIST: OK. Keep the image of his face in mind; remember it's just an image. You can do what you like to it. What do you need to happen to feel stronger and in control?

ANN: I've turned his face into a jack-in-the-box. He's a face on a spring (*lighter tone in voice*).

THERAPIST: A jack-in-the-box . . . er . . . what do you need now?

ANN: I need to close the box on his face.

THERAPIST: OK. Try to do that in the image.

ANN: . . . I'm pushing him down in the box . . . but he pops up again. I'm pushing him down again . . . but he pops up again . . . (*plaintively*) I'll never get rid of him.

THERAPIST: So, he pops up again. Try to change the image again to feel stronger and in control.

ANN: I'm cutting his spring.

THERAPIST: Cutting his spring . . .

ANN: He's bouncing around and is much smaller now.

THERAPIST: What do you want to happen now?

ANN: I'm chasing him down the street . . . Now an ice cream van comes round the corner and runs him over (*laughs*).

THERAPIST: OK, so an ice cream van runs him over. Keeping this in mind, how are you feeling now?

ANN: OK (*laughs*).

THERAPIST: How weak and helpless are you in reality now?

ANN: Not at all. It's just his face. I don't have to let him control me.

THERAPIST: Well done. Just focus on these feelings for a few moments more and what they mean.

The imagery that she employed to indicate a sense of strength and control over the image came as surprise to both her and the therapist. When asked about the significance of the ice cream van, she explained that on a number of occasions she was raped in the kitchen and she can remember hearing an ice cream van outside, as it was where it would stop in the summer on her estate. When she had the image of the face after this session, she brought to mind the ice cream van, which came to mean to her that she had survived, was safe, and was not weak or helpless. This case indicates how unexpected changes in imagery can have a powerful effect on meanings and that these changes cannot always be predicted or discussed in advance.

Working with images in recurrent nightmares

Sam was a Sierra Leonean asylum seeker in his early 20s and had experienced a number of traumatic events including witnessing family members being killed. His most distressing symptom was recurrent nightmares in which he was chased. These were not reliving nightmares but were clearly similar and were related to his actual experiences. The meaning of these nightmares for him was that he was 'going mad' and that he was 'weak'. There is evidence that rescripting the nightmares in imagery can cause a reduction in their frequency and severity (Krakow *et al.*, 2001).

THERAPIST: Which is the most common nightmare?

SAM: The machete one.

THERAPIST: The machete one. I'd like to go through that one again and for you to describe what you can see and what you can hear but also what you're feeling. And, as we go through it, to replay and put a new ending on it. For instance, at the worst moment they put the knife down and walk away so you have control over that image in your mind. Does that make sense?

SAM: Yes.

THERAPIST: OK. So if you could close your eyes and take yourself into that moment and describe what you can see, what you can hear and what you are feeling.

(*Pause*)

SAM: I can see them coming round. I don't know where they are coming from.

THERAPIST: What can you see right now?

SAM: I see myself and I see them. There were eight of them.

THERAPIST: Aha so there are eight of them.

SAM: Some of them have got a stick.

THERAPIST: Some of them have got a stick.

SAM: I . . . I was trying to hide [from] them. They are looking for me.

THERAPIST: What can you hear?

SAM: There is something they have that is making noise. On their body that is making noise.

THERAPIST: On their body that is making noise.

SAM: Like voodoo.

THERAPIST: As you see this how does this make you feel emotionally?

SAM: I'm scared.

THERAPIST: You're scared. What happens now?

SAM: I was trying to end it in a good way.

THERAPIST: What do you want to happen now?

SAM: For them not to be able to find me.

THERAPIST: Can you describe to me how that would happen?

SAM: . . . when they are searching I will try to be in the corner. They can't search there.

THERAPIST: In the corner of where?

SAM: In the corner of the shed. There is a shed down there. At the bottom, the back of the shed there is like a forest. And they are calling [to] themselves 'C'mon, we can't find him, let's go'.

THERAPIST: What do you see now?

SAM: They are going but one is still searching. He is going with them. He is going with them.

THERAPIST: He is going with them. What can you see now?

SAM: They've gone but I can still hear the voices.

THERAPIST: Still hear the voices.

(*Pause*)

THERAPIST: What's happening now?

SAM: I'm by myself.

THERAPIST: You're by yourself. And how do you feel emotionally at this moment by yourself?

SAM: I just don't want this to happen to me anymore.

THERAPIST: Don't want it to happen to you anymore . . . Have they gone now?

SAM: Yes, I can't hear them anymore.

THERAPIST: Can't hear them anymore. Do you feel safe right now?

SAM: Yes.

THERAPIST: I want you to focus in on this feeling of safety. I want you to keep your eyes closed for a few moments more. You've done really well. I want you to tune into this sense of safety and also the fact that you are here now in London and you have the car [small toy car as grounding object; Kennerley, 1996] as a reminder of that as well. These people who did bad things to you in the past can't get you now, can't get you here. This is a safe place. This is something you can remind yourself of. How are you feeling right now?

SAM: I'm feeling I'm safe.

THERAPIST: You're feeling you're safe. OK. I want you just to open your eyes and become aware of the room around you. So when you want to . . .
(*Opens eyes*)

THERAPIST: Well done. How was that?

SAM: I can't . . . I can't believe they just went back like that.

THERAPIST: So it's hard to believe that in those images they turned back. What do you make of the fact that in that imagery there they did turn back, that you could turn them back?

SAM: What did I make . . .??

THERAPIST: I was just wondering . . . what you make of that . . . what you've learned from that?

SAM: I'm just going to make them go back. I don't have to be scared no more.

THERAPIST: After today's session what should you do? How can you take this forward?

SAM: I will listen to the tape.

THERAPIST: Anything else you can do alongside that as well?

SAM: I'll have the car with me to remind me.

THERAPIST: So you'll have the car with you as well. That makes sense. I've been struck by how hard you've been working there, and impressed by how much you've put into it. I guess what I'm also thinking is that it will need more hard work from you between the sessions. If memories come into your mind you can change these images as you've done here. Do it during the daytime and it will help at night to get control over the dreams.

Following this there was a gradual reduction in the frequency and intensity of the dreams. Importantly, Sam did not think he was going mad for having such dreams and felt less weak as he was now seeing gradual improvements.

Summary

Intrusive images are the hallmark symptom of people with PTSD. However, the presence of images does not mean that the person necessarily meets criteria for PTSD. The images in PTSD are most commonly visual in nature. They may be exact replays of the events experienced or may be altered in a variety of ways that reflect meanings associated with the traumatic events. There is evidence that such images may function as a warning signal of the onset of trauma or when the meaning of the trauma changes for the worse.

There is extensive evidence that negative appraisals play an important role in the prediction and maintenance of PTSD symptoms. In particular, negative appraisals about the self, including the concept of 'mental defeat', are most strongly predictive. Although not well assessed by current measures, these appraisals are also encapsulated in the form of images. There is evidence that in the worst moments of traumatic memories (hotspots) over half of the associated meanings are related to psychological threat to the self rather than physical threat to the self.

Cognitive therapy for PTSD focuses on reducing the sense of current threat experienced by people. This concept of threat encompasses both psychological and physical threat. One of the main therapeutic aims is to update and better contextualise the traumatic memories (images). The key technique in this is imaginal reliving. In order to address the meanings associated with psychological threat, further cognitive techniques to update the memory within reliving may be beneficial. Whether such updating adds to existing treatments either through verbal restructuring or through imagery remains an open question at present. However, when meanings are encapsulated in imagery form, interventions are perhaps more easily attempted in the same modality. Direct imagery manipulations can give rise to new meanings or new meanings can be established in verbal discussion, which can then be reflected and experienced better emotionally through changed imagery.

Future research in this area may continue to examine factors such as why certain images intrude, the meanings associated with such images, and the relative effectiveness of different treatment strategies. In particular, there has been no research investigating the links between pre-trauma beliefs, peritraumatic meanings, and later appraisals and imagery in PTSD.

References

American Psychiatric Association (1994). *Diagnostic and statistical manual of mental disorders* (4th ed.). Washington, DC: APA.

Arntz, A., & Weertman, A. (1999). Treatment of childhood memories: Theory and practice. *Behaviour Research and Therapy, 37*, 715–740.

Birrer, E., Michael, T., & Munsch, S. (2007). Intrusive images in PTSD and in traumatised and non-traumatised depressed patients: A cross-sectional clinical study. *Behaviour Research and Therapy, 45*, 2053–2065.

Brewin, C.R. (2003). *Post-traumatic stress disorder: Malady or myth?* London: Yale University Press.

Brewin, C.R., Dalgleish, T., & Joseph, S. (1996). A dual representation theory of posttraumatic stress disorder. *Psychological Review, 103*, 670–686.

Clohessy, S., & Ehlers, A. (1999). PTSD symptoms, response to intrusive memories and coping in ambulance service workers. *British Journal of Clinical Psychology, 38*, 251–265.

Conway, M.A. (2005). Memory and the self. *Journal of Memory and Language, 53*, 594–628.

Conway, M.A., Meares, K., & Standart, S. (2004). Images and goals. *Memory, 12*, 525–531.

Conway, M.A., & Pleydell-Pearce, C.W. (2000). The construction of autobiographical memories in the self-memory system. *Psychological Review, 107*, 261–288.

Duffy, M., Gillespie, K., & Clark, D.M. (2007). Post-traumatic stress disorder in the context of terrorism and other civil conflict in Northern Ireland: Randomised controlled trial. *British Medical Journal, 334*, 1147–1150.

Dunmore, E., Clark, D.M., & Ehlers, A. (1999). Cognitive factors involved in the onset and maintenance of posttraumatic stress disorder (PTSD) after physical or sexual assault. *Behaviour Research and Therapy, 37*, 809–829.

Dunmore, E., Clark, D.M., & Ehlers, A. (2001). A prospective investigation of the role of cognitive factors in persistent posttraumatic stress disorder (PTSD) after physical or sexual assault. *Behaviour Research and Therapy, 39*, 1063–1084.

Edwards, D.J.A. (1990). Cognitive therapy and restructuring of early memories through guided imagery. *Journal of Cognitive Psychotherapy, 4*, 33–50.

Ehlers, A., & Clark, D.M. (2000). A cognitive model of posttraumatic stress disorder. *Behaviour Research and Therapy, 38*, 319–345.

Ehlers, A, Clark, D.M., Dunmore, E., Jaycox, L., Meadows, E., & Foa, E.B. (1998a). Predicting response to exposure treatment in PTSD: The role of mental defeat and alienation. *Journal of Traumatic Stress, 11*, 457–471.

Ehlers, A., Clark, D.M., Hackmann, A., McManus, F., & Fennell, M. (2005). Cognitive therapy for PTSD: Development and evaluation. *Behaviour Research and Therapy, 43*, 413–431.

Ehlers, A., Clark, D.M., Hackmann, A., McManus, F., Fennell, M., & Grey, N. (2009). *Cognitive Therapy for PTSD: A therapist's guide.* Manuscript in preparation.

Ehlers, A., Clark, D.M., Hackmann, A., McManus, F., Fennell, M., Herbert, C., & Mayou, R. (2003). A randomised controlled trial of cognitive therapy, self-help booklet, and repeated early assessment as early interventions for PTSD. *Archives of General Psychiatry, 60*, 1024–1032.

Ehlers, A., Hackmann, A., & Michael, T. (2004). Intrusive re-experiencing in posttraumatic stress disorder: Phenomenology, theory and therapy. *Memory, 12*, 403–415.

Ehlers, A., Hackmann, A., Steil, R., Clohessy, S., Wenninger, K., & Winter, H. (2002). The nature of intrusive memories after trauma: The warning signal hypothesis. *Behaviour Research and Therapy, 40*, 1021–1028.

Ehlers, A., Maercker, A., & Boos, A. (2000). Cognitive factors in chronic PTSD after political imprisonment: The role of mental defeat, alienation, and permanent change. *Journal of Abnormal Psychology, 109*, 45–55.

Ehlers, A., Mayou, R.A., & Bryant, B. (1998b). Psychological predictors of chronic posttraumatic stress disorder after motor vehicle accidents. *Journal of Abnormal Psychology, 107*, 508–519.

Ehring, T., Ehlers, A., & Glucksman, E. (2006). Contribution of cognitive factors to the prediction of post-traumatic stress disorder, phobia and depression after motor vehicle accidents. *Behaviour Research and Therapy, 44*, 1699–1716.

Foa, E.B., Ehlers, A., Clark, D.M., Tolin, D.F., & Orsillo, S.M. (1999). The Posttraumatic Cognitions Inventory (PTCI): Development and validation. *Psychological Assessment, 11*, 303–314.

Foa, E.B., & Rothbaum, B.O. (1998). *Treating the trauma of rape: Cognitive behavioural therapy for PTSD*. New York: Guilford Press.

Gillespie, K., Duffy, M., Hackmann, A., & Clark, D.M. (2002). Community based cognitive therapy in the treatment of post-traumatic stress disorder following the Omagh bomb. *Behaviour Research and Therapy, 40*, 345–357.

Grey, N. (2007). Posttraumatic stress disorder: Treatment. In S. Lindsay & G. Powell (Eds.), *Handbook of clinical adult psychology* (3rd ed, pp. 185–205). Hove, UK: Brunner-Routledge.

Grey, N., & Holmes, E. (2008). Hotspots in trauma memories in the treatment of posttraumatic stress disorder: A replication. *Memory, 16*, 788–796.

Grey, N., Holmes, E., & Brewin, C. (2001). Peritraumatic emotional 'hotspots' in memory. *Behavioural and Cognitive Psychotherapy, 29*, 367–372.

Grey, N., Young, K., & Holmes, E. (2002). Cognitive restructuring within reliving: A treatment for peritraumatic emotional hotspots in PTSD. *Behavioural and Cognitive Psychotherapy, 30*, 63–82.

Hackmann, A. (1998). Working with images in clinical psychology. In A.S. Bellack & M. Herson (Eds.), *Comprehensive clinical psychology* (Vol. 6, pp. 301–318). Oxford: Elsevier.

Hackmann, A., Ehlers, A., Speckens, A., & Clark, D.M. (2004). Characteristics and content of intrusive memories in PTSD and their changes with treatment. *Journal of Traumatic Stress, 17*, 211–240.

Halligan, S.L., Michael, T., Clark, D.M., & Ehlers, A. (2003). Posttraumatic stress disorder following assault: The role of cognitive processing, trauma memory and appraisals. *Journal of Consulting and Clinical Psychology, 71*, 419–431.

Holmes, E.A., Grey, N., & Young, K.A.D. (2005). Intrusive images and 'hotspots' of trauma memories in posttraumatic stress disorder: An exploratory investigation of emotions and cognitive themes. *Journal of Behavior Therapy and Experimental Psychiatry, 36*(1), 3–17.

Janoff-Bulman, R. (1992). *Shattered assumptions: Towards a new psychology of trauma*. New York: Free Press.

Kennerley, H. (1996). Cognitive therapy of dissociative symptoms associated with trauma. *British Journal of Clinical Psychology, 35*, 325–340.

Kleim, B., Ehlers, A., & Glucksman, E. (2007). Early predictors of chronic posttraumatic stress disorder in assault survivors. *Psychological Medicine, 37*, 1457–1467.

Krakow, B., Hollifield, M., Johnson, L., Kross, M., Schrader, R., Warner, T.D., *et al.* (2001). Imagery rehearsal therapy for chronic nightmares in sexual assault survivors with chronic posttraumatic stress disorder: A randomized controlled trial. *Journal of the American Medical Association, 286*, 537–545.

Lee, D. (2005). The perfect nurturer: A model to develop a compassionate mind within the context of cognitive therapy. In P. Gilbert (Ed.), *Compassion: Conceptualisations, research and use in psychotherapy* (pp. 326–351). Hove, UK: Routledge.

Lee, D., Scragg, P., & Turner, S. (2001). The role of shame and guilt in traumatic events. A clinical model of shame-based and guilt-based PTSD. *British Journal of Medical Psychology*, *74*, 451–466.

Marshall, G.N., & Schell, T.L. (2002). Reappraising the link between peritraumatic dissociation and PTSD symptom severity: Evidence from a longitudinal study of community violence survivors. *Journal of Abnormal Psychology*, *111*, 626–636.

Merckelbach, H., Muris, P., Horselenberg, R., & Rassin, E. (1998). Traumatic intrusions as 'worst-case scenarios'. *Behaviour Research and Therapy*, *36*, 1075–1079.

Michael, T., Ehlers, A., Halligan, S., & Clark, D.M. (2005). Unwanted memories of assault: What intrusion characteristics are associated with PTSD? *Behaviour Research and Therapy*, *43*, 613–628.

Mueller, M., Hackmann, A., & Croft, A. (2004). Posttraumatic stress disorder. In J. Bennett-Levy, G. Butler, A. Hackmann, M. Fennell, M. Mueller, & D. Westbrook (Eds.), *Oxford guide to behavioural experiments in cognitive therapy* (pp. 183–204). Oxford, UK: Oxford University Press.

National Institute for Health and Clinical Excellence (NICE) (2005). *Post-traumatic stress disorder: The management of PTSD in adults and children in primary and secondary care*. London: Gaskell and the British Psychological Society.

O'Donnell, M.L., Elliott, P., Wolfgang, B.J., & Creamer, M. (2007). Posttraumatic appraisals in the development and persistence of posttraumatic stress symptoms. *Journal of Traumatic Stress*, *20*, 173–182.

Resick, P.A., & Schnicke, M.K. (1993). *Cognitive processing therapy for rape victims: A treatment manual*. Newbury Park: Sage.

Reynolds, M., & Brewin, C.R. (1999). Intrusive memories in depression and posttraumatic stress disorder. *Behaviour Research and Therapy*, *37*, 201–215.

Richards, D., & Lovell, K. (1999). Behavioural and cognitive behavioural interventions in the treatment of PTSD. In W. Yule (Ed.), *Post-traumatic stress disorders: Concepts and therapy* (pp. 239–266). Chichester, UK: Wiley.

Smucker, M., & Dancu, C. (1999). *Cognitive behavioural treatment for adult survivors of childhood trauma: Rescripting and reprocessing*. Northvale, NJ: Jason Aronson.

Speckens, A.E.M., Ehlers, A., Hackmann, A., & Clark, D.M. (2006). Changes in intrusive memories associated with imaginal reliving in posttraumatic stress disorder. *Journal of Anxiety Disorders*, *20*, 328–341.

Speckens, A.E.M., Ehlers, A., Hackmann, A., Ruths, F.A., & Clark, D.M. (2007). Intrusive memories and rumination in patients with posttraumatic stress disorder: A phenomenological comparison. *Memory*, *15*, 249–257.

Steil, R., & Ehlers, A. (2000). Dysfunctional meaning of posttraumatic intrusions in chronic PTSD. *Behaviour Research and Therapy*, *38*, 537–558.

Chapter 7

Imagery and the self following childhood trauma

Observations concerning the use of drawings and external images

Gillian Butler and Emily A. Holmes

Clinical observations and challenges for CBT

The ideas in this chapter are drawn from clinical work with a series of people who were emotionally, physically and/or sexually abused during childhood and who also have a dysfunctional sense of self as adults. These people say such things as 'I don't know who I am', 'I'm a non-person', 'I don't exist', 'When I look inside there's no one there', 'There's no real me', 'I'm just an object'. The precise meaning of statements such as these is often not taken seriously or explored by cognitive therapists, possibly because it is quite clear that the person speaking knows that they exist, otherwise their suffering would not have brought them to treatment, and possibly also because existence is quite a difficult thing to talk clearly about.

In addition, more careful observation reveals that many of the people who say things like this also have serious practical difficulties during cognitive therapy. For example, they often find Socratic questions extremely hard to answer. When asked to provide a specific example of a problem or difficulty patients may be unable to do this, or they become entangled in the subjectivity of their experience, and cannot step back from describing what has (just) happened in order to think about it. Reference to the past, or associations to it, may trigger detachment or dissociation. Searching for alternative points of view during discussion is either impossible, as if this person had no access to, or experience of, other points of view, or it can become a purely theoretical, intellectual exercise. If you don't know who you are then maybe it is not surprising that you appear not to know what you think, or think different things at different times, or cannot easily develop new ways of thinking. Without a functioning sense of self it is as if there is no consistent framework or pool of resources to provide a clear cognitive basis for the work of cognitive therapy.

One solution: Working with meaning

We would like to suggest that cognitive-behaviour therapists will be better able to solve these problems if they develop the ways in which they think about and work with 'meanings'. In simple terms cognitive therapy involves identifying someone's thoughts; using a variety of techniques to re-examine those thoughts; searching for and developing alternative perspectives; and encouraging people to try out, or experiment with, ways of behaving that provide a reality base for new perspectives. Bringing all the elements together, in theory and in practice, helps people to feel better. The whole endeavour is based on understanding what thoughts mean: on trying to see things through someone else's eyes, or one's own eyes at another time point. Of course doing this, from both the therapist's and the patient's point of view, is always more complex than it sounds. One reason for this is that it involves working to make sense of how someone understands and interprets their experiences: what something means to them.

What is 'meaning'?

If cognitive therapists are concerned with understanding and helping to change meanings then it is important to define what they mean by 'meaning'. Often cognitive therapists ask their patients questions about meaning such as: 'What does that mean to you?' or 'What do you mean by that?'. One reason for the blank response that often follows is that the questions fail to distinguish between different aspects of meaning.

First, meaning can be about what is being referred to. Which event or episode or experience does the person have in mind? Are they referring to their history of neglect? To the despair that this engendered? Or to something else? Second, meaning can be about the significance of events, or experiences. 'What happened to me only happened because I was bad, and deserved nothing better.' 'It meant that I could never be like other people.' Third, meaning can be about the impact of what happened, for instance when being abused prevents a woman developing trusting relationships of any kind with men, or when shame destroys the sense of self-worth. Or when a person engages in risky behaviours without caring whether he lives or dies. Fourth, meaning can refer to the implications of what happened: 'Because of what happened I will never be able to enjoy sexual relations, or feel I have a right to exist'. 'Their behaviour took away my rights; I have no rights.' The fifth aspect of meaning is a more dynamic concept, and reflects the purpose or intention of the speaker: what they are doing when communicating, for instance with their therapist. They may be trying to test out the therapist's reactions, or to find out if they will be believed, or they may be avoiding touching on topics that might trigger too much distress or a dissociative episode. They may be seeking comfort, or affirmation, or finding out just how much their listener can be trusted.

Meaning is not just one thing, and representing meaning is therefore a complex business – especially for people who have not regularly been treated with respect nor learned to communicate openly with others. It is hardly surprising that patients find this difficult and as therapists we may have failed to pay sufficient attention to the persistence with which our patients continue to try to explain what they really mean, and to the creativity with which they solve this problem. Many people bring verbal and non-verbal material with them to therapy to contribute to the process of conveying information about themselves to their therapist. They may bring poetry, pictures, drawings, music or artifacts. They may use metaphor and analogy, or tell stories. A patient who found it difficult to talk about the neglectful and inappropriate parenting to which she was subjected recounted early in therapy a story that she had invented, as the oldest child in her family, to help her brothers and sisters through mealtimes, when they would all be subjected to torrents of criticism and ridicule. These actions affirm that meaning has many dimensions and is often complex, ambiguous and confusing. Representing meaning visually (or metaphorically) may enable people to capture diverse aspects of meaning in one place. It is not as if there is a clear meaning that the person is aware of and trying to convey to someone else, but rather as if the act of expression, the encouragement to try to explain, and the listener's full attention contribute to the discovery, or crystallisation, of (multiple) aspects of meaning.

Confusions in meaning

Confusion in terms of meaning (or failure to distinguish its multiple aspects) makes therapeutic work especially complex. We suggest that meanings can be particularly confusing and at times difficult to elucidate when the themes in therapy are, for example, linked to painful experiences in childhood, and when the child who seeks help as an adult suffered from neglect or abuse from an early age. There are many experiences we find relatively easy to describe, such as what we just did, or an interesting thing that happened last week. However, it can be hard for anyone to explain in words what their experiences meant to them when many such experiences took place over a long period of time (a general category of events rather than specific, separate events). For example, to convey to someone else what it was like to be a child in their family can be quite difficult to capture so it feels truthful. When negative childhood experiences have interfered with the normal development of a sense of self (among other things), this can be even harder. There are many reasons why clear meaning may be difficult to extract from aversive childhood/teenage life periods. We will focus here on just a few of the many possible strands in the literature, selecting those that link to the aim of the current chapter to explore imagery and the self. The links between the attempt to express and explore meanings that are hard to express, and inherently abstract, and the use of imagery are the main starting point for the ideas discussed in this chapter.

Autobiographical memory and meaning for self

The first two strands derive from (non-clinical) research on autobiographical memory. First, knowledge about the self in terms of general events (auto-biography) predominantly takes the form of generic visual images rather than verbal narratives, i.e. images derived from repeated experiences (Brewer, 1996; Conway, 1996, 2001; Rubin & Greenberg, 1998). Thus we may need to access images and not just verbal descriptions when discussing an extended period of time or repeated events with a client. Second, when adults are asked to recall self memories, regardless of how old they are when asked this question, they produce considerably more memories from the time period age 10–30 (mostly between the ages of 15 and 25) than from other times in their life. This time period is known as the 'reminiscence bump' (Conway & Holmes, 2005; Conway & Rubin, 1993; Rubin, 2002). The episodic memories recalled are by definition in the form of episodes encapsulated in clear mental images, and this batch of images is thought to be self-defining for adults. It has been proposed that, because they are self-defining experiences (e.g. a specific interaction with a teacher leading to development of long-term career goals; Pillemer, Picariello, Law, & Reichman, 1996), memories from the reminiscence bump retain enduring links to the sense of self (Conway & Pleydell-Pearce, 2000; Singer & Salovey, 1993). Such images may play a crucial role in the formation of a stable self system during late adolescence and early adulthood. This suggests that images from this period help to define identity and, because of this, they endure in memory in a highly accessible form (Conway & Holmes, 2005).

However, if the reminiscence bump were flattened or missing, and people were lacking specific image-based memories of this critical time period, what would this mean in terms of meaning for self? If we define ourselves through images of our experiences, then an absence of such image-based memories might lead to a 'hard-to-describe' sense of self. Further, it might be hard to identify meanings linked to these critical time periods. Perhaps this leads to just the sort of expressions we were confronted with at the beginning of this chapter, such as 'I don't know who I am', 'I'm a non-person', 'I don't exist'. We speculate that in order to capture (or recapture) meaning about self, or meaning about time periods crucial to the development of self, it may be particularly important to use images (rather than just words). So it may not be surprising that many of the patients described earlier have spontaneously used drawings, and other non-verbal methods, when communicating about their experiences – when asked, in various ways, about the meaning to them of these experiences.

How do we communicate about complex and abstract meanings? How do we represent them to ourselves, even? Increasing emphasis has recently been given to the roles played in this process by imagery, suggesting that it has a particularly powerful impact on emotion compared to verbal processing of the same material (Holmes & Mathews, 2005; Holmes, Mathews, Dalgleish, & Mackintosh, 2006). Recent work in cognitive therapy has pointed to the clinical value of learning to work with imagery: identifying it, reflecting upon its effects and its meaning so as to develop more complete formulations, and working to change it (for instance, through imagery rescripting; Arntz & Weertman, 1999; Holmes & Hackmann, 2004). Here we will focus on describing the different things that may be happening when people turn to imagery in order to explain themselves better when meaning is hard to convey.

Optical illusions: The need to externalise

A useful starting point has been provided in an experiment on the perceptual illusion in which an outline drawing can be seen as either a duck or a rabbit. As with other well-known illusions (the vase/silhouette; the young lady/old lady; the Necker cube), we know that people can switch between seeing the image one way or another. Analysing the processes involved in switching shows that the ability to do this depends on being able to externalise the image. People find it extremely hard to see the image another way in their 'mind's eye', without any external clues (i.e. to reframe meaning). It is as if the perceptual information has to be placed on a (metaphorical) external drawing board before it can be worked with (Chambers & Reisberg, 1985). This immediately suggests that when patients bring pictures or drawing to therapy they may, in addition to trying to explain themselves well, or to represent what something means to them (in one or many ways), be providing themselves with an external working space. The picture or drawing may become another tool for use in therapy, and therapists then need to think carefully about how they receive or work with such images, and about how they can use them to help people change. In essence we have limited working memory capacity (Baddeley, 1986): Our minds can only do so much of anything at one time. Once one has seen a duck, changing in one's mind's eye so as to be able to see a rabbit is nigh impossible (and vice versa). However, drawing the rabbit on a piece of paper allows you to look at it afresh so as to 'see' it – i.e. interpret its meaning – as being a duck (and vice versa). When we are just 'thinking about them', images cannot easily be seen from other angles or shifted. Externalising them can allow us to check out an alternative interpretation: Putting something 'out there' allows us to reflect on and talk about it. Therefore, it is also possible for us to be stuck with our interpretations of complex autobiographical mental images.

An example may help to illustrate this point. When a patient spoke early in therapy about all the terrible things that had happened to her, she started to make sense of her subsequent self-destructive and destabilising patterns of behaviour. Subsequently she drew a picture in which words for some of these experiences (abuse, poverty, filth, molestation, rape, neglect, violence, pornography – and many more) were buried in the ground from which some grass and trees were beginning to grow. Each growth point, still brown and leafless but embedded in green grass, was given the name of one of the constructive or positive sources of change that she had been able to find, both within therapy and outside of it. She entitled the picture: 'Shit makes good manure'. Externalising the image in a drawing seems to have allowed a reinterpretation through the combined use of verbal labels and the illustration of various 'growth points', so as to arrive at the picture's title.

In terms of episodic memory, we remember distinct moments in the form of images (although we usually communicate about them only in words). Following a trauma history there can, however, be a tendency to report general (or overgeneral) rather than specific memories, perhaps due to avoidance of specific trauma memories. One possibility is that when our memory is 'overgeneral' (Williams *et al.*, 2007), this is exactly when it is most difficult to come up with, or to use, imagery. It may also be important to do so in order to create a clearer or more elaborated sense of meaning.

Overgeneral memory has been linked to depression (Williams & Broadbent, 1986; Williams *et al.*, 2007), and could also result from the avoidance or dissociation that follows a history of traumatic experiences. It may also be linked to the salience, or discriminability, of events. In her account of the story of Mary Bell, who murdered two young boys when she was only 11, Sereny (1998) described Mary's memories (collected during extensive interviews with Mary as an adult) of the details of different times in her life. Mary reports specific memories of her early experience of neglect and abuse and specific memories of the murders. She reports overgeneral, non-specific memories of a long period of time in prison as an adult. For example, she was unable to link events, such as short-term friendships or unusually disruptive prison events, to any specific date. The explanation given by Sereny is not that Mary was depressed (which is possible, but for which there is no clear evidence) but rather that the daily, unvarying routine of prison life provided an indiscriminable environment. The point is that when someone says 'nothing happened', this may mean that nothing unusual to them happened.

With these ideas in mind, the rest of this chapter will be divided into two parts. In the first part we will describe some of the many functions of imagery, as observed in drawings collected by GB during therapy. In the second part we will think about the part played by the recipient of an image in developing an understanding of its meaning, and in furthering the various aims of therapy. This structure allows us to speculate on ways of using imagery to help people in the development of a more functional sense of self.

Some of the many functions of imagery

In this section we systematise our thinking about the use of drawings (and a few other types of imagery) by patients during therapy. Most of the examples described were provided by patients spontaneously, without any suggestion being made to them that they might find it useful to express themselves, or to represent the various meanings of their experiences using imagery. The context within which this appears to happen most readily is one in which the therapist attempts to explore the various aspects of meaning with the patient, and acknowledges that this is not always a straightforward or simple task. The images in some sense all serve the function of communication, but they appear to do so in different ways, and this is not their only function. Many of the pictures received included written words as well as images.

Enabling someone to talk about a traumatic experience

In the following examples, from early stages of therapy, the image provided by the patients appeared to help in referring to and describing, sometimes metaphorically, their experiences and their feelings about them. One patient drew a picture of a flood in which a stick figure was struggling. Another drew herself hiding in a cave that opened high up on a cliff face. In this picture she appeared three times: in the cave, hanging from the cliff face by her fingernails, and engulfed by flames as she fell. Another person described herself as stuck in a bramble bush so dense that to open her eyes would be to risk having her eyes pierced by thorns. A number of people represented themselves as 'blobs', or amorphous limbless shapes, with no clear definition. Describing herself as a jelly seems to be a verbal representation of a similar image.

These images appear to serve the externalising function mentioned at the start of this chapter, so that 'meanings' can be shared, explored, reflected on, and so on. A more elaborate, and symbolic, version of this was provided in a picture of an earthquake. The patient who drew this picture had been unable to talk about her past, but she was able to 'speak to the picture' without making eye contact. She described the picture as a representation of the after-shock that follows an earthquake, and of the time when rescue services are starting to arrive. In a clear, separated space above the earthquake she had drawn a stick figure opening a door, and another sitting at a desk. These represented her current sense of herself: attempting to go in and out in her daily life, and to do her work. She had come to therapy requesting help with current difficulties doing these things, and in this picture she recognised for the first time that she would have to acknowledge and think about the earthquake and the after-shock as well. It would not be possible to continue to ignore such momentous (traumatic) events.

Summarising and condensing

Imagery can be used to pull together threads of a story, and to capture the complex meanings of a long period of time. One patient drew her 'self portrait . . . the first 12 years' as a black square. She said 'This is the colour of my sadness. I felt so alone. There was no life. No touch unless it was violent or sexual'. She later drew a single picture to reflect the first 22 years of her life, in which she saw herself as most upright, whole and complete when she was born. During the following years she lived behind bars, being progressively forced into a smaller and smaller one-dimensional entity labelled 'high achiever'. The imagery in this picture also pulls together a particular life-defining period of time for this person, but one from which she emerged without knowing who she was. She used to say: 'I'm not a person; I'm just an object'.

A different type of summary was made by another patient at the end of treatment. First she drew an enormous picture on which she represented the main events of her traumatic childhood and subsequent years as an adult with no sense of who she was. She entitled the picture 'space for me', and explained that this reflected her conclusion that there was (now) space for her in the world: space for her to exist as herself, and space in which she could start to explore and to behave differently so as to 'discover herself'.

Linking things up

Images can be a powerful way of making connections between thoughts and feelings, between different aspects of experience, or between different periods of time. This observation was used with a patient who was extremely angry, and expressing her anger violently towards her partner and towards those trying to help her on the ward in which she was an inpatient. She came to therapy with a picture of her anger that she had drawn during Art Therapy: a red, black, yellow and white starburst or explosion. As the drawing appeared to interest her, she was specifically asked to draw rather than to describe the origins of her anger: to represent to herself 'where this anger really belonged'. She drew a series of 'cartoons' of her childhood experiences with her abusive father with schizophrenia, who beat her mother, destroyed the toys he had given her for Christmas, broke up the family piano and sexually abused her. However, for her the most meaningful picture was one of her life immediately after leaving home. She entered a convent and understood that she would be trained as a teacher, and instead was sent to a domestic science course. To her this confirmed that 'what is given will be taken away'. Subsequently, she linked the anger outbursts with her partner and the nursing staff on the ward to events in which her expectations of help (or rescue) were disappointed, and her angry outbursts ceased.

Illustrating processes

Various processes experienced by patients can be represented using imagery. The first example describes a patient's subjective experience of the fragmentary nature of memory. He described his memories of sexual abuse as pieces of a puzzle floating on moving waters. Occasionally two pieces would come together by chance, revealing parts of a picture that he could recognise (sometimes provoking flashbacks, sometimes provoking recognition of events that he had successfully not thought about for about 40 years). During therapy he 'completed the puzzle' and then was no longer subject to disturbing intrusions. Moreover, at this stage he was also able to 'rediscover' what it meant to 'be himself', rather than to live in ways that were designed to keep further harm at bay and to conceal from others the shame and wickedness that, until the pieces of the puzzle were sufficiently joined up, he had assumed reflected his inherent badness. This is not to suggest that the processes of change were mainly, or even predominantly, non-verbal, but rather that the imagery appeared to promote clearer understanding and calmer acceptance of a process over which this person had no apparent control once he had started to experience specific intrusions of earlier traumatic experiences. As the pieces of the puzzle started to come together in imagery this person also started to write his account of what had happened to him, and to explore how this had affected his sense of self.

The second example of a process represented in imagery was developed out of the words used during therapy, when an apparently minor event provoked a hugely disproportionate response in someone who was for the first time starting to engage in normal social activities. A minor disagreement with someone provoked a massive degree of distress. The patient drew a picture of a foot with an enormous scarlet, swollen big toe in which the word 'rejection' was written repeatedly. She realised through drawing the picture both that the event was no worse than stubbing your toe, and that her toe was particularly vulnerable, and likely to cause her much more pain than someone else's.

A third example was provided by someone who described her image of the process of change. She was opening a door high up in a tower, and letting in the light on her dark prison for the first time. Outside she could now see green fields and a whole new world. However, the door was high up in the tower, and there were no steps down to ground level. Opening the door was exciting, hopeful and terrifying all at once. The lability that can sometimes accompany profound change was represented by someone else as a bungy jump. The plunge having been taken, the rubber rope (safely attached to a harness) allowed the jumper to bounce up and down quite violently and suddenly before gradually coming to rest.

Responding differently

Images and drawings were sometimes used spontaneously by patients to deal with difficult situations or with episodes of intense feeling. Instead of resorting to her usual behaviours of cutting herself and drinking when distressed, one patient drew a picture of her feelings and wrote on the picture the words in her head when she was in great distress. Drawing the picture reduced the distress sufficiently for her to control her self-harming behaviours.

A patient who still felt that she did not deserve to be treated well, and who found it hard to rest, or to self-soothe when distressed (especially by flash-backs), made herself a lavender bag. The smell of the lavender she found calming and comforting, but she made the bag out of rough, scratchy canvas, in the shape of a cube. The hard edges and rough texture helped her to use the bag when she was upset as she no longer felt that this would be self-indulgent. She embroidered the initials of people from whom she had gained support on the sides. This textual object, rather than a 2-D picture, also represents a 'grounding object' (Holmes *et al.*, 2005; Kennerley, 1996).

The recipient's role in negotiating for meaning

In this section we will focus on the parts that can be played by the recipient of an image in developing an understanding of its meaning, and in furthering the various aims of therapy. A client may bring an externalised image (scrib-ble, sketch, painting, photograph, sculpture, etc.) to therapy and show or give it to the therapist. We use the term 'recipient' rather than 'therapist' henceforth in this section to underscore that the therapist does not need to be the 'instigator' who requested the image. The client may bring the image spontaneously, perhaps in an attempt to capture some aspect of meaning at a particular stage in therapy. The term 'recipient' also is intended to emphasise that the therapist needs to be open to receiving this form of signal or communication, and open to exploring all aspects of meaning.

First, it is clearly important to recognise the symbolic nature of representa-tion and the 'currency' of non-verbal languages. This is not the place to explore in depth the use of metaphors, analogies and symbols in the represen-tation of meaning, but to make reference to two central ideas that are relevant in this context. First, it is hard to talk about abstract concepts, and especially about emotions, without making them concrete. Metaphors and images help us to construct concrete representations of abstract matters, and therefore clarify our meaning. Second, there are conventional ways of doing this. Particular cultures, and people speaking the same language, develop meta-phorical and non-verbal languages that enable them to understand each other better when they speak about abstract matters. For instance, we can understand people who describe themselves as stuck in a hole or a rut, or as 'fragmented', or living in a dark tunnel. Often metaphors and images are drawn from our experience of the weather or terrestrial events (a stormy relationship; the earthquake referred to above), or from our understanding of life as a journey. We can be swept away by the current, or tossed by the waves. We can struggle up the mountain or get lost in the wilderness. Indeed, the concrete nature of these references is often missed as they are so often used.

In this context two points may need emphasis. First, the attempt to communicate about abstract concepts (violence, neglect, and so on) and about strong emotions (terror, humiliation, etc.) is normally facilitated by making the concepts concrete. We should expect to receive metaphors and images, and the process of exploring meaning, and of being aware of its many aspects, may therefore facilitate this normal process of communication. Second, the extreme and distressing nature of the experiences of the patients described here may make it more likely that they will want to protect themselves from the emotional distress caused by direct (verbal) reference to these events, and help them to make use of metaphor and imagery as distancing tools – as ways of both referring and not referring to what happened to them. It may also lead them to explore new, and less conventional, non-verbal languages.

So recipients of images should above all retain their curiosity. They can draw on their knowledge of conventions to understand (for example what it is like to be struggling up a hill with a weight strapped to one's back), and they can also remain open-minded and curious about the ways in which the conventions have been used, or set aside to provide new, idiosyncratic representations. A patient drew four faces on a large sheet of paper. Features were almost completely absent in the first, and became progressively clearer (though remaining blank of expression) in subsequent ones. When her therapist asked which direction the faces were progressing (i.e. in which direction to read the picture), this patient explained that she was beginning now to develop a sense of who she was but that this was unstable and it came and went. She was confused by the process and did not yet know if she was coming or going.

While they may not have actively requested the image, recipients need not feel passive in response, nor do they need immediately to appear to understand what is being communicated. Sometimes someone who has brought an image may be eloquent at sharing its meaning, either by describing it verbally or through a sense of clarity that the image is representing something useful. However, sometimes the client may be puzzled and confused. We have found it useful to acknowledge the courage it takes to bring and to show an image. Just as a therapist can at times 'just listen' to what someone has to say, so too can a recipient 'just look' at what has been brought. It may be important to shift the image, or to look at it jointly (or not if needed). It is of course fine to accept confusion – neither the image-bringer nor the recipient may be clear about the image and its meaning – indeed, a sense of joint bewilderment (or curiosity) may help in working together on this process ('gosh!').

Four main strategies could perhaps be distinguished. The first is to think of the pictures brought spontaneously to therapy as a means of communication. Sometimes the client is embarrassed to show the picture, and waits to produce it until the session is nearly over. In the vast majority of the cases described here the client did not wish to keep the picture, but gave it to the therapist just as one might give other forms of communication, with the clear sense that once delivered, the message belongs to the recipient and not to its creator. We might think of letters or emails in the same way. The second strategy is to seek to understand the various aspects of meaning that are being communicated. A picture (or piece of music, or artifact) may reveal information, attempt to explain it, elucidate the consequences or impact of experiences, or explore their implications for current difficulties or patterns of behaviour. It may also serve a function such as building up a sense of connection with another person. Different questions should be used to elucidate the different aspects of meaning, and when exploring these different aspects it is often helpful to make general requests and to ask very general questions first: 'Tell me about the picture . . . What is it about? How did it/does it make you feel? Help me to understand it'. Any aspect of the picture may carry important meaning, so it is important also to ask specific questions, for instance about the colours used, the juxtaposition of parts of the image, relative sizes and the significance of particular objects. In one picture a patient drew a clock to represent loss of time. In another the same patient put in a clock to illustrate how great periods of distress completely disrupted her normal routines. The changing symbolism might be missed if not explained.

A third strategy would be to think about the function of the picture for the patient, either at the time that it was made or, for example, at this stage in therapy. A picture might assist in the process of starting to reflect on traumatic experiences. It might be providing the external working space described earlier. It might help in drawing conclusions or summarising a piece of work, and it might assist in behaviour change (as in the example above when making the picture helped the patient to cope with intense distress with self-harm). There are numerous ways in which it might help with the process of self-discovery.

Finally, given the observations and ideas presented here, it would be possible for a therapist to use the process of drawing/image-creating to further particular aims of therapy. The work with the patient who suffered explosive bouts of anger described in the previous section provides an example in which a patient was helped by exploring and understanding the links between the roots of her anger in the past and current triggers for particular outbursts. A more complex example is provided next. For a patient whose identity at times fragmented into three parts, to each of which she gave a different name, the work involved imagining and drawing links between these three 'people', and eventually creating an image that represented all three of them together (at first as a drawing of a pansy, one of her favourite flowers, and which she knew could flower in the frost as well as in the sun). This helped her to integrate the fragments until she was able to think of them as being three aspects of herself (an angry child, a distressed and muddled teenager who both needed comfort and resented this need, and a mature adult). This integrative and symbolic work, spoken about during therapy sessions and subsequently worked on by her using pictures and images, seemed to help her to accept her different needs in different mood states, and to accept her variable moods and behaviours as belonging to the same person.

Together giver and recipient may put (simple) words to an image, saying briefly for instance what it may be of at a visual or surface level, e.g. 'It seems that . . . What do you think?'. To further explore meaning it can be helpful to encourage a climate of acceptance and exploration, and one in which suggestions can also readily be rejected ('Does that fit?'). Meaning for self may be tackled directly, e.g. 'What does this tell you about yourself?', 'How might you describe what this means for you?'. Processing meaning can happen through dialogue and gently exploring the (visual) language in the image, reflecting back, updating, trying again, and weaving a verbal narrative around what is represented. Meaning may become clear gradually. It may be helpful to think about the context in which the image was produced, e.g. 'At the time you made the image, what were we doing in therapy? What else was happening for you?'. This gentle, exploratory approach can be seen as one of the steps towards 'negotiating' a shared meaning over time, and it may take reflection and re-visiting. After having struggled to identify meaning in therapy, externalising an image that reflects self history, or sense of self, or implications for self, and putting this into words with another (affirming or validating) person can be very emotionally powerful. It also provides a development opportunity in realising meaning for the self.

Summary

In this chapter, rather than focusing predominantly on mental imagery within the mind's eye, our focus has been on externalised images as concrete representations such as scribbles, drawings and paintings. We began with examples of the struggle for meaning faced by clients who had spontaneously brought externalised images to therapy, a struggle with a sense of self or sense of history. We have discussed strands of research which in terms of self and autobiography suggest it may be important to represent these meanings in the form of images and not just words. Where clear self-defining imagery is lacking, it may be particularly useful to develop imagery. Rather than working on imagery solely at an imaginal level (i.e. as internalised mental representations) we have argued that it may be useful to externalise image-based representations to capture different aspects of meaning, in particular about the self. The functions of a series of such externalised images brought to therapy have been illustrated. We have discussed the role of the recipient of externalised images and how one might negotiate for meaning using these images during therapy. Finally, we have speculated that the advantageous attributes of imagery might be harnessed not only when clients spontaneously bring images to therapy, but by deliberately using these as a therapeutic tool. For example, one might consolidate meanings in a typical cognitive therapy blueprint by asking a client to create images deliberately to best represent this.

Those struggling maximally with a sense of self have illuminated the utility of this approach. While 'art therapy' is hardly a new discipline, perhaps we can now proactively take a cognitive psychology-informed approach to harnessing externalised image-making as part of cognitive therapy.

References

Arntz, A., & Weertman, A. (1999). Treatment of childhood memories: Theory and practice. *Behaviour Research and Therapy*, *37*(8), 715–740.

Baddeley, A.D. (1986). *Working memory*. Oxford, UK: Clarendon Press.

Brewer, W.F. (1996). What is recollective memory? In D.C. Rubin (Ed.), *Remembering our past: Studies in autobiographical memory* (pp. 19–66). Cambridge, UK: Cambridge University Press.

Chambers, D., & Reisberg, D. (1985). Can mental images be ambiguous? *Journal of Experimental Psychology: Human Perception and Performance*, *11*(3), 317–328.

Conway, M.A. (1996). Autobiographical knowledge and autobiographical memories. In D.C. Rubin (Ed.), *Remembering our past: Studies in autobiographical memory* (pp. 67–93). Cambridge, UK: Cambridge University Press.

Conway, M.A. (2001). Sensory perceptual episodic memory and its context: Autobiographical memory. *Philosophical Transactions of the Royal Society – Series B: Biological Sciences*, *356*(1413), 1375–1384.

Conway, M.A., & Holmes, E.A. (2005). Autobiographical memory and the working self. In N.R. Braisby & A.R.H. Gellatly (Eds.), *Cognitive psychology* (pp. 507–538). Oxford, UK: Oxford University Press.

Conway, M.A., & Pleydell-Pearce, C.W. (2000). The construction of autobiographical memories in the self-memory system. *Psychological Review*, *107*(2), 261–288.

Conway, M.A., & Rubin, D.C. (1993). The structure of autobiographical memory. In A.E. Collins, S.E. Gathercole, M.A. Conway, & P.E.M. Morris (Eds.), *Theories of memory* (pp. 103–137). Hove, UK: Psychology Press.

Giesen-Bloo, J., van Dyck, R., Spinhoven, P., van Tilburg, W., Dirksen, C., van Asselt, T., *et al.* (2006). Outpatient psychotherapy for borderline personality disorder: A randomized clinical trial of schema focused therapy versus transference focused psychotherapy. *Archives of General Psychiatry*, *63*(6), 649–658.

Holmes, E.A., Brown, R.J., Mansell, W., Fearon, R.P., Hunter, E.C.M., Frasquilho, F., *et al.* (2005). Are there two qualitatively distinct forms of dissociation? A review and some clinical implications. *Clinical Psychology Review*, *25*(1), 1–23.

Holmes, E.A., & Hackmann, A. (2004). Mental imagery and memory in psychopathology [Special Issue]. *Memory*, *12*(4).

Holmes, E.A., & Mathews, A. (2005). Mental imagery and emotion: A special relationship? *Emotion*, *5*(4), 489–497.

Holmes, E.A., Mathews, A., Dalgleish, T., & Mackintosh, B. (2006). Positive interpretation training: Effects of mental imagery versus verbal training on positive mood. *Behavior Therapy*, *37*(3), 237–247.

Kennerley, H. (1996). Cognitive therapy of dissociate symptoms associated with trauma. *British Journal of Clinical Psychology*, *35*(3), 325–340.

Pillemer, D.B., Picariello, M.L., Law, A.B., & Reichman, J.S. (1996). Memories of college: The importance of specific educational episodes. In D.C. Rubin (Ed.),

Remembering our past: Studies in autobiographical memory (pp. 318–341). Cambridge, UK: Cambridge University Press.

Rubin, D.C. (2002). Autobiographical memory across the lifespan. In P. Graf & N. Ohta (Eds.), *Lifespan development of human memory* (pp. 159–184). Cambridge, MA: MIT Press.

Rubin, D.C., & Greenberg, D.L. (1998). Visual-memory-deficit amnesia: A distinct amnesic presentation and etiology. *Proceedings of the National Academy of Sciences, 95*, 1–4.

Sereny, G. (1998). *Cries unheard: The story of Mary Bell.* London: Macmillan.

Singer, J.A., & Salovey, P. (1993). *The remembered self.* New York: The Free Press.

Williams, J.M.G., Barnhofer, T., Crane, C., Herman, D., Raes, F., Watkins, E., *et al.* (2007). Autobiographical memory specificity and emotional disorder. *Psychological Bulletin, 133*(1), 122–148.

Williams, J.M.G., & Broadbent, K. (1986). Autobiographical memory in suicide attempters. *Journal of Abormal Psychology, 95*(2), 144–149.

Chapter 8

Imagery and the negative self in eating disorders

Myra J. Cooper

Imagery, including mental imagery, is an everyday experience. It can be experienced in terms of sight, sound, taste, touch, smell and movement. One common way in which it is experienced is in creating or re-creating an experience in the mind. This is commonly referred to as 'mental imagery', and for most people it is a rich and multifaceted experience. It is also something most people take for granted as one aspect of normal, everyday life, and which they do not necessarily question or examine closely. Self is also an everyday experience that is not generally questioned. Most people have an ongoing, reasonably coherent everyday sense of self that is stable, and serves as a central reference point for organising and interpreting experience. From an everyday perspective, mental imagery and sense of self work together and help give our experience meaning in a range of ways, including value, worth, definition and impact.

Disturbance in mental imagery or self can have severe repercussions for how we interpret and find meaning in everyday experience. Clinicians will be familiar with how both of these everyday experiences can be disturbed and disrupted in those with an eating disorder. The majority of patients with an eating disorder, if asked to outline their problems or difficulties, will readily describe disturbances in their experience of both mental imagery and self.

Sheila MacLeod (1981, pp. 10–11) summarises her personal experience of an eating disorder as follows.

> In my experience, anorexia nervosa is not a matter of slimming which has somehow or other got out of hand and beyond the control of the anorexic herself. Neither does it signify an urge towards suicide, nor yet an aversion from sexuality. On the contrary, it is, like most other psycho-neurotic syndromes, a positive strategy aimed at establishing autonomy and resolving what would otherwise be unbearable conflicts in the life of the sufferer. These conflicts are partially related to and arising from the anorexic's individual history and personality structure – that is, they are intra-psychic. But they are also existential, that is, related to

being-in-the-world, which for human beings necessarily means being-in-a-body, and for women, being-in-a-female-body.

MacLeod's summary of her experience is informed by her reading of the scientific literature, thus it is not a completely naïve or everyday account. However, it clearly highlights both self, specifically autonomy, and internal conflicts, or disturbance in internal mental experience, as crucial aspects of having an eating disorder – both of which are the topic of this chapter. She also mentions a third aspect, the experience of 'being in a body' – the somatic dimension of an eating disorder, which has received very little attention in the scientific (particularly cognitive) literature.

Mental imagery, self and cognitive theory

Mental imagery is a relatively new topic of study for cognitive theorists and therapists, including for those interested in the psychology and psycho-pathology of eating disorders. Indeed, overall, mental imagery has received very little attention in the literature on eating disorders, and it is still an under-researched area. The self, however, has been considered an important topic historically in eating disorders, although interest in it had declined, and it is only recently that it has begun to attract renewed interest. In line with the popularity of cognitive approaches to theory and treatment, much of the recent research on mental imagery and the self has been conducted not with the everyday perspective described above in mind, but within a cognitive framework. This is true for eating and other disorders.

Cognitive perspectives in eating and also in other disorders have investigated mental imagery in two ways. Firstly, it has been investigated as an aspect of the psychopathology of the disorder, and secondly, it has been explored and developed as a potential treatment strategy. In relation to the self, the field is perhaps rather more advanced. Cognitive research not only has described the nature of the self, but has begun to incorporate self into revised cognitive models, including in eating disorders. Cognitive therapists have also begun to develop a range of novel treatments to modify negative self beliefs and their associated processing in those with eating disorders. Overall, self is receiving considerable attention in eating disorders, and is increasingly regarded as a central construct for understanding and success-fully treating bulimia nervosa and anorexia nervosa, as well as a range of 'not otherwise specified' eating disorders.

Self and mental imagery are known to be intertwined not only in everyday experience, but also in psychological theories. The relationship between them has begun to be explored in a number of psychological disorders, including very recently, in a small number of preliminary studies, in eating disorders. One exciting result of their interconnection is that mental imagery has begun to be developed as a strategy to modify self-related beliefs. There is now increasing interest in its use as a therapeutic strategy to modify self-related beliefs, particularly in those with eating disorders, and a small literature exists on the topic.

Aim of the chapter

The aim of this chapter is to examine the role of mental imagery, and its relationship to self, in eating disorders. A cognitive framework will be used as the primary theoretical perspective and the practical, clinical implications of the discussion for conducting cognitive-behavioural therapy (CBT) in those with eating disorders will be outlined. First, the terms 'eating disorders', 'mental imagery' and 'the self', as they are to be used here, will be defined. Second, historical and other references to food and eating imagery in eating disorders will also be identified, the potential clues these images provide about the nature of self will be noted, and treatment strategies (primarily non-cognitive) that have made use of food- and eating-related imagery will be briefly summarised. Third, body image and the broad scope of the term will be discussed. Those aspects that might fall under the definition of mental image that is used here will be identified. As for food and eating imagery, links to the self will be noted, and the use of imagery related to the body in therapy will be discussed. This will include its application in both cognitive and other approaches. Fourth, mental imagery as a feature of eating disorders will be discussed. Relevant empirical evidence related to mental imagery, self and their interrelationship in eating disorders will also be presented. Fifth, theoretical frameworks that might be used to understand the relationship between mental imagery and the self in eating disorders will be explored, including both cognitive theories and how these might begin to merge with developments in 'enactive' theories (and thus start to address McLeod's 'being-in-a-body'). Finally, strategies for using imagery to modify self beliefs in eating disorders, using a cognitive framework, will be briefly outlined.

Definitions of terms used in the chapter

Eating disorders

The term 'eating disorders' will be used here to include anorexia nervosa (AN), bulimia nervosa (BN), and the variants of these two disorders described in the DSM-IV-TR 'eating disorder not otherwise specified' (ED-NOS) category (American Psychiatric Association, 2004). It is widely believed that these disorders have common features, which distinguish them from both obesity (not currently classified as a psychiatric disorder) and binge eating disorder (currently classified as a subgroup of those with ED-NOS, but with criteria for research use only), although research supporting this claim is not currently extensive. In relation to cognitive theory, one important feature that they are thought to have in common is distorted or dysfunctional beliefs about the importance of control of eating, weight and shape, and this forms the basis for the transdiagnostic theory (Fairburn, Cooper, & Shafran, 2003), a cognitive theory that incorporates all eating disorder diagnoses. However, while the transdiagnostic argument is persuasive and clinically useful, it is important to realise that there is also evidence, for example from genome-wide linkage analyses, that the disorders are best considered distinct. In a recent review, Wonderlich, Joiner, Keel, Williamson, and Crosby (2007), while suggesting some changes to the current diagnostic groupings, make an argument for retaining the broad AN and BN categories as restricting vs binge-purge disorders and for integrating subclinical or ED-NOS variants into the full syndromes. This suggestion is consistent with large-scale latent class analysis studies (e.g. Keel *et al.*, 2004) that have identified clusters of different eating disorders, and is consistent with our definition of eating disorders as stated here. The separate AN and BN categories will be retained, and where applicable their ED-NOS variants will be discussed with the full syndrome equivalent.

Mental imagery

Mental imagery, or internal psychic representations, as defined by Horowitz (1970) is complex amalgams, not just a perception. This is an important point, as it has been noted that there has been a tendency to collapse image into perception and to treat it as a copy, or a faithful replication, of the external world. This has sometimes occurred, for example, in posttraumatic stress disorder (PTSD), where intrusive images of the trauma occur (Leys, 2006). However, Horowitz (1970, p. 4) notes, very clearly, that images are 'not merely imitations, but memory fragments, reconstructions, reinterpretations, and symbols that stand for objects, feelings or ideas'. The use of the term 'mental' refers to the fact that the image is an internal representation in one's head or mind, as opposed (for example, in relation to a visual image) to a drawing, or a picture captured on paper or canvas. Consistent with Horowitz's definition, Holmes and Hackmann (2004) note that the term imagery 'encompasses memories and dreams as well as spontaneously triggered and deliberately self generated images' (p. 390). By implication, these may not thus be veridical representations of real events, but include, for example, made-up events or those that exist purely in imagination. They can also include symbols and metaphor. These definitions are consistent with everyday understanding or definitions of imagery in the mind, for example, 'a set of mental images produced by the memory or imagination or conjured up by a stimulus' (Encarta, 1999). One important point, made by both Horowitz (1970) and by Holmes and Hackmann (2004), is that images are not confined to the visual, although much of the relevant research has focused on these. Horowitz's book, for example, primarily concerns visual images. Both Horowitz and others have emphasised that non-visual images exist, and may be important. These images can involve different representational systems, and can involve all the senses (i.e. visual, hearing, smell, taste, touch and movement).

The concept of the self

Self has been defined in countless ways, including within the field of psychology, and many of the definitions refer to rather different phenomena (Katzko, 2003). Indeed, it has been argued that the multitude of terms and definitions makes much of the work on self uninterpretable (Wylie, 1979). Harter (1999) notes the importance of defining any self-related terminology clearly in order to avoid ambiguity and confusion. In cognitive theory and therapy, self is typically reflected in the constructs of schemas and core beliefs about the self. The two terms are frequently used interchangeably in the literature and in therapy. However, Beck *et al.* define core beliefs as 'the content of the schema', while schemas are 'the cognitive structures that organise experience and behaviour' (Beck, Freeman, & Associates, 1990, p. 4). Consistent with this distinction, Padesky and Greenberger (1995, p. 5) note that core beliefs about the self are absolute ('I am strong') and dichotomous ('I am strong', 'I am weak'), with those core beliefs that are negative being more characteristically associated with psychopathology compared to those that are positive. Schemas, however, as used by both Beck *et al.* (1990) and Young, Klosko, and Weisshaar (2003), rather like mental images, are complex amalgams. As described by Young *et al.* (2003), schemas (termed 'early maladaptive schemas') comprise 'memories, emotions, cognitions and bodily sensations' (p. 7). They have other characteristic features, but overall (and when maladaptive) might be summarised as 'self defeating emotional and cognitive patterns that begin early in our development and repeat throughout life' (Young *et al.*, 2003, p. 7). Importantly, behaviours are not part of the schema; rather they develop as responses to a schema, and are driven by but are not part of the schema. Beck, Young, Padesky and other writers emphasise the all-encompassing pervasiveness of schemas, and as such their definitions are consistent with everyday definitions of self, for example, as 'somebody's personality or an aspect of it' (Encarta, 1999).

References to food and eating imagery in eating disorders and how these images relate to the self

Early clinical accounts of eating disorders note that the preoccupation with food and eating that is typical of those with an eating disorder often extends to mental imagery, and is typically focused on food and hunger. Bruch (1973), for example, describes the vivid dreams experienced and recorded in her writings by Ellen West, whose illness was described by Binswanger in 1944–5. These typically centred on food, and the dishes she did not allow herself to eat, but which she imagined herself being able to consume if only death were imminent. In a fictional account of an eating disorder, Margaret Atwood in *The Edible Women* (Atwood, 1980) describes the central character's visit to the supermarket for cake ingredients as follows: 'Her image was taking shape. Eggs. Flour. Lemons for the flavour. Sugar, icing sugar, vanilla, salt, food colouring' (p. 167).

Nevertheless, despite several rich accounts, mental imagery has not often been directly investigated in eating disorders, and plays little or no distinct role in the major models used to understand and treat these disorders. This includes the cognitive-behavioural models developed for anorexia nervosa (e.g. Fairburn, Shafran, & Cooper, 1999; Garner & Bemis, 1982) and bulimia nervosa (Fairburn, Cooper, & Cooper, 1986). Despite the fact that all these models emphasise food and eating, weight and shape concerns, there is no specific role for food and eating (or indeed, weight and shape) imagery. This is also true of recent revisions of these models, including the transdiagnostic model (Fairburn *et al.*, 2003), as well as revisions that attribute greater importance than earlier models to the role of the self, and to self-related beliefs (e.g. Cooper, Wells, & Todd, 2004; Waller, Kennerley, & Ohanian, 2007).

The relationship between starvation and imagery

One possibility is that images of food and hunger, which are known to be associated with starvation, are not a key part of the psychopathology of eating disorders. The adverse effects of dieting and, in the case of anorexia nervosa, starvation are emphasised in psycho-educational approaches and materials for eating disorders (e.g. Garner, Rockert, Olmsted, Johnson, & Coscina, 1985). Writers on the psychological impact of the 1944–1945 starvation study conducted at the University of Minnesota, where conscientious objectors were placed on semi-starvation diets, note not only preoccupation with food and eating, but also related daydreams, for example of 'eating senile and insane people' (Schiele & Brozek, 1948). Nevertheless, in the absence of scientifically robust experimental studies and detailed phenomenological descriptions of the images observed, it is difficult to be certain how similar the images observed in this study are to those characteristic of those with eating disorders, including anorexia nervosa. It is also likely to be an exaggeration to say that those with bulimia nervosa or many forms of ED-NOS are in a state of extreme starvation, thus its usefulness as a comparison when investigating the psychological sequelae of all eating disorders is unclear.

The relationship between dieting and imagery

Dieting is a very common behaviour and, unlike starvation, can form a realistic, easily obtainable comparison group in studies of imagery in people with eating disorders. This is particularly important as, although the evidence is limited, dieting is widely believed to generate some of the psychological symptoms that overlap with those typical of an eating disorder (e.g. Fairburn *et al.*, 1986). Perhaps more significantly, dieting is known to be a risk factor for the later development of an eating disorder; thus any study of novel psychological phenomena in those with eating disorders might be wise to include non-dieting control groups, in order to attempt to tease out potential markers of risk. Features associated with eating disorders that are also typical of those who are dieting are likely to be less informative in developing good models and effective treatments for eating disorders. However, to date, very little is known about mental imagery in dieters, making the need to use them as a comparison group particularly important.

Images of the self in eating disorders

Closer examination of the imagery in people with eating disorders suggests that they are not only concerned with food and eating. Many images appear to have clear meaning beyond the immediate content or context of food and eating. Not infrequently, there is consistency in the meanings attached. Most meanings would appear to concern the self. Indeed, inattention to self-related imagery and failure to perceive a link to self seem significant omissions when first-person accounts of eating disorders are studied, specifically when accounts of imagery are examined. A number of writers refer, for example, to changes in the vividness and accuracy of perception, intensity and change in content of dreams, and to rejection and distortion of images of the self as part of the subjective experience of an eating disorder, both in relation to food and eating and independently of such images (e.g. MacLeod, 1981). The distortion, intensity and emotional content of her self experience, and its extension from the literal to the metaphorical, are described by MacLeod as follows:

> In my rejection of the image I saw I was making a statement, the apparent text of which read, 'I don't want to look like (be) that'.
>
> (MacLeod, 1981, p. 79)

A passage in Aimee Liu's memoir *Solitaire* (Liu, 1979), the story of her eating disorder, contains a rich, detailed and evocative description of her memory of an imaginary banquet, and demonstrates how food and eating imagery can provide a window onto the self. The meaning of the imagined banquet is revealed in the message Liu reads on the slip of paper inside a Chinese fortune cookie: 'You eat – you die' (Liu, 1979, p. 85).

Bruch (1973) concludes her account of Ellen West by noting that although food and weight concerns are described, the central problem is an underlying deficit in self-awareness. The link to the self and the associated meaning for the self are evident in all the sources cited above, which describe imagery. It is either explicitly noted or clearly implicit. This link is important.

How imagery work has been used in therapy

Cognitive therapy

Just as imagery does not have a specific role in cognitive models of eating disorders, clinical work with mental imagery does not form part of routine cognitive therapy for eating disorders, where the emphasis is typically on working with verbal cognitions. Treatment manuals based on a cognitive-behavioural approach, and empirical papers evaluating the efficacy of CBT in those with eating disorders, rarely if ever mention or suggest working specifically with mental imagery. This is true of both BN treatment manuals (e.g. Fairburn, Marcus, & Wilson 1993; Schmidt & Treasure, 1993) and those for AN (e.g. Freeman, 2002; Treasure, 1997). Similarly, reports of treatment studies in both BN and AN (e.g. Agras, Walsh, Fairburn, Wilson, & Kraemer, 2000; Pike, Walsh, Vitousek, Wilson, & Bauer, 2003) do not mention work with or using imagery; rather verbal cognitions appear to be the main target of treatment when cognitions are addressed. One reason for its neglect may be that, as suggested above, food and eating images are often thought to be by-products of dieting or, in the case of AN, starvation. However, as noted above, not all the images described above relate only to food and eating; several also refer to the self, either in relation to food and eating or entirely independently of such a context. Nevertheless, despite the presence of some self-related images in first-person accounts, and the role given to the self by some writers and researchers, self has also not been a primary focus of these CBT interventions, so it is perhaps not surprising that self-related meanings have not often been addressed. This is true in relation to use of verbal as well as imaginal strategies.

Other psychological therapies

Other psychological therapies have a history of working with images in eating disorders, particularly those conceptualised within a psychodynamic and/or feminist framework. These include art therapy, which works with representations, including representations of self and feelings (e.g. Schaverien, 1994), and body image therapy, which may work with guided imagery, where patients are encouraged to generate images in response to theoretically important cues, such as maternal and paternal wishes and thoughts in anticipation of the patient's birth (e.g. Kearney-Cooke, 1989). Some therapies, for example psychodrama in combination with Gestalt therapy, seek to enhance patients' awareness of self, including internal thoughts, feelings and meanings, and work for example with posture, gesture, breathing, and movement (e.g. Hudgins, 1989). Body image work on dance and movement can also incorporate imagery work, and make use of guided imagery (Hutchinson, 1983). Overall, most work with images in those with eating disorders has been undertaken in the context of art therapy, or other experiential therapies. It is noteworthy that such work focuses primarily on self-related information, including emotion, as well as cognition. Work is not typically conducted with food and eating images, although these may form part of the work (Rust, 1987).

Body image in eating disorders

The word 'image' is used explicitly in relation to body image in eating disorders, but its precise meaning is often unclear. Disturbance in body image has been researched in eating disorders, often within a socio-cultural framework, but with some attempt to investigate the extent to which the disturbance might be cognitive in nature. However, as noted by Martin and Williams (1990), despite a relatively large literature on this, little direct work to modify imagery (body-related or otherwise) in anorexia nervosa (AN), bulimia nervosa (BN), or indeed the Eating Disorder Not Otherwise Specified variants of these (ED-NOS, American Psychiatric Association, 2004), has been conducted. Schilder (1950, p. 11) defined body image as 'the picture of our own body that we form in our mind', and this definition seems to be consistent with, for example, Horowitz's more general definition of image, and with the definition of mental image used here. Since Schilder, however, the term has become broader, and now includes, for example, 'a person's perceptions, thoughts and feelings about his or her body' (Grogan, 1999, p. 1). Thus, it has come to incorporate 'body size estimation', dislike of one's body, and a range of phenomena that reflect what Cash has termed 'your personal relationship with your body' (Cash, 1997, p. 2). In psychological research, three aspects of body image (the perceptual, affective and cognitive components) are often studied, and studies are not confined to investigation of internal mental images. For example, a range of measures have been developed to measure body dissatisfaction, or how one feels about one's body, and although this is not necessarily related to a mental image of one's body, the construct is usually included in any discussion of body image. In everyday use, the term usually refers to what people see, say in a mirror, or how they feel about their body. In psychological research there has been considerable interest in whether the 'distortion' is inside the person's head or not – that is, whether or not it is a veridical, true perceptual distortion. The role of body image in its various manifestations in eating disorders is not currently entirely clear, and it has its own 'body image' field of research and treatment. CBT does not normally tackle body image separately or specifically, although there has been some interest in what maintains 'dissatisfaction' with body, and how to decrease it. CBT has subsequently included work to reduce the body checking and body avoidance thought to maintain such dissatisfaction (e.g. Farrell, Shafran, Lee, & Fairburn, 2005), although to date this has not been systematically evaluated in people with eating disorders. Overall, body image has come to have a broader meaning than what is implied by the narrower definition of 'image', as has been used here, but nevertheless it contains within it the narrower meaning. Clinically, patients with eating disorders commonly experience internal, mental images of themselves as fat or thin. As well as being either distressing or rewarding, depending on their nature and context, such images may have a functional role, for example in enhancing motivation to lose weight or restrict eating.

The use of body image therapy to treat eating disorders

Body image therapy has made use of imagery, as defined in the narrower sense (see above). However, as suggested earlier it has not typically been developed as a treatment for eating disorders, but for those with disturbed body image. This includes cognitive-behavioural versions of body image therapy, developed not necessarily for those with an eating disorder, but for those unhappy with their body. Interestingly, within a CBT framework (e.g. Cash, 1997) the therapy does not make use of images as defined in their narrower sense. Cash's programme, for example, focuses primarily on self-acceptance and on learning to like your body using verbal strategies. Body image therapies based on different theoretical models, however, do use imagery as part of the treatment, both for those with body image problems and as part of treatment for those with an eating disorder. Treatments typically overlap with those described above in the section on food and eating imagery. As suggested above, this work is usually completed in the context of a psychodynamic or feminist framework, and may include a focus on self-related imagery, or other theoretically driven stimuli, including images of the self at different weights and sizes (e.g. Rust, 1987).

The relationship between body image and the self

Cognitive theory has long recognised that how patients with eating disorders feel and think about their body affects their self, specifically their self-esteem. Cognitive-behavioural therapy for eating disorders typically includes challenging of cognitions that reflect these beliefs. These strategies invariably employ verbal techniques, and are mostly designed to alter the dependence of self-esteem on evaluation of weight and shape. They do not usually extend to modifying the general negative self that is characteristic of those with an eating disorder. The link between self-esteem and weight and shape has been extensively researched and assessed (see, for example, Geller et al., 1998). Recently, however, it has become recognised that self is important in its own right in eating disorders, and empirical research has been conducted into its nature and function (see, for example, work by Cooper and colleagues and by Waller and colleagues).

Imagery and self in therapy

With the exception of some work conducted by experiential therapists that was mentioned above, the self has not often been tackled directly using imagery in eating disorders. However, one imagery-based treatment that focuses on self-experience is described by Esplen (Esplen & Garfinkel, 1998; Esplen, Garfinkel, Olmsted, Gallop, & Kennedy, 1998), and has been evaluated. It makes use of a series of guided images to promote self-soothing, including images designed to encourage comfort and relaxation, as well as images designed to promote self-exploration and self-experience. Preliminary evaluation suggests that the treatment is successful for some women with BN (Esplen et al., 1998) in decreasing bingeing and purging as well as improving their experience of aloneness and ability to self-soothe and self-comfort. Theoretically, the treatment draws on psychodynamic work including that of Winnicott and Bruch and on work in those with borderline personality disorder (as described by Esplen & Garfinkel, 1998).

Although not identified as a major treatment strategy, the use of guided imagery is described as a useful means of understanding the patient's personal identity structures (Guidano & Liotti, 1983), including patients with an eating disorder. Thus, it can be a useful assessment strategy rather than a specific treatment method.

With the development of revised cognitive theories (e.g. Cooper et al., 2004; Waller et al., 2007), which give self more importance, imagery rescripting has become an important strategy for challenging negative self or core beliefs. These strategies will be discussed in more detail later in the chapter.

Imagery and the self in eating disorders

The recent renewal of interest in imagery in anxiety disorders (e.g. Holmes & Hackmann, 2004) has generated a number of descriptive studies, and a growing number of experimental studies to describe the phenomena and to begin to pinpoint the function of imagery in different anxiety-related disorders. Inspired by this research, a small number of studies now exist that have investigated imagery in those with eating disorders. Two aspects have been studied to date: mental imagery as a feature of eating disorders and links between self-reported imagery and the self.

Mental imagery as a feature of eating disorders

There has been a growth in interest in mental imagery in various forms of psychopathology and some of the research on this topic has been brought together by Holmes and Hackmann (2004). This research conceptualises imagery within a cognitive framework, and there has been an emphasis on the potential implications for cognitive therapy. However, very little has been written about mental imagery as one aspect of the psychopathology of eating disorders, and this topic is not covered in Holmes and Hackmann (2004). The aim of this section, and those that follow, is to summarise what is currently known about the imagery reported by patients with eating disorders, with particular emphasis on its phenomenology in people with either anorexia nervosa or bulimia nervosa. As with anxiety disorder research, a general cognitive framework has informed much of the work that will be cited and emphasis will be placed on its relevance to cognitive therapy for those with eating disorders. Information relevant to the role and function of such imagery in eating disorders, as well as its general usefulness in providing access to other key beliefs, will also be presented.

The presence of imagery in eating disorders

Beck (1976), whose cognitive theory has informed much of current cognitive theory relevant to eating disorders, emphasised that mental imagery, in addition to verbal thoughts, might form an important route to the meanings that are the focus of cognitive therapy. However, in cognitive therapy and also in research, including eating disorders, most emphasis has been given to verbal thoughts. Clinically, patients' images have not often been enquired about in eating disorders, despite awareness that patients typically have mental representations of themselves, particularly in terms of physical appearance and size, that do not conform to reality. Prompted by research in other disorders, which has identified a role for imagery even though it has not traditionally been considered particularly important, and by clinical experience of the presence of imagery, a number of studies have now included an assessment of patient's spontaneous imagery, typically when they are asked to recall a situation related to their eating disorder concerns. Detailed semi-structured interviews have been employed in all these studies, allowing identification of patients' idiosyncratic images. The findings suggest that patients with eating disorders do indeed report spontaneous and also recurrent images related to their eating problems. For example, one very early study, in which imagery was not the main focus of the investigation, found that seven out of 12 patients with anorexia nervosa (AN) and six out of 12 patients with bulimia nervosa (BN) reported images when asked to talk about the last time that they had felt worried about their eating, weight and shape (Cooper, Todd, & Wells, 1998). More recently, a study of patients with BN in which imagery was the main focus of the investigation found that 12 out of 13 patients reported spontaneous images/impressions. This was significantly greater than the number of non-clinical controls (11/20) but not significantly different from the number reported by dieters (14/18)

(Somerville, Cooper, & Hackmann, 2007). This study will be discussed in more detail below.

The content and characteristics of imagery in eating disorders

Detail on the characteristic content and other features of the images reported is also available, particularly in Cooper *et al.* (1998), where a brief description of each spontaneous image is included. The majority of images concern body shape and size, either overall perception of themselves as fat/overweight or of one or more of their body parts being large and fat. Somerville *et al.* explored a range of other characteristics of their patients' images. Patients' images were recurrent and, compared to those of non-clinical and dieting participants, they were rated as more negative and anxiety-provoking. They also involved significantly more sensory modalities, with greater vividness ratings, than those of the other two groups. In particular, individuals with BN reported visual, organic (body-related) and cutaneous (tactile) sensations. Information on the sensory modalities of images associated with 'feeling fat' in patients with AN was reported by Cooper, Deepak, Grocutt, and Bailey (2007), and patients with AN reported a high number of visual and olfactory images (although no more than dieters and non-clinical controls), but more auditory, tactile and movement images than the other two groups. Many of the images in all modalities in those with AN were related to appearance of self, particularly seeing oneself as fat and overweight, including checking of arms and shoulders and pulling at one's stomach.

The role and function of imagery in eating disorders

The use of imagery in treatment, including in the context of cognitive therapy, has been described by several clinicians (see below). There has also been some discussion of how these interventions might fit into a theoretical framework. However, much less has been written on what the role and function of imagery as one manifestation of the eating disorder psychopathology might be; only one paper to date appears to have addressed this issue. Within the context of cognitive theory and therapy, imagery is thought to function as a maintaining factor for anxiety disorders (Holmes & Hackmann, 2004). A similar role and function for imagery in relation to BN has been suggested by Somerville *et al.* (2007), who argue that its role in maintaining the disorder is similar to that accorded to verbal automatic thoughts by cognitive theorists. Thus images, like verbal cognitions, may drive dieting and other weight control behaviours, which are thought by some cognitive theorists to lead to binge-eating (Fairburn *et al.* 1999). Alternatively, images may play a role equivalent to that of the negative beliefs about eating and related behaviours which, together with positive beliefs, encourage and maintain binge eating and its associated compensatory behaviours more directly (Cooper *et al.*,

2004). Like their associated verbal cognitions images may, therefore, need to be modified for treatment to be successful.

The clinical usefulness of imagery in eating disorders – imagery/body as a mirror to the self

Identifying imagery in patients with eating disorders may be useful, not only as a prelude to direct modification of such imagery (if indeed it plays a role in maintaining the eating disorder), but because evidence from anxiety disorders indicates that imagery provides a rapid way to access deeper level beliefs, including assumptions and core beliefs, and that the information obtained in this way is particularly rich and detailed, including when compared to information obtained via verbal cognitions (e.g. Pratt, Cooper, & Hackmann, 2004; see also the chapters on anxiety disorders in this volume). Although no direct comparison has been made between the two methods in patients with eating disorders, i.e. imagery vs verbal cognitions as an access strategy, there is evidence that imagery can provide a quick and useful route to core beliefs, and an abundance of detailed information about such beliefs and their characteristics, in patients with BN (Somerville & Cooper, 2007). Patients with BN reported significantly more negative self (core) beliefs than two non-clinical control groups. In addition, their emotional belief ratings for these negative self beliefs were higher than for their rational belief ratings. Specific themes were also identified in the patients' negative self beliefs. In decreasing order of frequency these involved self-value, failure, self-control and physical attractiveness (Somerville & Cooper, 2007). This finding is important given that such beliefs can be difficult and time-consuming to identify using more traditional verbal strategies. Interestingly, it suggests that images – typically of the self as fat/overweight, and rather as suggested by the first-person accounts of Liu (1979) – can provide a 'mirror' to the self. The example from Liu quoted above links food and eating with the self – thus eating has a meaning for the self. To date, food and eating imagery has not been explored specifically in empirical research with those with eating disorders, but it seems likely, as appears to be the case clinically, that this will also provide a mirror to the self, most likely mediated by images or thoughts of the self as fat or overweight.

The self in eating disorders

In contrast to writing and research on imagery, the concept of self has been extensively studied and reported on in eating disorders. Nevertheless, although there is a large literature, the nature, role and function of self, as opposed to weight- and shape-based self-esteem, have not been developed or widely studied in a cognitive framework. Research in a cognitive framework has looked in detail at the fact that self-esteem appears to be very dependent on weight and shape in those with eating disorders, but until recently has not paid so much attention to self as a broader concept. Much of the work on self has also been written from a psychodynamic rather than a cognitive perspective.

Cognitive views of the self in eating disorders

Historically, self did not have a particularly crucial role in early cognitive models of BN (e.g. Fairburn *et al.*, 1986), although the first cognitive model for AN (Garner & Bemis, 1982) did include a role for self. The role of self was highlighted in 1990 by Vitousek and Hollon, who included self-schema as a construct that was thought to be important in the development of both AN and BN. They used Markus' (1977) definition of self-schema, namely 'self schemata are cognitive generalisations about the self, derived from past experience, that organise and guide the processing of self related information contained in the individual's social experiences' (p. 64). More recently, cognitive models of BN and also AN have included low core self-esteem as a potential factor, albeit not in all patients with an eating disorder (Fairburn *et al.*, 2003). These models do not specify how low core self-esteem is to be conceptualised within a cognitive framework, nor provide detail on how it might be treated. Waller and colleagues have conceptualised self in eating disorders in terms consistent with Young's schema theory, and have developed schema theory to explain how AN and BN are differentially defined by the use of different schema-driven processes to deal with negative affect and cognitive distress. They have provided detail on how such beliefs and processes might be tacked in the context of cognitive therapy (Waller *et al.*, 2007). A similar framework for conceptualising self in terms of cognitive content and processes has been proposed by Cooper and colleagues (Cooper *et al.*, 2004), along with a detailed outline of how treatment based on their model, which differs also from previous models in its specification of maintaining factors, might proceed in BN (Cooper, Todd, & Wells, 2000, 2008).

Empirical research on the self in eating disorders

A relatively large body of work on the self in eating disorders (EDs), examined from a cognitive perspective, now exists. Two main approaches and groups have investigated self. Waller and colleagues have used the Young Schema-Questionnaire (YSQ: e.g. Young & Brown, 1994), which draws on Young's notion of early maladaptive schema, and established that patients with EDs typically score highly on several dimensions of this measure, and there appear to be links between some schemas and different behavioural symptoms, although the precise relationships are not always consistent. This research has been summarised recently in Waller *et al.* (2007). Waller and colleagues have also identified potential differences in the processing associated with self-schemas in those with BN compared to those with AN (e.g. Luck, Waller, Meyer, Ussher, & Lacey, 2005). Cooper and colleagues have devised and used the Eating Disorder Belief Questionnaire (EDBQ; Cooper, Cohen-Tovee, Todd, Wells, & Tovee, 1997). Unlike the YSQ, this was developed specifically for EDs, and the negative self-beliefs subscale provides a brief, easy-to-use measure of the core or negative self-beliefs characteristic of those with EDs. Again, high levels of these beliefs have been identified in those with EDs compared to controls, including women who are dieting. In a second line of research, Cooper and colleagues have investigated core beliefs using semi-structured interviews. This has been particularly fruitful in helping to identify core or negative self-beliefs that might not be captured on investigator-defined self-report measures, with the potential to uncover beliefs that might be specific to those with EDs rather than, for example, typical of other forms of psychological distress. It has also enabled the idiosyncratic processing associated with negative self-beliefs to be identified, in a way that the use of the Young-Rygh Avoidance Inventory (Young & Rygh, 1994), for example, may not permit (Woolrich, Cooper, & Turner, 2006).

Imagery and the self are linked in eating disorders

The evidence for a link between imagery in EDs and self-related beliefs has been outlined above, with a focus on the way in which identification and exploration of spontaneous imagery can provide a route or 'mirror' to the self. The research suggests, however, a complex relationship between imagery and the self, and a role for other factors.

When examined further, self-beliefs also have links with early memories, which, when recalled, are similar to spontaneous images in content and associated feelings and other characteristics. Spontaneous images thus often reflect early experiences/memories, including the meanings attached to them and the associated emotional experience. Such early memories may, of course, be experienced as images. The link between imagery and self in those with EDs therefore seems complex and involved; overall, the two seem to be extremely intertwined, both developmentally and in current experience of these disorders.

Models of imagery and the self in eating disorders

As noted above, imagery does not have a specific function or role in most cognitive theories, including those of EDs. This is in contrast to the self, which has a prominent position in several recent theories (Cooper *et al.*, 2004; Fairburn *et al.*, 2003; Waller *et al.*, 2007). Currently, theoretical understanding of how the two might be linked in EDs, and indeed in other psychological disorders, is not well developed. Existing models in cognitive theory have not been developed particularly with imagery in mind. For example, they do not explain its specific role or function, and tend to assume that imagery functions exactly like verbal cognitions. Some preliminary theoretical ideas about the link between imagery and the self that have been discussed in the literature, including one that relates particularly to EDs, are presented below.

Imagery, memory, and the self

A recent analysis suggests that the link between imagery and the self may be through memories, especially autobiographical memories of early experiences (Hackmann, Clark, & McManus, 2000). Studies in anxiety disorders, and also a study conducted by Somerville *et al.* (2007) in women with BN, found strong links between negative spontaneous imagery and early childhood memories, also termed autobiographical memories. These memories typically concern traumatic and negative experiences, and are linked to images in a range of ways. There is known to be a strong link between autobiographical memory and imagery, particularly visual imagery (Conway & Pleydell-Pearce, 2000), so this suggestion is consistent with research in several other (non-clinical) areas (see Conway & Pleydell-Pearce, 2000). More specifically, Hackmann and colleagues have suggested, including for bulimia nervosa (Somerville *et al.*, 2007), that memories may persist and fail to update, thus helping to explain why, in some disorders, apparently 'old' memories from childhood and early life continue to influence current experience.

Could images function as goals in eating disorders?

It has also been suggested that images are representations of goals, and that they relate specifically to ideal, standard or referent images in both negative and positive feedback loops (Carver & Scheier, 1999). When the standard is a negative image, plans are instituted to reduce any discrepancy between the standard and the perceived state of the world. Substituting a positive image can therefore change the negative image, and thus the negative self. Conway's 'cognitive motivational' model (Conway & Pleydell-Pearce, 2000), in which images are viewed as autobiographical memories that are related to goals, is consistent with this, and also Hackmann's memory analysis.

Other cognitive theories that are relevant to the link observed empirically between imagery and the self, including in EDs, are considered below.

The role of images in metacognitive theory

Cognitive theories aim to explain emotion, and most do this by identifying verbal or propositional information. A more recent theory, the interacting cognitive subsystems (ICS) theory (Teasdale & Barnard, 1993), explicitly incorporates non-verbal information, identifies a component of the model that corresponds to visual imagery, and outlines how non-verbal information is particularly important in 'hot' cognition, or the 'felt sense', which is termed 'implicational meaning' in the ICS model. Nevertheless, it does not outline a specific role or function for imagery or imaginal experience, although one implication of the analysis is that felt sense or hot cognition, i.e. emotion, might be best modified using non-verbal strategies, i.e. it is likely to be most useful to have a match between the modalities involved in the experience and in the techniques used to modify the experience.

In his metacognitive theory, Wells (2000) refers to both memories and goals. In addition, and unlike other theorists, he postulates a particular and specific role for imagery. Imagery (imagination) has an important function in knowledge compilation and modification, and Wells provides a detailed theoretical account of why this might be, identifying the unique role and function of imagery, with a profile that distinguishes it from alternative ways of acquiring new knowledge. This includes self-referent knowledge, such as self-beliefs. In this analysis, imagery encapsulates cause–effect and temporal relationships, and also combines information with behaviour, which facilitates a multimodal and multidimensional perspective on a situation, unlike verbal thoughts, which are generally unidimensional. One advantage of this rich complexity is that imagery can function as a virtual world, and can be used in therapy for maximum change in 'self' beyond the merely propositional.

Guidano and Liotti's cognitive theory of eating disorders

One exception to the lack of theory addressing the link between imagery and self in eating disorders is Guidano and Liotti (1983), who incorporate the idea of 'the quasi-imaginal representation of the fat body' (p. 281) into their cognitive structural analysis of eating disorders and highlight images as a key aspect of patients' personal identity structures, in addition to thoughts (and feelings). In this analysis, rather as in that of Beck in relation to anxiety disorders (Beck & Emery, 1985) and general cognitive therapy/theory, the specific role of images is not expanded upon in great detail, but would appear, as in Beck's account, to be similar to that of verbal thoughts. However, Guidano and Liotti go beyond discussion of the factors maintaining disorders. In their analysis, imaginal representation also forms part of the authors' account of the development and organisation of self-knowledge (see below), thus providing a unique developmental perspective not considered by others interested in imagery in psychopathology, including in EDs, to date. They argue that in infancy and the preschool years, imaginal rather than verbal representation predominates in the development of reasoning and problem solving, and is thus crucial in the early development of personal identity. Moreover, Guidano and Liotti describe an analogical code that processes 'images', with the imaginal stream being described as one of the more characteristic ways in which an individual's self-knowledge is manifested. As such, daydreams, nightmares, etc. may represent or reflect an important demand for change. This is not elaborated on greatly in their ED chapter, but it is useful in forming a theoretical basis, which also incorporates a clinical perspective (unlike normal developmental theory of self-concept), for some of the attributes and characteristics, qualities and properties attributed to images by Beck and others. Overall it gives imagery a special role in the development of self and personal identity.

Although many people have taken a cognitive approach to the development and nature of the self (e.g. Harter, 1999), others have also suggested that imagery is important in its development, including the development of the normal and abnormal self. Morin (1998), for example, argues that the role of imagery in mediating self-awareness and acquiring self-related information has not been given sufficient attention. He suggests that while it has a cognitive role, imagery also plays a part in the elaboration of other aspects of self- awareness and self-concept, specifically through images of one's physical self or 'autoscopic imagery' (Kitamura, 1985).

The preconceptual self in eating disorders

Morin's work prompts consideration of the preconceptual self, something that is rarely considered by cognitive theorists. Those who do consider it often refer to embodiment, i.e. the idea that representations, or the early origins, of the self are not necessarily mental, but body-based. Imagery is often defined as a picture in the mind, i.e. a mental phenomenon, but those interested in the role of the body ('embodiment') have extended this idea to include non-mental experience. For example, Johnson (1987) refers to 'image schema', synonymous with 'embodied schema', and notes that these 'are not rich, concrete, images or mental pictures' (p. 23); instead they have a kinaesthetic character, and reflect abstract patterns that 'emerge as meaningful structures for us chiefly at the level of our bodily movements through space, our manipulation of objects, and our perceptual interactions' (p. 29). Feedback at a very early age from physical and perceptual interaction with the environment lays the foundation for the self-concept, as experienced in later life. Self is thus not purely cognitive; the cognitive aspect is only part of the construct (Butterworth, 1999), and one that emerges relatively late in the child's development (Fonagy, Gergely, Jurist, & Target, 2002).

Broadening the definition of image to include 'embodied experience' might be particularly useful in eating disorders. Not only is the experience of the body a crucial aspect of the disorder, but it enables us to begin to understand some of the previously hard to explain phenomena, for example, patients' experience of feeling fat, and the re-experiencing of early emotional and physical sensations that appear more 'body based' than cognitive. Feeling fat is, perhaps, a good example of an aspect of the ED experience that has been hard to understand and conceptualise. It does appear to be related to a range of images, including in different modalities, and can provide information on the self in those with AN at a cognitive level. It thus also appears, like mental imagery, to provide a window to the self. Nevertheless, it remains elusive as a cognitive construct when experienced by patients – one possibility is that it fits the definition of an image schema (Johnson, 1987). As such it may be a precursor to mentalisation, cognition and thus mental images, but may also be connected developmentally to these, representing early experience, or an early stage of development of self – preverbal, and precognitive. The latter analysis is speculative, but overall it suggests that we may need to integrate more of what we know from normal developmental theory of the origins and development of different representational systems into our understanding of eating disorders and psychopathology in general.

Treatment of eating disorders involving imagery and the self

There is growing interest in the use of imagery to modify beliefs, including self-related beliefs, in patients with EDs. While much of this has lacked a strong theoretical rationale, the discussion above may help to begin to fill that gap. The literature to date that takes a cognitive perspective will be summarised below, and brief details of one procedure will be outlined together with, based on an experimental study, its suggested theoretical mechanism.

Ohanian (2002) first described a single case of 'imagery rescripting' for an ED. The treatment was conducted within the context of CBT, aimed to modify resistant emotionally held schemas, and was reported to be successful. The treatment was based on the strategies described by Edwards (1990) and by Layden, Newman, Freeman, and Morse (1993). Using similar strategies, as well as pictures, Mountford and Waller (2006) described use of imagery to modify the restrictive mode or tendencies in a patient with AN. Both approaches suggested that use of imagery strategies in those with EDs may be helpful. Clinically, a systematic protocol has been developed specifically using imagery to change strongly held emotional beliefs (Cooper et al., 2007, 2008). This commences with a detailed assessment of relevant core or negative self-beliefs, and then proceeds to identify an associated early memory related to the eating problems, within which the negative self-beliefs are typically encapsulated and contained. Working from the early memory, the core beliefs are modified collaboratively with the patient, with a focus on reducing the extent to which the patient believes them to be true in her current life. This is achieved by manipulating imagery in all the necessary and relevant modalities, and by bringing a trusted adult into the image, with whom the child interacts. Changes in belief are checked out at various points, and ratings taken, in order that the intervention can be appropriately targeted. As with the interventions described by others, it is not designed as a sole intervention, but to be used when emotional beliefs persist despite the use of traditional cognitive restructuring strategies. The efficacy of the protocol in modifying emotional belief has been demonstrated in an experimental study with women with BN (Cooper *et al.*, 2007b). Theoretically, it draws on the metacognitive model of Wells (2000) to explain its effects, particularly its specific impact on emotional belief. Specifically, bringing a trusted adult into the situation is thought to enable the patient to retrieve positive interoceptive and conceptual information, antagonistic to the negative information in the early memory. This then changes emotional belief, and also the relationship to the belief – illustrating the attention given in metacognitive accounts to altering the processes as well as the content associated with the belief.

Conclusion: Lived experience revisited

The lived or everyday experience of an eating disorder is rich and complex, and extends beyond the purely cognitive; focusing on imagery reminds us of this. Moreover, imagery can provide an important and useful mirror to the self, and the evidence to date suggests that the two are intimately linked. Research and relevant treatment approaches employing imagery are at a very early stage of development in EDs. Nevertheless, a small but promising literature is beginning to develop. There are also some preliminary theoretical ideas to explain the role and function of mental imagery. Within a cognitive framework Wells' (2000) metacognitive model has been useful, including in EDs, and has informed development of a treatment protocol and some preliminary research. This highlights the role of the processes involved in creating psychopathology, in addition to the content of any core beliefs. Research has confirmed the first-person accounts – that imagery is important, and that self is intimately linked to the imagery typically experienced by those with an eating disorder. It has also provided detail on the precise nature of these links, and identified others – for example, links to memories and to early experiences. It also reminds us that the body has a role – that eventually we may need to go beyond purely verbal, cognitive, and also mental, particularly if we are to understand the origins of the self. This may involve some redefinition of the term 'imagery', for example to include 'embodiment'. EDs are not a theoretical abstraction, or theoretical construct, but have an everyday aspect. An ED is experienced in a multidimensional way by the person who suffers from it – this has been referred to as 'lived experience'. Studying imagery, the self (and beyond) can remind us of that, and can help bridge the artificial gap between science and everyday life.

References

Agras, W.S., Walsh, T., Fairburn, C.G., Wilson, G.T., & Kraemer, H.C. (2002). A multicentre comparison of cognitive behavioural therapy and interpersonal psychotherapy for bulimia nervosa. *Archives of General Psychiatry, 57*, 459–466.

American Psychiatric Association (2004). *Diagnostic and statistical manual of mental disorders* (4th edition, text revised). Washington, DC: APA.

Atwood, M. (1980). *The edible woman*. London: Virago Press.

Beck, A.T. (1976). *Cognitive therapy and the emotional disorders*. New York: New American Library.

Beck, A.T., & Emery, G. (with Greenberg, R.L.) (1985). *Anxiety disorders and phobias: A cognitive perspective*. New York: Basic Books.

Beck, A.T., Freeman, A., & Associates (1990). *Cognitive therapy of personality disorders*. New York: Guilford Press.

Beck, A.T., Rush, A.J., Shaw, B.F., & Emery, G. (1979). *Cognitive therapy of depression*. New York: Guilford Press.

Beck, J.S. (1995). *Cognitive therapy: Basics and beyond*. New York: Guilford Press.

Bruch, H. (1973). *Eating disorders*. New York: Basic Books.

Butterworth, G. (1999). A developmental-ecological perspective on Strawson's 'The Self'. In S. Gallagher & J. Shear (Eds), *Models of the self* (pp. 203–211). Exeter, UK: Imprint Academic.

Carver, C.S., & Scheier, M.F. (1999). Themes and issues in the self-regulation of behavior. In R.S. Wyer (Ed.), *Perspectives on behavioral self-regulation: Advances in social cognition* (Vol. 12, pp. 1–105). Mahwah, NJ: Lawrence Erlbaum Associates, Inc.

Cash, T.F. (1997). *The body image workbook*. Oakland, CA: New Harbinger Publications.

Conway, M.A., & Pleydell-Pearce, C.W. (2000). The construction of autobiographical memories in the self-memory system. *Psychological Review, 107*, 261–288.

Cooper, M.J., Cohen-Tovee, E., Todd, G., Wells, A., & Tovee, M. (1997). The eating disorder belief questionnaire: Preliminary development. *Behaviour Research and Therapy, 35*, 381–388.

Cooper, M.J., Deepak, K., Grocutt, E., & Bailey, E. (2007a). The experience of 'feeling fat' in women with anorexia nervosa, dieting and non-dieting women: An exploratory study. *European Eating Disorders Review, 15*, 366–372.

Cooper, M.J. Todd, G., & Turner, H. (2007b). The effects of using imagery to modify core beliefs: An experimental pilot study. *Journal of Cognitive Psychotherapy, 21*, 117–122.

Cooper, M.J., Todd, G., & Wells, A. (1998). Content, origins and consequences of dysfunctional beliefs in anorexia nervosa and bulimia nervosa. *Journal of Cognitive Psychotherapy, 12*, 213–230.

Cooper, M.J., Todd, G., & Wells, A. (2000). *A self-help cognitive therapy programme for bulimia nervosa*. London: Jessica Kingsley.

Cooper, M.J., Todd, G., & Wells, A. (2008). *Cognitive therapy for bulimia nervosa*. London: Taylor & Francis.

Cooper, M.J., Wells, A., & Todd, G. (2004). A cognitive theory of bulimia nervosa. *British Journal of Clinical Psychology, 43*, 1–16.

Edwards, D.J.A. (1990). Cognitive therapy and the restructuring of early memories through guided imagery. *Journal of Cognitive Psychotherapy*, *4*, 33–50.

Encarta (1999). *World English dictionary*. London: Bloomsbury.

Esplen, M., & Garfinkel, P. (1998). Guided imagery treatment to promote self-soothing in bulimia nervosa: A theoretical rationale. *Journal of Psychotherapy Practice and Research*, *7*, 102–118.

Esplen, M.J., Garfinkel, P.E., Olmsted, M., Gallop, R.M., & Kennedy, S. (1998). A randomized controlled trial of guided imagery in bulimia nervosa. *Psychological Medicine*, *28*, 1347–1357.

Fairburn, C.G., Cooper, P.J., & Cooper, Z. (1986). The clinical features and maintenance of bulimia nervosa. In K.D. Brownell & J.P. Foreyt (Eds.), *Physiology, psychology and treatment of the eating disorders* (pp. 389–404). New York: Basic Books.

Fairburn, C.G., Cooper, Z., & Shafran, R. (2003). Cognitive behaviour therapy for eating disorders: A transdiagnostic theory and treatment. *Behaviour Research and Therapy*, *41*, 509–528.

Fairburn, C.G., Marcus, M.D., & Wilson, G.T. (1993). Cognitive-behavioral therapy for binge eating and bulimia nervosa: A comprehensive treatment manual. In C.G. Fairburn & G.T. Wilson (Eds.), *Binge eating: Nature, assessment and treatment* (pp. 361–404). New York: Guilford Press.

Fairburn, C.G., Shafran, R., & Cooper, Z. (1999). A cognitive behavioural theory of anorexia nervosa. *Behaviour Research and Therapy*, *37*, 1–13.

Farrell, C., Shafran, R., Lee, M., & Fairburn, C.G. (2005). Testing a brief cognitive-behavioural intervention to improve extreme shape concern: A case series. *Behavioural and Cognitive Psychotherapy*, *33*, 189–200.

Fonagy, P., Gergely, G., Jurist, E.L., & Target, M. (2002). *Affect regulation, mentalisation, and the development of the self*. New York: Other Press.

Freeman, C. (2002) *Overcoming anorexia nervosa: A self-help guide using cognitive behavioural techniques*. London: Constable Robinson.

Garner, D.M., & Bemis, K.M. (1982). A cognitive–behavioural approach to anorexia nervosa. *Cognitive Therapy and Research*, *6*, 123–150.

Garner, D.M., Rockert, W., Olmsted, M.P., Johnson, C.L., & Coscina, D.V. (1985). Psychoeducational principles in the treatment of bulimia and anorexia nervosa. In D.M. Garner & P.E. Garfinkel (Eds.), *Handbook of treatment for eating disorders* (pp. 513–572). New York: Guilford Press.

Geller, J., Johnston, C., Madsen, K., Goldner, E.M., Remick, R.A., & Birmingham, C.L. (1998). Shape and weight based self esteem and the eating disorders. *International Journal of Eating Disorders*, *24*, 285–298.

Grogan, S. (1999). *Body image: Understanding body dissatisfaction in men, women and children*. London: Routledge.

Guidano, V.F., & Liotti, G. (1983). *Cognitive processes and emotional disorders: A structural approach to psychotherapy*. New York: Guilford Press.

Hackmann, A., Clark, D.M., & McManus, F. (2000). Recurrent images and early memories in social phobia. *Behaviour Research and Therapy*, *38*, 601–610.

Harter, S. (1999). *The construction of self: A developmental perspective*. New York: Guilford Press.

Holmes, E.A., & Hackmann, A. (2004). A healthy imagination? Editorial for the special issue of *Memory*: Mental imagery and memory in psychopathology. *Memory*, *12*, 387–388.

Horowitz, M.J. (1970). *Image formation and cognition*. New York: Appleton-Century-Crofts.

Hudgins, M.K. (1989). Experiencing the self through psychodrama and Gestalt therapy in anorexia nervosa. In L.M. Hornyak & E.K. Baker (Eds.), *Experiential therapies for eating disorders* (pp. 234–251). New York: Guilford Press.

Hutchinson, M.G. (1983). Transforming body image: Your body, friend or foe? *Women and Therapy*, *1*, 59–67.

Johnson, M. (1987). *The body in the mind: The bodily basis of meaning, imagination, and reason*. Chicago: University of Chicago Press.

Katzko, M.W. (2003). Unity versus multiplicity; a conceptual analysis of the term 'self' and its use in personality theories. *Journal of Personality*, *71*, 83–114.

Kearney-Cooke, A. (1989). Reclaiming the body: Using guided imagery in the treatment of body image disturbances among bulimic women. In L.M. Hornyak & E.K. Baker (Eds.), *Experiential therapies for eating disorders* (pp. 11–33). New York: Guilford Press.

Keel, P.K., Fichter, M., Quadflieg, N., Bulik, C.M., Baxter, M.G., Thornton, L., *et al.* (2004). Application of a latent class analysis to empirically define eating disorder phenotypes. *Archives of General Psychiatry*, *61*, 192–200.

Kitamura, S. (1985). Similarities and differences between perception and mental imagery. *Journal of Mental Imagery*, *9*, 83–92.

Layden, M.A., Newman, C.F., Freeman, A., & Morse, S.B. (1993). *Cognitive therapy of borderline personality disorder*. Needham Heights, MA: Allyn & Bacon.

Leys, R. (2006). Image and trauma. *Science in Context*, *19*, 137–149.

Liu, A. (1979). *Solitaire*. New York: Harper & Row.

Luck, A., Waller, G., Meyer, C., Ussher, M., & Lacey, H. (2005). The role of schema processes in the eating disorders. *Cognitive Therapy and Research*, *29*, 717–732.

Markus, H. (1977). Self-schemata and processing information about the self. *Journal of Personality and Social Psychology*, *35*, 63–78.

MacLeod, S. (1981). *The art of starvation*. London: Virago.

Martin, M., & Williams, R. (1990). Imagery and emotion: Clinical and experimental approaches. In P.J. Hampson, D.F. Marks, & J.T.E. Richardson (Eds.), *Imagery: Current developments* (pp. 268–306). London: Routledge.

Morin, A. (1998). Imagery and self-awareness: A theoretical note. *Theory and Review in Psychology* (available at www.gemstate.net/susan/Imagry2.htm).

Mountford, V., & Waller, G. (2006). Using imagery in cognitive-behavioral treatment for eating disorders: Tackling the restrictive mode. *International Journal of Eating Disorders*, *39*, 533–543.

Ohanian, V. (2002). Imagery rescripting within cognitive behaviour therapy for bulimia nervosa: An illustrative case report. *International Journal of Eating Disorders*, *31*, 352–357.

Padesky, C.A., & Greenberger, D. (1995). *Mind over mood*. New York: Guilford Press.

Pike, K.M., Walsh, B.T., Vitousek, K., Wilson, G.T., & Bauer, J. (2003). Cognitive behaviour therapy in the post hospitalisation treatment of anorexia nervosa. *American Journal of Psychiatry*, *160*, 2046–2049.

Pratt, D., Cooper, M.J., & Hackmann, A. (2004). Imagery and its characteristics in people who are anxious about spiders. *Behavioural and Cognitive Psychotherapy*, *32*, 165–176.

Rust, M.J. (1987). Bringing 'the man' into the room: Art therapy groupwork with women with compulsive eating problems. In D. Dokter (Ed.), *Arts therapies and clients with eating disorders* (pp. 48–59). London: Jessica Kingsley.

Schaverien, J. (1994). The picture as transitional object in the treatment of anorexia. In D. Dokter (Ed.), *Arts therapies and clients with eating disorders* (pp. 31–47). London: Jessica Kingsley.

Schiele, B., & Brozek, J. (1948). 'Experimental neurosis' resulting from semistarvation in man. *Psychosomatic Medicine, 10*, 31–50.

Schilder, P. (1950). *The image and appearance of the human body*. New York: International University Press.

Schmidt, U., & Treasure, J. (1993). *Getting better bit(e) by bit(e): A survival kit for sufferers of bulimia nervosa and binge eating disorder*. Hove, UK: Psychology Press.

Somerville, K., & Cooper, M.J. (2007). The presence and characteristics of core beliefs in women with bulimia nervosa, dieting and non-dieting women accessed using imagery. *Eating Behaviors, 8*, 450–456.

Somerville, K., Cooper, M., & Hackmann, A. (2007). Spontaneous imagery in women with bulimia nervosa: An investigation into content, characteristics and links to childhood memories. *Journal of Behaviour Therapy and Experimental Psychiatry, 38*, 435–446.

Teasdale, J.D., & Barnard, P.J. (1993). *Affect, cognition, and change: Re-modelling depressive thought*. Hove, UK: Psychology Press.

Treasure, J. (1997). *Anorexia nervosa: A survival guide for families, friends and sufferers*. Hove, UK: Psychology Press.

Vitousek, K.B., & Hollon, S.D. (1990). The investigation of schematic content and processing in eating disorders. *Cognitive Therapy and Research, 14*, 191–214.

Waller, G., Kennerley, H., & Ohanian, V. (2007). Schema focused cognitive behaviour therapy with the eating disorders. In L.P. Riso, P.T. duToit, & J.E. Young (Eds.), *Cognitive schemas and core beliefs in psychiatric disorders: A scientist practitioner guide* (pp. 139–176). New York: American Psychological Association.

Wells, A. (2000). *Emotional disorders and metacognition: Innovative cognitive therapy*. Chichester, UK: Wiley.

Wonderlich, S.A., Joiner, T.E., Jr., Keel, P.K., Williamson, D.A., & Crosby, R.D. (2007). Eating disorder diagnoses: Empirical approaches to classification. *American Psychologist, 62*, 167–190.

Woolrich, R., Cooper, M.J., & Turner, H. (2006). A preliminary study of negative self-beliefs in anorexia nervosa: Exploring their content, origins and functional links to 'not eating enough' and other characteristic behaviors. *Cognitive Therapy and Research, 30*, 735–748.

Wylie, R.C. (1979). *The self concept: Theory and research on selected topics* (Vol. 2). Lincoln, NE: University of Nebraska Press.

Young, J.E., & Brown, G. (1994). *Young Schema-Questionnaire* (2nd ed.). In J.E. Young (Ed.), *Cognitive therapy for personality disorders: A schema-focused approach*. Sarasota, FL: Professional Resource Press (available at www.schematherapy.com).

Young, J.E., Klosko, J.S., & Weisshaar, M.E. (2003). *Schema therapy: A practitioner's guide*. New York: Guilford Press.

Young, J.E., & Rygh, J. (1994). *Young–Rygh avoidance inventory* (available at www.schematherapy.com).

Chapter 9

Evolved minds and compassion-focused imagery in depression

Paul Gilbert

Directed imagery exercises have been used for thousands of years as ways to try to create inner states of mind, deepen insights, and develop certain abilities. The most obvious examples are those of compassion-focused imagery as used in Buddhist practice (Leighton, 2003). In the past 100 years imagery has been used by a variety of psychotherapists – from Jung's (1875–1961) use of active imagination to explore archetypal processes, complexes and growth, to the work on imagery as a desensitisation process for painful emotions and memories. Major reviews of the tasks, forms, functions, difficulties, advantages and disadvantages, and dangers in the use of imagery in therapy now exist (Arbuthnott, Arbuthnott, & Rossiter, 2001; Frederick & McNeal, 1999; Hall, Hall, Stradling, & Young, 2006; Holmes & Hackmann, 2004; Rossman, 2000; Singer, 2006) and will not be explored further here. Rather this chapter will focus only on the theory and processes involved in the use of compassion-focused imagery.

These interventions were originally developed with, and for, people who have chronic, complex and severe depression, linked to high shame and self-criticism (Gilbert, 2000; Gilbert & Irons, 2005), a group that can be difficult to help (Rector, Bagby, Segal, Joffe, & Levitt, 2000). The chapter will outline how the potential potency of compassion-focused imagery arises from the interaction of a variety of evolved motivational, emotional and cognitive systems. These systems pertain to the importance of social relationships as major regulators of our emotions, and also to a host of ways humans have evolved 'imaginational competencies' that are often focused on 'self-in-relationship' to others and 'self-to-self' relating. Compassion-focused imagery is used to try to stimulate a particular type of affect regulation system (a soothing system) that is linked to social affiliation, care and well-being.

Evolved minds

If we start with the evolutionary story, then we can note that chimpanzees may share nearly 99% of our genes and certainly have many social goals in common with us, including forming caring attachments and friendships, living in groups, and concern with status. These social needs and motivations are basic to all mammals, but especially humans. Indeed, there is now good evidence that early care is central to human brain development and functioning, well-being, self–other evaluations/schemas, and affect regulation (Baldwin, 2005; Baumeister & Leary, 1995; Bowlby, 1969, 1973; Gilbert, 1989, 2003, 2007a; Guidano & Liotti, 1983; Safran & Segal, 1990; Schore, 1994; Siegel, 2001). The dynamic flow of moment-to-moment relationships affects our physiological patterns and states of mind (Cacioppo, Berston, Sheridan, & McClintock, 2000). In addition, previous experiences of relationships are coded in our minds as interpersonal schemas (Baldwin, 2005) and memories (Brewin, 2006) and can act as a lens that guides moment-to-moment processing of interactions and emotion.

When we consider the internal world of schemas, meaning, and meaning creation that influence our experience of ourselves as social beings, humans differ radically from other mammals in myriad ways by virtue of our ability to use language and symbols, to think and reason about ourselves (with heightened self-awareness and creation of a self-identity) and our self-in-relationship to others, and to represent internally models of the (social) world for inspection – that is, to imagine. From these qualities of mind we have evolved into a species that lives in two worlds: the world 'as is' and the world 'as imagined' (Singer, 2006). Wells (2000, p. 30) notes the evolutionary benefits of evolving a capacity for imagination to anticipate and cope with threats.

> In adaptational or evolutionary terms, the presence of a cognitive mechanism for facilitating the acquisition of plans for dealing with threat, without the need to repeatedly encounter the threat, would bestow on the individual a survival advantage. Imagery provides a 'virtual world' for programming procedural knowledge that avoids the dangers of on-line behavioural practice during exposure to actual danger.

Imagination evolved as an internal simulator, an onboard virtual reality system. As Singer (2006) and Wells (2000) point out, imagination is often dynamic and we can change what happens in it; imagine 'what would happen if . . .'. So, we can plan, conceptualise and anticipate. We can run lots of different simulations. In our imagination we can anticipate the fun of a holiday, the acclaim and life change if we achieve a goal (e.g. pass an exam), and the lost opportunities if we fail. Crucial to our imagination are a host of evolved competencies that enable us to imagine how we are viewed and felt about by others. These competencies relate to humans having a 'theory of mind' (Byrne, 1995), which literally means we can understand other people's behaviour by imagining and reasoning about their feelings and states of mind – i.e. we understand that their behaviour arises from how their minds are processing information (i.e. that they have feelings and motivations and can have accurate or inaccurate views). So when one thinks 'That person ignored me yesterday because they are depressed' this means one understands that a person can feel depressed and what depression feels like, and makes that the attribution for their behaviour. Peter Fonagy has referred to these abilities as 'mentalising' – which is the ability to appreciate, imagine and think about the mental states of others (e.g. see Fonagy & Target, 2006).

These abilities are also fundamental to how we experience ourselves during interactions. For example, experiences of self can arise from how we imagine we 'exist in the minds of others' (e.g. as liked, wanted and valued, or disliked, unwanted and devalued). We can never directly experience the feelings of others about the self, so have to infer/imagine them. Not only can we develop views of ourselves from how we think others view us, but our sense of feeling safe or threatened in the social world, and our self-conscious emotions such as pride and shame, are linked to whether we feel we create good or bad impressions in the minds of others (Gilbert, 2003, 2007b).

Imagination allows us to be creative and to invent and write stories of fictional characters who do not even exist. When we socially and culturally share and give meaning to imagined others, we can give birth to religions with gods and goddesses (Hinde, 1999). Our sense of self, life meanings, feelings and actions can be influenced by efforts to influence the 'mind' of these (imagined) gods and goddesses and our relationships to them (Bering, 2002). Many cultures believe that when people we love die, their essence can live on, that we can communicate with them, and that they still have an interest in our well-being.

So we have seen how powerful forms of social or relational imagination are, and their impact on the sense of self. There is one other aspect we should note about imagination that is important for understanding compassion-focused work with imagery exercises. This relates to the fact that imagination can exert a powerful stimulating effect on our physiological systems. For example, if we imagine a meal when we are hungry we can stimulate our saliva and stomach acids even in the absence of a real meal; if we imagine something sexual while lying alone in our beds we can stimulate sexual arousal. We can imagine the fun of a holiday and feel excited. Indeed, we can purposefully use and manipulate our imagination to create forms of arousal. Hence, internally generated stimuli (images) can stimulate specific groups of cells in the brain that regulate certain physiological functions (e.g. for eating or sexuality or excitement). Focusing on negative images can of course have more negative physiological impacts and be associated with stress arousal. Indeed, imagery is often used in functional magnetic resonance imaging (fMRI) to stimulate different brain areas for neuroscience research (George et al., 1995). Furthermore, with practice, various forms of imagery can produce changes in the brain, and can be used specifically to do so (Begley, 2007; Schwartz & Begley, 2002).

Compassion-focused imagery rests on these basic principles and seeks to help people develop imagery that they will find soothing and conducive to well-being. To do this requires some insight into the evolved physiological systems that underpin soothing and well-being because these are what we will seek to activate through compassionate imagery. Now there are many possible candidates for such a focus: for example, imagery that is associated with safe places, relaxation, or coping (Frederick & McNeal, 1999). Although we will not explore these here, this is not to demote their importance (see Chapter 3 for a discussion of these imagery techniques). Rather our focus is on imagery that stimulates an evolved affect regulation system, which is linked to evolved systems that underpin caring relationships.

Threat, the attachment system, safeness[1] and affect regulation

The world is a dangerous and threatening place, with 99% of all species that have existed now extinct. For many species, where parents do not provide care for their infants post-birth, mortality rates (from predation, diseases and starvation) are high, with only 1–2% surviving into adulthood to reproduce. An example that most people will be familiar with is turtles. In this threatening world all living things need to distinguish between the safe and not safe. Emotions such as anger, anxiety and disgust, and behaviours such as fight, flight, or curling up and withdrawing are basic defences for many animals, and are linked to threat-processing systems (Gilbert, 1989, 1993; Marks, 1987). For animals without attachment systems, these defences are linked directly to external threats.

Parental investment and attachment, however, evolve with having few offspring but protecting and caring for them early in life (Geary, 2000). This breeding strategy is basic to all mammals. Bowlby (1969, 1973) was one of the first to articulate the implications of the evolution of parental investment (attachment) in terms of basic motivations and affect regulation

---

1 In early work (e.g. Gilbert, 1989, 1993) I used the term 'safety system' to distinguish it from a threat system. However, the late ethologist Michael Chance pointed out to me that safe*ty* was a confusing term because it did not capture the essence of *safeness* as a state in which brain systems are organised and patterned. He noted that people can engage in a variety of defensive behaviours that could be called safety behaviours (e.g. aggression, avoidance or running away) that are aimed at coping and reducing threats. For example, a person might carry a gun to give a sense of safety, indicating that the sense of safety is very much linked to their perceived abilities to cope with a certain threat. Indeed, many psychologists use the terms 'safety behaviours' and 'defensive behaviours' interchangeably. Consequently, I (Gilbert, 1995) changed the term safe*ty* to safe*ness* to indicate the way our minds are organised when we feel safe (e.g. with relaxed and open attention, explorative and non-defensive; Gilbert, 1993). So the term 'safeness' is used to depict a 'state of being safe and content' where one's mind is not focused, attentive or concerned with threat, nor is one feeling that needs have not been met and thus one is 'wanting' (hence the issue of contentedness). The feelings of safeness arise from activity in soothing/content and safeness systems. We can contrast this with safety-seeking and safety that is linked to reducing threats.

for mammals. Adults evolve mechanisms to recognise their own offspring, take an interest in maintaining proximity to them, and respond to their (threat-aroused) distress calls. Infants in their turn evolve innate motivations to seek proximity to carers and to be physiologically responsive to their inputs; for example, infants can be calmed by parental signals. By the time humans arrive on the evolutionary stage, this basic strategy has given rise to a vast array of complex co-regulating interactions that are physiologically potent (Schore, 1994). Thus we know that humans are care-seeking animals who can regulate distress via access to care, and that the quality of care an infant receives from his/her parents affects the maturation of the brain and a host of regulating physiological processes, and influences important internal working models of self and others (Gerhardt, 2004; Mikulincer & Shaver, 2004).

Close kin-based attachments, however, are only one type of relationship that provides avenues for feeling safe or feeling threatened (Gilbert, 1989). As Baumeister and Leary (1995) and Bailey (2002) note, there are a host of 'value-based' relationships where people can feel safe because they feel they are like others, are accepted, valued and supported by others, and have a sense of belonging and community. Safeness derived from affiliation is therefore more than just nurturance, and includes feelings of 'being part of'. Indeed, when meditators have 'bliss states', they describe their experiences less in terms of feeling nurtured and more in terms of feeling 'part of the universe' and having a place within it (Coxhead, 1985). In addition we now know that throughout life humans often use supportive others to help them regulate threat arousal, and that the types of signals exchanged between individuals are powerful psychobiological regulators (Cacioppo *et al.*, 2000).

The study of attachment and affiliation has led to some surprising and deeply illuminating new findings about positive affect systems and their relationship to threat/stress systems. First is the finding that there are at least *two types* of positive affect regulation system (Depue & Morrone-Strupinsky, 2005). One gives us a sense of drive and vitality to seek out rewards and positive things; the other operates when we have consumed or achieved and no longer need to seek things (i.e. it turns off seeking and drive) – we are content. Both systems have been 'borrowed' and used by evolution to regulate behaviour in social relationships. Relationships are things that activate us and we seek them out – we get a real buzz when starting a new love relationship, or when we are chosen to be on the team. The contentment systems have also evolved into a system that registers care, love and affection, and signals acceptance and social safeness (Carter, 1998; Depue & Morrone-Strupinsky, 2005; Wang, 2005). When social signals of affiliation and 'being cared for and about' trigger this system we feel soothed by the support, kindness and care of others. These feelings are strongly linked to feelings of contentment, safeness and well-being and regulate both drive-seeking and threat systems.

Although the neuroscience is complex, and these systems are in constant states of co-regulation, a simplified model of these three affect systems is shown in Figure 9.1.

Social signals of affiliation and care have the qualities of soothing and involve neurohormones such as oxytocin and opiates (Carter, 1998; Depue & Morrone-Strupinsky, 2005; Panksepp, 1998; Uväns-Morberg, 1998). Signals and stimuli such as stroking, holding, voice tone, facial expressions, concerned interest/attentiveness and social support are *natural* stimuli that activate this system (Field, 2000; Uväns-Morberg, 1998; Wang, 2005). Depue and Morrone-Strupinsky (2005) link these two different positive affect regulating systems to different types of social behaviour. They distinguish affiliation from agency and sociability. Agency and sociability are linked to control and achievement-seeking, social dominance and the (threat-focused) avoidance of rejection and isolation. So when people are seeking these social outcomes they need drive and energy. Blocks on the path to these goals can be experienced as threats. In contrast, affiliation and affiliative interactions, operating via an oxytocin–opiate system, have a calming and soothing effect on participants, which also alters pain thresholds and has positive effects on immune and digestive systems. There is increasing evidence that oxytocin is linked to social support and buffers stress; those with lower oxytocin have higher stress responsiveness (Heinrichs, Baumgartner, Kirschbaum, & Ehlert, 2003). There is also increasing evidence that oxytocin reduces sensitivity in fear circuits of the amygdala, especially to socially threatening stimuli (Kirsch *et al.*, 2005). So evidence points to the role of an oxytocin–opiate system providing the basis for soothing and calming, and regulation of the threat system with a dampening effect on the production of the stress hormones such as cortisol (Carter, 1998; Depue & Morrone-Strupinsky, 2005; Field,

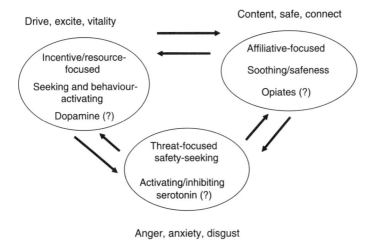

Figure 9.1 Types of affect regulation system.

2000; Wang, 2005). It can therefore be regarded as part of a 'safeness system' (Gilbert, 1989, 1993, 2005, 2007a; see Note 1 above).

From attachment and affiliation systems to compassion

The section above identified an evolutionary path for attachment and affiliation and the basic neurophysiological systems that have evolved to support them. Using this approach, we can posit that compassion is a complex, multi-faceted set of competencies that have emerged from the increasing elaboration of caring–providing/giving and social affiliation systems (Gilbert, 1989, 2000, 2005, 2007a). When we relate to others with a compassionate focus, we seek to alleviate their distress and promote their well-being. This requires that we are *sensitive* and able to recognise their distress and needs; can be *sympathetic* and emotionally moved by their distress; can *tolerate* their distress (rather than be avoidant or controlling); have *empathic* understanding of the causes, nature and alleviators of their distress (and what will promote well-being); and are non-judgemental and non-condemning. In addition, these responses are enacted with warmth. This combination of competencies has been called the compassion circle (Gilbert, 2005, 2009), which is illustrated in Figure 9.2.

When we encounter others who have this kind of disposition towards us, they are experienced as non-threatening and calming. They help us to feel safe. Moreover, there is now good research suggesting that if we have emotional memories of others having behaved in these ways towards us (e.g. loving and empathic parents, social acceptance), then these 'emotional memories' can be activated in times of stress and help us regulate stress (Baldwin, 2005). Based on the aspects of imagery noted above, we can therefore propose that developing imagery that incorporates the qualities of the compassion circle may have soothing and well-being-promoting properties.

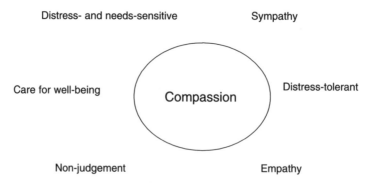

Figure 9.2 The compassion circle: Components of compassion from the care-giving mentality create opportunities for growth and change with warmth.

A brief history of compassionate imagery

As noted above, human evolution has given rise to abilities to imagine self-in-relationship to others and to feel comforted or threatened by such imaginations. This is because, just as imagining a meal or a sexual encounter can stimulate specific physiological systems, imagining certain types of self-in-relationship-to-others may stimulate specific affect systems (Gilbert, 2005, 2009; Gilbert & Irons, 2005). Indeed, there is a long history to the use of 'imaginary others' to help sooth the self. The most obvious of these is religious imagery. Armstrong (1994) points out that the concept of God has many functions. God can be seen as offering protection in exchange for obedience, but can also act as a focus for attachment needs, being cared for and cared about (Kirkpatrick, 2005). The exact nature of these images varies and is culturally constructed (Hinde, 1999). Prayer can be seen as efforts to engage in a relationship with an imaginary figure or figures, and through this form of relating one seeks to derive comfort and strength. There is evidence that some people can indeed derive much comfort and soothing by feeling 'in contact' with God and having imagery relationships with him or her (Kirkpatrick, 2005).

Buddhism has perhaps been the psychological system that is most identified with the concept of developing mindful compassion as an antidote to suffering (Dalai Lama, 1995, 2001; Leighton, 2003). There are various elements to developing and harnessing compassion, related to: (1) fostering a motivation to develop compassion to self and others; (2) meditative and imagery practices that engage with the feelings and states of mind of compassion (see below); (3) forms of thinking and acting that enhance compassion. In Mahayana Buddhism compassion qualities include generosity, ethical behaviour, patience, effort, and concentration, which are each divided into subtasks and guided by wisdom. Although Buddhist concepts are somewhat different to those derived from evolutionary theory (as depicted in the compassion circle in Figure 9.2), they are highly complementary and mutually informative.

Glasser (2005) has recently explored how Buddhist practice and compassion can be introduced into psychodynamic approaches, while Dowd (2007) has explored the implications of Buddhist psychology with a compassion focus for cognitive therapy. Although there are many different schools of Buddhism, all contain exercises that offer various practices for meditative imagery on the nature of compassion and the compassion Buddha (Walpola Sri Rahula, 1959/1997). Leighton (2003) has explored some of these images and their multiple forms, and offers the illuminating idea that they are designed to stimulate certain archetypal (innate) patterns of feelings, experiencing and 'being' within us. This fits well with the idea that different images, with different sensory cues, stimulate our physiological patterns. The Mahayana Buddhist view is also that the 'universe' is full of Bodhisattvas (those who have developed various levels of compassionate enlightenment) and one can imagine relating to them and tune into them, giving a sense of a shared journey, mutual support and a spiritual community – where all are seeking enlightenment through mindful compassion. Note that this focus is less on relating to an individual God or being nurtured by others, and more in terms of community and shared humanity, where 'all beings' are pursuing the same ends – enlightenment.

Leighton (2003) and Ringu Tilku Rinpoche and Mullen (2005) discuss some of the rituals and meditative practices that are designed to help participants tune into and feel compassion. For example, one set of imaginary practices involves a series of steps, each of which can take some practice. The steps are: imagining a certain type of Buddha; imagining the Buddha harnessing the compassion in the universe; imagining the Buddha directing that compassion energy to you (and what that feels like, i.e. being given and receiving compassion unconditionally); imagining the Buddha merging with you and you feeling the nature of compassion; imagining being full of compassion (being a compassion Buddha yourself); and then imagining giving compassion to all living things in the universe. As Leighton (2003) notes, there is no one compassion Buddha image, but instead there are a variety of images that have been developed for compassion imagery practices and which have different functions. There are also various imagery practices that are called loving kindness, where one focuses on giving loving kindness to self and then to others (Salzberg, 1995). Loving kindness meditation has been incorporated into mindfulness practice with good results (Shapiro, Astin, Bishop, & Cordova, 2005). Rein, Atkinson, and McCraty (1995) explored the impact of anger imagery and compassion imagery on a measure of immune functioning called S-IgA. Anger imagery had a negative effect on S-IgA, while compassion imagery improved it. Compassionate imagery, then, may do many things including altering neurophysiological systems.

Compassionate imagery

Developing compassionate imagery is part of what is called 'compassionate mind training' – literally training one's mind in the processes and feelings of compassion (Gilbert & Irons, 2004). It acknowledges the long history and traditions associated with the development and use of compassion imagery (Leighton, 2003). However, Gilbert and Irons (2005) have suggested that it is possible to use compassion imagery without recourse to religious symbols. Indeed, it might be wise at times to avoid these symbols because they are often culturally proscribed, may involve assumptions about other supernatural realms, and thus may be inappropriate for some people. In addition, we wanted to help people create, 'play with', discover, build and develop imagery that (a) was unique for them, (b) created an experience of soothing for them, and (c) incorporated experiences of compassion associated with the compassion circle, with sensitivity to their distress, sympathy, distress tolerance, empathy and non-judgement.

There is a range of imagery exercises that are designed to imagine creating, and then relating to, an inner friend, helper or guide (Frederick & McNeal, 1999; Rossman, 2000). Hall *et al.* (2006, pp. 61–62) offer an imagery sequence that involves walking up a mountain to find a wise compassionate other, noting his/her appearance as you sit beside him/her, and then imagining yourself looking 'through his/her eyes' at yourself. This is designed not only to induce certain feelings but also to alter perspectives for thinking about oneself.

The road to my approach in the use of compassion-focused imagery in CBT is of interest because it was first suggested by clients themselves. Back in the early 1990s, I became interested in how people with high shame and self-criticism struggled with basic cognitive-behavioural interventions. They could see the logic of generating alternative thoughts, but these did not help them to feel much different. Further exploration revealed that the emotional tone and the way that they 'heard' alternative thoughts in their head were often cold, detached or even slightly aggressive. With one particular lady, whom I will call Anne and who had chronic depression and suicidality, we pondered how she might generate more emotional warmth in her alternative thoughts: When she thought of alternative thoughts (to her depressing ones) or wrote them down, we wondered how she might focus on the feelings or warmth and reassurance in them. In fact, this revealed another key aspect of working with compassion: At first Anne was deeply frightened of developing warmth for herself, as I will discuss later. But it occurred to me that if the emotion system that gives rise to feelings of soothing and reassurance (what I had called a safety/safeness system [see Footnote 1 above]; Gilbert, 1989) was not sufficiently active then any 'alternative thoughts' could not generate such feelings – leaving a person with a logical understanding, but not being emotionally moved or reassured by alternative thoughts.

However, the point of the story is that gradually she did begin to practise warmth and told me that she found this a lot easier when she could 'personify it'. For her it was a female version of a compassionate Buddha – dressed as an Earth Goddess. Together we collaborated on various imagery experiments that focused on how she could use such images and I introduced my limited knowledge of compassion. We then wondered about whether she could bring a compassion focus into new styles of thinking about her predicament and her depression. For Anne, and now for many others, it seemed that if one offers some basic ideas about compassion, some people could generate their own images of a 'compassionate other' or of a compassion process. Rather than giving people specific images, as suggested by Buddhist and other traditional practices, people could generate their own (Gilbert, 2009; Gilbert & Irons, 2004). It turned out that once people had an idea of what they were trying to do, and why (to find images that stimulate the soothing system and feel safe and reassured), some (but not all) could come up with a variety of images that seemed helpful to them (Gilbert & Irons, 2004).

There is still debate and little research on what these images should entail, and whether culturally shared ones might work better than individually created ones, but in general it seems that the image of a compassionate other should be one that has a mind that can understand the mind of the client – i.e. it is not just some healing energy or entity. In addition, it should have all the qualities of the compassion circle. The reasons why the image should be sentient and have a mind that understands our own minds are complex and relate to various aspects of how our minds are attuned to what is going on in the minds of others (see Gilbert, 2005, 2007a, for a more full review; Fonagy & Target, 2006). Finally, the image should have had similar experiences to the self. Indeed, both the Buddha and Jesus Christ have credibility because they have lived a human life and know what human suffering is and have experienced it.

When I began this work, clients would use traditional cognitive-behavioural strategies of identifying various negative thoughts and then generating alternatives. However, as these alternative thoughts emerged, the client was asked to try to imagine their compassionate images and to try to 'hear and sense' their alternatives with as much warmth as they could, as if a compassionate other were speaking to them. In essence, the aim is to have an inner conversation with parts of the self through the use of imagery (Watkins, 1986).

Compassion-focused imagery of this form is therefore explained very much in terms of activating different parts of the self and learning how to use imagery to stimulate a particular affect system. Clients are encouraged to experiment and to allow images to change. We also advise that these images are not like clear pictures in the mind, but more like fragments and daydreams (Singer, 2006), and that it is their essence rather than any visual or other sensory clarity that is important. Anne never actually had clear images of her 'Buddha dressed as an Earth Goddess' but it 'came with an essence of warmth'. She noted that at times when she felt down she would close her eyes, take a few breaths and focus on her image, and on the feelings that came with it, and have an inner conversation. These 'alternative thoughts' emerged from the refocusing. From Anne and people like her, I developed the notion of the compassionate other as an ideal (see Appendix for notes on building a compassionate image). This could then act as a focus of attention and imagery in times of distress.

Lee (2005) has labelled this process the 'compassionate reframe', noting, as Anne did, that it is placing oneself in a particular frame of mind first and then re-examining one's distressing feelings and thoughts that can be helpful. In other words, one imagines one's compassionate ideal and 'what the compassionate image would say to the self and how s/he would say it'. This has some similarity to the more traditional cognitive intervention of 'imagining what a friend or someone who cares for you might say; imagine seeing yourself through their eyes. Then imagine how you feel if you focus on that'. Lee (2005) has used the term 'Perfect Nurturer' to depict the ideal compassionate image that has all the qualities and attributes that one would ideally want from such a figure. While this is very helpful for some people, it is useful to keep in mind that the concept of 'a nurturer' can have different meanings for different people. It is, for example, unclear how this concept relates to Buddhist notions of compassion imagery (Leighton, 2003). Indeed, in these traditions, the concept of a guru or mentor is less about nurturing in the sense of protecting, taking care of and providing for, and more about acceptance, sharing in the journey of suffering, teaching, guided practice and enlightening. Thus, as Lee (2005) notes, her view of nurturance is broadly focused and, like the concept of care, is multifaceted and changes with developmental stages and needs. Consider also that it can be important for people to feel cared about by aging parents, noting the difference between being 'cared for' and being 'cared about'. With their frailties they can no longer nurture us and, indeed, we may need to nurture them. What is key is how we feel we exist for them, as a loved, esteemed or valued person, the knowledge that they worry for us and have our well-being at heart. Thus, the issue is about how we come to feel about ourselves via how we think and imagine others feel about us (Gilbert, 2003) – and this is the key to the psychotherapy relationship (Gilbert, 2007b) and to the compassionate image. These aspects are crucial to work with the client's needs and experiences and to explore with them what fits for them.

So here then is a simple 'technique' of imagining an 'ideal compassionate other' that one imagines relating and conversing with in one's mind (see Appendix). We stress that this is an inner creation with the sole purpose of trying to bring on-line the soothing systems. There are a number of variants to this, such as recalling the voice tones, dispositions, and facial expressions of someone who was caring of the self, and imagining what they might say and how they might say it. This can trigger helpful emotional memories. The key here, however, is not so much the content (although this is obviously important) as the felt experience – feeling the care, concern and warmth of the imagined other. For some people this has dramatic effects. For others, though, it can be frightening, as I will note below.

Working with shame and self-criticism

So far we have explored the idea that evolution has designed our brains to be highly sensitive to social inputs, able to be soothed and calmed because we have brain systems that respond to care stimuli, and able to imagine and reason about social relationships and how we exist in the minds of others. We can feel soothed by imagining/believing that others care about us. Our basic experiences of threat and safeness are forged in and through our early attachments, and social relationships shape these inner imaginations (Baldwin, 2005; Schore, 1994). However, by late childhood humans begin to treat 'self-as-an-object' for self-evaluation. We can become self-accepting, nurturing and compassionate or deeply self-critical and hostile. Compassionate mind training (Gilbert, 2000, 2009; Gilbert & Irons, 2005) was first designed for people who struggled with high levels of shame, self-criticism and even self-hatred: people who are known to have chronic problems and who are difficult to help. They can be locked into a self-harassment cycle where – when stressed – they become self-critical, ruminative or reactivate shame memories. These increase stress (e.g. cortisol), leading to further stress, which reduces their ability to 'stand back' and re-evaluate situations.

Although many therapies have focused on the importance of self-acceptance as an antidote to self-criticism, compassionate mind training focuses on a series of steps for moving from self-criticism to self-compassion. First we focus on self-criticism as a safety behaviour that has various functions (i.e. a functional analysis is important rather than seeing self-criticism merely as a cognitive distortion for which alternative evidence is sought). Thus, we do not seek to undermine self-criticism directly if this is too frightening for a person, but rather to teach the person how to redirect attention and thinking to a more compassionate focus. Second, we focus on teaching the nature and value of self-compassion. Third, we work on developing a set of exercises that seek to promote self-compassion – some of which involve imagery – and activate the soothing system (Gilbert, 2007a, 2009).

As in classical behaviour therapy (using emotional reciprocal inhibition), the goal here is to try to bring on-line a new affect system that counters the aversive emotions that are recruited and stimulated in self-criticism. Keep in mind that, as noted above, the oxytocin–opiate system can regulate the amygdala, and it is the amygdala that is the probable source for the feelings engendered by self-criticism. Although awaiting research data, compassionate imagery may be one way of activating this soothing. Here, people learn to detect and note their self-criticism, but then to refocus their attention to the compassionate image and its qualities. We are not seeking to (just) teach people to generate alternative views or evidence *against* self-criticism (in a point-to-point debate that may be rebutted with 'yes buts') but to create a new affect that provides an important emotional base for alternative thinking – that is, to generate alternative thinking and meaning-making from a different emotional position.

Self-compassion and the compassionate self

Self-acceptance is just one aspect of self-compassion: Many therapists and theorists see *self*-compassion as a complex, multifaceted process. The cognitive therapists McKay and Fanning (1992), who have developed an important self-esteem programme, view self-compassion as made of understanding, acceptance and forgiveness. Neff (2003a, 2003b), from a social psychology and Buddhist tradition, sees compassion as consisting of three bipolar constructs related to kindness, common humanity and mindfulness. *Kindness* involves understanding one's difficulties and being kind and warm in the face of failure or setbacks rather than harshly judgemental and self-critical. *Common humanity* involves seeing one's experiences as part of the human condition rather than as personal, isolating and shaming; *mindful acceptance* involves mindful awareness and acceptance of painful thoughts and feelings rather than over-identifying with them. Neff, Kirkpatrick, and Rude (2007) have shown that self-compassion is different to self-esteem and is conducive to many indicators of well-being (see also Gilbert & Irons, 2005; Leary, Tate, Adams, Allen, & Hancock, 2007).

My own approach to self-compassion is to use the compassion circle as a self-directed focus for work (see Figure 9.2). Thus, compassion is the focus of the therapeutic relationship (Gilbert, 2007b) and self-compassion the task for the client's development. Self-compassion involves learning to understand what self-care is (in contrast to only self-protection) and to be motivated to engage with it; to be *sensitive* and able to recognise our own distress and needs, including how we have come to develop, and at times be trapped by, safety behaviours; how we can be *sympathetic* and emotionally moved by our distress and life stories; how we can learn to *tolerate* our distress (rather than be avoidant or controlling or using various defences such as denial or dissociation); how we can develop *empathic* understanding of the causes, nature *and alleviators* of our distress (and what will promote our well-being); and how we can become non-judgemental and non-self-condemning.

To help people explore the feelings of compassion we can use the notion of compassion 'coming in' from others to self or 'flowing out' from self to others. For both, one can use imagery from emotional memories. For example, one can try to recall a time someone was very kind to one and what that felt like, trying to bring to mind as many details as possible. Or one can recall a time one was kind and helpful to someone else and what that felt like – again trying to recall as many details as possible. In using imagery experiences one can close one's eyes, take a few breaths, and imagine a child or cared-for person in distress and really wanting to help and care for the child or person. We note what that feels like and our thoughts and behaviours. People who can do this note major differences in these feelings and bodily sensations from if they (say) feel anxious or angry with someone. This helps to illuminate what compassionate feelings are like. Following this, the person may be asked to imagine directing those same feelings towards themselves (as is common in loving kindness meditations). Often this is where blocks emerge and require work.

The compassionate actor

An extension of this approach is to use what is sometimes used in acting, where the actors have to 'get into role' by imagining themselves to be a particular type of person in order to convince an audience of the role; that is, they have to create certain states of mind within themselves to 'feel into' the role. This is a form of imagination that is about creating states of mind within oneself. To do this for compassion one might offer the following instructions.

> Now for a moment, imagine a wise and compassionate person. Imagine becoming that person. Think of the ideal qualities you would like to have as a compassionate person. It does not matter if you are actually like this, because this is about feeling yourself into a role and way of being. Breathe gently and feel yourself slowing and inner calmness. Think about your age and appearance, your facial expressions and postures, your wisdom, your inner emotions of, say, gentleness. Now, like an actor about to take on a part, feel yourself into this role – becoming this person.

Recall, as noted above, that one of the stages in some Buddhist imaginary exercises is imagining fusing with and becoming a compassion Buddha. This has some similarity with that exercise. One can elaborate on these as is helpful. For example, noting that it does not matter if the person feels genuine or not, the idea is to explore 'playfully' what it is like to try to put oneself into a compassion role, focusing on these qualities. The practice, then, is to learn how to inwardly create and enter this role when distressed, recognising that it is possible to create these roles because as human beings, who have long been interested in acting and actors, this is part of what we can do. Then one can teach the person to look at their anxious, depressed or self-critical self 'through the eyes of this inner compassionate self'. The idea is to shift self-processing into the soothing systems.

So we can shift processing by imagining relating to an ideal compassionate other or perfect nurturer, to see our self 'through their eyes' and/or imagine their source of wisdom, strength, warmth and non-judgement for us, and how that feels to receive it and how it changes our thinking. Or we can focus on our own inner capacities for compassion, feeling into this sense of self (like an actor taking on a role and becoming that person) and then from there we may engage in whatever CBT, memory or emotion-focused work as is appropriate. Sometimes it is just the sense of soothing that occurs from these shifts in imagery that can be helpful. All the time the collaborative focus is on finding ways that stimulate the compassionate and soothing qualities of our minds – a kind of physiotherapy for the mind (Gilbert & Irons, 2005). Both 'compassionate other' imagery and 'compassionate self' imagery can be practised each day and in certain situations. We also stress that compassion is not about submissiveness or just being 'nice'. We can then learn to explore the thoughts of our inner compassionate self. Indeed, compassion may mean being honest about, and working with, great rage or hatred.

Compassionate letter writing

To help in the practice of developing these feelings, and directing them towards the self, we can invite people to write compassionate letters to themselves. Some people like this because it involves a more narrative and dialogic approach than only working with specific thoughts. Compassionate letter writing can be used in different ways and has been suggested by other approaches to therapy (Mahoney, 2003). In compassionate mind training, we teach people to first imagine themselves in the compassionate role and to spend some time just feeling their way into that role and then we ask them to write themselves a letter. This letter will have the qualities of the compassion circle: that is, it will have a focus on care for the self; it is distress- and need-sensitive; it has sympathy and is moved by the individual's pain. The letter is also distress-tolerant, emotionally robust and patient, and it is empathic, understanding, and non-judgemental. In the letter, the person may focus on becoming more mindful and aware of common humanity issues (Gilbert, 2007a; Leary *et al.*, 2007; Neff, 2003a, 2003b). In other words, the person has to try to create a compassionate mindset and look at his/her own distress from that point of view. If the person has some familiarity with the way that thoughts can become biased by emotions, and how we can become rather black and white in our thinking (for example) as we become depressed, this can also help here because this awareness enables him/her to try to take a more balanced view, accompanied by feelings of warmth and compassion. Thus, we are blending in some cognitive alternatives.

Often compassionate letter writing will take time to shape up and at first the letters can be rather dismissive or cold. Indeed, asking people to write a compassion letter can be very revealing because at times very harsh, invalidating and 'advice giving (you should)' can be seen as 'compassionate'. So you need to check on the *emotional tone* and felt experience. For example, a person wrote from her compassionate self: 'Dear X, I am sad you are feeling so upset. This has been an upsetting time for you and your upset is very understandable. However, you know you tend to be very black and white about things and this is another example. Maybe you are over-reacting . . .' Now while the first couple of sentences felt helpful, the 'However, you know you tend to be very black and white about things and this is another example. Maybe you are over-reacting' was felt to be rather condemning and really an appeal to 'stop making mountains out of molehills'. Thus there was actually a sense of shame for 'over-reacting' that crept through, and it was not at all empathic or warm. However, this had not been apparent to the person at first because she was so used to 'helpful' others talking to her this way. So, gradually she learned the difference between an invalidating and a validating message to herself. One notes and discusses this in a non-judgemental way, helping the person to refocus on compassionate feelings because it is the feelings of the letters that are important. So, collaboratively one might come up with 'This has been an upsetting time for you and your upset is very understandable, especially given things that have happened to you. Humans are upset by things like this and they can disturb us [common humanity]. You have felt like this before though and shown a lot of courage in getting through it and were pleased you did [redirect attention to strengths in a person]. Let's focus on that courage and what would be helpful to you right now ...' Interestingly, in the letters it is sometimes a 'you' have felt upset and at other times 'I' have felt upset. My impression is that over time the wording changes from 'you' (as if it is another person writing) to 'I' and 'me' as if it is becoming internalised. We need research to explore the importance of these aspects further.

One explains that tuning into compassion can be difficult, which is understandable as people are not used to treating themselves this way, but (as in behavioural experiments) let's see what happens over time as we practise. Although research on the value of this approach is scant at present, in a series of recent studies with students, Leary *et al.* (2007) found that this type of writing can be helpful in dealing with negative life events.

It can also help for the therapist to gently, and with a slow, warm voice, read their letters back to them and see if they have feelings of understanding and warmth via the tones of the therapist. You note that it is their words you are reading and therefore they have the compassionate insights they need.

When compassion is frightening

Working with compassion can often activate strong grief and sadness, and people may cry. For some this is very helpful because they are better able to work on their pain (rather than avoiding it, getting angry with it, or trying to bully themselves out it), and this can be followed by feeling more peaceful. For others, though, these feelings are frightening and any possibility of having sympathy for their own distress, or sadness at how alone they have felt, is felt to be alarming, shaming, or makes them vulnerable and they may shut down or even dissociate. Here we note this and return to the 'three circles' (Figure 9.1) and slow down – recognising and discussing the fear of warmth for the self.

Compassion-focused work is relatively straightforward with mild to moderate depressive difficulties. One spends a lot of time on psycho-education explaining the 'three circles' and that what one is trying to do is to access and develop a soothing system and integrate this into other cognitive-behavioural, dialectical-behavioural or emotion-focused approaches. Compassion becomes a way of being with oneself. Thus, there is active understanding and collaboration in trying to develop one's self-soothing systems. So whether one is trying to generate alternative thoughts or work on behavioural experiments and tasks, develop acceptance or tolerance or work with situations or feelings one is frightened of, one can learn to do these with warmth and compassion for the difficulties in doing so. One learns to be supportively encouraging, attending to the inner warm voice.

However, for more complex difficulties, especially those associated with early attachment difficulties and trauma, this is far more complex. As Bowlby (1973, 1980) noted, for some people kindness is frightening. When frightened or alarmed, people will activate self-protective defences. The reason for this is the following. Under normal circumstances, parents are sought out and provide sources of comfort. The child experiences his or her parents as comforting in times of stress and empathic to his or her emotions. The soothing system then operates as it was designed to. But if parents are neglectful or abusive, rather than experiencing comfort and understanding the child experiences threat. If, when a child is distressed and seeks comfort, valuing or understanding, there is 'no-one there' to help and soothe, or they are pushed away or punished, or if attachment people (e.g. parents) are associated with abuse and shame, then the soothing, and the felt need for soothing, becomes associated with yearning, grief or punishment and threat. This is related to insecure and disorganised attachment styles (Liotti, 2000, 2002). The processes and consequences of this are shown in Figure 9.3.

In these contexts, if a person experiences kindness and warmth from a therapist or in imagery work, this will access the soothing systems that underpin attachment and internal working models of relationships. This in turn will reactivate emotional memories of (say) 'no-one there and aloneness', neglect, abuse or shame that have not been dealt with, and trigger conditioned emotional reactions (e.g. fight, flight, avoidance). As these memories and emotions are activated, they may feel overwhelming and activate a secondary set of defences to control the feelings in that moment. Thus, the person can become anxious and avoidant, or aggressive, or shut down, or dissociate. Even the feelings of warmth can be alien and frightening.

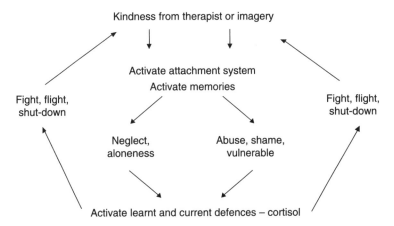

Figure 9.3 Ways in which kindness and compassion can relate to threat and avoidance.

Case example 1 (with details changed)

John had a severe depression. He had grown up with an older sibling who was very ill and who died in early adolescence. Mother was depressed and sometimes hospitalised. The family was soaked in sadness and anger and not able to meet each other's needs. There was emotional neglect, and his mother told him that he cried every night for the first years of his life. When he engaged in compassion imagery he felt alarmed and frightened. In imagery, he had a sense of falling into darkness and there being no-one there – being totally alone forever. Exploring what would help him produced a spontaneous idea of someone coming to rescue him and 'turn a light on'. He was then able to consider how these feelings might be echoes of real memories of fear and crying in the night in his room alone, and no-one would come, with a conditioned emotional shut-down response. These were being reactivated via working on soothing and the attachment system. Not surprisingly, he tried to avoid these feelings. He recognised that when he engaged in compassionate imagery work these might be the unprocessed emotional memories that came back for him, triggering feelings of fear and grief (and later anger) that were felt to be overwhelming.

Case example 2 (with details changed)

Jane had been abused by a neighbour but felt too ashamed and confused to tell her parents. However, she became depressed and irritable as a child and her parents labelled her as difficult and 'naughty'. She felt that it was extremely difficult to imagine a compassionate image being genuinely understanding and kind, and instead the imagery was associated with feelings of her being bad in some way, and with feelings of anger and confusion. Thus, imagery work had reactivated the attachment systems and the memories associated with early attachment figures and these were felt to be frightening and overwhelming.

For both cases, the work involved is similar to that of exposure work with traumatic memories (Clark & Ehlers, 2004; Lee, 2005). Briefly, this offers a lot of psycho-education so that people can stand back and understand how their emotions and emotional memories may be working, collaboratively working out how to engage with these emotional memories and the pacing, to distinguish the emotional memories from the 'now safe experience' and working with powerful grief, fear and anger feelings. In addition, via collaboratively agreeing to gradual exposure and desensitisation work, with care given to the therapist's voice tones, grounding, gentleness and encouragement, the person may begin to reprocess these memories in the presence of a caring other.

Therapeutic clarity can help by explaining that it is understandable why warmth is frightening and why the person can be confused with new emotions that may involve wanting to withdraw from or even hurt the therapist – these can be natural consequences of their attachment history and will take time to work through. In addition, compassion-focused work can illuminate beliefs such as: 'Compassion is weak; it is letting one's guard down; letting oneself off the hook; only by criticising myself can I succeed and be accepted; I am so bad I do not deserve compassion'. For many of these beliefs the focus is on the fear – for example, ask 'What is your greatest fear of/in: letting your guard down; letting yourself off the hook; reducing self-criticism, or having something you think you do not deserve; or seeing that certain things were really not your fault, that you are not bad?'. This illuminates the (sometimes intense) fears of becoming self-compassionate and these are key themes to work with in the process of using compassion – how people can be compassionate towards these fears.

Finally, we should note that compassion-focused work is a way for doing, and being in, therapy, conceptualising difficulties in terms of evolved affect regulation systems and social mentalities, and conditioned emotions and memories (Gilbert, 1989, 2005, 2007a, 2007b). It can thus be easily integrated with basic CBT approaches (Beck, Freeman, Davis, & Associates, 2003), dialectical-behavioural therapy (DBT; Linehan, 1993), and multimodal therapies (Lazarus, 2000) that offer comprehensive therapy procedures. For example, Liotti (personal communication, 10 March 2007) has pointed out that DBT (Linehan, 1993) can help people with problematic attachment systems because it offers strong boundaries and affirmations, including being able to call the therapist if distressed and suicidal. This helps to reactivate the attachment and soothing systems through the therapeutic relationship and may be a necessary precursor to in-depth compassion work.

I have found that explaining the 'three circles' and how emotional memories can work can offer something to 'hold on to' with the idea that we can gently, and with compassion, retrain our brain (Begley, 2007; Gilbert, 2009). This can help the therapeutic alliance, develop imagery as 'mind training' and offer 'grounding' thoughts that can be useful in times of stress: e.g. 'these feelings are how my brain is trying to work through my pain'. Via collaboration, one finds what is helpful to the person in regard to these grounding ideas and frameworks. One client who was a caver noted that 'it is like going into the cave prepared with the right gear and with a guide rather than being naked and getting lost'.

Conclusion

Imagery is only one aspect of compassion-focused therapy and compassionate mind training, but it is an important one because it is a vehicle for experiencing compassionate feelings and for reactivating key evolved affect regulation systems. This chapter has outlined some of the theory and neuroscience reasoning behind compassion-focused imagery and how compassionate imagery can be a practice in its own right (as in meditations or active imagination), and used in activities such as generating alternative thoughts and compassionate letter writing. It was also noted that compassionate imagery can be used when we have to engage in behavioural tasks and experiments that we find difficult and that require courage. While evidence for the use of imagery is now well established (see Arbuthnott *et al.*, 2001 and other chapters in this volume), evidence for the effectiveness of a compassion-focused approach is only just beginning (Gilbert & Proctor, 2006; Leary *et al.*, 2007). Currently we are also planning to explore the different types of changes that take place in the brain when people engage in self-criticism in contrast to self-compassion, with the hope that one day we will be able to develop better imagery and other exercises that focus on changing various brain systems (Begley, 2007). This is because compassion-focused work makes specific predictions about the neurophysiological systems underpinning it and the mode of its effectiveness. It is thus testable and is changing in the light of research. As for mindfulness, learning to develop our own compassionate imagery and work on compassionate practice can be helpful in our own self-development and therapeutic practice.

Finally, I noted that compassion-focused work can reactivate fears and overwhelming feelings that are probably coded in early memories of attachment, care and protection. These cases are usually more complex and can take much longer to work with. Compassion from a therapist or generating compassionate images for these people can be alarming, frightening or overwhelming, and the person may avoid them or act out in the therapy. Having a view of attachment memories and how they may be activated in therapy can alert the therapist to these possibilities and open discussion of the issues with the client. Openness, psycho-education (e.g. of our innate needs, affect regulation systems, and conditioned emotional memories), gentleness, encouragement, and discussion of the understandable feelings and how to approach them can all be helpful.

References

Arbuthnott, K.D., Arbuthnott, D.W., & Rossiter, L. (2001). Guided imagery and memory: Implications for psychotherapies. *Journal of Counselling Psychology*, *48*, 123–132.

Armstrong, K. (1994). *A History of God*. London: Mandarin Books.

Bailey, K.G. (2002). Recognizing, assessing and classifying others: Cognitive bases of evolutionary kinship therapy. *Journal of Cognitive Psychotherapy*, *16*, 367–383.

Baldwin, M.W. (2005). *Interpersonal cognition*. New York: Guilford Press.

Baumeister, R.F., & Leary, M.R. (1995). The need to belong: Desire for interpersonal attachments as a fundamental human motivation. *Psychological Bulletin*, *117*, 497–529.

Beck, A.T., Freeman, A., Davis, D.D., & Associates (2003). *Cognitive therapy of personality disorders* (Second Edition). New York: Guilford Press.

Begley, S. (2007). *Train your mind, change your brain*. New York: Ballantine Books.

Bering, J.M. (2002). The existential theory of mind. *Review of General Psychology, 6*, 3–34.

Bowlby, J. (1969). *Attachment. Attachment and loss*, Vol. 1. London: Hogarth Press.

Bowlby, J. (1973). *Separation, anxiety and anger. Attachment and loss*, Vol. 2. London: Hogarth Press.

Bowlby, J. (1980). *Loss: Sadness and depression. Attachment and loss*, Vol. 3. London: Hogarth Press.

Brewin, C.R. (2006). Understanding cognitive behaviour therapy: A retrieval competition account. *Behaviour Research and Therapy, 44*, 765–784.

Byrne, R.W. (1995). *The thinking ape*. Oxford, UK: Oxford University Press.

Cacioppo, J.T., Berston, G.G., Sheridan, J.F., & McClintock, M.K. (2000). Multilevel integrative analysis of human behavior: Social neuroscience and the complementing nature of social and biological approaches. *Psychological Bulletin, 126*, 829–843.

Carter, C.S. (1998). Neuroendocrine perspectives on social attachment and love. *Psychoneuroendorinlogy, 23*, 779–818.

Clark, D.M., & Ehlers A. (2004). Posttraumatic stress disorder: From cognitive theory to therapy. In R.L. Leahy (Ed.), *Contemporary cognitive therapy: Theory, research and practice* (pp. 141–160). New York: Guilford Press.

Coxhead, N. (1985). *The relevance of bliss*. London: Wildwood House.

Dalai Lama (1995). *The power of compassion*. New Delhi, India: HarperCollins.

Dalai Lama (2001). *An open heart: Practising compassion in everyday life* (edited by N. Vreeland). London: Hodder & Stoughton.

Depue, R.A., & Morrone-Strupinsky, J.V. (2005). A neurobehavioral model of affiliative bonding. *Behavioral and Brain Sciences, 28*, 313–395.

Dowd, T. (2007). Elements of Buddhist philosophy in cognitive psychotherapy: The role of cultural specifics and universals. *Journal of Cognitive and Behavioral Psychotherapies, 7*, 67–79.

Field, T. (2000). *Touch therapy*. New York: Churchill Livingstone.

Fonagy, P., & Target, M. (2006). The mentalization-focused approach to self pathology. *Journal of Personality Disorders, 20*, 544–576.

Frederick, C., & McNeal, S. (1999). *Inner strengths: Contemporary psychotherapy and hypnosis for ego strengthening*. Mahwah, NJ: Lawrence Erlbaum Associates.

Geary, D.C. (2000). Evolution and proximate expression of human parental investment. *Psychological Bulletin, 126*, 55–77.

George, M.S., Ketter, T.A., Parekh, P.I., Horwitz, B., Herscovitch, P., & Post, R.M. (1995). Brain activity during transient sadness and happiness in healthy women. *American Journal of Psychiatry, 152*, 341–351.

Gerhardt, S. (2004). *Why love matters: How affection shapes a baby's brain*. Hove, UK: Routledge.

Gilbert, P. (1989). *Human nature and suffering*. Hove, UK: Psychology Press.

Gilbert, P. (1993). Defence and safety: Their function in social behaviour and psychopathology. *British Journal of Clinical Psychology, 32*, 131–153.

Gilbert, P. (2000). Social mentalities: Internal 'social' conflicts and the role of inner warmth and compassion in cognitive therapy. In P. Gilbert & K.G. Bailey (eds.), *Genes on the couch: Explorations in evolutionary psychotherapy* (pp. 118–150). Hove, UK: Routledge.

Gilbert, P. (2003). Evolution, social roles, and differences in shame and guilt. *Social Research, 70*, 1205–1230.

Gilbert, P. (2005). Compassion and cruelty: A biopsychosocial approach. In P. Gilbert (Ed.), *Compassion: Conceptualisations, research and use in psychotherapy* (pp. 9–74). Hove, UK: Routledge.

Gilbert, P. (2007a). Evolved minds and compassion in the therapeutic relationship. In P. Gilbert & R. Leahy (eds.), *The therapeutic relationship in the cognitive behavioural psychotherapies* (pp. 106–142). Hove, UK: Routledge.

Gilbert, P. (2007b). *Psychotherapy and counselling for depression* (Third Edition). London: Sage.

Gilbert, P. (2009). *The compassionate mind: A new approach to the challenges of life.* London: Constable and Robinson.

Gilbert, P., & Irons, C. (2004). A pilot exploration of the use of compassionate images in a group of self-critical people. *Memory, 12*, 507–516.

Gilbert, P., & Irons, C. (2005). Focused therapies and compassionate mind training for shame and self-attacking. In P. Gilbert (Ed.), *Compassion: Conceptualisations, research and use in psychotherapy* (pp. 263–325). Hove, UK: Routledge.

Gilbert, P., & Procter, S. (2006). Compassionate mind training for people with high shame and self-criticism: A pilot study of a group therapy approach. *Clinical Psychology and Psychotherapy, 13*, 353–379.

Glasser, A. (2005). *A call to compassion: Bringing Buddhist practices of the heart into the soul of psychotherapy.* Berwick, ME: Nicolas-Hays.

Guidano, V.F., & Liotti, G. (1983). *Cognitive processes and emotional disorders.* New York: Guilford Press.

Hall, E., Hall, C., Stradling, P., & Young, D. (2006). *Guided imagery: Creative interventions in counselling and psychotherapy.* London: Sage.

Heinrichs, M., Baumgartner, T., Kirschbaum, C., & Ehlert, U. (2003). Social support and oxytocin interact to suppress cortisol and subjective response to psychosocial stress. *Biological Psychiatry, 54*, 1389–1398.

Hinde, R.A. (1999). *Why gods persist: A scientific approach to religion.* London: Routledge.

Holmes, E.A., & Hackmann, A. (eds.) (2004). *Mental imagery and memory in psychopathology* [Special Issue: *Memory, 12*, 4]. Hove, UK: Psychology Press.

Kirkpatrick, L.A. (2005). *Attachment, evolution and the psychology of religion.* New York: Guilford Press.

Kirsch, P., Esslinger, C., Chen, Q., Mier, D., Lis, S., Siddhanti, S., *et al.* (2005). Oxytocin modulates neural circuitry for social cognition and fear in humans. *Journal of Neuroscience, 25*, 11489–11493.

Lazarus, A. (2000). Mutlimodal replinishment. *Professional Psychology: Research and Practice, 31*, 93–94.

Leary, M.R., Tate, E.B., Adams, C.E., Allen, A.B., & Hancock, J. (2007). Self-compassion and reactions to unpleasant self-relevant events: The implications of treating oneself kindly. *Journal of Personality and Social Psychology, 92*, 887–904.

Lee, D.A. (2005). The perfect nurturer: A model to develop a compassionate mind within the context of cognitive therapy. In P. Gilbert (Ed.), *Compassion: Conceptualisations, research and use in psychotherapy* (pp. 326–351). Hove, UK: Routledge.

Leighton, T.D. (2003). *Faces of compassion: Classic Bodhisattva archetypes and their modern expression*. Boston: Wisdom Publications.

Linehan, M. (1993). *Cognitive behavioral treatment of borderline personality disorder*. New York: Guilford Press.

Liotti, G. (2000). Disorganized attachment: Models of borderline states and evolutionary psychotherapy. In P. Gilbert & K. Bailey (eds.), *Genes on the couch: Explorations in evolutionary psychotherapy* (pp. 232–256). Hove, UK: Psychology Press.

Liotti, G. (2002). The inner schema of borderline states and its correction during psychotherapy: A cognitive evolutionary approach. *Journal of Cognitive Psychotherapy, 16*, 349–365.

Mahoney, M.J. (2003). *Constructivist psychotherapy: A practical guide*. New York: Guilford Press.

Marks, I.M. (1987). *Fears, phobias and rituals: Panic, anxiety and their disorders*. Oxford, UK: Oxford University Press.

McKay, M., & Fanning, P. (1992). *Self-Esteem: A proven program of cognitive techniques for assessing, improving, and maintaining your self-esteem* (Second Edition). Oakland, CA: New Harbinger Publishers.

Mikulincer, M., & Shaver, P.R. (2004). Security-based self-representations in adulthood: Contents and processes. In N.S. Rholes & J.A. Simpson (eds.), *Adult attachment: Theory, research, and clinical implications* (pp. 159–195). New York: Guilford Press.

Neff, K.D. (2003a). Self-compassion: An alternative conceptualization of a healthy attitude toward oneself. *Self and Identity, 2*, 85–102.

Neff, K.D. (2003b). The development and validation of a scale to measure self-compassion. *Self and Identity, 2*, 223–250.

Neff, K.D., Kirkpatrick, K., & Rude, S.S. (2007). Self-compassion and its link to adaptive psychological functioning. *Journal of Research in Personality, 41*, 139–154.

Panksepp, J. (1998). *Affective neuroscience*. New York: Oxford University Press.

Safran, J.D., & Segal, Z.V. (1990). *Interpersonal process in cognitive therapy*. New York: Basic Books.

Rector, N.A., Bagby, R.M., Segal, Z.V., Joffe, R.T., & Levitt, A. (2000). Self-criticism and dependency in depressed patients treated with cognitive therapy or pharmacotherapy. *Cognitive Therapy and Research, 24*, 571–584.

Rein, G., Atkinson, M., & McCraty, R. (1995). The physiological and psychological effects of compassion and anger. *Journal for the Advancement of Medicine, 8*, 87–105.

Ringu Tilku Rinpoche & Mullen, K. (2005). The Buddhist use of compassionate imagery in mind healing. In P. Gilbert (Ed.), *Compassion: Conceptualisations, research and use in psychotherapy* (pp. 218–238). Hove, UK: Routledge.

Rossman, M.L. (2000). *Guided imagery for self-healing*. New York: New World Library.

Safran, J.D., & Segal, Z.V. (1990) *Interpersonal process in cognitive therapy*. New York: Basic Books.

Salzberg, S. (1995). *Loving-kindness: The revolutionary art of happiness*. Boston: Shambhala.

Schore, A.N. (1994). *Affect regulation and the origin of the self: The neurobiology of emotional development*. Hillsdale, NJ: Lawrence Erlbaum Associates, Inc.

Schwartz, J.M., & Begley, S. (2002). *The mind and the brain: Neuroplasticity and the power of mental force*. New York: Regan Books.

Shapiro, S.L., Astin J.A., Bishop, S.R., & Cordova, M. (2005). Mindfulness-based stress reduction for health care professionals: Results from a randomised control trial. *International Journal of Stress Management, 12*, 164–176.

Siegel, D.J. (2001). Toward an interpersonal neurobiology of the developing mind: Attachment relationships, 'mindsight' and neural integration. *Infant Mental Health Journal, 22*, 67–94.

Singer, J.L. (2006). *Imagery in psychotherapy*. Washington, DC: American Psychological Press.

Uväns-Morberg, K. (1998). Oxytocin may mediate the benefits of positive social interaction and emotions. *Psychoneuroendocrinology, 23*, 819–835.

Walpola Sri Rahula (1959/1997). *What the Buddha taught*. Oxford, UK: Oneworld.

Wang, S. (2005). A conceptual framework for integrating research related to the physiology of compassion and the wisdom of Buddhist teachings. In P. Gilbert (Ed.), *Compassion: Conceptualisations, research and use in psychotherapy* (pp. 75–120). Hove, UK: Routledge.

Watkins, M. (1986). *Invisible guests: The development of imaginal dialogues*. Hillsdale, NJ: Analytic Press and Lawrence Erlbaum Associates, Inc.

Wells, A. (2000). *Emotional disorders and metacognition: Innovative cognitive therapy*. Chichester, UK: Wiley.

Compassion-focused websites

- www.compassionatemind.co.uk
- www.self-compassion.org
- www.mindandlife.org

Appendix: Building a compassionate image

This exercise is to help you *build* up a compassionate image for you to work with and develop (you can have more than one if you wish, and they can change over time). Whatever image comes to mind or you choose to work with, note that it is *your* creation and therefore your own personal ideal – what you would really like from feeling cared for and cared about. However, in this practice it is important that you try to give your image certain qualities. These will include *wisdom, strength, warmth* and *non-judgement*.

So, in each box below think of these qualities (wisdom, strength, warmth and non-judgement) and imagine what they would look, sound and feel like.

If possible we begin by focusing on our breathing, finding our calming rhythm and making a half smile. Then we can let images emerge in the mind – as best we can; do not try too hard – if nothing comes to the mind, or if the minds wanders, just *gently* bring it back to the breathing and practise compassionately accepting.

Here are some questions that might help you build an image: Would you want your caring/nurturing image to feel/look/seem old or young; male or female (or non-human looking, e.g. an animal, sea or light)? What colours and sounds are associated with the qualities of wisdom, strength, warmth and non-judgement? Remember your image brings compassion to you and for you.

How would you like your ideal caring–compassionate image to look – visual qualities?

How would you like your ideal caring–compassionate image to sound (e.g. voice tone)?

What other sensory qualities can you give to it?

How would you like your ideal caring–compassionate image to relate to you?

How would you like to relate to your ideal caring–compassionate image?

Chapter 10

Imagery and memories of the social self in people with bipolar disorders

Empirical evidence, phenomenology, theory and therapy

Warren Mansell and Sarah Hodson

The idea of the self as a single, unitary entity is one that pervades our culture and may well apply to most people most of the time. However, the consensus within social psychology is that there are multiple self-concepts that are differentially accessible within different contexts (for a review, see Markus & Wurf, 1987, and see Chapter 2). Indeed, there is evidence to suggest that the more identities an individual possesses, the better is their mental health (Kessler & McRae, 1982), yet this may only be the case when the identities are successfully integrated with one another (Thoits, 1983). This chapter makes the case that the self-concept can often develop through early experiences to become fragmented and poorly integrated. Moreover, when the expression of different facets of the self is closely linked with different internal states, a person will experience swings in their mood that often have an impact on people around them. We propose that at the extreme, this process expresses itself as a bipolar disorder, or alternatively as another condition characterised by mood swings such as borderline personality disorder. Effective therapy helps people to gain an awareness of these changes in self and then to alter their behaviour in ways that transform and integrate recurrent self-images, and this allows them to go on to develop healthier, more flexible and less mood-dependent self concepts.

In order to develop this proposal, several areas of empirical and theoretical literature will be reviewed and new empirical and clinical work will be presented. First, studies on the self-concept in bipolar disorders will be reviewed, followed by research on the self specifically within a social context. Then the empirical literature on autobiographical memory and images of the self will be covered and illustrated by a qualitative analysis of memories from an earlier study (Mansell & Lam, 2004), together with examples from clinical practice. The potential theoretical explanations for the data reviewed up to this point will then be briefly covered, homing in on accounts involving multi-level representations and control of perception, followed by examples of clinical interventions that may be effective in this client group. Finally, areas for future research and development will be highlighted.

Bipolar disorders

The term 'bipolar disorders' refers to a range of psychological disorders that are characterised by extreme mood swings. Bipolar I disorder, previously termed 'manic depression', was the first defined and is characterised by a history of at least one depressive and manic episode. The defining features of mania are elevated, expansive or irritable mood, and three or more (or four if mood is irritable) of the following for a week or more: inflated self-esteem or grandiosity, decreased need for sleep (e.g. feeling refreshed after less than three hours per night), pressure of speech, thoughts racing, distractibility, increased goal-directed activity and pleasurable risky activities (e.g. promiscuity, overspending) (American Psychiatric Association [APA], 2000). For these symptoms to constitute mania, they need to lead to a significant disruption in functioning, or hospitalisation, or they need to be accompanied by psychotic symptoms such as delusions, thought disorder and hallucinations. In addition, detailed studies reveal that the symptoms of mania can also include dysphoria, worry, panic, aggression and hostility (e.g. Cassidy, Forest, Murry, & Carroll, 1998).

A second condition, bipolar II disorder, is characterised by a history of hypomania rather than mania. During hypomania, patients experience the same clusters of symptoms as a manic episode, but they fall short of mania in several ways. The symptoms do not include psychotic experiences, and last for at least four days rather than for over a week. Although other people notice that their behaviour is clearly different from when they are in their normal state of mind, the symptoms do not lead to clinically significant social impairment or hospitalisation (APA, 2000).

Further diagnoses such as cyclothymia, rapid cycling bipolar disorder and bipolar disorder not-otherwise-specified complete the spectrum of bipolar disorders. This spectrum extends into the non-clinical domain. For example, in a general community study, 55% of 28–30 year-olds who had experienced hypomania in the previous year did not have a history of unipolar depression (Wicki & Angst, 1991). A recent student survey revealed that the majority of 167 psychology undergraduates reported hypomanic symptoms at some point in their lives (Udachina & Mansell, 2007).

Most of the work reviewed in this chapter refers to individuals with bipolar I disorder unless stated otherwise. Nevertheless, the evidence of a bipolar spectrum helps to explain why an approach based on theories of 'normal' cognitive processing and those shared with other conditions (or 'transdiagnostic' approaches; Harvey, Watkins, Mansell, & Shafran, 2004) are likely to be helpful in understanding more disruptive states of mind.

Self-concept in bipolar disorders

The self-concept within bipolar disorders has rarely been studied in relation to imagery and memory. Yet the literature on self-concept provides a good starting point before going on to explore imagery and memory directly.

Negative self-concept

It is evident that individuals with bipolar disorders often hold an excessively negative self-concept. The simplest form of evidence comes from the clinical syndrome of depression, which is defined by feelings of worthlessness and thoughts of death or self-harm. Therefore, two critical questions arise. First, is a negative self-concept a necessary feature of bipolar disorder, or are there exceptions? Second, is the negative self-concept present throughout a person's life, whether depressed, manic or euthymic? With regard to the first question, there is a small minority of individuals who appear to experience only manic, and not depressive, episodes even when monitored over 20 years (Solomon et al., 2003). However, there have been no psychological tests on these individuals to rule out the presence of an excessively negative self-concept that might be present during sub-clinical depressed states.

To answer the second question, studies have used various methods to try to elicit self-concept in the different phases of bipolar disorder. In terms of explicit self-reported self-esteem, certain studies suggest that it is similar to non-clinical populations during euthymia (Pardoen, Bauwens, Tracy, Martin, & Mendlewicz, 1993; Winters & Neale, 1985) and during mania (Lyon, Startup, & Bentall, 1999). However, there are several exceptions to these findings. Some studies have found lower self-esteem in bipolar disorder than in non-clinical controls during euthymia (Blairy et al., 2004). There are also indications that the apparently normal 'average' self-esteem measured at one point in time over a group of people with bipolar disorder is not a stable measure; in fact, it fluctuates more widely from day to day in people with bipolar disorders (Jones et al., 2006). Moreover, implicit measures of self-concept such as unexpected recall of self-rated adjectives have revealed a bias for negative self-relevant words during mania (Lyon et al., 1999) and during remission (Winters & Neale, 1985). Scott and Pope (2003) assessed positive and negative self-esteem separately during different phases and found that both positive and negative self-esteem tended to be higher during hypomania than during depression or remission. However, no non-clinical control group was included to assess whether either of these were abnormally elevated. Taken together, it appears that a negative self-concept can often be identified at points during the course of bipolar disorders, even though it is not always evident within the explicit descriptions that individuals provide. These findings are consistent with the notion of a manic defence (Abraham, 1911/1953; Bentall, 2003; Neale, 1988), which suggests that mania is a strategy used to avoid feelings of failure and negative self-esteem. The notion of avoidance of the perception of a negative self-concept is one that we will return to several times in this chapter.

Positive self-concept

The diagnostic symptoms of mania and hypomania include inflated self-esteem or grandiosity. Thus, a positive self-concept would at least seem to be explicitly present in many people with bipolar disorder. However, this symptom is not *necessary* for a diagnosis of mania or hypomania (APA, 2000). Thus, a valid empirical question is whether (hypo)mania is typically associated with an elevated (or 'hyperpositive') self-concept, and whether an elevated self-concept can be identified during other phases of the condition. With regard to the first question, there is mixed evidence. As noted above, Lyon *et al.* (1999) found similar levels of self-esteem in mania to non-clinical controls, yet this finding may obscure a difference between positive and negative self-esteem, which may both be elevated during hypomania (Scott & Pope, 2003). Goldberg, Wenze, Welker, Steer, and Beck (2005) used a cognitive checklist for mania and compared the differences in subscales between manic, non-clinical controls and unipolar depressed patients. Perhaps surprisingly, subscales assessing self-importance and interpersonal grandiosity were not significantly higher in the manic group. Thus, although an elevated positive self-concept seems to be present in many cases of mania, there is no evidence that it is always present.

With regard to an elevated positive self-concept during other phases, there is little evidence to suggest that this is the case. For example, Lam, Wright, and Sham (2005) assessed the extent to which patients with bipolar disorder value and perceive that they possess a range of positive self-dispositional traits (e.g. dynamic, creative, successful), using the Sense of Hyper-Positive Self Scale. They found that patients who had scored higher on this scale prior to treatment showed increased rates of relapse of hypomania or mania after cognitive therapy, but they did not compare baseline levels on this scale with non-clinical controls.

The evidence suggests that positive self-esteem may at least be similar to non-clinical controls at times, but that it fluctuates more, and may be more evident in explicit measures than in implicit ones.

Self-discrepancy and elevated personal goals

An alternative way of looking at self-concepts is to assess people's concepts of their hypothetical selves. Bentall, Kinderman, and Manson (2005) explored Higgins' (1987) distinction between how people currently describe themselves (actual self), how they would like to be (ideal self), how they should be ('ought' self) and how other people would view them (self–other) (self-discrepancy theory is discussed in more detail in Chapter 2). The sample was formed from four groups: patients currently experiencing mania, currently depressed bipolar patients, patients during remission from a bipolar episode, and non-clinical controls. The individuals experiencing mania showed greater consistency between their actual and ideal self-descriptions compared to healthy controls, whereas the depressed patients reported discrepancies between the actual and ideal self and between the actual and ought self, owing to lowered actual self ratings. This study again suggests a fluctuation in self-concept in different phases, with some indication of an elevation in self-concept during mania (as indexed by the degree to which one is fitting in with one's ideal self), and a drop in self-regard during depression. However, while the depressed patients in this study showed a more negative actual view of the self, there was no evidence that the manic patients had a more positive view of themselves than the non-clinical controls. The degree of positivity of the ideal and ought selves was not reported in this study.

There are other ways to assess whether their views of themselves, as they could or should be, are particularly positive. Some indirect evidence comes from studies that have shown elevated goal attainment beliefs in people with bipolar disorder relative to people with unipolar depression (Lam, Wright, & Smith, 2004), but this study did not have a non-clinical control group. Further suggestive evidence comes from a study by Johnson and Carver (2006), who found that students who scored higher on the Hypomanic Personality Scale (HPS; Eckblad & Chapman, 1986) reported more extreme socially oriented goals for themselves, such as being famous and politically influential. The HPS has been found to predict the onset of bipolar disorder in a 10-year longitudinal study (Kwapil *et al.*, 2000).

Thus, it could be the case that people with bipolar disorder have views of themselves in the future that are particularly positive and hard to attain when compared to their current perception of themselves. Yet this evidence is indirect, and there seems to be little work unpacking the nature of the 'hypothetical selves' in bipolar disorder, in terms of exploring their related imagery and origins. In other words, it is likely that the self-concept is not merely held in an abstract form, but is formed from detailed sensory representations of the self that are brought into awareness and held for comparison during current goal-directed behaviour. It is possible that more detailed analyses may reveal these more extreme and idiosyncratic images of possible selves than could be evident in questionnaire studies. Data will be presented later that begins to address this omission in the literature.

Dissociated self-concepts

We have reviewed evidence for both positive and negative self-concepts within bipolar disorder, which are evident at different times and deviate to different extents from the individual's self-ideal depending on whether they are depressed or manic. One study has explored the extent to which these self-concepts form separate clusters in bipolar patients during remission (Power, de Jong, & Lloyd, 2002). Using a Q-sort technique, Power *et al.* found that people with bipolar disorders displayed self-concepts that coalesced into completely positive or completely negative categories, in contrast to the more mixed and balanced concepts of healthy controls and individuals with a chronic physical illness (diabetes). This study provides support for a greater dichotomy of the self-concept within bipolar disorder that is consistent with the findings covered earlier and deserves replication. One key question that remains is whether the expression of these self-concepts varies only as a function of the kind of episode (mania, depression, remission), or whether smaller mood changes can reveal them.

Mood-dependent conflicting self-concepts

Owing to some intricate diary studies by Bentall and colleagues (e.g. see Bentall, Tai, & Knowles, 2006), good evidence is now emerging that the self-concept fluctuates in people with bipolar disorders more than in non-clinical controls, even outside episodes. For example, a study involving a twice-daily mood diary reported by Bentall *et al.* (2006) found that remitted bipolar patients showed extreme fluctuations in self-esteem that were not present in remitted unipolar depression. The evidence reviewed so far indicates an explanation for this – if disconnected positive and negative self-concepts were held in memory then they would have the capacity to express themselves at different times and influence current ratings of self-esteem. However, what leads to the expression of one versus another? One suggestion is that people with bipolar disorder make more extreme personal appraisals of changes in internal states and that it is these internal states that precede changes in self-concept (Mansell, Morrison, Reid, Lowens, & Tai, 2007). For example, one may believe the following: 'When I feel good, I know that I am a very important person', or 'When I feel restless and agitated I know I am about to have a breakdown'.

Two studies have found that people with bipolar disorder have stronger beliefs in statements of this kind compared to non-clinical controls (Mansell, 2006; Mansell & Jones, 2006). Mansell *et al.* (2007) have proposed that people with bipolar disorder make a variety of conflicting extreme personal appraisals of themselves as a function of their internal state, and that these are not simply divided between positive and negative. These appraisals are markers of a range of cognitions and perceptions of different extreme aspects of the self, which are tied to different internal states that can be discovered through further interview with the individual. They relate to earlier interpersonal experiences and influence current behaviour in ways that can perpetuate cycles of escalating mood swings. For example, clients who interpret their high state of energy as indicating a breakdown may experience an image of themselves being criticised and controlled by others during a previous episode, which they try to suppress through self-critical self-talk and social withdrawal, which then contributes to depressed and irritable mood. We will discuss this model further when considering the clinical implications of exploring imagery and the self in bipolar disorder.

The social self

The 'self' is often discussed in relative isolation. However, most theories of the self point to the social origins of the self within early development and later interpersonal interactions (Beck, 1967; Bowlby, 1969; Markus & Wurf, 1987; Rogers, 1951; see also Chapter 2 for further discussion of the relational self). The neglect of this issue is particularly surprising for bipolar disorder, where interpersonal behaviour varies so widely between different mood states. During the approach of a manic episode, people with bipolar disorder often seek out other people for stimulation, validation and coercion into their ambitious ideas (e.g. encouraging them to join them in a religious revival or risky business venture). They are often very irritable and critical towards those around them. Systematic studies of hypomania and mania support these views (Goodwin & Jamison, 1990; Jamison, Hamman, Gong-Guy, Padesky, & Gemer, 1990; Janowsky, Leff, & Epstein, 1970). For example, Jamison *et al.* (1990) found that individuals with bipolar disorder rated themselves as more sociable during hypomania compared to euthymia, yet also more uncooperative and 'wild'. In contrast, during depression they reported being more compliant and dependent on other people than non-clinical controls (Rosenfarb, Becker, Khan, & Mintz, 1998).

The cognitive approach of Mansell *et al.* (2007) takes these observations into account by considering how other people's reactions to the individual's behaviour during different mood states can confirm their extreme personal appraisals. For example, when relatives and friends become more critical during the build-up of a high, the individual may interpret this as jealousy or competitiveness, thereby confirming the belief that in this energised state one has fantastic ideas that must be pursued alone, no matter what the consequences. In therapy, the clinician needs to be particularly aware of these processes, and develop ways to understand them together with the client.

It is important to consider how much self-concepts in the preceding account represent social-self-concepts. Most self-related traits have an interpersonal quality. A 'positive' self could involve directing and influencing other people or it could involve listening to, and understanding them in a considerate way. Similarly a 'negative' self could be controlling and domineering, or it could be passive, aimless and compliant. There is clearly a necessity to explore many factors in relation to the self: 'positive' versus 'negative' self-concepts; whether they are hypothetical or actual; their cohesiveness and expression over time; plus the interpersonal qualities of these self-concepts.

Imagery and memory may prove to be the key. Thus, owing to the importance of the social side of the self, the empirical and clinical work covered in the remaining chapter will return to it in detail.

Imagery and memories of the self

Memories of the self are examples of autobiographical memory, which can be defined as an 'explicit memory of an event that occurred in a specific time and place in one's personal past' (Nelson & Fivush, 2004). It is thought that the primary function of autobiographical memory is to represent past events in the present so that an individual maintains a sense of being a coherent and consistent person over time (Conway, Singer, & Tagini, 2004; Nelson, 2003).

Evidence across psychological disorders

Within recent years, there has been a resurgence of interest in the phenomenology of imagery of the self in psychopathology, as evident from this volume, a previous special issue of *Memory* (Hackmann & Holmes, 2004), a review of recurrent imagery across psychological disorders (Harvey *et al.*, 2004) and earlier work by Ann Hackmann and colleagues (e.g. Hackmann, Clark, & McManus, 2000). This chapter will not review these studies in detail as they will be covered in other chapters. In essence, they have illustrated that people with a wide range of psychological disorders report recurrent, distressing, intrusive, multi-modal, self-relevant imagery that relates to their personal concerns and can typically be related in theme and content to earlier distressing experiences. These findings have been explained within disorder-specific models (e.g. Clark & Wells, 1995; Ehlers & Clark, 2000) and within broader conceptual frameworks (e.g. Dual Representation Theory; Brewin & Holmes, 2003; Self Memory System; Conway, Meares, & Standart, 2004), and have also informed treatment techniques within cognitive therapy. This chapter will return to the theoretical and clinical aspects of self-imagery and memory within bipolar disorder later. At this point, it is important to focus on the research on self-imagery and memory within bipolar disorder, which is at an early stage compared to conditions such as anxiety disorders, depression and even psychosis.

Bipolar disorders

Experimental evidence suggests that imagery has a stronger effect on both positive and negative emotional states than verbal thoughts (Holmes & Mathews, 2005; Holmes, Mathews, Dalgleish, & Mackintosh, 2006). This suggests that imagery may have a particularly strong role in driving the conflicting emotional states observed in bipolar disorder. The literature on memory in bipolar disorder begins with early studies of mood-dependent memory, leading on to studies in which the quality and content of the memories have been studied in more detail.

Mood-dependent memory refers to the phenomenon whereby what one remembers during a given mood is determined in part by what one learned when previously in the same mood. In bipolar disorder, two studies on memory used the natural mood swings in individuals with rapid-cycling bipolar disorder to investigate mood-dependent memory using either autobiographical memory (Eich, Macaulay, & Lam, 1997) or free associations to words (Weingartner, Miller, & Murphy, 1977). Both studies found that more memories were recalled when moods at encoding and retrieval were matched than when moods were different.

A key distinction has been made between *general* and *specific* autobiographical memories (Williams & Broadbent, 1986). General memories refer to whole classes of events, or events that occur over a long period of time, whereas specific memories of an event happened at a particular place and time. Williams and Broadbent (1986) demonstrated that individuals with a history of suicide attempts recalled a higher proportion of general versus specific memories than healthy controls. Since this study, overgeneral memory has been associated with a range of psychopathology (see Harvey *et al.*, 2004, for a review).

Scott, Stanton, Garland, and Ferrier (2000) found that individuals with remitted bipolar disorder showed an overgeneral memory bias and poor problem-solving ability compared to a group of non-clinical controls. Similarly, Mansell and Lam (2004) found that relative to a group of remitted unipolar depressed patients, the remitted bipolar group recalled more general than specific negative memories and reported more frequent recollections of the negative memory during their everyday lives. The study observed that specific memories were much more likely to be recalled as images than general memories. Nevertheless, some general memories were encapsulated by images of generic kinds of situations (e.g. being depressed) and were therefore not coded as specific. This study also gave examples of the content of the negative memories: the experience of depression; being perceived as a failure by others; and trauma. However, no systematic analysis was conducted.

The finding of an overgeneral memory bias and poor problem-solving ability was further replicated in a study of individuals with bipolar I disorder or unipolar depression compared to non-clinical controls, and was found to be maintained in both clinical groups at 12-week follow-up (Tzemou & Birchwood, 2007). They used a memory interview developed for unipolar depression by Reynolds and Brewin (1999). This study also found that the clinical groups reported recurrent, distressing traumatic memories that were not present in the control group. They included memories of sexual abuse, rape, car accidents, witnessing death, physical restraint during hospital admission, and loss of employment. The study suggested that it was the individuals who showed less overgeneral memory bias that reported intrusions, which led to the conclusion that an overgeneral memory bias can serve to block traumatic memories from awareness. The study indicated little change in these observations at different phases of bipolar disorder. In contrast, a single case study of a man with rapid cycling bipolar disorder found that days of depression tended to be associated with more overgeneral and negatively toned memories, whereas days of mania were associated with more specific and positively toned memories (Lam & Mansell, 2008).

Delduca and Jones (2007) carried out a study of autobiographical memory in students with a high or low vulnerability to hypomania. They found that the high-risk group recalled more specific (rather than general) memories in response to negative cue words than the low-risk group, and that these memories were also recalled faster. These findings support the view that the negative self-concept is particularly accessible in individuals with a proneness to bipolar disorder, and fit with the findings concerning intrusive memories in diagnosed individuals. It is possible that, unlike the patients in the study by Mansell and Lam (2004), these individuals had not developed a generic memory for repeatedly occurring negative situations (e.g. episodes of depression), or that they did not use overgeneral recall as a way to suppress unpleasant imagery as suggested by Tzemou and Birchwood (2007). Interestingly, this study also found a trend for the high-risk group to be quicker to recall memories to the cue word 'successful' than the low-risk group. This provides a suggestion that positive autobiographical memories can be facilitated, but may be specifically around the theme of personal success; this links to the work described earlier highlighting the positive 'ideal self' in bipolar disorder and the self-report of extreme personal goals in the public arena such as the pursuit of fame and political influence.

In summary, there is convergent evidence that people with bipolar disorder experience intrusive, distressing memories, and an overgeneral memory bias; and suggestive evidence that their relative expression may vary between individuals, and that overgeneral memory bias may develop as a form of avoidance of these memories later in the course of the condition. The study of positive memories is sparse, but certain positive themes relating to success may have enhanced accessibility. What is required is more information on the nature of both the negative and positive memories in people with bipolar disorder. In particular, the themes and quality of memories in earlier studies have been described in insufficient detail to delineate the most important features. Therefore, we conducted a detailed qualitative analysis of memories in bipolar disorder to address this omission in the literature.

A detailed exploration of positive and negative autobiographical memories in bipolar I disorder

In order to explore the nature of the memories in bipolar disorder in more detail, we conducted a new analysis of an earlier cohort (Mansell & Lam,

2004, 2006), in which interviews with people with remitted bipolar I disorder were transcribed and analysed using Interpretive Phenomenological Analysis (IPA; Osborn & Smith, 1998; Smith, 1995). The aim of the study was to analyse the experience of autobiographical memories, including their content, themes and characteristics, with the expectation that these memories would provide further information about the individual experiences of autobiographical memories.

The participants were recruited as part of two earlier studies (Mansell & Lam, 2004, 2006), where full details regarding recruitment procedures, inclusion criteria and diagnosis are outlined fully. Of the 32 participants, 21 were female ($M = 42.24$, SD $= 11.5$) and 11 were male ($M = 51.45$, SD $= 11.8$). However, three of these participants were excluded from the current study, one due to an inability to transcribe the interview recording adequately and two because of the limited nature of their transcription material.

The materials relevant to this study included two lists of four words presented to the participants during a prior study (Mansell & Lam, 2004). One list contained positive words (optimistic, success, adored, confident); the other contained negative words which were antonyms to the positive words (pessimistic, failure, hated, unconfident). During the study, the participants had been presented with either the positive or the negative list of words before being asked to tell the experimenter as soon as a memory of a specific event in their lives came to mind. After being asked to provide several ratings about the memory, the experimenter asked them to describe the memory, trying to recreate the scene or impression in as much detail as possible, describing what they saw, heard or felt. These memory descriptions were tape-recorded, with each recorded interview lasting approximately four to five minutes, although this varies between interviews. This procedure was then repeated using the alternative word list.

As stated above, IPA (Smith, 1995) was used in the analysis of the memory transcripts to allow an exploration of the memory content. Although IPA often involves semi-structured interviews rather than analyses of recordings, it was deemed appropriate given their phenomenological content. As per Osborn and Smith (1998) and Smith (1995), the analysis initially involved repeatedly reading each memory text while making unfocused notes regarding broad themes. Themes that characterised sections of text were identified and tentatively organised. These were then analysed in relation to one another, while returning to the original texts, leading to further development of theme definitions and content. Therefore, these themes led to a consistent and meaningful account of the participants' experiences, which was based within their own words. This means that the emergent transcript themes are not constructs predicted in advance, but those proposed by the participants themselves. Some of the personal details have been changed to preserve anonymity. To ensure the accuracy of the analysis, as proposed by Osborn and Smith (1998), discussions were held between the experimenter and two independent sources regarding the initial analysis of a set of eight transcripts and the themes emerging from those transcripts. The final analysis was verified by these two sources in order to ensure that the analysis presented was systematically achieved and supported by the data.

Negative memories

Table 10.1 gives the results of the analysis. Five superordinate themes emerged within the transcripts of the negative memory recollections, none of which emerged in the analysis of the positive memory transcripts. These were 'negative self-concept', 'victimisation', 'isolation', 'substantiation' (the degree to which memories were justified through describing their context) and 'illness'. The 'negative self-concept' theme was inherent throughout the other emergent themes and is illustrative of the internal tone of the negative memories recalled, in that the primary focus of these memories was the negativity of the self. Expressions of this negative self-concept ranged from outright assertions of low self-worth, for example, '*I really wasn't worth much*' (P96) and '*I didn't like myself*' (P49), to more detailed descriptions such as being weak, helpless or inadequate. This sense of personal weakness demonstrated by the participants was magnified by the impression that this inadequacy is related not only to an inability to act ably, but also to possessing insufficient confidence to decide on appropriate action. These feelings of confusion exacerbated their perceived inability to deal with a situation and, therefore, highlighted their inadequacies at the time.

The superordinate theme of victimisation was demonstrated by the participants in two ways, with the participants describing themselves in terms of being victims and, less often, by providing images of others as victims. They described experiences of physical abuse, bullying and overt criticism, which were noted in the original paper (Mansell & Lam, 2004).

The theme of isolation was very prominent. There were frequent descriptions of feeling '*catastrophically alone*' (P55), '*very isolated*' (P96) and '*like an outsider*' (P49). These feelings of detachment were acutely felt and were portrayed as being stronger than simply feeling 'alone' or 'lonely'; rather as an '*extreme experience of failure and loneliness*' (P55). The sense of isolation was projected along different sub-themes. The first of these was the notion of 'not belonging'; the second was a disconnection from their surroundings. In the portrayal of 'not belonging', descriptions incorporated elements of irrelevancy and a personal lack of importance that could not be overcome. The participants positioned themselves as being dissimilar to others; for example, a participant who is a descendant of German Jews involved in the Holocaust states, '*I think I'm the only person in my family who really has a continuing contact with Germany*' (P75). This 'not belonging' then led to the sensation of being 'disconnected'. In describing this notion, Participant 49 used the metaphor of being in a 'goldfish bowl' to depict not only the

Table 10.1 Results of the qualitative analysis of autobiographical memories in remitted bipolar I disorder

Memories	Themes	Sub-themes	Examples
Negative	Negative self-concept	Low self-worth	'I really wasn't worth much' (P96)
		Inadequacy/Personal weakness	'I felt inadequate, just making mistakes and worrying' (P18)
		Indecision/Confusion	'I just don't know what to do...It's me watching them, but I was too small' (P80)
		Hopelessness/Helplessness	'I'm sitting on the floor feeling hopeless' (P1)
	Victimisation	Self as a victim	'they backed away from me or they said things that weren't very nice' (P65)
		Others as victims	'when I see injustices done to vulnerable people...I get very angry' (P76)
		Critical/Hostile others	'my...grandmother was hostile' (P55)
	Isolation	Not belonging	'a sense of antipathy and placelessness, having no pertinence' (P4)
		Being 'different'	'I'm the only person in my family who really has a continuing contact with Germany' (P75)
		Disconnection from surroundings	'I couldn't communicate with people' (P49)
	Illness	Depression	'I felt very dejected and severely depressed' (P11)
		Illness and life-events	'that led to my breakdown' (P18)
		Being 'different'	'everybody...didn't seem to have mental health problems where I...did' (P49)
		Suicidality	'I wanted to die when I come out and I very nearly did' (P48)
	Substantiation	Validate accuracy	'if I don't give you some background it will sound most peculiar' (P27)
		External responsibility	'the job, they shouldn't have given it to me, it was too much for me' (P18)
Positive	Positive interaction with others	Positively perceived interactions	'for the first time in my life I started to really make friends' (P3)
		Companionship	'we were all quite merrily chatting and drinking' (P31)
		'Centre of attention'	'it was a wonderful feeling to be on the platform viewing the whole school' (P7)
	Positive feedback	Inferred emotional feedback	'seeing my psychotherapist's face and just the reflection back of a...positive feeling' (P55)
		Overt verbal feedback	'the feedback from all the people I would coach, I mean, was very positive' (P8)
		Acceptance/Approval	'I felt that she would feel good about me having made that decision' (P11)
	Positive perception of others	General descriptions	'my niece looking adorable and smiling and laughing' (P40)
		Physical descriptions	'Suzy was very beautiful' (P58)
		Absolute language	'he was so perfect' (P96)

feeling of a barrier between her and those around her, but also her inability to communicate with others. This isolation perpetuated not only the individuals' view of themselves as being victims, but also their negative self-concepts and the perception that they were 'unable' to 'connect' with others. The sense of being 'different' to others was an important element of this, and one that seemed intrinsically linked to the participants' perceptions of themselves in terms of their illness.

In recalling their negative memories, the participants repeatedly character-ised themselves in terms of their disorder, which constituted the third theme of 'illness'. This did not occur in the positive memory transcripts. The vast majority of the participants, in characterising themselves as *'sick'* (P81), referred to feelings of depression; for example, *'I felt very dejected and severely depressed'* (P11) and *'[I was] feeling depressed'* (P55). There were only two descriptions in which mania was referred to, with the first being an afterthought to the memory description, *'I didn't realise it at the time, but I was quite excitable'* (P8), while the second used mania as a comparator to depression, *'the memory is of a period of depression after a period of mania'* (P4).

The inclusion of the participants' disorder was expressed in two ways: by relating their illness to life-events and by connecting it to their 'difference' to others. Descriptions of their experience of bipolar disorder in relation to their life-events were causal, although this causality was reported in both directions, with the life-events causing the disorder, *'I became ill only about 15 months after'* (P8) and *'that led to my breakdown'* (P18), as well as the disorder causing the life-events, *'incidentally that was my first depressive episode'* (P75) and *'I didn't do my best as a mother because I was sick'* (P81). The notion of being 'different' included how others' perceptions of the parti-cipants' disorder further separated them; for example, as *'a nutter'* (P66), or, as Participant 49 stated: *'everybody had, just didn't seem to have mental health problems where I quite obviously did'* (P49). The negative positioning of the self relative to others was also connected to the participants' recollections of the ways in which others view them in terms of their illness, as illustrated when a participant outlines a verbal attack by the daughter of a neighbour:

> *she turned round and she said if you come near my mother I'm going to call the police and tell them that as you're a nutter you should be dragged off to the nuthouse and they should lock you up and throw away the key* (P66).

Another participant combined the themes of illness, negative self-concept and critical others:

> *I felt that I couldn't leave the room to join them . . . I was really daunted by it and, yeah, it's people that I, I know really well. It's just, shouldn't have been intimidated by* (P40).

One of the interesting findings within the analysis was that three memories recalled by different participants described almost identical situations that had been pinpointed by Mansell and Lam (2004). These were expressive descriptions of a time during a period of depression where the image was of being alone in bed while having an awareness of events unfolding around them and of an acute knowledge of time passing (P4, P31 and P40). These descriptions involved elements of disconnection and isolation already discussed, but demonstrated that this can be an effect of bipolar disorder. However, further than this, there was imagery of the participant having an awareness of 'another world' separate to their own, while still being aware of the passing of time in their own 'world'. This, again, highlighted the notion of 'not belonging' or being 'different'. Finally, a subordinate but prominent theme that also emerged under 'illness' was that of 'not existing', found in relation to memories describing periods of depression. At times this notion of not existing can be seen to have elements of escapism, *'I just wanted to disappear'* (P27). This was intrinsically connected to the notion of hopelessness, with suicidal ideation being a minor but potent element of the negative memories recalled, *'I wanted to die when I come out and I very nearly did'* (P48). With this, there was the notion that recollections of severe depression also serve a function; as Participant 40 stated, *'it reminds me of how bad things can get when I get depressed'*.

The final superordinate theme that emerged from the analysis of the negative transcripts was that of 'substantiation'. This is different from the other themes as, while the others can be described as 'content' themes, 'substantiation' is actually a method of description itself. However, this particular method of description occurred only in the negative transcripts and was found in the majority of those analysed, which rendered it prominent enough to be considered as a superordinate theme. Substantiation involved prolonged descriptions of the background or history of the event that they were describing, to situate it within a context. This served the purpose of validating the accuracy of what was said to the listener. It also often involved attributing responsibility for the event to these external factors. They would attribute responsibility for the events either to others, for example, *'it was decided that I would work at the headquarters'* (P9) and *'the job, they shouldn't have given it to me, it was too much for me'* (P18), or to situational factors, such as their disorder, *'I was handicapped, well, by . . . a lot of things to do with the environment'* (P8), and:

> *I'd applied for . . . Harvard entrance and everyone, everyone else in the family went to Harvard so it, so there, so it's a, quite a stack of people because I'm the youngest of five of us and my parents went there as well and . . . my, sort of, grandmother was . . . hostile and I hadn't been able to concentrate on doing any work and feeling depressed and . . . catastrophically alone* (P55).

The second of these examples, provided by Participant 55, is a good illustration of how the themes of accuracy validation, attribution of external responsibility, victimisation, illness, isolation and negative self-concept are interconnected and combine to form a particular perception of the participants' experiences.

Positive memories

In contrast to the negative memories, the way that participants were perceived by 'others' in positive memories was of particular importance. Here, three superordinate themes emerged, which were not apparent in the analysis of the negative memories. These themes were, 'positive interaction with others', 'positive feedback' and 'positive perception of others'.

'Positive interaction with others' is an umbrella theme, which incorporated elements of the other themes, 'positive feedback' and 'positive perception of others'. However, these sub-themes were separated for ease of analysis and because participants' descriptions did not necessarily include elements of all three themes. The theme of 'positive interaction with others' emerged in three ways, in which intensity of interaction can be seen to increase hierarchically. The recollections reflecting this theme that can be classed within the first level described interactions between the participant and one or more others, in which the participant is viewed in a positive light. Those at the second level detail interactions in which a close companionship is felt with the other(s). The third type of interaction demonstrated that participants felt that they were the 'centre of attention' or the focus of the interest of other(s). These level definitions, while subtle, emerged prominently in the analysis.

In analysing the positive interactions between the participant and other(s), there were elements of equality between the actors described, in which the interaction between them was mutually beneficial; for example, *'we were drawn to each other ... We did have some very good times'* (P58), *'we soon became very attached to each other'* (P9) and *'the stimulation of peer group students'* (P3). These descriptions often emphasised the importance of positive affirmation gained from positive interactions. The second sub-theme, that of companionship, tended to be described in relation to the participants being a part of a mutually supportive group that has a positive focus. The third theme within 'positive interaction with others' outlined the ways in which the participants described themselves as being the focus of the attention of other(s); for example, *'it was a wonderful feeling to be on the platform viewing the whole school'* (P7).

Within the theme of 'positive feedback', there were references to emotion displayed by another towards the participants, as well as actions or verbalisations that were complimentary to them. These two sub-themes are inherently different in that the first requires that the participant infer the positivity from the feedback given, while in the second, the positivity is overtly presented by the 'other'. Despite these themes emerging within positive memories, the notion of 'positive self-concept' did not emerge in the way that 'negative self-concept' emerged from the negative memories. An additional element denoting the importance of others' perceptions was a strong need for approval, often from critical or hostile others.

In the final superordinate theme in the positive memories, the participants focused on their extreme positive perceptions of certain others. The instances were often very strong descriptions, with the frequent use of absolutes; for example, *'incredible'* (P31), *'perfect'* (P96) and *'it was a wonderful experience'* (P7). This strongly descriptive language used by the participants in their descriptions of others illustrated two important issues: that the language used by the participants emphasises the positivity in others, and that it emphasises the lack of positivity in the participants towards themselves.

Overview of the analysis

It was clear from this analysis that the negative self-concept within the sample was often extreme, detailed and pervasive. This is consistent with the review of the literature on negative self-concepts and intrusive memories presented earlier. In many cases, participants' memories described the negative experience of depression, including feelings of worthlessness, helplessness, isolation, hopelessness and lack of purpose. It is important to consider that the experience of depression itself can form a rich autobiographical memory that may influence an individual's future goals. Thus, there was strong support in the study for the notion of an extreme negative self-concept linked to the low mood and activation levels of the depressed state. It seems from the analysis that the diagnosis itself, and subsequent stigmatisation, can further exacerbate the depressed state, imbuing it with a sense of disconnection and alienation. Despite the negative self-concept that was described, it was also clear that the participants were very aware of the external factors that could also be responsible for their condition, which naturally bred feelings of resentment and anger. Thus, the concept of significant others as over-critical, over-demanding and sometimes hostile or victimising towards the self was evident from the descriptions, which is consistent with the role of negative beliefs about close others in the cognitive model. Within the negative memories, there was typically a view of a helpless self dominated and controlled by others, which illustrated the interpersonal elements of autobiographical memory very clearly.

It is possible that the negative self-concepts in these accounts might also be expected in people with a history of unipolar depression, although the symptoms themselves could be more extreme and worsened by the stigma within bipolar disorder, as suggested by the analysis. The other aspects of the memories that may be more unique to bipolar disorder are less clear, but it may be the nature of the positive memories that is key. There were many autobiographical memories that might be expected in other individuals, including experiences of positive feedback and companionship. However, the elaborated positive memories of being the centre of other people's attention are notable, and may indicate the kind of self-concept for which people with bipolar disorder strive as a way to overcome their problems and evade criticism. These memories could influence the kinds of extreme socially oriented goal-attainment beliefs reported by people with a proneness to hypomania (Johnson & Carver, 2006). More specifically, the positive self-concept may depend on the activation and excitement of excelling in a public arena. There were also indications, in some cases, that the participants in the memories were often striving to gain the approval of the same individuals that were displaying criticism and hostility towards them. This would put them at risk of failing to reach these standards if these critical individuals indicated that the person's performance was 'never good enough'. In addition, the cognitive model would suggest that people with mood swings use states of high activation to strive to match these high standards, but that they may simultaneously appraise their internal states in negative ways when they fail either to reach or to maintain the levels of activation they require, or when they become fearful of losing control over their thoughts and behaviour during these highly activated states. A further related feature of the memories is the observation that many of the positive memories were vivid descriptions (e.g. adorable, perfect) of the desirable characteristics of certain others (e.g. pets, children). It is possible that in doing so, the participants were safely and vividly articulating the highly socially attractive ideals that they themselves strive towards.

What seemed to be conspicuously absent from the accounts was a positive sense of self that is internalised, coherent, and independent of others' evaluations, which could respond assertively and effectively to manage other people's hostility or criticism. This finding seems consistent with the literature on the positive self-concept in bipolar disorder; there is actually little evidence that it is elevated in empirical studies especially when explored at a deeper, implicit level. It is possible that a controllable, flexible and contextualised positive self-concept is less available in people with chronic mood swings. The cognitive model would suggest that these individuals could improve their long-term well-being through understanding the conflicted nature of their internal-state-driven selves and, in turn, through developing a self-concept that integrates these and builds on them according to long-term goals and values held by the individual. We will return to this when discussing treatment.

Theoretical explanations

The findings of the literature review and the qualitative investigation are summarised in Table 10.2. We have already explained how an integrative

Table 10.2 Summary of the evidence for different properties of self-concepts and autobiographical memory within bipolar disorder

Property	Example reference
More negative self-esteem compared to non-clinical controls	Lyon et al. (1999)
Overt positive self-esteem similar in level to non-clinical controls	Winters and Neale (1985)
More negative implicit self-esteem compared to non-clinical controls	Lyon et al. (1999)
Recurrent, distressing intrusive memories in contrast to controls	Tzemou and Birchwood (2007)
Overgeneral memory bias	Scott et al. (2000)
Multiple possible selves	Bentall et al. (2005)
Fragmented, dichotomous or contradictory self-concepts	Power et al. (2002)
Greater fluctuations in self-esteem over time	Jones et al. (2006)
Elevated success-related goals	Lam et al. (2004)
Conflicting extreme positive and negative self-concepts closely related to changes in internal state	Mansell (2006)
Striving to achieve a highly activated, socially oriented (but fragile and problematic) positive self-concept in order to overcome the perception of personal vulnerability at the hands of others who are perceived as critical, controlling or hostile	This chapter

cognitive model of mood swings and bipolar disorders might account for these (Mansell, 2007; Mansell *et al.*, 2007): The imagery and memories of the self that people with bipolar disorder report represent stored information relating to the extreme and conflicting appraisals they hold of themselves during different internal states. This model provides a helpful link between the content of imagery and the themes of personal meaning. However, it does not provide an actual mechanism. It is a model that is simple enough to translate into a collaborative individualised formulation, but it is not a psychological theory about the role of imagery and autobiographical memory. To provide this, more complex frameworks of the mind would be required. While it is beyond the remit of this chapter to describe these in detail, it may be helpful to summarise some potential frameworks here, particularly in order to help relate the findings within bipolar disorder to other conditions, and to theories of cognition and emotion more generally.

Theories of memory and representation

Several explanatory frameworks have been developed within the clinical arena. These include Dual Representation Theory (DRT; Brewin, Dalgleish, & Joseph, 1996) and Schematic-Propositional-Analogue-Associative Representations (SPAARs; Power & Dalgleish, 1997). Both of these theories have drawn attention to the different *levels of meaning* that different kinds of information provide. In essence, imagery is regarded as a direct analogue of actual perception whereas verbal information is regarded as a way of recoding information in the form of *propositional* statements that do not have a direct analogue in reality. According to DRT, imagery tends to form situationally accessible memories (SAMs) that become triggered and intrude into awareness in response to cues in an automatic manner, whereas verbally accessible memories (VAMs) are under voluntary control and form the coherent, verbalisable memories of our experiences. Normally, SAMs naturally convert into VAMs as they are integrated into the existing knowledge base, but this becomes blocked in psychological disorders owing to behaviours such as suppression, worry and avoidance. Thus, it is possible that the imagery and memories reported by individuals with bipolar disorder remain unintegrated for the same reason. Nevertheless, this account seems to require an explanation of what motivates behaviours such as thought suppression within a richer model of the organisation of memory.

Conway and colleagues (Conway & Pleydell-Pearce, 2000; Conway, Singer, & Tagini, 2004) have provided a model of autobiographical memory that has similarities to the above clinical models, yet provides more detail about the nature and organisation of autobiographical memory and imagery. According to this account, representations within autobiographical memory are strongly influenced by the nature of the 'working self'. The individual is motivated to represent themselves in certain ways, such as loyal, strong and kind. Memories that do not fit with these desired self-goals remain unintegrated with the remaining self-knowledge. These examples of event-specific knowledge (ESK) are the equivalent of the SAMs in DRT, and remain highly sensory in nature and emotionally charged. The individual is motivated to keep them from awareness through behaviours such as active suppression and avoidance of triggering situations. It has been suggested that overgeneral memory – difficulty recalling specific events resulting in general, non-specific statements – is another way to avoid these memories. Thus, within bipolar disorder, it is possible that the images of multiple, extreme selves represent ESKs that are regarded as conflicting with the individual's self goals, and are therefore suppressed or distorted; the individual is driven by avoiding their awareness of aversive selves (e.g. worthless; criticised) rather than through more functional progress towards their own self-generated goals.

In a later paper, Conway *et al.* (2004) elaborated on the earlier model through highlighting two principles that they propose guide the organisation and content of autobiographical memory: *coherence* and *correspondence*. They propose that correspondence is often sacrificed to maintain self-coherence. It is possible that the negative and positive memories within bipolar disorder are influenced by the tension between these principles. From the results of this review and the qualitative analysis, we can now speculate that the theme of the working self in bipolar disorder could be 'energetically excelling to overcome the extreme vulnerability caused by hostile or critical others'. The model suggests that individuals with chronic mood swings would experience lack of correspondence between their memories and their environment to the extent that they maintain this self-theme through distorting or suppressing inconsistent information, and that successful therapy relies on building up a self-concept that fits better with experience and existing self-knowledge rather than struggling to maintain coherence in this way. This still leaves the question – how does this occur?

Perceptual Control Theory

Conway and colleagues' approach seems to fit well with the findings, and could provide the impetus for further research in bipolar disorders to explore individuals' goals and their ESKs that conflict with them. Nevertheless, it is likely that there is a further level to explore before a truly mechanistic account of the role of imagery in bipolar disorder (or any other mental health problem) can be put forward. Psychological frameworks require a theory that is informed by the biological systems that underpin them, leading to a reverse-engineering account of human behaviour that can form principles through which working simulations of certain phenomena can be developed. Perceptual Control Theory (PCT; Powers, 1973) is such a theory.

According to PCT, all behaviour is driven by the control of perception. The individual is intrinsically goal-oriented and these goals (or reference values) are specified at every level of perception within a hierarchy, from intensity of stimulation through object perceptions to system concepts that would include the self. According to PCT, behaviour is observed as individuals attempt to match their current perception with internal references. Thus, if a person is maintaining a certain self-concept, this implies that there is a control system hierarchy that connects in a detailed way to perceptions at lower levels (e.g. behavioural routines, images, feelings) that constitute that self-concept. Within PCT, there is no obvious limit to the number of control systems, and therefore conflict between control systems is inevitable. Conflicting reference values lead to a range of difficulties in managing behaviour, and the individual typically oscillates in an unstable manner between them. According to Powers (1973/2005), chronic, unresolved internal conflict is at the heart of psychological problems (see also Mansell, 2005). An example of conflict is as follows: A 'good companion' self-perception would involve the goal of sharing personal experiences, whereas a 'protect from criticism' self-perception may involve the goal of keeping personal experiences secret.

Conway and colleagues' concepts of correspondence and coherence could be understood from a PCT perspective. The drive for correspondence would be a result of control systems directing behaviour so that perception (of the environment) matches with internal reference values, which is the key function of an individual control system. The drive for self-coherence would form part of a wider aim of reducing internal conflict between the reference values of different control systems so that they function effectively. It is likely that the theme we have identified within bipolar disorder (rising above the vulnerability caused by hostile others through excelling in a public arena) would entail a rich constellation of reference values of the self and other within a hierarchical control system. PCT would suggest that it is not this theme *per se* that leads to problems in people with mood swings, but the degree to which it leads to conflict. This conflict could reside within the system itself (e.g. trying to reach standards of performance that are perceived to attract criticism), with other systems (e.g. those governing other essential reference values such as safety and companionship) or with those of other individuals (e.g. other people's standards of 'normal behaviour').

According to PCT, if the conflicting internal references are kept from awareness (for example through overgeneral memory or suppression) then the conflict cannot be resolved and the individual continues to experience the consequences. Therapy might work by focusing awareness on the conflicts between control systems at various levels so that 'reorganisation' can take place. This process occurs without any direction from the individual, and appears similar to 'insight' or a shift in perspective; it naturally resolves conflict between reference values and is accompanied by the development of a higher level of organisation beyond that which currently controls behaviour. A therapeutic technique known as the 'Method of Levels' has been developed to aid this process and is described elsewhere (Carey, 2006).

In this brief section we aimed to clarify different kinds of explanation that can be applied to autobiographical memory, and these are summarised in Table 10.3 (see also Barnard, 2004). Arguably, the appropriate type of explanation depends on three facets: who (e.g. people with bipolar disorder; humans in general), what (e.g. memory; control) and how (e.g. heuristics; simulation). The strengths of CBT models of psychological disorders are that they lend themselves well to shared explanations and formulations of experience, yet they say a limited amount about how psychological processes work. More detailed conceptual frameworks like the SPAARs and Dual Representation Theory provide much more detail as to the processes at work, yet are difficult to personalise for formulations and still fall short of providing working simulations of the key process involved. Frameworks like PCT and ICS (Interactive Cognitive Subsystems; see Barnard, 2004) form a more mechanistic understanding of psychological processes, yet in full they are too complex for shared formulations with clients and are generally less well specified at higher levels of abstraction (e.g. content of values, beliefs, etc.). The following section on interventions takes strategies that follow from some of these forms of explanation, but it is possible that a less eclectic and more focused approach could be taken in the future.

Interventions

Clinical case examples of self imagery

Table 10.4 describes the 'possible selves' that emerged during individual cognitive therapy with a number of clients with bipolar disorder. They are organised in a way that reflects the conflicting self-concepts relating to different internal states within the cognitive model (Mansell *et al.*, 2007). Typically, one self-state operates to seek safety and escape from an aversive self-state; this more 'positive' self-state then also becomes aversive as its negative consequences become apparent. For example, Client 1 reported her earliest memories of witnessing domestic violence at home. She vividly remembered trying to 'grow taller and stronger' at a very young age, in order to try to protect her mother from her father's attacks. This potentially positive self-image conflicted with memories of the interpersonal impact of this activated self – becoming too impulsive and being punished by her mother for her behaviour. One escape from this paradoxical activated self was deactivation – a state of emotional distance and numbing. However, in this state of mind she became more vulnerable to being manipulated and controlled by others, which led to a further attempt to recapture a positive state of activation to overcome other people's perceived attempts at controlling her. Her life experiences of trauma, activation, deactivation and retraumatisation could

Table 10.3 Summary of different kinds of explanation used to conceptualise autobiographical memories in bipolar disorder

Name of explanatory framework	Sample (Who?)	Domain (What?)	Form (How?)
Integrative Cognitive Model of Bipolar Disorder (Mansell et al., 2007)	People with mood swings or bipolar disorders	Beliefs, behaviour, physiology, environment, cognition, behaviour, metacognition	Heuristic to guide formulation, shared understanding and hypothesis testing
Dual Representation Theory (Brewin et al., 1996)	Clinical populations, involving trauma	Memory	Heuristic to explain nature of, and relationship between, memory representations
SPAARs (Power & Dalgleish, 1997)	Humans in general	Multi-level representations	Heuristic to explain nature of multiple levels of representation
Self Memory System (Conway & Pleydell-Pearce, 2000; Conway et al., 2004)	Humans in general	Multi-level autobiographical memory and related goal-oriented processes	Heuristic with aspects of processing detail relating to hierarchical organisation of memory and mechanisms of access and change
Interacting Cognitive Subsystems (Barnard & Teasdale, 1991)	Humans and animals	Multi-level representations and processing	Mechanistic; simulation
Perceptual Control Theory (Powers, 1973/2005)	Living systems	Control of multiple levels of perception; conflict; reorganisation	Mechanistic; simulation

Table 10.4 Clinical examples of self imagery and memories in clients with a bipolar disorder categorised by level of activation and personal appraisals

Client details	Safety-seeking activated	Aversive activated	Safety-seeking deactivated	Aversive deactivated	Intervention	'Reorganisation memory' examples
(1) 37F, BPI	Child Self growing taller and stronger to help save mother from father's physical attacks; Adult Self saves others in the present	Child Self knocking rapidly on mother's bedroom door, worried whether she has died, only to get punished by mother for waking her	Adult Self cut off from feelings to escape the emotional pain	Adult Self manipulated and controlled by others especially when emotionally cut off; Child Self physically constrained by father	Grounding during traumatic memories; formulating transition between self states; restructure childhood memories; build healthy deactivated self using mindfulness	Being assertive and firm with a long-term abusive friend rather than being submissive or aggressive
(2) 33F, BPI	Adult Self feels larger than other people; Child Self as the child in the village who is known by everyone for smiling all the time	Adult Self as irritable, restless and making endless lists	Unknown	Depressed Adult Self looking unattractive and unlikeable; Child Self looking in mirror and trying to smile rather than look 'ugly' in eyes of mother	Develop healthy deactivated self using an image of self from recent experience; experiment with seeing people when depressed; restructure childhood memories	Enjoyable weekend with friends where positive experiences were shared and there was minimal irritability and good sleep

(3) 38M, BPII	Adult Self as trying very hard, doing everything more quickly to avoid failure at work	Adult Self as 'schizo' and out of control, attacking or shouting at other people	Adult Self as 'content' and free of any distressing emotions; often requires alcohol	Adult Self as depressed, inactive, 'black' inside head and suicidal; being controlled and blamed by others	Experiment with activated state during session to test beliefs about lack of control; reduce avoidance when depressed; monitor and increase 'content' periods without alcohol	Facing a past abusive individual without losing control of temper
(4) 43M, BPI	Adult Self as overcoming depression by being extremely creative, active and intelligent in artistic career	Adult Self as 'desperate for praise' in social situations; image of Child Self red in face after seeking praise from father and being slapped	Unknown	Adult Self as depressed, worthless and suicidal; Child Self being physically abused and controlled by brothers	Test beliefs during social situations using feedback from others; formulate avoidance when depressed and reduce; discuss and reframe childhood memories	Facing a work colleague who witnessed his mania and tolerating the anxiety when usually he would have avoided them
(5) 38F, BPII	Adult Self as full of great ideas and a perfect, active, responsible mother	Adult Self as a 'gibbering over-the-top weirdo' and others reacting by laughing and rejecting	Unknown	Adult Self as a useless, depressed, irresponsible mother; Child Self as abandoned by 'selfish' father	Formulate development of different self states; experiment with 'letting ideas go'; build up healthy self	Memory of self on a recent holiday when felt happy and optimistic, and not irritable or 'over the top'

F, female; M, male; BPI, bipolar I disorder; BPII, bipolar II disorder.

be conceptualised as oscillations between these self-states. The remaining cases demonstrate a similar pattern. In the following sections, the way that these self-images can be explored to therapeutic effect will be discussed. We will conclude with the description of recovery-related autobiographical memories that seem to arise during therapy and demarcate reorganisations of the self-concept that are more adaptive.

'Going up a level'

In the first instance, talking about images, *as images*, is likely to be therapeutic. Until this point they often seem to be conceptualised as potential or actual realities for the self rather than as cognitive phenomena. It also appears that access to the sensory information within the images is state-specific. However, during therapy, the client can become aware of these cognitions during different internal states and begin to take a more overarching and contextualised view of them. For example, describing how they come and go at different times, how they may be different from current reality, and exploring their origins can all help to provide a richer 'metacognitive' understanding of imagery. It is possible that this aspect of therapy is one of the most active ingredients and drives the shifts in appraisal and self-perspective that characterise moments of change. This suggestion would be consistent with metacognitive models of psychopathology (Wells & Matthews, 1994), as well as the development of 'higher level' control of self-concepts within PCT.

Formulation

The discussion of imagery can aid formulation for bipolar disorder for several reasons (see also Mansell, 2007; Mansell & Lam, 2004). First, it promotes an understanding of mood swings that is based on the client's first-person experiences rather than on assumptions about bipolar disorder as a fixed biological illness over which the client has no control; this sets the stage for a cognitive formulation. Second, the images often encapsulate appraisals of the self during different internal states that form the key components of a cognitive formulation according to Mansell *et al.* (2007); the conflicts between beliefs that form part of the model are made more explicit to the client when explained in terms of their own multiple self-images. Third, the images often provide a direct access to the past experiences that form part of the model; often memories of the self or others contribute to these self-images. Discussing their origins can help to disengage their past meanings from their present interpretations and promote greater understanding of how the clients have come to perceive themselves in these potential ways.

Active interventions

Beyond the description and formulation of imagery and memories, certain therapeutic techniques can be applied to the imagery in a similar manner to other conditions (Hackmann & Holmes, 2004). Perceptual discrimination is a useful technique with its origins in the treatment of PTSD. For example, a client experienced intrusive memories of past assaults when she was involved in a verbal argument with her current partner. She felt as though the past physical assaults were happening at that moment, leading her to be increasingly frightened and aggressive. Through talking about the memories in detail, she became more able to differentiate them from her experiences in the present moment that did not involve actual physical assault. In turn, she was better able to reappraise these intrusions as understandable memories of a past trauma rather than as a sign that 'it was all happening again' and that 'I am about to relapse again'. This client often found it overwhelming to talk about her past trauma. She was reminded that it was up to her to decide when to talk about it; there was no rush; and on occasions she was provided with a 'grounding device' (a rubber stress ball) to help her focus on the present and prevent detachment during these sessions (cf. Holmes *et al.*, 2005; Kennerley, 1996).

Other techniques can provide more direct reappraisals through restructuring of imagery. Client 2 in Table 10.4 was helped with her aversive memory of being told she was ugly when she was sad, which seemed to drive her need to look happy all the time as an adult. She was helped to imagine returning as an adult with the knowledge she has now, to tell her child self that she understands how she feels – but she does not need to look happy all the time; it's OK to look and feel sad occasionally.

A final technique also follows from the fluctuating and aversive nature of the self-images in bipolar disorder. Many individuals find it hard to visualise an image of themselves that is realistically positive, healthy and achievable, and therefore fall back on the aversive images they have used in the past. Often during the latter stages of therapy, when clients have learned to disengage from the less healthy self-images or reappraise them, they find it helpful to develop a template of a healthy self-image as a target. For example, Client 3 developed a realistic positive image of himself as successful at work but not trying too hard, which could think logically and be caring towards himself and others. He could cite certain times in his recent past when he attained this self-image, which then provided anchor points for this image in order to attain these experiences in the future. Other examples are provided in Table 10.4. These 'reorganisation memories' in bipolar disorder may be important to understand if we wish to help clients to be more resistant to relapse and improve their quality of life. Some therapists may be interested as to how this approach links in with the role of imagery in generating and building a compassionate self in individuals who experience shame and self-attacking (Gilbert & Irons, 2004; Kohut, 1977).

Conclusions

The role of imagery and memories of the self in bipolar disorders has not been studied in detail. In this chapter we have endeavoured to address this omission through a comprehensive empirical review and a new phenomenological investigation leading to a theoretical discussion, and by discussing the implications for clinical practice and future research. The dynamic multifaceted self-concept within bipolar disorder could be regarded as an extreme archetype of the shifting self-concept that appears to be present in all individuals, and that is intrinsically an interpersonal construction. We tentatively suggest that the key personal theme within bipolar disorder is 'striving to achieve a highly activated, socially oriented (but fragile and problematic) positive self-concept in order to overcome the perception of personal vulnerability at the hands of others who are perceived as critical, controlling or hostile. Consistent with Mansell *et al.* (2007), we suggest that it is the internal and external conflict generated by this personal goal (and its constituent lower order references such as images of the self) that leads to the disruption associated with the condition. Future research could explore this proposition in more detail, using interviews about imagery and memory during relevant situations, and by empirical tests of the associations between beliefs assessed by the Hypomanic Attitudes and Positive Predictions Inventory (HAPPI; Mansell, 2006) and the content of recurring imagery and memories. It would be fascinating to study whether a 'metacognitive' treatment directed at self-relevant imagery and memories could be efficacious for people with bipolar disorder in itself.

We hope that our work here will encourage clinicians to enquire about imagery and memories in their clients, and work with them to heighten and broaden their own awareness of these conflicting self-concepts and facilitate the development of other self-concepts that enhance well-being and combat the damaging effects of severe mood swings. The extent to which working with imagery in bipolar disorder could contribute to full recovery remains to be established, but we hope that its potential is clear.

Acknowledgements

Thank you to Lusia Stopa for providing the opportunity to write this chapter, to Emily Holmes for her helpful feedback, and to Craig Murray for invaluable help with the qualitative analyses.

References

Abraham, K. (1911/1953). Notes on the psycho-analytical investigation and treatment of manic-depressive insanity and allied conditions. In K. Abraham (Ed.), *Selected papers on psychoanalysis*. New York: Basic Books.

American Psychiatric Association (2000). *Diagnostic and statistical manual of mental disorders* (4th Edition, Text Revision). Washington, DC: American Psychiatric Association.

Barnard, P.J. (2004). Bridging between basic theory and clinical practice. *Behaviour Research and Therapy, 42,* 977–1000.

Barnard, P.J., & Teasdale, J.D. (1991) Interacting cognitive subsystems: A systemic approach to cognitive–affective interaction and change. *Cognition and Emotion, 5,* 1–39.

Beck, A.T. (1967) *Depression: Clinical, experimental and theoretical aspects.* New York: Harper and Row.

Bentall, R. (2003). *Madness explained: Psychosis and human nature.* London, UK: Penguin.

Bentall, R.P., Kinderman, P., & Manson, K. (2005). Self-discrepancies in bipolar-affective disorder. *British Journal of Clinical Psychology, 44,* 1–18.

Bentall, R.P., Tai, S.J., & Knowles, R. (2006). Psychological processes and the pathways to mania: Exploring the manic defence hypothesis. In S.H. Jones & R.P. Bentall (Eds.), *The psychology of bipolar disorder* (pp. 117–137). Oxford, UK: Oxford University Press.

Blairy, S., Linotte, S., Souery, D., Papadimitriou, G.N., Dikeos, D., Lerer, B., *et al.* (2004). Social adjustment and self-esteem of bipolar patients: A multicentric study. *Journal of Affective Disorders, 79,* 97–103.

Bowlby, J. (1969). *Attachment and loss: Vol. 1. Attachment.* New York: Basic Books.

Brewin, C.R., Dalgleish, T., & Joseph, S. (1996). A dual representation theory of posttraumatic stress disorder. *Psychological Review, 103,* 670–686.

Brewin, C.R., & Holmes, E.A. (2003). Psychological theories of posttraumatic stress disorder. *Clinical Psychology Review, 23,* 339–376.

Carey, T.A. (2006). *The method of levels: How to do psychotherapy without getting in the way.* Hayward, CA: Living Control Systems Publishing.

Cassidy, F. Forest, K., Murry, M., & Carroll, B.J. (1998). A factor analysis of the signs and symptoms of mania. *Archives of General Psychiatry, 55,* 27–32.

Clark, D.M., & Wells, A. (1995). A cognitive model of social phobia. In R. Heimberg, M. Liebowitz, D.A. Hope, & F.R. Schneier (Eds.), *Social phobia: Diagnosis, assessment and treatment* (pp. 69–93). New York: Guilford Press.

Conway, M.A., Meares, K., & Standart, S. (2004). Images and goals. *Memory, 12,* 525–531.

Conway, M.A., & Pleydell-Pearce, C.W. (2000). The construction of autobiographical memories in the self-memory system. *Psychological Review, 107,* 261–288.

Conway, M.A., Singer, J.A., & Tagini, A. (2004). The self and autobiographical memory: Correspondence and coherence. *Social Cognition, 22,* 491–529.

Delduca, C.M., & Jones, S.H. (2007). *A preliminary investigation of the effect of hypomanic personality on the specificity of autobiographical memory recall.* Manuscript submitted for publication.

Eckblad, M., & Chapman, L.J. (1986). Development and validation of a scale for hypomanic personality. *Journal of Abnormal Psychology, 95,* 214–222.

Ehlers, A., & Clark, D.M. (2000). A cognitive model of posttraumatic stress disorder. *Behaviour Research and Therapy, 38,* 319–345.

Eich, E., Macaulay, D., & Lam, R.W. (1997). Mania, depression, and mood dependent memory. *Cognition and Emotion, 11,* 607–618.

Gilbert, P., & Irons, C. (2004). A pilot exploration of the use of compassionate images in a group of self-critical people. *Memory, 12*, 507–516.

Goldberg, J.F., Wenze, S.J., Welker, T.M., Steer, R.A., & Beck, A.T. (2005). Content-specificity of dysfunctional cognitions for patients with bipolar mania versus unipolar depression: A preliminary study. *Bipolar Disorders, 7*, 49–56.

Goodwin, F., & Jamison, K. (1990). *Manic-depressive illness*. Oxford, UK: Oxford University Press.

Hackmann, A., Clark, D.M., & McManus, F. (2000). Recurrent images and early memories in social phobia. *Behaviour Research and Therapy, 38*, 601–610.

Hackmann, A., & Holmes, E.A. (2004). Reflecting on imagery: A clinical perspective and overview of the special issue of *Memory* on mental imagery and memory in psychopathology. *Memory, 12*, 389–402.

Harvey, A.G., Watkins, E., Mansell, W., & Shafran, R. (2004). *Cognitive behavioural processes across psychological disorders: A transdiagnostic approach to research and treatment*. Oxford, UK: Oxford University Press.

Higgins, E.T. (1987). Self-discrepancy: A theory relating self and affect. *Psychological Review, 94*, 319–340.

Holmes, E., Brown, R.J., Mansell, W., Fearon, R.M.P., Hunter, E.C.M., Frasquilho, F., *et al.* (2005). Are there two qualitatively different forms of dissociation? A review and some clinical implications. *Clinical Psychology Review, 25*, 1–23.

Holmes, E.A., & Mathews, A. (2005). Mental imagery and emotion: A special relationship?. *Emotion, 5*, 489–497.

Holmes, E.A., Mathews, A., Dalgleish, T., & Mackintosh, B. (2006). Positive interpretational training: Effects of mental imagery versus verbal training on positive mood. *Behavior Therapy, 37*, 237–247.

Jamison, K.R., Hamman, C., Gong-Guy, E., Padesky, C., & Gemer, R.H. (1990). *Self-perceptions of interpersonal functioning in unipolar and bipolar men and women*. Unpublished data.

Janowsky, D.S., Leff, M., & Epstein, R.S. (1970). Playing the manic game: Interpersonal maneuvers of the acutely manic patient. *Archives of General Psychiatry, 22*, 252–261.

Johnson, S.L., & Carver, C.S. (2006). Extreme goal setting and vulnerability to mania among undiagnosed young adults. *Cognitive Therapy and Research, 30*, 377–395.

Jones, S.H., Tai, S.J., Evershed, K., Knowles, R., & Bentall, R. (2006). Early detection of bipolar disorder: A pilot familial high-risk study of parents with bipolar disorder and their adolescent children. *Bipolar Disorders, 8*, 362–372.

Kennerley, H. (1996). Cognitive therapy of dissociative symptoms associated with trauma. *British Journal of Clinical Psychology, 35*, 325–40.

Kessler, R.C., & McRae, J.A. (1982). The effects of wives' employment on the mental health of married men and women. *American Sociological Review, 47*, 216–227.

Kohut, H. (1977). *The restoration of the self*. New York: International Universities Press.

Kwapil, T.R., Miller, M.B., Zinser, M.C., Chapman, L.J., Chapman, J., & Eckblad, M. (2000). A longitudinal study of high scorers on the hypomanic personality scale. *Journal of Abnormal Psychology, 109*(2), 222–226.

Lam, D., & Mansell, W. (2008). Mood-dependent cognitive change in a man with bipolar disorder who cycles every 24 hours. *Cognitive and Behavioral Practice, 15*, 255–262.

Lam, D., Wright, K., & Sham, P. (2005). Sense of hyper-positive self and response to cognitive therapy for bipolar disorder. *Psychological Medicine, 35*, 69–77.

Lam, D., Wright, K., & Smith, N. (2004). Dysfunctional assumptions in bipolar disorder. *Journal of Affective Disorders, 79*, 193–199.

Lyon, H., Startup, M., & Bentall, R.P. (1999). Social cognition and the manic defence: Attributions, selective attention and self-schema in bipolar affective disorder. *Journal of Abnormal Psychology, 108*, 273–282.

Mansell, W. (2005). Control theory and psychopathology: An integrative approach. *Psychology and Psychotherapy: Theory, Research and Practice, 78*, 1–40.

Mansell, W. (2006). The Hypomanic Attitudes and Positive Predictions Inventory (HAPPI): A pilot study to select cognitions that are elevated in individuals with bipolar disorder compared to non-clinical controls. *Behavioural and Cognitive Psychotherapy, 34*, 1–10.

Mansell, W. (2007). An integrative formulation-based cognitive treatment of bipolar disorders: Application and illustration. *Journal of Clinical Psychology, 63*, 447–461.

Mansell, W., & Jones, S.H. (2006). The brief HAPPI: A questionnaire to assess cognitions that distinguish between individuals with a diagnosis of bipolar disorder and non-clinical controls. *Journal of Affective Disorders, 93*, 29–34.

Mansell, W., & Lam, D. (2004). A preliminary study of autobiographical memory in remitted bipolar and unipolar depression and the role of imagery in the specificity of memory. *Memory, 12*, 437–446.

Mansell, W., and Lam, D. (2006). 'I won't do what you tell me!' Elevated mood and the assessment of advice-taking in euthymic bipolar I disorder. *Behaviour Research and Therapy, 44*, 1787–1801.

Mansell, W., Morrison, A.P., Reid, G., Lowens, I., & Tai, S. (2007). The interpretation of and responses to changes in internal states: An integrative cognitive model of mood swings and bipolar disorder. *Behavioural and Cognitive Psychotherapy, 35*, 515–541.

Markus, H., & Wurf, E. (1987). The dynamic self-concept: A social psychological perspective. *Annual Review of Psychology, 38*, 299–337.

Neale, J.M. (1988). Defensive function of manic episodes. In T.F. Oltmanns & B.A. Maher (Eds.), *Delusional beliefs*. New York: Wiley.

Nelson, K. (2003). Self and social functions: Individual autobiographical memory and collective narrative. *Memory, 11*, 125–136.

Nelson, K., & Fivush, R. (2004). The emergence of autobiographical memory: A social cultural developmental theory. *Psychological Review, 111*, 485–511.

Osborn, M., & Smith, J.A. (1998). The personal experience of chronic benign lower back pain: An interpretive phenomenological analysis. *British Journal of Health Psychology, 3*, 65–83.

Pardoen, D., Bauwens, F., Tracy, A., Martin, F., & Mendlewicz, J. (1993). Self-esteem in recovered bipolar and unipolar outpatients. *British Journal of Psychiatry, 163*, 755–762.

Power, M.J., & Dalgleish, T. (1997). *Cognition and emotion: From order to disorder*. Hove, UK: Psychology Press.

Power, M.J., de Jong, F., & Lloyd, A. (2002). The organization of the self-concept in bipolar disorders: An empirical study and replication. *Cognitive Therapy and Research, 26*, 553–561.

Powers, W.T. (1973/2005). *Behaviour: The control of perception*, New Canann, CT: Benchmark.

Reynolds, M., & Brewin, C.R. (1999). Intrusive memories in depression and post-traumatic stress disorder. *Behaviour Research and Therapy, 37*, 201–215.

Rogers, C. (1951). *Client-centred therapy: Its current practice, implications, and theory.* Boston: Houghton Mifflin.

Rosenfarb, I.S., Becker, J., Khan, A., & Mintz, J. (1998). Dependency and self-criticism in bipolar and unipolar depressed women. *British Journal of Clinical Psychology, 37*, 409–414.

Scott, J., & Pope, M. (2003). Cognitive styles in individuals with bipolar disorders. *Psychological Medicine, 33*, 1081–1088.

Scott, J., Stanton, B., Garland, A., & Ferrier, I.N. (2000). Cognitive vulnerability in patients with bipolar disorder. *Psychological Medicine, 30*, 467–472.

Smith, J.A. (1995). Semi-structured interviewing and qualitative analysis. In J.A. Smith, R. Harre, & L. Van Langenhove (Eds.), *Rethinking methods in psychology.* London: Sage Publications.

Solomon, D.A., Leon, A.C., Endicott, J., Coryell, W.H., Mueller, T.I., Posternak, M.A., *et al.* (2003). Unipolar mania over the course of a 20-year follow-up study. *American Journal of Psychiatry, 160*, 2049–2051.

Thoits, P.A. (1983). Multiple identities and psychological well-being: A reformulation and test of the social isolation hypothesis. *American Sociological Review, 48*, 174–187.

Tzemou, E., & Birchwood, M. (2007). A prospective study of dysfunctional thinking and the regulation of negative intrusive memories in bipolar I disorder: Implications for affect regulation theory. *Psychological Medicine, 37*, 689–698.

Udachina, A., & Mansell, W. (2007). Cross-validation of the mood disorders questionnaire, the internal state scale, and the hypomanic personality scale. *Personality and Individual Differences, 42*, 1539–1549.

Weingartner, H., Miller, H., & Murphy, D.L. (1977). Mood-state-dependent retrieval of verbal associations. *Journal of Abnormal Psychology, 86*, 276–284.

Wells, A., & Matthews, G. (1994). *Attention and emotion: A clinical perspective.* Hove, UK: Lawrence Erlbaum Associates.

Wicki, W., & Angst, J. (1991). The Zurich study: X. Hypomania in a 28–30 year-old cohort. *European Archives of Psychiatry and Clinical Neuroscience, 240*, 339–348.

Williams, J.M., & Broadbent, K. (1986). Autobiographical memory in suicide attempters. *Journal of Abnormal Psychology, 95*, 144–140.

Willig, C. (2001). *Introducing qualitative research in psychology: Adventures in theory and method.* Maidenhead, UK: Open University Press.

Winters, K.C., & Neale, J.M. (1985). Mania and low self-esteem. *Journal of Abnormal Psychology, 94*, 282–290.

Index